# AYRSHIR
# DISCOVERING A COUNTY

## DANE LOVE

## FORT PUBLISHING LTD

First published in 2003 by Fort Publishing Ltd, Old Belmont House,
12 Robsland Avenue, Ayr, KA7 2RW

Cover painting: 'A view of Culzean Castle' by Alexander Nasmyth
(1758–1840). Reproduced by kind permission of The National Trust for
Scotland.

Typeset by S. Fairgrieve (0131–658–1763)

Printed by Bell and Bain, Glasgow.

ISBN 0-9544461-1-9

# Contents

# List of Illustrations

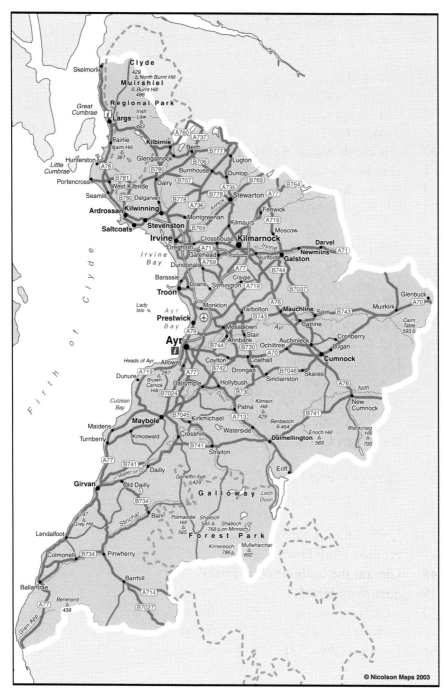

Ayrshire

# Preface

THE FORMER COUNTY OF Ayrshire is now divided into three local authorities, but to Ayrshire residents the county is still something of a special entity, one that is dear to their hearts. The former shire of Ayr was made up of three divisions, Cunninghame to the north, Kyle between the rivers Irvine and Doon, and Carrick to the south. In total the county was 1,132 square miles in extent, or around 724,234 acres. This made it the seventh largest county in Scotland.

Ayrshire has been described in various places as being like a huge natural amphitheatre, with a circle of hills and high moorland dropping down to the better agricultural land and the wide sweep of Ayr Bay. From the northernmost point at Kelly Burn, on the border with Renfrewshire (now Inverclyde), to the southernmost at the Galloway Burn, on the border with Wigtownshire (now Dumfries and Galloway) is sixty miles in a direct line, but if one stays on dry land and follows the road, these places are ninety miles apart. At its widest, which is halfway from north to south, the county is twenty-eight miles wide, stretching from the Heads of Ayr to Glenbuck Loch.

Anciently, in the second century, this part of Scotland was part of the kingdom of the Damnonii. A version of Gaelic seems to have been spoken after the withdrawal of the Romans, and it continued in use in some areas as late as the sixteenth century. In the eighth century the Kyle and Cunninghame divisions were part of the kingdom of Northumbria, Carrick still being part of Galloway.

Ayrshire was created around 1130–50 when the three ancient land divisions of Cunninghame, Kyle and Carrick were merged, under the jurisdiction of one sheriff, and his deputies. This was organised by Sir Hugh de Morville at the command of King David I. The hereditary sheriff of the county was the Earl of Loudon, and the county town was Ayr. Two Royal Burghs were created (Ayr and Irvine), a parliamentary burgh (Kilmarnock), and in later years Police Burghs created at Ardrossan, Cumnock, Darvel, Galston, Girvan, Kilwinning, Largs, Maybole, New-milns, Prestwick, Saltcoats, Stevenston, Stewarton and Troon. The county was divided into around fifty parishes, but some of the smaller ones were merged to create larger parishes, leaving forty-six in 1891.

In 1975, Scottish local government was reorganised and Ayrshire lost its independence. The county was absorbed into a large Strathclyde region, with its headquarters in Glasgow, and the region was sub-divided into smaller districts. The former Ayrshire was divided into four of these second-tier forms of local government, namely Cunninghame, centred on Irvine, Kilmarnock and Loudoun, Cumnock and Doon Valley, and Kyle and Carrick, centred on Ayr.

The two-tier system of local government was abolished in 1996, and replaced by a single tier system once more. At this time the former county of Ayrshire was divided into three authorities, South Ayrshire being virtually the same area as Kyle and Carrick centred on Ayr, East Ayrshire was created out of the Kilmarnock and Loudoun and Cumnock and Doon Valley districts, and North Ayrshire out of Cunninghame district. North Ayrshire also includes the islands of Arran, Great and Little Cumbrae, which, in 1975, had been placed within Cunninghame district, formerly being within the county of Bute.

The Earls of Loudoun were Campbells, an early branch of the great Argyllshire clan, and they were influential in county politics for many years. Other major landowners include the Kennedys, so important at one time that they were styled 'Kings of Carrick', owning much of the county south of the river Doon. The Wallaces of Craigie, Stewarts of Dundonald, Cunninghames of Kilmaurs, and Montgomeries of Eglinton were other major landowners, each with a number of branches establishing dynasties of their own.

Apart from the major landowners, there were numerous long-standing smaller lairds, each holding considerable sway in their own parish. Among these the Fergussons of Kilkerran, Crawfords of Kilbirnie, Boswells of Auchinleck, Brisbanes of that Ilk, Blairs of that Ilk, Dunlops of that Ilk, and Boyds of Kilmarnock became influential.

Ayrshire has played its part in many events from national Scots history. Some of Robert the Bruce and William Wallace's early escapades took place here in the late thirteenth century, when the country was ruled by England. Indeed, the county lays claim to being the birthplace of both heroes, though this is contested by Renfrewshire in the case of Wallace, and Dumfriesshire in the case of Bruce.

From 1250 until 1550 the county was in the grip of the church, abbeys being created at Kilwinning and Crossraguel, and lesser ecclesiastical centres existing at Fail, Mauchline, Dalmilling, and elsewhere. The church took an active part in the governance of the county, most parishes being linked to an abbey or cathedral, many distant from these boundaries, such as Glasgow, Paisley or Melrose. The Reformation, which took place around 1560, wrestled the county's wealth from these abbeys, but it was transferred to local landowners in most cases, building up their strength. The Roman Catholic adherents did not accept Protestantism without a fight and, in a number of cases, continued to worship in their usual manner for much longer.

One of the most significant events in the religious history of the county was the time of the Covenanters. Charles I wished to impose Episcopacy on the Scots, to bring the county into line with England, but the Presbyterians could not accept this. They were also against his claim of the 'Divine right of kings'. Ayrshire, like most of south-west Scotland, was very much against this, and most supported the National Covenant, that was drawn up in Edinburgh. Government soldiers persecuted the Covenanters, many being martyred for their beliefs. The 'fifty years struggle' lasted until 1688 and included a number of famous deaths, including that of John Brown of Priesthill, brutally executed in front of his family.

Two of Scotland's greatest literary figures were Ayrshire men. Robert Burns has gained an international renown as a poet, famed for his works such as *Tam o' Shanter* and 'Auld Lang Syne'. James Boswell was celebrated for his *Life of Johnson* during his lifetime, but in the late twentieth century found fame anew with the discovery and publication of his detailed and intimate diaries, which record life in London, Europe and Scotland during the second half of the eighteenth century.

The county has produced a number of important novelists, including John Galt, noted for his *Annals of the Parish* and *The Ayrshire Legatees*, and many other works. George Douglas Brown is noted in Scots literary circles as the man who killed the 'kailyard school' of writing with his major work, *The House with the Green Shutters*. If he had lived longer, who knows what other masterpieces he would have produced.

Ayrshire has a long history as an agricultural county, with the celebrated Ayrshire cow being bred here for its milk-producing qualities. This breed was developed around 1780 and became the standard animal throughout the county. Similarly the county is known for developing Dunlop cheese, Ayrshire bacon and 'Girvan' potatoes. The uplands have been used for rearing beef cattle, sheep and, in more recent years, growing coniferous trees. Although agriculture has been the most important industry in the county for centuries, in the last couple of hundred years it has been eclipsed by heavier industry.

The natural resources of the rocks in the county have resulted in the development of coal and ironstone mining over the centuries. The Ayrshire coalfield was one of the most productive in Scotland, and most of the central and northern parts of the county had coal reserves. These were probably always worked on a small scale, there being evidence that the monks of Fail worked seams near Tarbolton in the fourteenth century, but with the arrival of the railway and the development of the iron works at various locations resulted in the industry burgeoning.

Mines were sunk in hundreds of locations and, adjacent to most, simple miners' rows were built to accommodate the workers. Such was the growth of the industry that workers were brought in from other counties, and even Ireland, to supply the labour that was required.

The ironstone in the county was worked for many years, until it was discovered that a better quality ore could be imported. The smaller iron-works that relied on local ores to start with were eventually closed, leaving only that at Glengarnock to continue working until relatively recently.

Engineering was carried on at various locations, shipbuilding being important at Ayr, Irvine, Ardrossan and elsewhere. Trains have long been produced in Kilmarnock, as have major engineering components, in particular valves for the water industry. At a later period tractors were manufactured in Kilmarnock.

Railways brought industry to the county on a scale never seen before, and the ease of transport for goods resulted in a prosperity only dreamed of previously. The growth of Glasgow and the towns in central Scotland resulted in parts of the county being now close enough to be affected by the 'second city' of the British Empire. Many of the industrialists and affluent businessmen of the city established holiday homes for themselves along the Ayrshire coast, creating a new industry in tourism.

The demise of heavy industry has been replaced by more diverse manufacturing over the years. Some of these industries have come and gone, whereas others have gone from strength to strength. Whisky is an important employer, and although the county has no malt whisky distilleries, there are major whisky plants associated with Johnnie Walker, Grants, Chivas and the House of Campbell, producing grain whisky, blending and bottling. Various smaller businesses also produce whisky products.

The woollen industry has been important in the shire, and still employs many people. Wool was spun and created into clothing, blankets, and carpets, the famous BMK brand originating here. Wool was also used to produce the famous Kilmarnock bonnets, 4,000 people being employed in the trade at one time.

Cotton and other cloth manufacturing have been carried out at various places. Beith and Kilbirnie were noted for the manufacture of linen, and the village of Catrine was celebrated for its cotton works, second only to New Lanark in importance at one time. Weaving was carried out in many homes throughout in the eighteenth and nineteenth centuries, many of the distinctive single-storey cottages in the villages around the county being erected for this purpose, with a room kept for the loom.

At Prestwick and Monkton the aircraft industry is associated with Prestwick Airport. British Aerospace has produced various models of light aircraft over the years, and a number of other businesses undertake the servicing and repair of aircraft. Similarly, at Irvine, Volvo manufactured buses and trucks for a period.

The computer age has resulted in a number of large manufacturing plants across the county, though these seem to be somewhat erratic as to their existence and employment. Major companies such as Digital Equipment, Fullarton Computer Industries, Prestwick Circuits, SCI and Compaq have had plants, some of which no longer exist.

Chemicals are produced in major plants at Dalry (Roche) and Irvine (Glaxo SmithKline), kelp is processed near Girvan, wood is pulped for paper at Irvine and chipped for chipboard at Irvine and Auchinleck. The glass bottle works at Irvine is a major supplier to the whisky industry.

The population of Ayrshire has been increasing gradually over the years. The population at various stages has been:

| | |
|------|---------|
| 1750 | 60,000 |
| 1800 | 80,000 |
| 1850 | 190,000 |
| 1900 | 250,000 |
| 1950 | 320,000 |
| 2000 | 368,000 |

This last figure is made up of 112,000 residents in South Ayrshire, 120,000 residents in East Ayrshire, and 136,000 residents in North Ayrshire. Ayrshire means many things to many people. I trust that this book will inspire those who read it to find out more about this splendid county.

The number of people who have supplied snippets of information for this book cannot be counted, and the author is frightened to try and name them all, from fear of missing one or a dozen out. Suffice to say, that I wish to thank all those folk who have filled in the blanks or added to my knowledge over the years, perhaps for other books or none. It all seems to get filed away, either at home or in the mind, to be drawn back out and used for projects such as this. No doubt many of these folk will recognise their contribution in the following pages. For these I express my thanks.

Dane Love
Auchinleck, 2003.

# 1

# Skelmorlie, Largs and Fairlie

THE VILLAGE OF SKELMORLIE is not an ancient one: the lands were feued by the proprietors from 1850 as a fashionable seaside resort. Wealthy businessmen from Glasgow and Renfrewshire were attracted to the area, away from the smog and pollution of the city, and here they built desirable cottages and miniature mansions for themselves. With the arrival of the railway at nearby Wemyss Bay (across the Kelly Burn and consequently on the Renfrewshire side of the border), commuting to the city became relatively easy.

The oldest building in the village is the Italianate Beach House, which dates from 1844, and was built as a holiday villa by George C. Arbuthnott, father-in-law of John Burns of Castle Wemyss. Arbuthnott was the third son of Sir William Arbuthnott, Baronet, Lord Provost of Edinburgh. Today it has been extended and is occupied as a nursing home. Most of Skelmorlie's buildings were constructed from the local rich red sandstone, the natural rock visible on the cliffs that separate Upper and Lower Skelmorlies. A number of these buildings along the main shore road are hotels, while others are nursing homes or private residences.

Upper Skelmorlie seems to be a world away from the lower part of the village, and lies on the land above the cliffs, its attractive roadways lined with trees and expensive houses. The conglomerate cliffs were created by the erosive waves, but the sea has long-since receded, leaving the raised beach. In the cliff side are a number of caves, many of which are now features within residents' gardens.

The houses and cottages of Skelmorlie are rather grand Tudor or Gothic-style buildings. Among them is the village manse, designed by the noted Glasgow architect John Honeyman in 1874. Skelmorlie House dates from the 1890s. Tudor House is an apt description for a grand home designed in 1904 by Watson & Salmond. The Craig Memorial Home was erected in the Victorian period as West Park House. It is a baronial building and at one time was the home of Hunter Craig MP. It is now divided into flats. Croftmhor is an English manorial style house of 1904, designed by H. E. Clifford. Skelmorlie Golf Course is located on the hillside to the east of the village. The eighteen-hole course is a par 65, and is 5,030 yards in length.

At one time Skelmorlie had a hydropathic establishment. This was located on the cliff-top above the main road, but from 1941 the hotel had the convenience of a mechanical lift down the cliff-face to the main road below. When the hotel was erected between 1868 and 1873 it had the benefit of Turkish, salt-water and other baths. Dr Ronald Currie, who was a member of Professor Joseph Lister's surgical class in Glasgow, established the hydro. Designed in a baronial style, the hotel fell on hard times and was demolished in 1987.

The parish church in Skelmorlie stands at the north end of the village by the side of the main road. The oldest part of the church buildings is the hall of 1856, to which the present church was added in 1895. This was also designed by John Honeyman. Working with him as an apprentice at that time was a young architect, Charles Rennie Mackintosh, and it is thought that the future doyen of Scottish architecture and design may have been responsible for designing the unique wrought-iron lamp stand that is located by the side of the steps. Stained glass in the church includes work by William Morris & Co. (dated 1900), as well as windows brought from St Andrew's Church in Greenock. Skelmorlie's former United Presbyterian Church of 1874, which stands next to the Kelly Bridge, has been converted into a domestic dwelling. In Upper Skelmorlie is the Evangelical Church, originally the village hall, erected in 1904 to the plans of H. E. Clifford.

Skelmorlie Castle lies about half a mile south of Skelmorlie village. Perched on a narrow promontory above the Skelmorlie Glen, the old part of the castle is the foursquare tower. This dates from around 1502 but was restyled around 1600. Sir Robert Montgomerie added other wings in 1636. Between 1856 and 1864 large baronial wings were added to the castle for a tenant, John Graham. The architect was William Railton of Kilmarnock. Graham (c.1795–1886) was a successful Glasgow textile merchant and was noted for his art collection. A disastrous fire in 1959 damaged much of the old tower and one of the wings. The wing was demolished, but the tower was restored to plans by Noad & Wallace of Glasgow, completed in 1962, to create the present castle, which still remains a substantial pile. Skelmorlie Castle has long been a seat of the Montgomerie family, later represented by the Earl of Eglinton and Winton. The Montgomeries acquired the lands in 1461 from the Cunninghams. The family were granted a baronetcy in 1628, but it became extinct in 1735, whereupon the heiress married a cousin.

Skelmorlie Glen is a narrow wooded valley, the Skelmorlie Water dropping quickly from the moors. The moors hereabouts are used for shooting grouse. At the head of the water, on Ferret of Keith Moor, are the remains of a Bronze Age hut circle, located on a low knoll near the foot of Martin Glen. Another ancient mound can be found near to Skelmorlie Mains; its history is unknown.

The Skelmorlie Water joins the Firth of Clyde at a small hamlet known as Meigle. There are one or two cottages hereabouts, and at one time there was a chapel, constructed in 1876 of concrete. This was the gift of the Misses Stewart of Ashcraig. The building is now converted into a house. There is also a much older earthwork that was known locally as the Serpent Mound from its curved shape. It is speculated that this may have had some early connection with the cult of sun worship.

South from Meigle to Largs the coastline is home to a few largish country houses, some of which have been converted into hotels. One of the most prominent is the Manor Park Hotel, distinguished by its square tower. This building was erected in 1843 as a country house known as St Fillans. The architects responsible were David & James Hamilton. The house was also at one time known as Blackhouse. Extensions were added in 1905 and, in 1910, Fryers & Penman of Largs designed the balustraded tower. The association with St Fillan originates from the fact that there was at one time a chapel dedicated to the saint on the moors hereabouts. On Blackhouse Moor St Fillan's Well can still be discerned on the ground. The site of the chapel, which was located nearby, has long since been lost.

Overlooking the firth from its dominant position above the raised beach cliff is Knock Castle. This large tudoresque edifice dates from 1851–2 and was designed by John Thomas Rochead, a noted architect who was responsible for many churches, as well as the Gothic spire that forms the William Wallace monument at Bridge of Allan. Knock is one of his finest works, and the castle contains many fine examples of high Victorian interiors. The castle was built for Robert Steele, a rich industrialist from Greenock. It was extended in 1908 to plans drawn up by Fryers & Penman.

A few hundred yards north of the present castle are the remains of the older Knock Castle, rebuilt and adapted as a gardener's cottage and something of a parkland folly in 1853. The old castle probably dates from 1603–4, when the Frasers erected it. The Frasers of Knock were long established, being a branch of the highland Frasers of Lovat. They acquired Knock around 1380 by marrying the heiress and retained it for almost 300 years. One of the last of the family fought with Montrose at the Battle of Philiphaugh in 1645. The castle was sold in 1674 to the Montgomeries of Skelmorlie.

Knock Castle takes its name from The Knock, a conical hill which, although only 712 feet in height, is a prominent landmark to the north of Largs. Trackways from either Manor Park or Brisbane Mains can be followed to its summit, which of course affords extensive views of the firth, encompassing Arran, the Cumbraes and the mountains of Argyll. The summit of the Knock is crowned with a prehistoric hill fort; the rampart encircles an area 165 feet by 95 feet, beyond which are traces of a ditch, in some places cut into the natural rock. The rampart walls themselves have traces of vitrified stonework within them, indicative of timber lacing that has been set on fire, either by accident or perhaps design, in order to increase its strength.

South of Knock estate is Quarter House, dating from around 1812 when it was built by James Wilson of Hailey. Soon one enters the northern houses of Largs, built along the raised beach. Routenburn Golf Course, an attractive 18-hole course, occupies the land above the wooded cliff. This is 5,604 yards in length, a par 68, and was founded in 1920.

The main road crosses the Noddle Bridge and enters Largs proper at its northern end. The bridge was formerly a high arched bridge, but this was demolished and a new lower and wider structure erected in 1824. The present bridge of 1977 in turn replaced this.

At the Noddle Bridge stands the former gatehouse to Netherhall. The gatehouse itself has been rebuilt, the former arched pend through the building being enclosed with glass to create a larger domestic living place. On the wall of the building is a plaque commemorating Sir William Thomson (1824–1907), later Lord Kelvin of Largs, who built Netherhall House and lived there when not working at Glasgow University. William Thomson was born in Belfast but moved with his parents to Glasgow in 1832 when his father was appointed Professor of Mathematics at the university. A prodigy, young William enrolled at the university at the age of 10, and at 16 moved to Cambridge University. At the age of 22 he was appointed professor of mathematics and natural philosophy at Glasgow, remaining such until 1899. He was one of the greatest physicists of all time, and it was he who worked out that the temperature scale started at absolute zero, now known as the Kelvin scale. He also established the Second Law of Thermodynamics, researched magnetism, hydrodynamics and vortices. His patent for the mirror galvanometer resulted in him earning a fortune. He invented numerous other electric and hydrodynamic devices, and his Glasgow home was the first in the city to have electric lights.

Thomson, using plans supplied by Campbell Douglas & Sellars, erected Netherhall House in 1876–92. Similar to a French chateau in style, the house was notable for its early use of electric lighting, the first in Scotland, and for including an elevator. In the year that the work was completed, at a cost of £12,000, Thomson was raised to the peerage as 1st Baron Kelvin of Largs. When Kelvin died he was buried in

Westminster Abbey, near to Isaac Newton. Today Netherhall has been subdivided into smaller homes, and much of the grounds built on.

The Noddsdale Water has carved a distinctive valley through the hills of north Ayrshire. It is quite an atmospheric place, as though it is unsure of itself, and even the name of the watercourse has caused some trouble over the years. Current Ordnance Survey maps name the burn the Noddsdale Water, but it has also been given the alternative spelling of Noddle. Even the name of the glen is shared between Noddsdale Glen and Brisbane Glen. In Largs the roadway heading for the valley is known as Brisbane Glen Road.

The name Brisbane is usually associated with the large city in Queensland, Australia, but it existed here first. Indeed, it was a local lad who took it to Australia. Brisbane House formerly stood up the glen, about one mile from its foot. An old Scots-style mansion, it had been erected in 1636 but was demolished in 1942. The original front door is now preserved 'down under' in Brisbane's City Hall. A stable block of around 1808 by James Gillespie Graham survives. The house was originally known as Kelsoland, at one time the property of the Kelso family, but it was sold to James Brisbane of Bishopton in 1671. The Brisbanes of that Ilk are first recorded in the fourteenth century when they acquired the £10 lands of Gogo and Killincraig. In 1595 the Brisbane lands were erected into the Barony of Gogoside. In 1650 the title was renamed Barony of Noddle. Following the acquisition of Over Kelsoland the barony was in 1695 renamed Brisbane.

Sir Thomas MakDougall Brisbane was a noted soldier, and governor of New South Wales. He was born at Brisbane House in 1773 and joined the army at the age of 16. He moved through the ranks quickly, and by 1813 was a major general. In his years of service he was active at Flanders, West Indies, Spain and North America. In 1821 he was appointed governor of New South Wales. During his term of office he reformed the currency, revised the system of land grants and improved overall efficiency. Sir Thomas married the heiress of the Border estate of Makerstoun, after which he adopted the surname MakDougall Brisbane.

A very keen astronomer, Sir Thomas built an observatory at Brisbane, Largs, which had pillars to assist in alignment. Three of these survive on the Green Hill, which itself was at one time the town's moot hill, where justice was dispensed. In Australia he built an observatory at Parramatta, near Sydney, in 1822, which was used to map out the stars of the southern hemisphere and he catalogued 7,385 stars there. Brisbane returned to Britain in 1825 and built and endowed the Brisbane Academy in Largs. He also gifted the Broomfields Park to the people of Largs. Created a baronet in 1836, he died in 1860 and was buried in the old Brisbane vault in Largs kirkyard. The last Brisbane to live in Largs was Miss Florence Brisbane, who died in 1932.

On the opposite side of the river from Brisbane, near to Middleton Farm, can be found a short pathway from the road leading down to a shady nook next to a small stream. There is an old recumbent gravestone here, known locally as the Prophet's Grave. This marks the resting place of William Smith who was the minister of Largs in 1647 when the town was struck by plague. A number of inhabitants were sent outwith the confines of the village to live in Brisbane Glen, and Smith went with them. He contracted the disease and died. According to a tradition, if the branches of two holly trees that grew at the graveside ever touched, then pestilence would return to Largs. Smith was 28 when he died, and had only been minister in Largs for three years.

Further up Brisbane Glen the hills become steeper and higher, particularly to the east. The highest in the immediate area is Burnt Hill, its rather flat summit being 1,596 feet above the level of the sea. Dropping from the high moors here are some fast-flowing streams, most of which have at least one distinctive waterfall. The high rainfall experienced on the moors has been harnessed for drinking purposes, with reservoirs at Middleton and Noddsdale, and a larger reservoir at Outerwards, originally constructed by Largs Town Council. On the moor beyond Outerwards farm, occupying a low summit, are the fragmentary remnants of a Roman fortlet.

The road through Brisbane Glen meanders into more open countryside beyond Outerwards, crossing over a low pass into the glen formed by the North Rotten Burn. Again this stream has its waterfalls, one of the more significant being known as the Black Linn. When the road crosses the Rottenburn Bridge it leaves Ayrshire and enters Renfrewshire. Near to the bridge, downhill from the Black Linn, are the ruins of an old shepherd's cottage known by the unusual name of Ferret of Keith. Alternatively known as 'Back o' the World', this cottage had the distinction of being the most northerly habitation in Ayrshire, further north than Paisley or even Glasgow!

The town of Largs stands at the foot of the Gogo Water, another quick-flowing stream that falls from the moors hereabouts. Largs has long been an important seaside resort, and to this day is popular with day-trippers and holidaymakers. The promenade around Largs Bay is a fashionable stroll and, though the beach is too stony for sandcastles, it maintains a pleasant atmosphere. Tourists flock to the town in the summer, though perhaps not so many as in the heyday of trips 'doon the watter' from Glasgow, to take in the views, have an ice cream at the renowned Nardini's café, or catch the ferry for Cumbrae and the quieter resort of Millport.

The bay is protected by the island of Great Cumbrae from the worst of the westerlies, and when the effect of the North Atlantic Drift is added it has allowed palm trees to flourish. The Romans knew of Largs's qualities, for they are known to have established a bath house here. Excavations in 1820 in the garden of Mrs Hall, the local postmistress, revealed remnants of this. Later, baths were erected to allow fashionable Victorians to take the waters, and in Bath Street can be seen the former Bath House of 1816, distinguished by its bowed ends. James VI created Largs a Burgh of Barony in 1585 for John Brisbane and his wife Anne Blair. It became a Police Burgh in 1876.

The parish of Largs extends to 14,610 acres, but much of this is high moorland of poor agricultural value. Historically, the town was something of a market and fishing centre, with many employed in the weaving trade. A pier was established at the foot of Main Street and with the advent of Clyde steamers Largs quickly became an important stopping point. The pier of today is an L-shaped structure, erected in 1834 at a cost of £4,275, protecting a tiny harbour that is mainly used by Caledonian MacBrayne for the Great Cumbrae ferry. At the landward end of the pier is a granite sculpture of a quasi-Viking longship, unveiled on 20 August 1993 by Stewart Dewar, convener of Cunninghame District Council. Overlooking the pier is the modern block known as the Moorings, erected in 1990 to plans by MacMillan & Cronin of Largs, but copying to some extent the older Moorings of 1936 by James Houston.

Main Street is a busy shopping area, the everyday shops of a small town supplemented by the gift and ice cream shops that are popular with visitors. The street widens out into the former Market Place, but today this is a bustle of passing cars. There are some quite attractive buildings in the street, as well as the usual more modern boxes, the commercial need apparently more important than aesthetic criteria. The banks had the wherewithal to create some attractive buildings – the Bank of Scotland dates from around 1860, while the Royal Bank of Scotland structure was erected in 1900 in a Dutch renaissance style. But perhaps the most attractive is the former British Linen Bank of 1907–8, designed by Sir Thomas Washington Browne in a style more suited to the Cotswolds. The railway station is located behind the façade of the shops.

The railway reached Largs on 1 June 1885, but proposals to continue the line further north, linking with the railway at Wemyss Bay were vigorously, and successfully, resisted by local landowners. Other schemes that envisaged the railway swinging round to the foot of Gogo Water and along the front to a rebuilt pier also failed. The station building at Largs dates from 1936 but was seriously damaged on 11 July 1995 when a train failed to stop and crashed through the buffers. The station was rebuilt thereafter, but much of its original elegance has been lost.

The old churchyard in the centre of the town is a quiet spot that is worth searching out. It is located off Main Street, in a lane called Manse Court. Although not very large, the kirkyard contains many old and interesting gravestones. Notable also are the two burial mausoleums, the larger being the resting place of the Montgomeries of Skelmorlie, the smaller the burial place of the Brisbanes of that Ilk. The Skelmorlie Aisle, for it was once attached to the long-demolished parish church, dates from 1636 and is a fine building erected to house the remains of Sir Robert Montgomerie. The exterior is quite plain, apart from the windows and the coat of arms over the doorway, but inside is a spectacular memorial to Sir Robert Montgomerie of Skelmorlie and his wife, Margaret Douglas. Sir Robert erected the vault in memory of his wife, who was killed by a kick from a horse at Largs Fair. The memorial within is a finely-carved canopy-tomb in the Renaissance style, although the effigy is either missing or was never actually made. If the quality of this wasn't enough, the barrel-vaulted ceiling is lined with wood and is richly painted with scenes of the seasons, signs of the Zodiac, and what may be the only known illustration of the original church of Largs. This was the work of J. S. Stalker in 1638. The aisle is now protected by Historic Scotland and is regularly open to the public. The Brisbane vault is a dinky little stone structure by comparison. Roofed with large stone slabs, the vault was erected in 1634. Next to this vault is a Bronze Age burial cist, relocated here in 1906 from a site near to the Haylie burial chamber. Within was found a human skeleton.

Largs Museum is located in Kirkgate House, an old building next to the kirkyard gate. Built into the wall are some old stones rescued from the Gogo Bridge, recording dates of erection. The bridge was carried away in a flood in 1831 but quickly rebuilt. The museum, which is operated by volunteers from Largs & District Historical Society, contains much of interest, and also mounts a range of exhibitions. Here can be seen various relics from Largs's past, in particular Victoriana, Mauchline Ware and items reflecting the town's links with Australia.

The seafront at Largs, known variously as the Esplanade, or Victoria Esplanade, is where the day-tripper heads. The southern part of it is the Gallowgate, one of the old streets of Largs. Here can be found the amusements and bars of the seaside resort, which quickly recede from sight as one walks north, where the front is occupied by open grassland and flower beds. Overlooking the Esplanade is Nardini's restaurant, famous the world over for its delicious ice cream. Pietro Nardini and his three sons, Augusto, Sandrino and Nardino, founded the café in the early 1900s, when they bought an old mansion on Largs seafront for £10,000. The present building is a noted Art Deco structure, designed by Charles Davidson in 1936, and still furnished in the style of the period. The café and associated business was placed on the market in 2001.

Brooksby House is now a convalescent home. It was erected in 1837 to plans of David Hamilton for Matthew Preston, a Glasgow merchant. The stone for the house came from Girvan, and was transported to the site by ship. One of these sank en route, but some of the stone was salvaged and it is said that some of the discoloured stone on the stable block was a result of this. Moorburn House dates from 1876, and is now council offices. Further north, on the landward side of the Esplanade, stands Vikingar! an exciting visitor and leisure centre. This incorporates the former Barrfields Pavilion, erected in 1929 to plans by

Largs: the promenade with St Columba's Church (left)
and the Clark Memorial Church (right)

William Barclay. The centre contains a five-hundred-seat theatre and cinema, an eighty-feet swimming pool, and a visitor centre detailing the association of the Vikings with Largs. There are also fitness rooms, a play area, and a winter garden, complete with an award-winning display of trees and plants.

Largs is distinguished by a fine selection of churches, erected with the bountiful patronage of some of the settlers to the town. One of the largest stands on the promenade, at the junction with Gallowgate. This is St Columba's Parish Church, constructed in 1891–3 to replace the old church of 1812 that stood on the same site and which in turn had replaced the kirk in the kirkyard. The architects were Henry Steele and Andrew Balfour, and the building was constructed with rich red sandstone, its tower, spire and clock dominating views of the bay. Within can be seen some fine stained glasswork, executed by Cottier & Co., Douglas Strachan, and Alfred & Gordon Webster, an oak pulpit by M. S. Gibson, and a war memorial by Sir Robert Lorimer. The organ is by 'Father' Henry Willis. A memorial within commemorates Sir Thomas MakDougall Brisbane. The church is open to visitors during the morning.

Further north along the Esplanade is St Mary's Star of the Sea RC Church. This is a modern building, erected to the plans of A. R. Conlon, of Reginald Fairlie & Sons, in 1962. Its statue of Our Lady, Star of the Sea, by the Scots sculptor, Hew Lorimer, distinguishes the chapel. Within are tapestries. At Aubery Crescent, to the north end of the Esplanade, is St Columba's Scottish Episcopal Church. Built in 1876 to plans by Alexander Ross and Robert J. Macbeth, this church was unfortunate in that its tower was never completed. Inside can be seen memorials to Lord Kelvin and MakDougall Brisbane.

Back in the centre of town, just off Main Street, are two other notable church buildings, standing side by side. The largest, and most distinguished, is the Clark Memorial Church, built 1890–2 of red sandstone from Locharbriggs and Corsehill. The main aisle of the church is an early English Gothic building, with statues of Moses and St John at the west end. Adjoining, but quite separate from the main block, is a tall steeple, with a peel of bells. John Clark of the Anchor Thread Mills in Paisley gifted the church, which started out as a United Presbyterian place of worship, to Largs. He employed William Kerr of T. G. Abercrombie, architects from Paisley, to design the building. Inside are a fine hammer-beam roof and a Willis organ. The stained glass is a good example of the arts and crafts movement, the work of Stephen Adam, Meikle & Sons and C. W. Whall.

Easily dwarfed by the massive bulk of the Clark Memorial, but distinguished in its own way, is the Romanesque church of St John's, originally erected as a Free Church but now part of the Church of Scotland. This was erected to plans by A. J. Graham in 1886. There are two other churches in Largs: the United Free in Brisbane Road (1929) and the Brisbane Evangelical Church at the junction of School and Boyd streets.

There are no churches south of the Gogo Water. This is quite significant, for over many years the parishioners in that part of the town campaigned to have a place of worship close at hand to prevent them having to ford the Gogo in spate during the winter months, and at other times when heavy rain caused a quick run-off from the moors. Proposals for moving the parish church to Fairlie were never carried out, and the church that was eventually erected there as a chapel of ease was established after the Gogo had been bridged.

Although there are no churches south of the Gogo, in Mackerstoun Place, occupying a former hotel, is a Benedictine monastery. At the southern end of the building is a museum of Scottish Christianity, which gives an account of worship in Scotland over the centuries. On display are twelfth century statues, reliquaries, embroidery carried out by nuns in the early nineteenth century and numerous other artefacts.

Further south along Broomfield Crescent is Curlinghall, now a group of modern flats. The name comes from the former mansion that was erected there in 1813. This was the home of Dr John Cairnie, who was a very keen aficionado of the sport of curling. Indeed, at Curlinghall he erected the very first indoor curling rink in the world. Cairnie was instrumental in founding the Royal Caledonian Curling Club in 1838, becoming its first president. He had placed an advertisement in the *North British Advertiser* calling on those interested in curling to a public meeting in the Waterloo Hotel in Edinburgh. Cairnie was late, by which time the dozen or so interested men were thinking of going home, believing they had been hoaxed. However, once Cairnie got things in motion they were so impressed by him that he was voted on as chairman.

The Elderslie Hotel consists of two buildings: Priory Lodge erected in 1829–30 to plans by David and James Hamilton, and Elderslie House of 1812, originally the UP manse. Proposals in 1911 to extend the buildings and create what was to be Largs Hydropathic were hampered by the Great War.

The land hereabouts was where the Battle of Largs took place in 1263. A memorial stone at Curlinghall commemorates the victory of the Scots over the Vikings, and though the battle was not a major one, the victory was instrumental in bringing about the end of Viking rule over the western seaboard of Scotland. The Norsemen had been making a number of raids on the west coast of Scotland and were proposing trying to reclaim some lands they had lost to King Alexander III of Scotland. King Haco of Norway came with a fleet of around 160 long ships, manned by thousands of Vikings, though the number varies depending on which account of the battle is consulted. The Scots were camped west of Kilbirnie, awaiting an attack. However, a storm blew many Viking ships onto the coast on 2 October 1263 whereupon the Scots attacked the sailors. Haco sent more men as a backup, but the Scots were successful in defeating them also. Some form of truce seems to have resulted, and Haco is thought to have obtained permission to bury the Viking dead in the nearest Christian site to the battle. This is thought to have been at the Chapel of St Vey, on the island of Little Cumbrae. Excavations there revealed numerous bodies with steel helmets. Some of the ancient cairns in and around Largs were traditionally claimed to be burials of Viking dead, but later historians have proved them to be much older, dating from the Bronze Age.

The more striking memorial to the Battle of Largs stands on a low headland at Far Bowen Craigs, at the southern extremity of the town, next to the Largs marina. The memorial is known locally as 'The Pencil' because of its shape, and even some modern housing has been given the street name, Pencil View. The memorial, the design of which is based on a Pictish round tower, was the work of J. S. Kay of Newton Stewart. Rising seventy feet in height, the monument was opened on 10 July 1912.

On the hillside east of the town is the Inverclyde Scottish National Recreation Centre, opened by Queen Elizabeth in 1958. This residential sports centre offers many courses, and is used regularly for football training by the Scotland national team among others. The main house at Inverclyde was erected in the late nineteenth century as a private house, at that time known as Burnside House. It was later used as the Whitehills Hotel.

Gogo Glen strikes east of Largs. The name Gogo is supposed to be Celtic, meaning a branching river. The glen is steep and narrow, with no road through it, other than a small track from Flatt to the Greeto Bridge and some sheep pens. The Greeto Water is a tributary of the Gogo, but is the larger watercourse, dropping from the Waterhead Moor. Both the Gogo and the Greeto are adorned with a multitude of waterfalls, including the Black Linn and Maiden's Loup. At the head of Greeto Water is the Hill of Stake, at 1,711 feet the tallest hill in the Ayrshire and Renfrewshire heights.

The Haylie Brae is one of the main routes out of Largs; the A760 climbs up the hillside and makes its way over the hills to the Garnock valley. On the brae is Largs cemetery. Here can be seen the grave of shipping magnate and art collector Sir William Burrell (1861–1958), who gifted the Burrell Collection to the City of Glasgow. The Burrells were regular holidaymakers at Largs, renting Auchenean in Nelson Street, now the site of Nardini's Restaurant. Also buried here is Lord Kelvin's wife. There are two viewpoint indicators on low hillsides above the road, one at the Haylie Reservoir (which was constructed by Ayr County Council for water storage) the other on a rocky knoll to the north. This second viewpoint is also accessible by climbing a steep path from Douglas Park.

North of this second viewpoint is a low knoll known as Castle Hill, on which are the remains of a prehistoric hill fort. This is quickly reached from the roadside and affords spectacular views over Largs, and of any attacking marauders for that matter. Lying on the hillside below the fort is the remote cottage of Cockmalane, at one time a popular view on old picture postcards of the area.

The growth of the southern side of Largs has been checked by the 18-hole golf course and policies of Kelburn Castle. Largs Golf Club's course extends south, through part of Kelburn Park, east of the main road. It is 5,707 yards in length and a par 68. The opposite side of the road is occupied by the very busy Largs yacht haven. A road crosses the railway to a car park and facilities for sailing and cruising yachts. The marina is modern, having only been established in the mid 1980s. Pontoons behind two large breakwaters provide a safe berth for hundreds of pleasure craft.

The attractive lands hereabouts form the policies of Kelburn Castle, seat of the Earls of Glasgow. The castle policies are now home to a country park, popular throughout the summer months with visitors. Here can be seen the attractive park centre, formed out of an old steading, an assault course and the children's favourite, the 'Secret Forest'. Attractive woodland walks can be taken up and down the side of the Kel Burn, which here drops suddenly from the moors to the coastal plain. Above the castle is a notable waterfall, the water cascading into a deep pool. Just beyond this the path leads to an attractive memorial to the 3rd Earl of Glasgow. This was the work of Robert Adam in 1775. The Plaisance is a formal walled garden, in which grow two-thousand-year-old yew trees. An eighteenth-century sundial, ice house and laundry museum can also be seen.

Kelburn Castle itself is one of the finest country houses in the north of Ayrshire. The oldest part is the tower of 1581, to which various additions have been made, although it is claimed that work from the twelfth century is incorporated. The tower rises four storeys in height, and has turrets and towers at the corners. The William and Mary block dates

Kelburn Castle: the old tower with the William and Mary wing to the left

from 1700 and is an attractive extension to the old tower. A Victorian wing was added in 1879. The castle is open to visitors during the months of July and August, when tours can be booked at the park centre. Within one can see a fine selection of antique furniture, paintings, William Morris wallpaper and collections of taxidermy.

Kelburn has been the seat of the Boyle family since 1140. They were hereditary coroners of Largs. In 1699 David Boyle was created Lord Boyle of Kelbourne and in 1703 was raised in the peerage to Earl of Glasgow. He was instrumental in promoting the Act of Union. The 7th Earl was Governor of New Zealand from 1892–7. The Earls of Glasgow still own the castle and estate.

South of Kelburn parklands we enter the coastal village of Fairlie. This is built along the shore at the foot of the hills, most vehicles passing through the village and not stopping to enjoy the atmosphere. Near the north end of the village is a road out to a headland, where there is a parking and picnic area. This was where Fairlie Pier once stood, a popular halt for Clyde steamers in their heyday. Today it is the location of a modern sewage-treatment works, erected in 1995.

Fairlie was originally a small fishing village, the boats lugged up onto Fairlie Sands. Here also was an old inn that was established for those folk travelling by ferry to, or from, Cumbrae. The Fairlie Inn was later converted into a private house, now known as Rockhaven. With the arrival of the railway (opened on 1 June 1880) the village began to grow and, as with most coastal communities, became a popular location for summer villas and retirement homes. The railway required a tunnel beneath the main street of the village, at 4,000 yards in length one of the longest tunnels in southern Scotland. The village even had two railway stations at one time, the village station, which is still in use, and a station at Fairlie Pier. The pier and station there were opened on 1 July 1882 and as it offered the shortest crossing to Campbeltown, was a popular halt with fast trains from Glasgow.

Immediately to the north of the pier headland is the former NATO base, with its jetty out into Fairlie Roads, the name for the stretch of water between Great Cumbrae and the mainland. A railway siding out onto the pier allowed ships to be restocked, but today the site is no longer used by the military.

A walk along Bay Street can be made from the picnic area. At the north end, in the gusset between the shore road and the main street, stands the parish church. This was erected in 1833–4 to seat 300, but in 1883 it was extended to plans by J. J. Stevenson, when the squat tower and spire was added. The church has some fine stained glass, the work of Morris & Co., Powell Brothers, Gordon Webster and Heaton, Butler & Bayne. Within the church can be seen a 'Breeches' Bible of the sixteenth century, wherein Adam and Eve made themselves breeches, and the tenth or eleventh century Fairlie Stone, which is probably part of an early Christian cross. Found when the Chapel House was demolished, the stone has carvings of a man and two wild animals. There is also a mural plaque commemorating Alan Boyle, noted for flying the first British monoplane in 1909. The former Free Church, erected in 1879 and subsequently the parish church hall, was in 1998 converted into a private house.

The Village Inn and Mudhook Restaurant is an old, traditional Scots inn. On the external wall is a plaque commemorating the boat-building yard of William Fife, which formerly occupied the ground across the street, as well as the founding of the Mudhook Yacht Club in 1873 by five Clyde yachtsmen. The Fairlie Yacht Club was founded in 1961 by a small group of keen sailors who moored their yachts in Fairlie Bay. The Club now has over 400 members and runs a popular racing series at Largs and Inverkip, as well as weekend passage races to places throughout the Firth of Clyde.

William Fife (1785–1865) established the boatyard in 1812. One of the first significant ships built there was the *Industry*, in 1814. Later in time Fife's yard was the birthplace of some famous racing yachts, including the Marquis of Ailsa's *Bloodhound* (1864) and *Shamrock* (1899) and Sir Thomas Lipton's *Shamrock III* (1903). During the Second World War the yard was requisitioned for military use, when it played home to the Anti-Submarine Experimental Establishment. Fife's sold out in 1947 but yacht building continued for a number of years under the name of the Fairlie Yacht Slip Company. The yard was eventually closed in 1985 and the sheds demolished soon afterwards.

Fairlie village hall is an attractive, if rather diminutive, structure. Like the parish church it was designed by Stevenson, and was the gift of Charles Stuart Parker. He was the MP for Perthshire (1868–74) and Perth (1878–92).

Between the older part of Fairlie village and the mouth of the Fairlie Burn are some fine houses. Fairlie House was erected in 1816 for Charles Parker and remained in Parker hands until 1934. Mrs Parker's sister and her husband, Hugh Tennent, built Creich House, now known as Fairhaven. It was Hugh Tennent who brought back the recipe for lager from Europe, brewing the well-known Tennent's Lager in Glasgow from then onwards. Fairlie Cottage was the home of Sir James Dobbie (1852–1924), a noted chemical engineer responsible for inventing various instruments used in the maritime industry. John Honeyman designed Fairlie Cottage and his trainee, Charles Rennie Mackintosh, may have influenced some of the early Art Deco designs.

Fairlie Burn cascades through the narrow defile known as Fairlie Glen, the stream tumbling down over a series of falls. Above some waterfalls, and affording extensive views over the Clyde, stands the square tower of Fairlie Castle. Sir Robert Fairlie of that Ilk, whose family held these lands from the fourteenth century, erected this in 1521. The tower rises four storeys in height, the wallheads surrounded by an ornate chequerboard corbel course. Around 1660 the Fairlies sold the tower to the neighbouring Boyles of Kelburn. Elizabeth Halkett, Lady Wardlaw (1677–1727), set much of her ballad 'Hardyknute' at Fairlie Castle.

Southannan House was latterly used as a children's home but has now been sub-divided. It was at one time a magnificent mansion. It has its origins as a castle, which was designed by Lord Sempill from a design which he procured in Italy, and was one of the most ambitious buildings built during the reign of James VI; Mary Queen of Scots came to Southannan in 1563 to visit Lord Sempill. The name comes from St Annan or Innan, for in the grounds formerly stood a chapel dedicated to the saint, and not from South Annan, for there is no North Annan. The ruins of Underbank still exist in the grounds. This was an extensive building built around 1500 by Lord Sempill.

On the hillside above Southannan House can be found a natural rock on which Bronze Age man has carved a cup and ring marking. What these symbols were is unknown, but this one can be found on a rock at the Diamond Hill. Diamond Hill is a lower eminence of Kaim Hill, which rises 1,270 feet above the village. Kaim Hill was at one time quarried for its stone, a stratum of breccia (white sandstone containing quartz) being in great demand for making millstones. In 1837 thirty stones were produced per annum. The stone was taken down to Fencebay where a small production unit created high quality stones that were exported as far away as Australia. This industry died out with the introduction of more modern methods of grinding. Explorers can find half a millstone lying at the north end of the quarry.

The Southannan Sands and Fence Bay have been developed as a large ore terminal. British Steel created a large stockyard on the level ground, extending out into the bay, at a cost of over £160 million in 1979. The architects were Frank Mears & Partners. A long pier with tall cranes was built out into the deep water of Fairlie Roads, allowing ships to unload iron ore. This was then transported ashore on long conveyors, before being loaded onto railway wagons. The Hunterston Ore Terminal, as it was known, was closed in 1992, but Clydeport reopened it for the importation of coal.

2

# West Kilbride, Portencross and Hunterston

THE PARISH OF WEST Kilbride occupies 10,032 acres, and is located on a large headland west of the Crosbie and Knockewart hills. The cafe on Boydston Shore marks the southern limit of the parish today. The low-lying land here is a raised beach, the steep Boydston Braes being the original cliffs. Along the cliff top are a series of prehistoric defences, a dun below Boydston farm, a homestead above Glenfoot House, and an earthwork further south at Ardrossan. On Boydston Shore can be found some ancient stone-fish-traps, created by building stone walls between low and high tides in which fish were trapped as the tide receded.

The village of West Kilbride is an ancient one, but it may have originally been located further to the south-west, near the present Seamill, until it was found more prudent to 'hide' the village inland, away from raiders from the sea. West Kilbride was renowned for its five mills (two for oats, one for flax, one for grinding bark for tanning purposes and the fifth for milling charcoal into a powder, used in foundries). It was also noted for weaving and sewing muslin, and some of the traditional styled single-storey weavers' cottages are still extant. In 1837 there were around one hundred handlooms in the village, working for agents in Paisley and Glasgow. Due to its location inland the centre of West Kilbride is thus bypassed by all those who do not need to go there, leaving the village somewhat forgotten up its little glen.

Kirktonhall House stands at the east end of the Main Street. It was originally erected in 1660 but was extended in 1791 and 1807. Now used as council offices, Kirktonhall was the birthplace of Professor Robert Simson (1687–1768). In the garden is a sundial dated 1717, thought to have been designed by Simson himself. It also contains the initials of his father and mother. The Glen, now a park but originally part of Kirktonhall's grounds, was gifted to the village in 1924 by Robert Barr.

In Arthur Street, just off Main Street, can be found the rather interesting West Kilbride Museum. This is located in the upstairs of what was at one time the Public Hall, erected in 1899 to plans by Alexander Paterson. There are displays on various themes, including local castles, weaving, Ayrshire embroidery, and even beachcombing, as well as temporary exhibitions on a variety of subjects.

The churches of West Kilbride are quite distinctive in their architecture.

24

Overton Church was erected in 1883 to the plans of Hippolyte J. Blanc. It has some fine stained glass from various periods, including windows by William Meikle, C. E. Stewart, Gordon Webster and the Towerlands Studio. The Webster windows depict some local historical connections, including Arran, Hunterston 'A', Crosbie and Law castles and Sir William Wallace. Built as a UP church, it cost £2,500 and could seat 400 worshippers. St Andrews Church dates from 1881 and was designed by James Ritchie in a French style. Originally the Free Church, it had to go one better than the parish church – its spire was 120 feet in height. Built at a cost of £3,500, it could seat 450. The former Barony Church dates from 1873 and was the work of Henry Blair, using Early English influences. This could seat 610 and is distinguished by a spire measuring 100 feet. In 1995 its stained glass windows were removed illegally and subsequently lost. St Bride's RC Church was built in Hunterston Road in 1908 and to celebrate its fiftieth anniversary a Marian shrine was erected in the grounds. One of West Kilbride parish's early ministers, Revd George Crawfurd, 'was deposed in the strick times of the Covenant for wardly mindedness and selling a horse on the Sabbath Day.'

The railway reached West Kilbride on 1 May 1878 on its way searching for the holidaymakers of Largs and the coast. The station buildings are attractive, dating from around 1900, the work of James Miller.

West Kilbride cemetery is located on the lower slopes of Drummilling Hill. From a distance one memorial is larger than the rest – the Simson Monument. This was designed by F. T. Pilkington in 1865 and commemorates Robert Simson, born on 14 October 1687, the eldest of seventeen sons born to John and Agnes Simson. The style of the memorial is rather overpowering, incorporating Egyptian-style motifs. Simson is known as the 'Restorer of Greek Geometry', having spent much of his time researching the ancient Greek mathematicians and piecing together fragments of their work. He was particularly interested in Euclid, and translated and edited his works. Simson commenced his studies at London, and became professor of mathematics at Glasgow University in 1711, remaining there for fifty-eight years. He died in Glasgow on 1 October 1768 and was buried in the city's Blackfriars burial ground. He was never married, and Kirktonhall passed to his great-nephew who later sold it. Dr Trail of Belfast wrote a memoir of Simson's life and work in 1812.

Other illustrious sons of West Kilbride include General Sir Robert Boyd (1710–94), who was the lieutenant governor of Gibraltar at the time of the siege in 1782. His parents tenanted a small farm in the parish, but Robert moved at an early age to Irvine where he was brought up. He worked as a sailor in the port there before being impressed into the navy. He later became a soldier and worked his way up through the ranks.

The passing motorist will be better acquainted with the Seamill part of the village, where coastal villas and hotels were erected in more peaceful times, when attack from the sea was unlikely. On entering the village from the south the road splits at Chapelton Farm, now converted into houses. In 1871, on the farmlands, a plough unearthed a hoard of 300 silver coins, mainly dating from the reign of Queen Elizabeth. The coast road passes smart bungalows to the foot of the Kilbride Burn, where the old Sea Mill survives as a domestic residence. Visible from the roadside is the former storage pond and the millwheel. Across the road from Sea Mill is a house known as The Fort, so-called from the fact that it occupies the site of an ancient hill-fort. Excavations here in the 1830s unearthed charcoal, bones and antlers. In 1833, when the present coast road was being created near here, two Bronze Age urns were uncovered.

Up the Kilbride glen is the large building now used as a Christian residential centre. It was built in 1893–4 as the Glasgow and West of Scotland Co-operative Society convalescent home. Another large property, Holland House in Ardneil Bay, was a former Children's Home, erected in 1893, as part of the Glasgow Fresh-Air Fortnight Scheme, and another was a Young Men's Christian Association hostel, which accommodated 250, and dates from 1893. The Paisley Convalescent Home was erected in 1885 for use of patients from Paisley Infirmary, at the expense of James Arthur of Carlung. It was doubled in size in 1897 by which time it could accommodate 100 residents. Today it is the West Kilbride community centre.

Seamill Hydro Hotel is still popular for holidays, having been extended considerably since the hydropathic was first erected in 1871. The hotel was extended in the 1920s by Thomas Marwick, in the 1960s by Hay Steel & MacFarlane, and again in recent years. The main road climbs steeply now, passing through a busy part of the village, to the crossroads. The upper road leads into West Kilbride centre, while the lower drops down to the shore.

On the lower slopes of Law Hill, at the east end of West Kilbride, stands the foursquare tower of Law Castle, sometimes known as Kilbride Castle. Local tradition holds that it was erected for Princess Mary, daughter of King James II, who married Thomas, the Master of Boyd. Thomas was to become Earl of Arran, but he and his father were attainted in 1569 for supposedly plotting against the king (who was a minor) and had to flee the country. The castle is said to date from 1468 but may have taken until around 1510 to complete. The tower is rectangular in plan, and rises through four floors to an open parapet. The castle was for many years abandoned, but recently has been restored to plans of Ian Begg, a noted architect in this field, who actually built a modern castle for himself near Kyle of Lochalsh.

A range of prominent hills rises to the east of West Kilbride, starting with Law Hill. This is crowned with a wireless transmitter. Further east is Blackshaw Hill, and then the highest of this group, North Knockewart Hill, at 794 feet above sea level. This too is topped with a wireless station, but of more interest is the ancient burial cairn. In the low-lying ground between Blackshaw and North hills can be found an ancient enclosure and a cup-and-ring-marked rock. The South Knockewart Hill is better known as Knock Jargon, rising 758 feet in height. A hill fort that comprises two walls enclosing an area approximately 150 feet by 100 feet adorns the summit. South of this are further mounds and ditches. Within the fort is a burial cairn, fifty feet in diameter.

The old trackway from Law Castle alongside the north of Law Hill then south of Blackshaw Hill and into Glen Garnock is known locally as the King's Road. Tradition has it that the dead kings and queens of Scotland were brought this way to Portencross, from where they were ferried across the firth to Argyll and thence to Iona for burial. Within West Kilbride they were taken along the road known as the Halfway.

Portencross: castle, village and old harbour

From West Kilbride the B7048 strikes west to the little village of Portencross. South of this road is West Kilbride golf course, an 18-hole, par 71 course, of 6,452 yards length. Tom Morris senior, winner of four Open Championships in the nineteenth century, designed the course. An attractive hamlet, there is little here other than a few large houses in secluded grounds and a couple of rows of former fishermen's houses in addition to the ruined castle. And yet Portencross played an important part in the history of the area, out of all proportion with its size today. The castle was originally known as Ardneil, a name that survives for a farm on the road into Portencross. The barony that Portencross Castle was the caput for is known as Ardneil.

The castle is the most prominent building in the village. It was probably erected in the fourteenth century, its elongated L–plan being the result of the narrow rock headland on which it stands. Built by the Boyds, who held the barony since the Bruce gave it to them, the castle remained in their hands until 1785 when Robert Boyd died unmarried. It then passed to the Fullarton family. The tower stands on the bare rocks of the shore, and would have been an important lookout for Clyde boats. To the immediate north of the castle is a narrow rocky inlet, officially the old harbour, where the castle could originally have kept a boat or two. The castle rises over three floors, the ground and first floors being vaulted. The lesser tower has an extra storey. An inventory of the contents of the castle made in 1621 stated that there were 'ten fedder beddis' within it. Latterly fishermen's families occupied it. The roof has gone, being blown off in a storm in January 1739, but it was capped in the twentieth century with concrete.

A hundred yards or so to the north is the 'new' harbour, little more than an inlet of the sea, surrounded by dry-stone walls and a few anchoring rings. This harbour was constructed around 1800. The harbour dries out at low tide, but was at one time a popular haven for fishing vessels and ships up to forty or fifty tons burden could sail in at high water. A further few hundred yards north are the remains of a pier projecting out into the firth. It was built of concrete and opened on 11 July 1912 with the intention of allowing Clyde cruisers to tie alongside, in the expectation that it would bring tourists and custom to the village. The hoped-for railway that would have allowed these developments to materialise never came, and the pier was quickly abandoned. Proposals in 1969 by Standard Oil (or Esso as it is better known in this country) to construct an oil terminal here also came to nought, much to the delight of the locals who feared that it would totally destroy the historic atmosphere of the area. The large house overlooking the pier is Auchenames, built in the early nineteenth century for the Craufurd family. The walled garden is dated 1839. Additions were made to the house in 1904 for W. Adam of Overton, who had bought the estate from the Craufurds.

One of the ships from the Spanish armada that was sailing in the vicinity in 1588 sank in water ten fathoms deep when it was wrecked off the headland. An early diving expedition in August 1740 by Sir Archibald Grant and Captain Rae recovered numerous brass and iron guns from the wreck. One of these, a cannon, on which the Spanish arms and crown could just be discerned, was for over two hundred years affixed to the rocks next to the castle. It is now at Hunterston visitor centre. It is said that the ship was sunk at the command of Geils Buchanan, a local witch. Daniel Defoe wrote of the diving expedition in his *A Tour Through the Whole Island of Great Britain*. He noted that 'Captain Rae immediately went down and found the vessel to be very entire, to have a great number of guns on board, but to be full of sand.' The ship itself has never been recovered and lies beneath the waves to this day.

The sailing ship, *Lady Margaret*, ran aground in a storm on the rocks south of Portencross Castle in January 1770. The cargo was worth £14,000 and it was decided to abandon the ship, which was worth only £2,600, and to salvage the goods in the hold instead. A large hole was cut in the side of the vessel, facilitating the salvage operation. After the ship was emptied of all that could be rescued, it was destroyed by the waves on 11 February 1770.

The hill above Portencross is known as the Auld Hill, probably from the fact that its summit has the remains of a fort and dun upon it. The fort is badly damaged, but is of particular interest due to the fact that some of the stonework is vitrified. The fort covers an area 100 feet by 50 feet, and two external ditches enhanced the defences. The dun is located at the southern end of the fort, and was constructed at a later date. Measuring forty-five feet by twenty-five feet, the dun is protected by thick walling.

A track passing the new harbour and the pier continues through a narrow gap in the rock cliffs, known as the Throughlet, and makes its way north to Northbank Cottage. This is a rather undistinguished building, typical of many thousands, but here in 1913 there took place the 'Portencross Murder' which is unsolved to this day. The cottage was home of Alexander MacLaren and his wife, Jessie, as well as his sister-in-law, Miss Mary Speir Gunn. On 18 October the three were in the house reading when the window was broken and shots were fired. Mary Gunn was hit by three bullets and died instantly. Jessie MacLaren was wounded but survived while Alexander MacLaren was uninjured. He went outside immediately but saw no one and then ran to Portencross to raise the alarm. No one was ever caught, though some believe that MacLaren was the culprit, plotting the murder of his wife so that he could then marry Mary Gunn, her younger and more attractive sister. The case has never been solved, and remains a mystery to this day.

North of West Kilbride stands Carlung House, built in 1932 for the Arthur family. The house is a fine English Manorial building, designed to look older than its actual date of construction, and was the work of J. Austin Laird. The house occupies the site of various earlier buildings, including an old tower house of around 1560, a replacement of 1799 and a third of 1845–53. The lodge house is contemporary with the mansion, but the oval walled garden probably dates from the mid nineteenth century. The Baronetcy of Carlung, created in 1903, is still held by the family. The first baronet, Sir Matthew Arthur (1852–1928), was a director of the Glasgow and South West Scotland Railway Company and chairman of Arthur & Co. of Glasgow. Sir Matthew was created Baron Glenarthur in 1918. Today the house has been divided into flats. The smallholdings named Thirdpart occupy much of the ground to the north.

A roadway from the A78 strikes northwest towards Hunterston Castle, still the property of the Hunter family. The Hunters were given the lands in the thirteenth century, and Ailmer de la Hunter's name appears in the Ragman Roll of 1296. The lairds have been active in Scottish affairs, John Hunter being killed at Flodden and Mungo Hunter killed at Pinkie.

The castle is an old tower house of the sixteenth century, to which various extensions have been added, in particular in 1847. The tower rises through four storeys, the ground floor of which is vaulted. In 1913 Sir Robert Lorimer was employed by the Hunters to restore the castle, which he did admirably, though it would have been better without the large double doors into the tower. Internally there is much fine crafts-manship, in particular the carved stone lintel in the great hall that bears the Hunter arms, and is the work of Lorimer. The castle was restored again in 2001 and is now the centre of the Clan Hunter Association worldwide. There are occasional tours of the castle for visitors.

A number of old trees at Hunterston were of local interest. One of these, the Resting Tree, had a large hollow cut out of one side, into which a bench was placed. The tree, which had originally been used as the local dule tree, died, but an oak seedling was planted to replace it in 1985 by Neil Aylmer Hunter, the twenty-ninth clan chief.

North of the castle, and its successor, stands the large bulk of Hunterston House. Erected around 1800 by Robert Caldwell Hunter, the house is a block of three storeys plus attic. Extensions were added in 1835, the 1880s and later. The house has various bays and a prominent tower, though its view of Great Cumbrae has been spoiled somewhat by the creation of Hunterston Oil Rig Construction Yard just off Hunterston Sands. The house, however, remains the seat of the Hunters.

Hunterston 'B' power station

Along the shore is a wide road leading to Hunterston Nuclear Generating Stations. There are two power stations sitting side by side here, Hunterston 'A' and 'B', the former now redundant and in the process of being decommissioned. Hunterston 'A' was erected in 1957–64 to the plans of Howard V. Lobb & Partners. Distinguished by its large glazed tower, the station was a Magnox-type generator, comprising two 160-megawatt gas-cooled reactors. The station was opened in 1964 by Queen Elizabeth, the Queen Mother, at which time it was the most powerful nuclear plant in the world. It was closed in 1990 and a 135-year decommissioning programme was instituted.

Hunterston 'B' was built between 1967 and 1976, Robert Matthew Johnson-Marshall & Partners providing the plans for a basic box shape, which is considerably less attractive than the older station. Sir Monty Finnieston officially opened the power station in 1976. Within the main building the two advanced gas-cooled reactors can produce 1,288 megawatts of electricity. A visitor centre has been established to allow the story of nuclear power to be told, and from it guided tours of the main building are given.

Beyond Hunterston 'A' the road can be followed to a pier, on the landward side of which is an enclosure used by British Nuclear Fuels Limited for training purposes. Behind it, beneath the cliffs of Hawking Craig, can be found the Holy Cave. This is traditionally associated with St Kentigern, or St Mungo as he is better known. He is the patron saint of Glasgow, as well as other places, and it is said that he came to this cave for some quiet reflection. At the mouth of the cave is a very deep wishing well, to which pilgrimages were made for many years. The water in the well was said to have curative properties.

The cliffs of Hawking Craig extend south from here to Portencross, at various points the rock formations being known as the Three Sisters, Meg, Jean and Lizzie. These cliffs are also sometimes known as the Three Jeans or Three Nuns. A path along the shore makes a pleasant stroll to Portencross Castle, visible on its headland to the south.

It was in the vicinity that two workmen digging ditches in 1826 found the Hunterston Brooch. On cleaning it up they discovered that it was a very fine piece of craftsmanship, dating from around AD 700. Made of solid silver, the brooch has gold filigree ornamentation, and a later inscription in runes that was probably added in the tenth century. This was translated as 'Malbritha owns this brooch'. It may have been the work of Anglo-Saxon craftsmen based either somewhere in the west of Scotland or else in Ireland, where the Celtic designs with which the brooch is decorated was common. The National Museum in Edinburgh acquired the brooch for £500 in 1891, but a replica was made and is on display in Hunterston.

On the opposite side of the main road from Hunterston the land rises to the Crosbie Hills, the tallest of which is known as Caldron Hill. This eminence, 1,081 feet above sea level, is crowned by a prehistoric burial cairn, a second cairn being located on the Little Caldron nearby. A third cairn is located on Biglees Hill further to the west. A roadway makes its way round the north side of these hills from Fencebay, dropping again down to Dalry. As it climbs its follows the Glen Burn, which tumbles over a couple of waterfalls as it makes its way seaward from the Glenburn reservoir. One of the falls is known as Linnford. Below the fall, within the wood, is a prehistoric homestead known as the Castle Hill.

From the Crosbie Hills a stream known as the Crosbie Burn drops down to Crosbie Castle and soon changes its name to the Kilbride Burn, passing through West Kilbride. Crosbie Castle (or Crosbie Towers as it is sometimes known) is an ancient building to which various alterations have been made over the centuries. The oldest surviving part probably dates from 1676, though the site is much older. This part is T-shaped, and rises three storeys in height. Extensions were made to the old tower around 1896, and it is thought that Thomas MacGibbon and David Ross were responsible for these. Crosbie stands on a cliff above the Crosbie Burn, and no doubt the south side at one time had a moat or ditch for defence. It is claimed by some that Sir William Wallace, the great freedom fighter, was actually born here, for his mother was a Craufurd and she may have gone home to give birth. More plausible is the fact that he simply sheltered here for a time with his uncle, Reginald Craufurd. The Craufurds may have been granted the lands in 1263 for their part in the Battle of Largs. A later owner was nicknamed 'The Fish' for some reason – he was a friend of Fox and Gibbon. From 1941–59 Crosbie served as a youth hostel, followed by a caravan site, but has returned to private ownership. Within the grounds of Crosbie are two ancient mounds of unknown provenance, the Bushglen and Glen mounts.

# 3

# Ardrossan, Saltcoats and Stevenston

WHAT IS KNOWN LOCALLY as the 'Three Towns' consists of the burghs of Ardrossan, Saltcoats and Stevenston. To the outsider, passing along the 'High Road' they are hard to separate, but to the resident they are quite distinct and the boundaries well known. Ardrossan is the community furthest to the west. The town is ancient, for it has an old castle ruin perched on the Castle Hill. This existed at the time of the battles for independence in the thirteenth and fourteenth centuries. William Wallace is associated with a cunning ploy that started when he set one of the houses in the village alight. The English, who held the castle at the time, came out to assist in dowsing the flames, only to find themselves under attack. The attack was so successful that the Scots managed to fill one of the castle's vaults with English corpses. Since that time the vault has been known as 'Wallace's Larder'. In 1829, when a cutting was being made for the railway, a large bronze ring, with signet, was discovered, on which the initial 'W' was marked. It is thought this belonged to Wallace himself.

Ardrossan Castle

The earliest owners of Ardrossan, including the castle, appear to have been the Barclays, and later the Ardrossans of that Ilk. The Montgomerie family probably erected the castle that we see today on Castle Hill in the fifteenth century. It consisted of a major tower with vaults on the ground floor. The remains of a sally port survive, as well as part of a wall around the courtyard. On the south side of the court-yard a smaller building has survived, complete with vault, which was probably the kitchen. The castle was used as the principal seat of the Earl of Eglinton in 1528 after the Cuninghames sacked Eglinton Castle. Cromwell is said to have used some of the stone to build his citadel at Ayr, and certainly by 1689 the castle was in ruins. Further plundering took place in 1746 when the 10th Earl used stone to build a wall around a new park he had created.

North of the castle, but still on the hill top, can be seen the remnants of the old parish church. This was probably erected in the twelfth century but was abandoned in 1696 when it was seriously damaged by a storm. An old graveyard surrounded it, and a particularly fine stone sarcophagus found here in excavations in 1911 is now located in the museum at Saltcoats.

The church was replaced by a second building that stood next to the Stanley Burn, north of Parkhouse Road. This was erected in 1697 and served for almost fifty years. The church was then dismantled and re-erected in Saltcoats in 1744. Fragmentary remains of the Stanley building can just be made out on the ground within the public park. Also on the Castle Hill is an obelisk erected in memory of Dr Alexander MacFadzean (1788–1849). He was instrumental in having Ardrossan designated as a Burgh of Barony for £5 householders in 1846.

The old castle and church are all that remain of the original community of Ardrossan. The town was totally rebuilt in the late eighteenth century by the 12th Earl of Eglinton, when he decided to create a port here. He was created Baron Ardrossan in 1806. The plans originally included a canal from here to Glasgow, passing through the Garnock valley, but other than a short stretch that can be discovered in the vicinity of Ardeer, little of the canal was built.

Ardrossan's main street is known as Glasgow Street. Its strikes in a north-easterly direction from the cross, the spine of a gridded community. Much of the street has been redeveloped over the years, though some of the rebuilding work is not as attractive as it could have been. In the street stands the Congregational Church, dating from 1903 and the work of the architect, John B. Wilson. The adjoining hall was formerly the primary school. The civic centre dates from 1851 when it was known locally as Graham's Castle after its owner, Duncan Graham, who came to the town from the north of Scotland. He built his 'castle' in a gothic style, with battlements and arched windows. Properly known as Castlecraigs, the building was purchased by Archibald Russell in 1894, and sold to the Ardrossan Dockyard Company in 1920. They extended the building with the addition of recreation rooms. In 1933 it was used as a Masonic lodge, but in 1946 it was acquired by Ardrossan Burgh Council and became the town's civic centre. Almost next door is the Church of the Nazarene, built in 1857 as the Park Church of Scotland. The architect was Thomas Wallace.

West of Glasgow Street, and running parallel with it, is Montgomerie Street. Here stood the large houses of the professional classes, but these have gone and the street has been rebuilt over the years. Some of the derelict harbour-side property is currently being redeveloped. A large area of ground, now an industrial estate, was formerly the Shell Mex oil distribution and refining plant. This was established in 1925 and oil tankers of up to 11,000 tons could land crude oil at the harbour ready for refining. The works closed in 1986. At the corner of Montgomerie and Barr streets are modern flats, occupying the site of St John's Church, erected in 1859 as the Free Church. The church closed in 1987, having merged with the Barony Church, and the building was demolished in 1991. The Fire Station in Barr Street dates from 1933. The bottom end of the street turns sharp left into Princes Street. Here is Ardrossan library. The Eglinton Hotel was built in 1813 by the 12th Earl of Eglinton at a cost of £10,000. It was destroyed by fire in the 1980s.

Near Ardrossan Cross was the former town hall, erected in 1856 and adorned by a clock. Ardrossan was elevated to a Burgh of Barony in 1846. From Ardrossan Cross, Harbour Street and Harbour Road lead out onto the headland on which the town was built. The industrial landscape here has seen better days, and most of the old industries have gone. Here was the shipyard of the Ardrossan Dry-dock and Shipbuilding Company, where vessels of up to 6,000 tons were erected. The yard operated between 1910 and 1930.

The harbour at Ardrossan today comprises of the Eglinton Dock, which has been redesigned as the Clyde Marina and is a popular haven for sailing yachts and pleasure boats. The Eglinton Tidal Basin is still sometimes used for small cargo vessels. The Old Tidal Basin is now the Arran Ferry terminal, from where the Caledonian MacBrayne ferry service leaves for the island of Arran. The service is popular all year round, and the Ardrossan Harbour station brings tourists and commuters almost to the dockside by rail.

The outer harbour is protected by a large breakwater, which has its terminus on the East Crinan Rock, one of the large rocks in the vicinity potentially hazardous to shipping. There have been various grandiose schemes for extending the harbour over the years, some of which included building piers out to the Horse Isle, but none came to fruition. The Chinese paddle steamer *Chusan* ran aground on the Crinan Rock on 22 October 1874. The vessel broke into two, and fifteen lives were lost. A memorial in Ardrossan cemetery commemorates these sailors.

Ardrossan harbour has had a varied career. It was built for the export of coal, but in the 1920s and 1930s it was the British base of the Hudson Bay Company, and numerous cargoes of fur, sealskin, fish and oil were landed here. The port was also an important landing point for Baltic timber, which was converted into railway sleepers in the yard of William Christie & Co, at the Inches. The yard suffered a major fire in 1913, after which the business, which had exported railway sleepers as far as India, collapsed.

The South Bay is Ardrossan's high spot. Here a fine selection of villas from the early nineteenth century stands in a wide crescent overlooking the sandy South Beach. At the west end stands the Bath Villa, erected in 1807 by the 12th Earl of Eglinton. This was a fashionable facility in which tourists could bathe in a series of pools, containing hot, cold and salt water. The Bath Villa was an inn operated on the tontine principle, but was closed when the Earl died in 1819. In 1833 Dr MacFadzean, who also introduced a bath for the use of the poor, who did not have to pay, reopened the facility. Although there was accommodation for some overnight residents, this hydropathic establishment was never as large as the hydro hotels. Today modern sheltered housing surrounds Bath Villa.

The Barony Church stands across the street from Bath Villa. This was erected in 1844 when it was known as the New Parish Church. The church is distinguished by its rather quirky belfry and spire, with clock, designed by Black & Salmon. In stark contrast with the Barony St John's Church (as it has been known since 1988) is the Roman Catholic St Peter-in-Chains Church. This is a fine twentieth century building of 1938, its use of brick being quite distinctive. The architect was T. Warnett Kennedy, a partner of Jack Coia (1898–1981), who was given an award for the design. The tower is a notable landmark, and has been compared to that at Stockholm Town Hall. St Peter's occupies the site of the former Pavilion, the Earl of Eglinton's local townhouse. This was erected by him in 1831 but was demolished in the 1930s.

Across the street from St Peter's, in an area of garden on the Esplanade, is the memorial to the crew of HMS *Dasher*, an Archer Class

Escort Carrier. This ship was carrying out manoeuvres in the Firth of Clyde when it sank on 27 March 1943 with the loss of 379 lives. An explosion occurred and the vessel sank within six minutes. The memorial comprises a large boulder bearing an inscribed slab.

The large memorial commemorating the dead of the First World War is in the form of a cross, the faces of which have carved panels (by James A. Young of Glasgow) depicting a number of great Scots. The architect was Peter MacGregor Chalmers, a noted Scots architect who specialised in historic buildings, and built new ones in traditional styles. Chalmers died during the execution of this memorial, and it was completed by his successor, J. Jeffrey Waddell. The panels depict St Columba, Robert the Bruce, Robert Burns, David Livingstone and James Watt, and the memorial was unveiled on 5 May 1923.

The South Bay buildings contain a house occupied by the Verona Fathers (No. 8). This was formerly the home of Hugh Hogarth, who was the founder of H. Hogarth & Sons Ltd, better known as the Baron Shipping Line. Among their many vessels was the *Baron Ardrossan*, the bell of which is now in the Saltcoats museum.

The last building in Ardrossan, before one crosses the Stanley Burn and enters Saltcoats, is St Andrews Episcopal Church. This was erected in 1874 to the plans of David Thompson, but its proposed tower was never built. Next door is St Peters RC Primary School, though when it was erected in 1882 it was Ardrossan Academy. The Academy was transferred to its present location in Sorbie Road in 1933, though it has been extended considerably since that time.

The north-west section of Ardrossan overlooks the North Bay to Horse Isle. Here are the two main roads, Eglinton Road and Montgomerie Road, named after the two main titles held by the Earl who established the town. This part of the town is home to some sizeable bungalows and houses, enjoying the more open aspects away from the more industrial area on the headland. Among the fine houses is Seafield House, now a Barnardo's home. The house is a baronial building, with hints of Jacobean detail, now painted a rather gaudy colour. The designer was Thomas Gildard, who was more a historian and writer on architectural matters than an architect. The first part of the house was completed in 1820, at a cost of £7,500, with extensions in 1858.

West of Seafield are the modern houses at Montfode. A prehistoric earthwork can be seen above the Montfode Burn. A farm road leads over the raised beach and climbs to Montfode Farm. Here can be found the remains of Montfode Castle. This probably dates from the sixteenth century and was the seat of the Montfodes of that Ilk. The family became extinct in the seventeenth century, when John Montfode of that Ilk died, and today there is probably no one of the surname Montfode living in Ayrshire. The castle comprises of little more than a circular stair turret with a doorway and gunport. In the nineteenth century James Carrick Moore, brother of Sir John Moore of Corunna fame, owned the estate. On the low hill above the farm are five underground tanks associated with the Shell refinery.

It was from Ardrossan's North Shore that the first short-wave radio messages were transmitted across the Atlantic. The American Paul F. Godley came to Britain in 1921 to try and send or receive messages from the United States, a distance of over 3,000 miles. His first attempts in London failed but, on 11 December 1921, he was successful in receiving a message at the North Shore, a spot he had selected for its quietude. On Abbotsford House nursing home a plaque, erected by the Radio Society of Great Britain, commemorates his achievement.

In the bay off Ardrossan's North Beach is Horse Isle. A low-lying rocky islet, this has since 1961 been protected as a nature reserve by the Royal Society for the Protection of Birds. Some people believe that the isle was given its name because horses were quarantined here for a few weeks before being taken ashore. Another theory claims that it was named after Philipe Horsse, son-in-law of Sir Richard Morwell. The islet extends to around twelve acres at high tide. On the island is a tapering stone beacon, fifty-two feet in height, erected in 1811 by the Earl of Eglinton at the suggestion of Sir Thomas Ross, the celebrated Arctic explorer. The tug *Brigadier* ran aground on the island after being engulfed by a large wave and forced onto a reef in October 1960. The harbour pilot, Neil MacDonald, had observed the tug and had already launched a rescue before the distress flares were sent up. Fortunately no lives were lost.

From Ardrossan, Dalry Road climbs slowly up the hillside behind the town before dropping down to Dalry. On the way it passes three reservoirs, or, to be more precise, it passes two and seems to pass through the third. The lower reservoir, Mill Glen reservoir, lies east of the road, beyond Mill Farm. The Busbie Muir Reservoir lies between some smallish hills, the dam originally constructed by Ardrossan Town Council to store water for the burgh. Down the other side, in the Garnock basin, is the Munnoch Reservoir, originally constructed by Irvine and District Water Board in 1877–8. The road (the B780) crosses the reservoir by means of a causeway. The Munnoch Burn forms the Ardrossan parish boundary.

A minor road from Munnoch Reservoir passes by way of Meikle

Ittington and Muirlaught farms before joining the Dalry Road, which links Saltcoats with Dalry. West of this road, on the low hill of Knockrivoch (464 feet), is the ancient earthwork known as Knockrivoch Mount. The road drops down to Saltcoats, the upper part of which comprises of various housing schemes. Within one of these schemes, in Corrie Crescent, is St Brendan's Roman Catholic Church, erected in 1965 to plans by Rennie & Watson of Saltcoats. The church is built of brick and timber, and has brightly coloured southerly windows and a detached bell tower. The unique crucifix was designed locally and made from steel. Saltcoats North Parish Church stands at the crossroads with the A78, extended in 1963, and near to which is the Bethany Hall of 1964. From here Sharphill Road continues down to the older part of Saltcoats.

Saltcoats is an old community, created a Burgh of Barony for the Earl of Eglinton in 1528 and a Police Burgh on 23 May 1885. It does not have a parish of its own, being divided between Ardrossan and Stevenston parishes. The name of the town comes from the cots, or small cottages associated with the salt workers. At one time there were two salt pans at Saltcoats, one at the site of the Apollo cinema and another nearer Stevenston. Sea water was evaporated to create rock salt, which was in demand for curing herring. With the importation of a finer grade of salt from Liverpool, the industry collapsed. Saltcoats was the first place in Scotland to make Epsom Salts (magnesium sulphate), which was then exported to London, Europe and New York.

Saltcoats from the harbour

Saltcoats has an old harbour, which consists of little more than a pier. Sir Robert Cuninghame (d. 1715) began its construction in 1684, but winter storms invariably hampered the works. It was eventually completed around 1700, having cost £1,000. The pier was damaged in a storm in January 1739 but it is recorded that ten masons rebuilt it within two weeks, being paid ten pence and a quantity of whisky each day. The pier was enlarged in 1797. Today only the odd pleasure craft uses the basin, but at one time this was an important port. Coal was brought from the local pits and transferred to ships for export to Dublin and elsewhere. The town council bought the pier in 1914, but by then the harbour was in terminal decline, having been surpassed by the nearby port of Ardrossan.

On the pier is a bricked-up building that was formerly an old store-house. There was at one time a customs house (erected 1805) here also, latterly used as an inn, but this was demolished in 1924. Within the shingle basin of the harbour can sometimes be seen fossilised tree stumps, which are perhaps 250 million years old. Only visible at low tide, these stumps were first noticed in the early 1960s. There are around thirty of them in total. The harbour formerly had a shipbuilding yard, but all of this has been cleared. The harbour wall was built in 1924 and restored in 1988. Along the promenade can be seen a large anchor, representing the former shipbuilding industry, and an unusual sundial.

The old parish church of Saltcoats has since 1958 been used as North Ayrshire Museum. The building, which dates from 1744, still stands in its graveyard. This, in fact, was the Ardrossan parish church, for there is no Saltcoats parish, the whole of the town falling within the parishes of its neighbours. The old church is a plain block, the only real ornamentation being the small belfry. The church was damaged in a storm in 1773 and rebuilt the following year. The church was closed in 1908 when the present parish church was opened in Caledonia Road. The museum is of considerable interest, for here can be seen a variety of antiquities from the locality, including old mine working implements, the burgh regalia of the 'Three Towns', old photographs and books, maps and paintings and many other fascinating relics. A replica cottage has been built, and the cist that was discovered between the High Street and Boglemart Street has been rebuilt here. The stone coffin and elaborate lid found on Ardrossan's Castle Hill are also here, as is the fragment of St Winning's Cross, found built into an old cottage in Kilwinning in the 1930s.

Near the old parish church is the Erskine Church of 1866, built to the plans of William Stewart, which has a spire rising above a Venetian facade. There are four stained glass windows, commemorating former ministers and congregation members.

In Countess Street stands the Town House, originally erected to the plans of Peter King in 1825. The steeple, which rises over six floors and includes a public clock, was erected by subscription the following year. Within the façade is a circular opening which allowed fresh air and light into the cell of the tolbooth. Here also was a domestic dwelling where the artist, Sir John Lavery (1856–1941), spent some of his childhood. Born in Belfast, he was a noted portrait artist and painted Queen Victoria's state visit to Glasgow in 1888. He was knighted in 1918. The adjoining town hall was opened on 22 October 1892, designed by W. D. Howie & H. D. Walton of Glasgow. There had been an architectural competition the previous year but all seventeen entries were rejected. The north end of the street is the location of the railway station, the buildings dating from 1894. The railway here was opened on 4 September 1888, at which time it was part of the Caledonian Railway.

Countess Street becomes Quay Street once it crosses Dockhead Street. In the street is Clytus House, which occupies the site of the home of Betsy Miller (1792–1864). She was the daughter of a ship owner in the town. By all accounts she was a very determined woman, and persuaded her father to allow her to go to sea. She eventually became the captain of the brig *Clytus* and was the only female sea captain listed in the British Registry of Tonnage.

Harbour, Hill and Nineyard streets lie at the east end of Saltcoats main shopping area. Here can be found two of the town's oldest inns, the Grange Hotel and the Windy-ha'. The Grange Hotel was originally known as the Saracen's Head Inn and was established in the years when coaches needed facilities for horses to be changed. The Windy-ha' dates from around 1900 and is distinguished by its tower and small spire.

In this vicinity can be seen the Saltcoats Free Church, which was built in 1858 as the Free Church Academy. In 1882 the school was closed and it later was converted into a church. The original Free Church in the town was erected in 1843 to plans of David Cousin. The first minister was the Revd Dr David Landsborough (1779–1854) who was instrumental in bringing about the Disruption, which led to the formation of the Free Church of Scotland. Landsborough remained at Saltcoats until 1855. He is also remembered as a notable naturalist, discovering seventy species of plants and animals, some of which were named after him. Landsborough also wrote a number of renowned books on botany and a volume about the island of Arran.

In Nineyards Street is the large baronial building of 1866, 1874 and

1888 (designed by H. & D. Barclay) that was erected as the Glasgow Mission Coast Home. This was originally used to allow Glasgow people the chance to take a holiday away from the city's pollution. Dominating the streetscape with its octagonal tower, the building is now used by the Come to God campaign.

The main shopping thoroughfare is Dockhead Street, which strikes west from the cross. It is now pedestrianised and home to a fine selection of shops. Halfway along the street can be seen the Hope Christian Fellowship Church, located in the former Trinity Church, which had been erected in 1889. Previously this church was Trinity and Landsborough Church, formed in 1969 when the Trinity Church joined the Landsborough Church. The building includes some stained glass by Ballantine and Gardiner, and Ward & Partners. The Landsborough Church was demolished after it was closed. Other old churches in Saltcoats that have been lost include the Saltcoats North Church, erected in 1836 and demolished around 1966.

Dockhead Street turns into Hamilton Street west of the junction with Windmill Street. Striking north from the same junction is Chapelwell Street, the north end of which is dominated by the Erskine Church, erected in 1866. Its spire distinguishes the church. In Hamilton Street is the Congregational Church, erected in 1863. Ardrossan Road continues westward from the war memorial, which was unveiled on 27 May 1922. On the left is Our Lady Star of the Sea Roman Catholic Church, erected in 1856 to plans by Alexander Baird of Airdrie. At the far end is the Baptist Church, dating from 1867 when it was known as the Saltcoats Free Gaelic Church.

Climbing over the railway from the war memorial is Caledonia Road. On the opposite side of the railway from the older part of the town is the present Ardrossan parish church, known today as St Cuthbert's South Beach Church. It was built in 1908, becoming the fourth parish church. The architect was Peter MacGregor Chalmers, who provided the town with a fine building, complete with clerestory, balustraded tower, and Romanesque detailing. Within the church is a model of a French frigate, brought here from the old parish church. William Dunlop made this in 1804 as a thanksgiving for having survived the Napoleonic wars. The stained glass windows include work by Gordon Webster and William Wilson. On the other side of Campbell Avenue from the church is Argyle Primary School, originally erected in 1876 in a French Gothic style to plans by Alexander Adamson.

Windmill Street strikes south from the junction with Hamilton Street. The name comes from an old windmill that formerly stood here.

Remains of it can be found behind number 51, but when it was built is unknown. The oldest maps of the area depict it as a ruin. The Beach Pavilion stood in Winton Circus. It was erected in the early twentieth century for leisure purposes, but during the Second World War it became an important cartographic centre. Here the maps used for invasions of the continent in 1944 were prepared. The Pavilion was demolished in 1999 and the present Apollo cinema erected on the same site.

The most easterly of the three towns is Stevenston. The town is quite old, having been established early in the twelfth century, but it did not achieve burgh status until 1952, giving it the distinction of being the newest burgh in Ayrshire, and the second last to be created in Scotland. The name is thought to have come from Stephen Lockhart, who lived here in the twelfth century, his father acquiring the whole parish in 1170. Although linked with the other two towns, Stevenston is the more detached and, by contrast with the other two, does not owe its origin to the sea, for here the coast is too sandy and the sea too shallow to establish a port. There is little left of the old part of Stevenston, for the town centre has been redeveloped over the years, leaving it rather open and some-what undistinguished.

Sir Robert Cuninghame purchased Stevenston parish, which extends to 4,268 acres, in 1656. His nephew of the same name succeeded in 1678 and immediately began developing the economic potential of the estates. The first deep pit sunk in the area was known as the Deep Shank Pit, which was established in 1678. This stood in the glen east of the church, and a water wheel was used to pump the water from the mine. In the Auchenharvie area were various coal pits, some of which were susceptible to flooding, either by high tides or from the Stevenston Burn bursting its banks. Numerous lives were lost as a result, and at one time the underground workings collapsed, leaving the surface level of the ground much lower and filled with water. This depression became known locally as the Sits. Auchenharvie Colliery was located at the west end of Stevenston. It was the scene of a mining disaster on 2 August 1895 when water from the old Deep Shank pit burst through into the Number 4 pit. Over 120 men were below ground at the time and, of these, fourteen were trapped. Five of the men were released two days later, but nine men lost their lives: Henry, John, James and William Glauchan, James and Peter Mullen, Duncan Gallagher, John MacGee and Robert Conn. A cairn on the golf course at Auchenharvie com-memorates the disaster.

The High Kirk of Stevenston occupies a picturesque location on a knoll above the Stevenston Burn. It was erected in 1832–3, but it stands on an ancient site. The church was erected to plans by Thomas Garven. Within are murals by James Wyllie, depicting the church in the four seasons. Stained glass includes work by Oscar Paterson of around 1900. On the tower is a sundial commemorating Revd Dr David Landsborough. He was ordained to this church in 1811 but at the Disruption he left his charge to join the Free Church, becoming minister at Saltcoats. Landsborough was buried in the kirkyard here, where a Gibbsian-style memorial marks his grave.

The manse nearby is a distinguished old building, part of which dates from 1700, though the bulk of it was finished in 1787 and added to in 1885 to plans by John Burnet. Landsborough's son, William, who was born in 1825 in the manse, emigrated to Australia. He led an expedition through the centre of the country, from the Gulf of Carpentaria to Melbourne, searching for the explorers Burke and Wills, who had failed to arrive at the appointed time. Simultaneously, John MacDouall Stuart, another Scot from Fife, travelled from Adelaide to Darwin, meaning that both men were the first to cross the continent, but in opposite directions.

The main street of Stevenston comprises Main Street and Townhead Street, where can be seen the baronial Post Office of 1939. In Schoolwell Street stands the Champion Shell Inn, an old establishment that was run by monks for the benefit of travellers. The inn gets its name from the unique drinking contest held there whereby competitors had to drink as much mead as possible in one gulp from a carved Pectan shell goblet. The winner of this local version of a yard of ale became the Champion Shell Drinker.

Off the High Road, here known as Glencairn Street, on a pathway leading to Sinclair Street, is a short obelisk commemorating Lesley Baillie, the 'Bonnie Lesley' of the Robert Burns song, 'O saw ye bonie Lesley'. The obelisk was originally erected at Mayville in 1784, but was repaired and relocated in 1929. Baillie was born in Mayville House, which still stands in Schoolwell Street. The house dates from 1720 when it was built for Robert Baillie, a sea captain. It is made of stone and distinguished by its pediment with urns, probably added around 1773, along with a sundial bearing that date.

In Hayocks Road is St John's RC Church, erected in 1963 at a cost of £40,000 to plans by James Houston junior. The frame has laminated trusses supporting the roof and windows by M. Gabriel Loire of Chartres. This modern church replaced the old chapel-school in Moorpark Road, which had been used since 1905. The former Hayocks House, which was erected in the nineteenth century, latterly survived as a hotel and public house in the midst of the housing scheme, overlooking what was used as Ardeer Thistle Football Club's park from 1952–73. The house was also known as Ardchoille, when it was a seat of the MacGregors, but it is now demolished.

Up Kerelaw Road from the town is Kerelaw School, a former List D establishment that still caters for pupils with difficulties. It was opened in 1966. Within the grounds are the remains of Kerelaw Castle. The castle originates from the fifteenth century, but it was rebuilt in a fanciful style around 1830 to act as a folly within the grounds of Kerelaw House. Kerelaw House dated from the 1780s and was built for Alexander Hamilton, but was demolished around 1970. One of the later owners of Kerelaw was Gavin Fullarton, who owned plantations in the West Indies. A keen botanist, he introduced many exotic plants to his garden here.

New Street, which heads south from the town centre to Ardeer, is one of the most interesting parts of the town. Here is the cemetery, where memorials to victims of accidental explosions in the Nobel works can be seen. Here also can be seen a memorial commemorating the 606 cholera victims who died between 5 August 1845 and 15 April 1871. Workers from the Ardeer ironworks put up the memorial. Glencairn Primary School lies on the east side of the street. Built into the wall is a stone from its predecessor, Stevenston Public School, dating from 1875. This was burned down in 1982 and the present school was erected in 1984. The Ardeer Halls of 1911 now form a youth and community centre. The former police station building of 1899 is now the Caley Centre. The War Memorial Institute has panels on the front wall listing those who fell in action.

Stevenston was an important coal-mining community. In 1772 a canal from here to the harbour at Saltcoats was started and remains of it, known as the Master Gott, can be seen within Ardeer Park. The canal was constructed by the coal masters to avoid paying the tolls levied on the road. This made it the first commercial canal in Scotland. The line of the canal followed the ancient route of the river Garnock, which used to flow west from where the present railway bridge crosses it, through the bogs at Dubbs and Ardeer Park, before joining the sea near Saltcoats. Ardeer Park was at one time an industrial site, being home to a coal pit and quarry, but it has been landscaped to create a popular park with loch and miniature golf course.

The Ardeer Quarry was renowned for its 'Stevenston Stone' which could be dressed like marble and which was in considerable demand for making floors, chimneypieces and cladding for walls. Much of it was exported to Dublin and Belfast. The Parkend Quarry produced a fine Osmond Stone, used for making ovens and lining furnaces.

There was also a large ironworks at Ardeer, established soon after

1851 by the Glengarnock Iron Company. Five large blast furnaces were built on the foreshore, and at one time there were 850 men employed there, producing between 900 and 1,000 tons of pig iron each week. Ownership passed to Merry & Cunningham Ltd, who tried to build their own pier head in the bay, thus avoiding the duty payable for landing ore at Ardrossan. Slag was dumped out into the bay, but the idea was abandoned once it was realised that the firth was too rough for ships to dock. The promontory created, however, still survives and is known locally as the Slag Point or Old Pier. The ironworks were closed in 1931 and demolished in 1935.

Ardeer House was a Georgian mansion erected in the early nineteenth century for the Warner family, but was demolished in 1968. A columned doorway from the house was saved, and now stands near the ICI recreation building. Livingstone Church stands at the junction of New Street with Old Quarry Road. Built in 1887 as a Free Church, it replaced the older building of 1845, which became the Woodside Hall. It was named after Revd John Livingstone, minister at the time of its completion. The Trust Bar in Station Road, which was erected in 1906 and designed by Hugh Thomson, was founded as a Gothenburg inn. This meant that the public house was run by the locals for the benefit of the community, with all profits being ploughed into good works in the town.

The southern part of Stevenston is known as Ardeer, and the Ardeer church stands impressively with its octagonal tower. In Moorpark Road West is the Kingdom Hall of Jehovah's Witnesses, and the 'Wee Tin Kirk', or Ardeer United Free Church, is located in Ardoch Crescent. The Glengarnock Iron & Steel Company gifted the ground for this in 1890 and a mission Church of Scotland existed until 1942. In 1943 the church became a United Free charge, linked with Ayr for ministerial purposes since 1985. Trelawney Terrace is named after the sailing ship of that name which ran aground on the shore on 22 January 1819. The ship broke up and nineteen lives were lost, including that of four men from Ardeer who engaged in a rescue attempt

West of Ardeer and Stevenston is the Beach Park and Auchenharvie Park. At a place known as Saltcoats Campbell is the Sandylands caravan site. North of this, in Auchenharvie Park, is a large loch and west of here is Auchenharvie golf course. The course is nine holes and 5,203 yards in length, a par 66. Within the course can be seen the Auchenharvie engine house, looking somewhat like an old ruined Cornish tin mine. Only a gable and parts of the walls survive, but this building dates from the early 1700s, when it housed the second Newcomen steam engine to be used in Scotland. The engine was used to pump water from the coal mines.

North of the A738 lies Auchenharvie Academy and Harvey's leisure centre, which incorporates a swimming pool and ice rink. The school and leisure centre were built on the site of Auchenharvie House, originally known as Seabank. The original house was erected in 1708 but in the early nineteenth century this was extended for Robert Reid Cuninghame. It survived until 1972, by which time it was used as a special school, before being demolished. On the hillside above can be seen the base of a Martello tower, erected sometime before 1812 by Robert Reid Cuninghame of Auchenharvie (1744–1814) when there was a threat of invasion from France or America. It was known locally as Nelson's Tower. Auchenharvie Academy was opened on 26 August 1971.

The Ardeer peninsula extends south from Stevenston for two miles to the Irvine Bar, and the present mouth of the rivers Garnock and Irvine. This peninsula comprises many acres of sand dunes, and it is said that after a great storm the sand was blown over acres of cultivated soil. Indeed, when the Misk pit was sunk, the colliers dug through many feet of sand before arriving at a layer of soil. Within this they found an entire tobacco pipe that was in such good condition that they were all able to take a puff at it!

The Ardeer peninsula is home to the massive Stevenston complex owned by ICI. This vast area consists mainly of sand dunes, but built within them were a multitude of small buildings used for the manufacture of explosives. In 1873 the British Dynamite Company opened a factory here for the manufacture of what was known as 'guhr' dynamite. This was the first time that dynamite was produced in a safe manner, incorporating nitro-glycerine. The company later became known as Nobel's Explosives Company Limited, after Alfred Nobel (1833–96) who had started the works. On 8 May 1884 an explosion killed ten women and injured four others. Alarik Liedbeck designed the oldest buildings that survive in the Ardeer site. In 1926 the company was merged as part of Imperial Chemical Industries Limited (ICI). The works originally had a very tall cooling tower, visible for many miles around, but in 1973 it collapsed during a storm. Within the complex is the Africa House, so called because it was used at the Empire Exhibition in Glasgow in 1938 to house the Africa exhibition. The style of the building has nothing to do with that continent, however, for its ornate gable is more Dutch in style. Nobel House was erected in 1966, a massive office block designed by Sir Basil Spence, Glover & Ferguson. The Ardeer works have been reducing in size over the last few years, so that today it only employs a fraction of its former number. In its heyday the works were so significant that a street in the town was named Dynamite Road, and a stick of dynamite appears on the burgh arms.

# 4

# Kilwinning and Irvine

IRVINE IS THE THIRD largest town in Ayrshire. In 1966 it was designated by the Scottish Development Department as the fifth and last New Town to be created in Scotland. New Towns were established to create jobs and revitalise the community. The area designated for Irvine New Town consisted of two old burghs, Irvine and Kilwinning. The New Town designation ended in 1986, leaving the town to continue growing by itself. Although part of the New Town, Kilwinning still retains much of its independence, and is physically separate from Irvine, there being stretches of open countryside (and the Irvine and Kilwinning bypasses) between them.

Kilwinning lies to the north of Irvine, straddling the river Garnock at a point where the river could be bridged. The name comes from the Irish saint, Winning or Winnin, who is thought to have settled at the foot of the

Garnock in AD 715. He established a cell, or *cille*, here from which we get the burgh name. The abbey later occupied the site of the cell. Kilwinning was often known as Segdoune, or Saigtown, meaning saint's town. St Winning's Well was located near to the manse, which is located off St Winning's Road. In 1889 the town was constituted as a Police Burgh.

Kilwinning Abbey

The town itself is ancient, and here stands the remains of Kilwinning Abbey, founded between 1140 and 1191 for the Tironensian monks by Hugh de Morville. The abbey was attacked in 1559. In 1571 the last abbot, Gavin Hamilton, was killed in a skirmish at Restalrig, near

Edinburgh. Between 1561 and 1591 most of the abbey, which was said to have covered several acres, was dismantled, the stones being used for building purposes. A new parish church was built on the site of the abbey in 1590, but this was demolished in 1774 when the present church was erected. Known as Kilwinning Abbey Church, it was built by John Garland, mason in Kilwinning, and John Armour, wright in Kilwinning, at a cost of £546. An old stone dated 1593 and bearing the arms of the Eglinton family is incorporated in the wall. A very plain building, it has stained glass windows commemorating the Countess of Eglinton, the Conn family, Thomas Borland, Alexander Stewart, the Hendrie family, James Gaul and Reverends Archibald Hunter and William Lee Ker. These include work by Abbey Studio, Stephen Adam, W. & J. J. Kier, J. T. & C. E. Stewart and Gordon Webster. Within is a gallery for the Eglinton family.

The old abbey steeple was struck by lightning in 1809 but survived until 1814 when it collapsed, just as plans for strengthening it were about to start. The present 103 feet-tall clock tower was erected in 1815 at a cost of £2,000 to plans by the architect David Hamilton. It now houses a visitor centre dedicated to local history. The original south transept gable still stands in the old graveyard, pierced by a round window and four lancet windows. The remains are protected by Historic Scotland. Here the papingo, or popinjay, is hung every July, to allow the Ancient Society of Kilwinning Archers to take part in an archery contest. This society has been in existence since at least 1488. The papingo is a wooden target, based on a parrot. The winner has the honour of accepting the magnificent silver trophy that dates from 1724, usually displayed in the public library. The papingo shoot is an ancient tradition, one that Sir Walter Scott referred to in his novel, *Old Mortality*, although he transfers the location to the Upper Ward of Clydesdale:

> When the muster had been made, and duly reported, the young men, as was usual, were to mix in various sports, of which the chief was to shoot at the popinjay, an ancient game formerly practised with archery, but at this period with fire-arms. This was the figure of a bird, checked with party-coloured feathers, so as to resemble a popinjay, or parrot.

The kirkyard has a number of interesting memorials, including the burial aisle of the Earls of Eglinton and Winton. Here also are memorials to the Glasgows of Montgreenan, Revd Dr James Steven, mentioned in Burns's 'The Calf', and David Muir of Woodgreen (1666–1741) who left his estate to the poor of the parish.

Kilwinning has always been an important railway junction, the present station being opened on 23 March 1840. A second station on the former Barrmill to Ardrossan line of the Lanarkshire & Ayrshire Railway (the Caledonian line) was opened on 4 September 1888 and a third opened in 1890. Kilwinning East station was closed on 28 July 1930.

Main Street, Kilwinning lies to the north of the kirkyard. The street has been pedestrianised for some time, a relief road bypassing it to the north. At the east end of Main Street is the Garnock Bridge. Soon, on the right, one can see the old burgh cross, the upper part made from wood. The cross originally stood on the Corsehill (cross hill) to the east of the town centre, marking the pilgrim's way to St Winning's shrine.

A lane leads north from Main Street to the Erskine Church, erected in 1838. Also in the town centre is Kilwinning Free Church, located in the former Original Secession Church of 1759. The Free Church in Vaults Lane was founded in 1738. The Congregational Church lies on the north side of the bypass road in Woodwynd. The congregation was founded in 1844 and the building dates from 1846. A hall was erected in 1979. In Church Street is the former Pentecostal Church, but this has been taken over by the Cornerstone Church. A further place of worship is the Bridgend Gospel Hall, located on the east side of the bridge over the Garnock.

On the south side of Main Street is the Masonic Lodge building, opened in October 1893, the work of John Armour. This is the 'mother lodge' of the Masonic movement, the oldest known lodge in Scotland. It is thought to have been founded around 1150 when the abbey was built. When lodges were originally given numbers, Edinburgh was designated Number 1, but when Kilwinning proved that it was older it was given the numeral zero, thus it remains Lodge No. 0 to this day. The lodge has had many distinguished visitors over the centuries. King James I patronised it in the early fifteenth-century and presided for a time as Grand Master.

At the west end of Main Street is the former Mansfield Church, erected in 1861 and distinguished by its steeple. The church was closed on 18 June 2000 and the Rainbow Nursery now occupies the building. Near to this church is St Winin's RC Church, erected in 1937 to plans by T. Cordiner to seat 400. A plaque on the wall of 178–180 Main Street commemorates the celebrated 'Bard of the Yukon', Robert William Service (1874–1958). Service was born in Lancashire but moved to Kilwinning in 1880 where he lived with his paternal grandfather, who was the postmaster of Kilwinning. He spent the next three years here, writing his first poem at the age of six. In 1894 Service emigrated to Canada where he worked in a bank in Victoria, British Columbia. Service later lived in France. He was a keen poet, and in 1907 his book,

*Songs of a Sourdough,* was published. Other volumes followed, including a number of novels, but today he is remembered mainly for his humorous works, such as 'The Shooting of Dan McGrew' and 'The Cremation of Sam McGee'.

On the corner of Dalry Road stands Caley House, named after the former Caledonian Railway station that stood here. Caley House was erected in 1984 to plans by Irvine Development Corporation and provides accommodation for young people. West of the railway lines are the modern housing schemes of Whitehirst Park and Pennyburn, most of which were erected as part of the New Town project. In Stevenston Road, at the road into Whitehirst Park Primary School, is the Mansfield Trinity Church, opened on 23 March 2001, the first new church to be opened in Scotland in the third millennium AD. The building is circular in plan, rising to a clear dome. The Trinity appellation is taken from the Holy Trinity, as well as from the fact that it serves the western part of Kilwinning, which comprises three housing schemes! There are two Catholic schools in this area, St Luke's Primary School and St Michael's Academy. Pennyburn Primary School is located in the eastern half of the housing estate. At the south side of Pennyburn is the West Byrehill Industrial Estate, home to various factories and bonded warehouses.

The former Eglinton Ironworks stood east of Nethermains Road. The great Scottish industrialist William Baird established the works at the Blacklands following an invitation from the Earl of Eglinton. The furnaces went into blast on Christmas Eve 1846. The works were closed in the 1920s and the site has either been built on or landscaped to form a recreation ground.

Dalry Road (A737) leads north towards the town of that name, with most of the route remaining within Kilwinning parish. Kilwinning Academy is passed on the right, and MacGavin Park on the left, presented to the burgh in the will of John MacGavin (1806–81). Just before the park is a lane leading to the Abbey Primary School. There are two other primary schools in Kilwinning – Corsehill Primary on the east side of the river Garnock, and St Winning's Primary in St Winning's Road.

At the north end of the town is Melvin House, formerly a training centre associated with the Water Industry Training Association. The house dates from 1898–1901, when it was known as Ledcameroch, built to plans by J. J. Burnet for Robert C. King, a solicitor in the burgh. An Arts and Crafts style building, the house has been extended in recent years. Soon the open countryside is reached, and to the left is Smithstone House. Distinguished by its large bay windows, Smithstone dates from around 1800 and is used as a training centre for boys planning to enter the priesthood. On the level holm of the Garnock at Woodend were ancient mounds that were known as the Druid's Grove.

Another half mile brings one to Dalgarven, where there is a hotel and, down by the river, an old water-driven flourmill. The oldest part of the mill dates from 1620 and is the only surviving watermill in Scotland. The Ferguson family converted Dalgarven Mill into a museum of country life and costume. On display is a fine collection of furniture, clothing, utensils and tools. Visitors are welcome all year round, and among the facilities offered is a tearoom. Within the grounds of Dalgarven Hotel is a stone arch which tradition claims was taken from Kilwinning Abbey.

The next significant place on the Dalry Road is Monkcastle, a small estate on the west side of the road. The present house dates from between 1802–5 and may have been the work of James Gillespie Graham. A square block, the house rises from a basement storey to two storeys plus attic. The original Monk Castle ruins can still be seen standing on a prominent position above a small stream. The castle is T-shaped in plan, and probably dates from the early seventeenth century. An older castle must have occupied the site, as its existence was recorded in 1536. It was in all probability a summer lodge for one of Kilwinning's monks. The house latterly became the property of the Earl of Abercorn (one of whose subsidiary titles is Baron Mountcastle, a corruption of Monkcastle) but in 1723 was acquired by Alexander Miller. Over the re-entrant doorway is a panel with three grotesque carvings. In the small rocky glen next to the castle are some interesting waterfalls. At High Monkcastle was a fireclay mine, the clay taken down to the brickwork that stood next to the railway junction, by the side of the Garnock.

Dalry Road continues north of Monkcastle and drops to the Caaf Bridge, which marks the northern boundary of Kilwinning. There is little of any great significance within the parish to the west of the Dalry Road, the land being occupied by farms. Stevenston, or Ashgrove, Loch marks the junction of Kilwinning, Ardrossan and Stevenston parishes. The loch was at one time considerably larger than its current extent. Ashgrove House was a fine Georgian mansion of the eighteenth century but was demolished in 1960.

The eastern half of Kilwinning parish is comprised of the former estates of Eglinton and Montgreenan. Eglinton Castle today is a sorry ruin comprising little more than a small façade and a solitary round tower, rising to a lookout point. In its heyday the castle was one of the grandest country houses in Ayrshire. The castle was designed by John Paterson and erected between 1796–1802 for the 12th Earl of Eglinton. It consisted of a massive block, four storeys in height, but with a fifth floor in the four corner towers and the great central octagonal tower. Lesser wings spread to either side, creating one of the largest buildings in the county at that time. The castle occupies the site of the original Eglinton Castle, which may have dated from the fourteenth or fifteenth century. It was a substantial tower house, rising through four storeys to a parapet. The noted architect, William Adam, altered this in the early eighteenth century for the 9th Earl. In 1775 John Baxter was commissioned to supply plans for the extension of the castle, but the plans never came to fruition.

One of the most significant events in the life of the castle was the Eglinton Tournament. The 12th Earl was a keen historian and was concerned at the lack of pageantry at Queen Victoria's coronation. He decided to organise a grand tournament based on mediaeval lines in 1839, which attracted no less than 80,000 spectators. The event was held over two days, and boasted jousting, parades, and Queens of Beauty. The weather proved to be the event's downfall, and it was often blamed for the fall of the Eglinton family, although they lost money in many other ventures.

In December 1925 the Eglinton family vacated the castle and the roof was removed shortly after. The Royal Engineers used it for target practice, leaving the shell a total ruin. In the 1970s the Clement Wilson Foundation, which had bought the estate, removed most of the structure, and made safe the surviving fragments. Today the castle ruins form the centrepiece of a large country park, opened in 1986, which extends to almost 1,000 acres. The former Home Farm is now a visitor centre where there is an education room, café, interpretation hall and shop. A memorial near to the visitor centre commemorates Hugh Montgomery, who died at the age of six years and a few months. His grandfather, the Earl of Eglinton, erected the fluted marble column. From here a pathway climbs to the top of a low hill, now planted with trees in a Belvidere form. The summit has a stone-built rotunda, erected in recent years. The Lugton Water meanders through the Eglinton policies, crossed by a few bridges. One of these, west of the castle, is known as the Tournament Bridge, even although it was erected in 1811, the architect being David Hamilton. Extensive paths and bridleways wander through the grounds, and a sizeable lochan is located in the former Deer Park. On the south side of the park, next to the Long Drive, is an old doocot dating from the early eighteenth century.

Eglinton House dates from 1798, a rather strange building, and probably the work of John Paterson. It is located within Eglinton's policies and was originally the gardener's cottage. Within the park area is a former factory that was used for the manufacture of canned meats and other produce before being closed in 1996. Robert Wilson & Sons created this out of the original stable block, the canning business having been established in Kilwinning itself in 1849. The Clement Wilson Foundation also donated the gardens to the town and a small statue of Robert Burns can be seen therein.

Between Eglinton and Montgreenan are the small villages of Benslie and Montgreenan. These owe their origin to the former Fergushill Colliery, and miners' rows were erected to house the workers. Montgreenan had even a railway station at one time, and still has a church with a short steeple. This was erected in 1879 to plans of William Railton. The village of Doura has little left of it, other than a former school, later converted into the Lochlibo Inn. Torranyard is another little community, complete with inn and the Braemoor Christian Holiday Village, a large residential caravan site.

The roadway into Montgreenan House is lined with old milestones, taken from the roadsides of Ayrshire. The house is a rather fine Georgian structure, with a bow front overlooking the open countryside, and a pillared portico on the entrance front. The house was erected between 1810–17 for Dr Robert Glasgow, who had earned a fortune in St Vincent in the West Indies and had purchased the estate in 1794. His grandfather, Revd John Glasgow, had been minister in Kilbirnie. The architect of the mansion is unknown, but may have been John Paterson. The house was leased as a school for a time, and was later owned by Lord Weir, but it is now a fine country house hotel.

Within the policies of Montgreenan, in a loop of the Lugton Water, are the remnants of Montgreenan Castle, though this actually stands across the border in Stewarton parish. The castle was anciently a possession of the Rosses then Cuninghames. Alexander Cuninghame was given a charter of the lands in March 1582–3, but he was later to be killed in the famous feud between the Cuninghames and Montgomeries. Thomas Cuninghame, who succeeded his father in 1674, was a noted Covenanter, and took part in the Pentland Rising in 1679. On 8 January 1683 he was indicted for treason and rebellion. The estate then passed to the Stevenson family, who remained until 1778. There are also two fine stable courts in the Montgreenan grounds, one contemporary with the house and ornamented with a clock tower; the other is perhaps Victorian.

On the opposite side of the Lugton from Montgreenan Castle is Clonbeith Castle, another ruin. The castle stands in the midst of a farm steading. Clonbeith dates from 1607, according to a date over the doorway. This is Clonbeith's finest feature, the overdoor comprising a baroque-style pediment, surmounted by a unique series of corbels. The castle was probably built for William Cunningham.

To the west of Clonbeith is Monkredding House, an old building that is noted for its round tower and conical roof. The oldest part of the house perhaps dates from 1602, which date appears on a stone. Other work was dated 1638 and in 1905 a large extension was added to plans by Hugh Thomson of Saltcoats. Monkredding was anciently a Kilwinning Abbey property, but in 1532 was acquired by Thomas Niven. In 1698 the estate passed to the Cunninghames of Clonbeith.

East of Clonbeith are the farms of Fergushill Hall and Hill of Fergushill. The name is all that survives of Fergushill Castle, which was at one time the seat of the Fergushills of that Ilk. The countryside hereabouts is rather flat and scrubby, the ground quarried for sand and stone and mined for coal over the years. At the north-eastern extremity of Kilwinning parish is Auchentiber, a small community of houses and an inn. West of here are the Auchentiber, Cockinhead and Dykeneuk mosses, and the dispersed farming community of Auchenmade. At North Auchenmade was a station on the former Caledonian Railway.

The town of Irvine is of ancient origin, perhaps even occupying the site of the Roman centre of Vindogara. The oldest part is centred on the crossroads at the junction of High Street, Bridgegate and Bank Street. This was designated a burgh around 1140 by David I for his Great Constable, Hugh de Morville. In 1371 the burgh was granted a charter elevating it to the status of a Royal Burgh. From then the town has expanded over the centuries, most notably in the twentieth when it was designated a New Town. Extensive housing schemes and industrial estates were added and Irvine now has a population of 33,000.

The centre of the town is still quite traditional in appearance, though here and there modern buildings have been built in a quite incongruous manner, destroying the traditional street line. The errors of the 1960s and 1970s seem to have been acknowledged, and most of the new buildings within the core of the old town have a design that complements the scale and appearance of the townscape. High Street starts at the Town House and leads north through Irvine Cross. The Town House is a fine building of 1859–61, designed by James Ingram. The building now contains council offices and is topped with a notable tower and octagonal lantern containing a clock, visible for miles around. The war memorial was erected in 1921 to commemorate the dead of the Great War. The style of the memorial was based on the old market cross that formerly stood nearby, its site marked on the roadway with cobbles.

The streetscape here is quite traditional, even the modern infill of 1979 by Irvine Development Corporation architects (85–93 High Street) being traditional in style. The Royal Bank of Scotland is a fine classical building of 1856, the work of Peddie & Kinnear. Just beyond the cross two old inns stand facing each other across the street – the Eglinton Arms and the King's Arms. The King's Arms was used for accommodating a number of important people attending the Eglinton Tournament. It was here Prince Napoleon (later Napoleon III of France) stayed. At 167 High Street can be seen a plaque (sculpted by Robert Bryden) commemorating John Galt (1779–1839) one of Scotland's most eminent novelists. Galt was born in a house that formerly stood here, the son of a shipmaster. He moved to Greenock at the age of ten where he received much of his education. He went to London in 1804 where he started writing, and his early works included school textbooks (written as Revd T. Clark). He later became a popular novelist, and many of his books are still in print, being classic examples of Scottish literature. These include *The Provost* (1822), *The Entail* (1823), *The Ayrshire Legatees* (1820) and *Annals of the Parish* (1821), the last-named being regarded as his masterpiece. In 1826 Galt emigrated to Canada, where he was responsible for founding the town of Guelph in Ontario. His Canadian ventures failed, and he returned to Scotland in 1829, writing many other works, including historical romances and a biography, *Life of Byron* (1830). Galt is buried in the Inverkip Street cemetery in Greenock.

John Galt

High Street continues its northward route with the new name Wellwood Street. Wellwood House is home to Irvine Burns Club, which was founded in 1826 and claims to be the oldest club in continuous existence. The founder members included Dr John Irvine, whose wife, Helen Miller, was one of Burns's 'Mauchline belles'. The first vice-president was 'Dainty' David Sillar. The club preserves a fascinating collection of original Burns manuscripts and artefacts, and many historical items associated with Irvine. The club often bestowed honorary membership on various notables, and as a result has a fine collection of letters written by them, including Charles Dickens, Sir Arthur Conan

Doyle, Sir Alexander Fleming, Sir Edmund Hillary, Yehudi Menuhin, George Bernard Shaw, Lord Tennyson and Margaret Thatcher. The building has some interesting stained glass and a rather fine mural depicting scenes from the poet's life. This was the work of Ted and Elizabeth Odling. At the end of the street is the Turf Inn, 'established a long time ago' according to the mural on the wall.

Striking downhill from the west side of the High Street is the Seagate. This is one of the oldest streets in the town, and it preserves its traditional atmosphere. On the north side stand the ruins of Seagate Castle, erected between 1562 and 1585 by the Montgomeries as their town house. The castle stood overlooking the old harbour area of the town (Seagate means the road to the sea) and though it is adorned with towers and small guardrooms, there are no real defensive features. A vaulted pend leads through part of the building, and the bosses of the roof contain the arms of the 3rd Earl of Eglinton and his wife, Margaret Drummond of Innerpeffray, whom he married in 1562. The castle is said to have had Mary Queen of Scots as a visitor in 1563, but there is little evidence of this. The house remained occupied until around 1746 when the 10th Earl of Eglinton had the roof timbers removed and used in a new church he was building at Ardrossan.

At the foot of the Seagate, in Castle Street, stands a statue that is known locally as the 'Black Man'. It was erected in the High Street in 1865, the statue sculpted by John Steell, but was moved to its present location in 1929. The statue actually commemorates David Boyle of Shewalton (1772–1853) who was born in a house in Irvine's High Street known as Boyle's Parterre, a grandson the of the 2nd Earl of Glasgow. He was educated in the town, and then Edinburgh, where he qualified as a solicitor. Boyle became the Lord Justice General of Scotland and Lord President of the College of Justice in 1841. He is remembered as the man who sentenced the political martyrs, John Baird, Andrew Hardie and James Wilson, and it was he who was responsible for sentencing William Burke, one half of the murderous duo, Burke and Hare. Boyle was friendly with Sir Walter Scott and dined regularly with him. He died at his home of Shewalton House, which he inherited in 1837, and was buried there.

Annfield House, now a hotel, occupies the other side of Castle Street from the Seagatefoot. This was erected around 1850 for Provost Thomas Campbell who was involved in the erection of the Victoria railway bridge, better known in Irvine as Campbell's Bridge. Behind Annfield House, in Academy Road, is the former Irvine Royal Academy building. This was erected in 1900–2 to plans of John Armour, and it replaced an older building of 1816 by David Hamilton that stood on the same site. The school closed in 1993 when it merged with Ravenspark Academy to form the present Irvine Royal Academy, located in the Ravenspark building in Kilwinning Road. The old sandstone building, distinguished by its domes, is now Sovereign House, occupied by offices.

In West Road are two churches, St Mary's RC Church and the Mure Parish Church. St Mary's was erected in 1875 to plans by J. & R. S. Ingram. The Mure Church was erected in 1850. Here also is the former Relief Church of 1773, established when many of the congregation disagreed with the Earl of Eglinton's choice of minister that he presented to the parish church. The Buchanites had their early foundations with this congregation. The church closed in 1977 when a new Relief Church was opened at Bourtreehill, the hall being taken over by the British Legion and the former church building now being used by the Pentecostal Church.

Between the river and West Road area is Irvine's Low Green. This stretch of grassland is now a quiet park area, but it was at one time a busy part of the town, where the slaughterhouse was located. There were even limestone quarries and a coal mine here, and boats navigated the river to the original harbour.

From Irvine Cross the road known as Townhead strikes eastward. There are some traditional buildings here, but also some new build. At the foot of an old lane to the east of the newer part of the parish kirkyard is St Inan's Well, which is supposed to be associated with the early founder of the town. To the east of this are the Golf Fields, an open space that seems to have had no connection with golf, the name being a derivative of Goat Fields or Goal Fields. A powder magazine can be seen in the fields, dating from the seventeenth century. It was rebuilt in 1801.

On the other side of Townhead a road known as the Glasgow Vennel strikes north. This was originally the main road from Irvine to Glasgow, before Bank Street was created. The Vennel contains some very interesting old buildings, most of which have been sensitively restored, so much so that the restoration earned Civic Trust awards and a Europa Nostra Award in 1985. The reason this place was looked after was because of its associations with Robert Burns. The poet came here in 1781 to learn how to heckle flax, and lodged in a house that survives as number 4, known as the Lodging House. The Heckling Shop, where he learned the trade, is still in existence (number 10), and today the building is operated as a small museum and gallery. The heckling shop was destroyed by fire in 1781 but Burns remained in the burgh until March 1782.

Some of the other buildings in Glasgow Vennel are of interest. Patrick

Hunter's house was the place where Buchanites had their meetings. The eponymous Elizabeth Buchan (1738–91) was born in Banffshire but moved to Irvine in 1783, where she managed to persuade the minister of the Relief Church that she had heavenly powers, and that she was the woman referred to in Revelations 12. Ousted from the church for her unorthodox beliefs, she and some followers formed a sect in 1784, known as the Buchanites. They were eventually expelled from Irvine and forced to travel around south-west Scotland, settling for a time at Closeburn in Dumfriesshire before moving on to Crocketford in Kirkcudbrightshire. There they built a convent of sorts and remained for some time. After Buchan herself died, the group disbanded.

Bank Street is one of the main streets in Irvine town centre that has remained open to traffic. It starts at the cross, and heads in a north-easterly direction to the Stanecastle Roundabout. The street was laid out as a replacement for Glasgow Vennel in 1828, the new route being better for access to the harbour. Near the junction with East Road stand the Baptist Church (1879) and the Templar's Hall (1871). Beyond East Road is the modern Galt House office block, after which the street is lined with large sandstone houses, a number of which are now used as commercial offices or which have been divided into flats. The Irvine annexe of Kilmarnock College was formerly the Bank Street school, opened in 1875.

Just before the street crosses the bypass stands the modern Church of Jesus Christ of Latter Day Saints (perhaps better known as the Mormons). In the roadway behind the church (MacKinnon Terrace) can be found a stone cairn, erected in 1976. This commemorates the 'Drukken Steps' which was a favourite haunt of Robert Burns when he lived in Irvine. The actual steps were located 700 yards north-west of here, the site now covered by the bypass road. Originally the Drukken Steps was known as St Bryde's Well.

The housing scheme west of here is quite considerable. At its heart is St Andrews Parish Church, dating from 1957, which was gifted to the town to commemorate the centenary of the death of John Ferguson, founder of the Ferguson Bequest. Rennie & Bramble of Saltcoats designed the church, and there is stained glass by Mary Wood (1957), Ann Marie Docherty (1998) and one that dates from 2000. The St Andrews Episcopal Congregation shares the building with Church of Scotland worshippers, who in 1981 were responsible for adding a new chapel or meeting room, designed by R. L. Dunlop of Troon. At the opposite end of the estate the roadways rejoin Kilwinning Road, a continuation of the High Street and Wellwood Street. Kilwinning Road is another street lined by rather fine houses. Some of the largest have gone, such as Williamfield, but surviving is Burnside House, latterly a children's home, and Heathfield House, extended in 1986 to create a sheltered housing complex.

Academy Gardens occupies the site of the annexe to the old Irvine Royal Academy, erected in 1932. Behind the houses is an open stretch of grassland, originally linked to the Low Green but now divorced by the creation of the bypass link, Marress Road. On this grassland can be found a series of stone cobbles marking the site of the old gallows, where the Irvine Covenanters were hanged. Further out is a statue of Robert Burns, erected in 1896. The statue was carved by the Scottish sculptor, James Pittendreigh MacGillivray (1856–1938), and depicts the poet standing with his dog. Beyond the statue the grassland opens out into the Town's Moor. On the Moor is an elliptical racetrack used by the Cadgers for horse racing. The Cadgers were the local carriers who hauled coal and other goods through the town towards the harbour.

By the side of the present Irvine Royal Academy building (erected in 1969 as Ravenspark Academy), Sandy Road leads down over the Moor to Bogside Golf Course, home of Irvine Golf Club. The course is 18 holes, 6,408 yards in length, a par 71. North of Sandy Road is the 18-hole municipal Ravenspark golf course, 6,500 yards in length and a par 71. Beyond Bogside golf course is the disused Bogside Racecourse. The 12th Earl of Eglinton established this in 1807 and the first steeplechase in Scotland took place here in 1838. There were quite considerable viewing pavilions overlooking the course. The original Scottish Grand National was run here from 1947 until 1965 when the course was closed and the racing event was moved to Ayr.

Along Sandy Road from Bogside is the former Ravenspark Hospital, established in 1905. At the north end of Sandy Road, where it crosses the river Garnock, is a low-lying stretch of boggy ground. This is now protected as a nature reserve, known as the Garnock Floods. Ayrshire Central Hospital lies on the east side of Kilwinning Road. The hospital was erected in 1936 and some buildings still display contemporary architectural features. The Redburn Hotel was formerly a dower house associated with Eglinton Castle. Opposite it is the entrance to the former Volvo truck and bus factory, established in 1975 within an old army vehicle-recovery-depot, but closed in 2001.

Back at the cross, the Bridgegate leads down towards the site of Irvine Bridge, now occupied by the large shopping centre. Bridgegate was rebuilt along its northern side, so that today there are only modern buildings there. The southern side is more interesting, for here can still be found some traditional buildings, still functioning perfectly well as shops and other businesses. Hill Street strikes off the Bridgegate, heading towards the old Parish Church. The street is one of the town's most attractive ones, for here the eighteenth and nineteenth century buildings have been restored, and together with the cobbled roadway forms an attractive scene. The Parish Church is an old building of 1774. The main block of the church is a simple building with hipped roof, the only real adornment being the tall steeple containing a clock over the west end. Within can be seen a number of fine stained glass windows, including work by W. & J. J. Kier. A window by J. Blyth and W. Blair commemorates St Inan. This also shows the symbols of the Irvine trades as well as a view of the harbour.

The parish church occupies an ancient site. Within the graveyard can be seen some interesting old graves, among them a Covenanting martyrs' memorial, commemorating James Blackwood and John MacCall. These men were taken at the Battle of Rullion Green and sentenced to be hanged in Irvine. The burgh hangman refused to carry this out, even under torture, and one of the Covenanters due to be hanged in Ayr was forced into carrying out the deed on 31 December 1666. The present memorial was erected on New Year's Eve, 1823. The graveyard also contains the grave of David Sillar (1760–1830), associate of Robert Burns. He was a minor poet himself, and Burns regarded his work highly. Sillar was for a time a schoolteacher, grocer and navigation lecturer. Stones also commemorate victims of shipwrecks, such as William Crooks, captain of the *Abyss*, who perished in 1791. There is an old, but restored, memorial to *IHON PEBLIS OF BROVMLANDIS*, provost in 1570 and 1596. A memorial commemorates John Ferguson of Cairnbrock (1787 –1856) who bequeathed £500,000 to be used for religious and educational purposes in the six counties of south-west Scotland. The Ferguson Bequest is still distributed.

Kirkgate is an old street that has been rebuilt in modern years; prior to the Reformation it was known as Friarsgate. Here can be found the Orange Lodge, established in 1872, making its Scotland's oldest. The Trinity Church is an attractive building built from a variety of sandstones. It has a tall steeple that is a local landmark. Trinity Church was erected in 1863 and was designed by the celebrated architect, F. T. Pilkington, and is one of only three remaining examples of his ecclesiastical work. The church was closed for worship in 1966 and became a community centre, but is now closed, perhaps awaiting conversion into flats.

The shopping centre opened for business in 1973 on the site of the old Irvine Bridge. A couple of panels rescued from the bridge are built into the present building next to the windows overlooking the river. The Forum centre was added to the Mall in 1984. Across the river Irvine from the town centre is the district known as Fullarton. This was in fact at one time unconnected with the burgh, being in a different parish. In fact, Fullarton was created a burgh in 1707. The independence of the Fullarton residents caused some strife for the Irvine burghers over the years. Today the heart of Fullarton has been destroyed. The old central part has been more or less demolished and a totally new street layout placed on top. The shopping centre that crosses the Irvine extends over much of the old town centre, and the acres of parking around it occupy more ground that at one time was home to houses, shops and other buildings.

Still surviving, however, is the former Wilson Fullarton Free Church, now standing by the side of a large roadway and almost dwarfed by the large concrete box that is the shopping centre. The church was erected in 1873 and later became part of the Church of Scotland. In 1963 the congregation merged with that of Trinity, but in 1974 the congregation was disbanded. The building was later used as the Fullarton Church Hall, and is now the Fullarton Centre, still associated with the Fullarton Church. Cunninghame House is a modern office block that contains council offices and the local library. Within is preserved the famous Eglinton Trophy that was created in 1842 and presented to the 13th Earl of Eglinton to commemorate the Eglinton Tournament of three years earlier. Next to Cunninghame House is a more attractive glass-roofed tax office, known as Marress House.

Across the road is the Fullarton Parish Church, an unusual church building, Tudor-like in appearance, with tiny spirelet turrets and bell-cote. The church was designed by James Ingram and erected in 1836–8 as Fullarton Free Church. The church has a stained glass window by G. Maile, and there is also a memorial stone commemorating James Montgomery (1771–1854). Adjoining it is the church hall, originally erected as the Free Church School in 1840. Marress Road bypasses the town centre (replacing the Irvine Bridge) and swings over the river by means of the 1973 bridge to join Kilwinning Road. The name comes from an old farm that formerly existed here, the grounds of which now form the Marress playing fields.

Fullarton Street (originally laid out in 1776) passes south through the present residential homes of Fullarton. On the east are five blocks of multi-storey flats, erected in 1968. Beyond the houses are industrial and trading estates.

The railway passes through the town on a north–south axis, linking Ayr with Glasgow. The Glasgow-to-Ayr line first passed through the town in 1839, and the railway station was opened on 5 August 1839. A former branch line struck off south of the station and headed east to Dreghorn, Springside and ultimately Kilmarnock. Most of this branch is now either used for roads (the former bailey bridge used by trains makes an unusual road crossing across the river Irvine), or else as a public walkway. West of the railway is the harbour area of Irvine. After years of decline this area is now alive, the old buildings restored and attractive modern buildings erected in the gap-sites. Ayrshire Metals was at one time Irvine shipyard. Various yards had existed along the harbour side, but in 1912 the large four-berth shipyard was built and leased to Mackie & Thomson of Govan. Lithgow's took over in 1928 but the yard declined, and the last two ships (which had lain on the stocks for five years) were launched in 1936. Nearby is the Kingdom Hall of Jehovah's Witnesses, erected 1992–4.

Montgomery Street was named in honour of James Montgomery, who was born at number 26 (now demolished) in 1771, the son of a Moravian pastor, who tried to establish a church in Irvine. Montgomery became a journalist in Sheffield, where he edited the *Sheffield Iris*. Montgomery's views were contentious at the time, and in 1795 he was fined and imprisoned for printing a 'seditious' poem. He was also against slavery, and did much to try and end this trade. He became noted as a poet and writer of many hymns, some of which are still sung in churches to this day. He died in Sheffield where a statue in the town centre commemorates him.

The Scottish Maritime Museum has various buildings open to the public along the harbour side. On the north of Montgomery Street is the Winch House. South of the street, in Gottries Road, is the Linthouse building, one of the finest examples of shipyard architecture in Scotland. This was originally erected at Linthouse in Govan in 1872–3 to plans of William Spence, where it formed part of the yard of Messrs Alexander Stephen. The whole building was dismantled in 1988 and brought to Irvine in 1991 where it now houses many artefacts preserved by the museum. In the yard in front of the building can be seen the Longhope lifeboat and other artefacts.

The Maritime Museum also protects the Shipyard Worker's flat, at 122A Montgomery Street, which is furnished as it would have been in 1907 when the tenement block was erected.

Within the harbour itself are pontoons to which have been moored a selection of vessels. These form an important part of the maritime museum's exhibits, and include an old tug boat, a coastal puffer named *Spartan*, coaster, experimental vessel, and the *Antares*, a fishing boat that sank off Carradale on 22 November 1990 with the loss of all four crewmen. It was later refloated and brought here.

Irvine harbour showing vessels at the Maritime Museum

The harbour front has an attractive line of old and modern buildings, overlooking the tidal part of the river Irvine that forms the natural harbour. Some old inns overlook the quayside, the oldest of which is the Ship Inn. This was originally erected in 1597 as an ostler's. In 1754 it obtained a license to allow it to sell alcohol. The Harbour Arts Centre occupies another waterside building. Here various local groups meet and enjoy live music, photography, theatre and special exhibitions.

Art is something that Irvine is proud to promote. There are various sculptures dotted around the town, commissioned by the Development Corporation and other organisations. Down by the harbour side is a statue of the Carter's Horse, commemorating the horses used to haul goods around the town. Further out, at the mouth of the river, is a stone sculpture of a small fisherman in a boat, hauling a massive net of fishes through a huge wave. Another sculpture down in the beach park is the stone dragon, perched on a low knoll overlooking the beach.

The Magnum Leisure Centre is a modern building containing a swimming pool, ice rink, theatre, cinema and other leisure facilities. The building was erected in 1976 to plans by Irvine Development Corporation architects. The Harbour Master's Office is one of the last of the original buildings along the harbour side. The house dates from the early eighteenth century. On the wall is a clock. A footbridge, known as the Millennium Bridge of Scottish Invention, links the south side of the river with the Big Idea inventor centre. The bridge is unique in that it can be retracted to the north side of the river at night, when the visitor centre is closed, or at any time of the day when a yacht or boat needs to sail past. On the bridge are metal panels with cutaway images reflecting the genius of twenty-three Scottish inventors over the centuries.

The Big Idea building has a large glazed front to it, but the rest is composed of a large dome, the surface of which is covered with grass. From the sea and other angles it looks as though it is one of the large sand dunes on the Ardeer peninsula, on which it stands. The centre was designed by Building Design Partnership of Glasgow and opened in April 1999. Within, the visitor is encouraged to get involved with the exhibits, and interact with the displays. There are 40,000 square feet of exhibits, and visitors are supplied with an inventor's kit. There is a history of explosions' exhibition and a puppet theatre and library. Visitors can also enjoy a snack in the café or browse in the gift shop.

Near the mouth of the river stands the square tower of the signal station. This unique building was erected in 1904, having been designed by the Irvine harbour master, Martin Boyd. The tower has a pole surmounting it on which was suspended twelve large balls. These were connected by ropes and pulleys to floats in the water, and as the tide ebbed and flowed the balls moved up and down. Sailors could tell by looking at how many balls were visible just how deep the water was at the mouth of the river, known as Irvine Bar, which is a notorious watercourse to navigate. At night time, when the balls could not be seen, lamps were positioned behind windows and screens moved up and down, blocking or revealing them, and so the depth of water could still be told.

The Beach Park stretches south from the Magnum and the harbour side. Some of the land was reclaimed from old bings, created from iron oxide residue. A large pond was formed, adding to the attractions. There was for a time a Seaworld exhibition area at the harbour mouth, but this was closed and the building converted into a children's play centre. South and east from the Beach Park is an industrial estate, home to many local employers. The Portland Glass Company was established in 1920, its works now operated by Rockware. ICI established a chemical works here in 1935. Further out is the Glasgow Gailes golf course (18-hole, par 71, 6,539 yards), founded in 1892 by the Killermont Golf Club of Glasgow, and between the railway and the beach, Western Gailes golf course (18-hole, par 71, 6,709 yards), established 1897. These courses are popular with the members of the clubs associated with them. A new course was created in the early 2000s, known as Southern Gailes. Shewalton cemetery is located by the side of Ayr Road, a remote spot for a burial ground of this age. A few houses are located on the Irvine side of the cemetery, and behind them is the Shewalton Pits Nature Reserve. Quarrying for sand formed the pits. Today the reserve is home to a fine selection of wild birds.

East of the Irvine bypass are a number of modern housing schemes, all forming part of the new town. The most southerly of the communities is Dreghorn, originally a small village in its own right, complete with a parish of 5,661 acres. This was formed in 1668 by uniting Dreghorn with Perceton parishes. Today the village has been extended to the west and subsumed into the larger town. The old part of Dreghorn still displays its age, the Main Street heading east from the crossroads being the original part. Here can be seen Dreghorn Primary School, erected in 1908 in a massive sandstone bulk. Next door is the small Ebenezer Hall, built in a Gothic style with blonde sandstone.

The parish church (formerly known as Dreghorn and Pearston, now Dreghorn and Springside) at the crossroads is quite a distinguished building, being octagonal in plan and having a clock tower topped by a slender spire. The church was erected in 1780, perhaps with the guiding hand of Archibald, 11th Earl of Eglinton. In 1876 the internal arrangements were altered, creating seats for 500. It contains windows by Susan Bradbury and Gordon Webster. At the kirkyard gate is a small building, now used as the Session House. It was erected in 1774 as a school, but was converted into the meeting place for the kirk session around 1890. The Parish Church Hall is located on the opposite side of Townfoot, being erected of Ballochmyle stone in 1903 to plans by John Armour & Sons.

Another church stands in Main Street. The Congregational Church (originally the Evangelical Union Church) was a fine sandstone edifice erected in 1864, but is now unfortunately closed, the building used for storage purposes. East of the main village, at Corsehill, there was formerly another church, the Perceton & Dreghorn Church, built as a Free Church in 1877. This became disused and was put up for sale. The purchasers did not convert it into a house or workshop, as with many other abandoned places of worship. Instead, they dismantled it stone by stone and shipped it off to Japan, where it now forms a wedding chapel within one of the country's theme parks. The Japanese had searched the world for a building like this, where the entrance doorway was opposite the pulpit, and so the building stands there to this day! On the Mount behind the site of the church is the parish war memorial.

The Dunlop Memorial Hall commemorates John Boyd Dunlop (1840–1921) who was born in the Plough Inn, which was next door to the present Eglinton Arms. He was a keen cyclist, and strove to make his ride more comfortable. This resulted in his reinvention of the pneumatic tyre, which he patented in 1888. The Dunlop Rubber Company, which took his name, had no connection with the inventor of the tyre. Dunlop became a veterinary surgeon, practising in Dublin. On the wall of the hall is a bronze plaque incorporating a bas-relief of Dunlop's head. Adjoining the hall are more modern library and social work offices. Dreghorn Station was located north of the village across the Annick Water. It lay on the branch line from Crosshouse Station to Irvine and was opened on 22 May 1848. The station was closed on 6 April 1964.

Across the Annick Water from Dreghorn are the communities of Broomlands and Bourtreehill. Both of these modern schemes stand on small estates or farms of some antiquity. The site of Bourtreehill House is now a local park. The house was built in 1682 for the Montgomeries of Skelmorlie but damaged by fire in 1879. Robert Ingram drew up plans for the restoration work, but the house was demolished in the 1970s. There is little of any historical interest existing within the schemes. The parish church that serves Bourtreehill is known as the Relief Church, for this replaced the old Relief Church that formerly existed within Irvine's West Road. The foundation stone of the Bourtreehill building was laid on 18 September 1976, the architects being Hay Steel & MacFarlane. Almost next door is St John Ogilvy RC Church, a striking edifice rising to central tower. The architects of this fine building were Douglas Niven & Gerard Connolly, and the church was erected in 1982. In Gigha Terrace at Broomlands is the Broomlands-Bourtreehill Baptist Church.

The next two communities to the north, Stanecastle and Girdle Toll have more of interest to be seen. Stanecastle gets its name from the old tower of that name, which still stands by the side of the large Stanecastle roundabout. The tower was erected in the sixteenth century. It rises over four storeys to a corbelled parapet, but the large Gothic windows are later additions. The Francis family anciently owned the lands, but in 1508 an heiress took the estate to the Montgomerie family, marrying the third son of the 1st Earl of Eglinton. It was he, William Montgomerie of Greenfield, who built the present tower. Later owners moved to Broom-lands House, but the castle remained the property of the Eglintons until fairly recently.

A roadway from the roundabout leads into South Stanecastle and the Knadgerhill cemetery. By the side of the entrance gates is a memorial commemorating a skirmish that is thought to have occurred here in 1297 involving Sir William Wallace. Part of the Girdle Toll area predates the New Town, the name deriving from an old toll house that stood on the Glasgow Road. The scheme to the north is known as Lawthorn. Here can be seen an ancient burial cairn on a low knoll known as Lawthorn Mount. A modern set of standing stones can be seen on a low hill north of Cairnmount Road. The church at Lawthorn was created from the original Littlestane Farm, which had an old limekiln at it.

Across the Annick Water from Lawthorn is Perceton, again an old, if small, community that has been extended in recent years. The houses here are much larger, built in the grounds of Perceton House. This building was erected in 1770 and was occupied by William MacCredie at that time. The Barclay family occupied the earlier house, and were created Baronets of Pierston (the spelling seems to be changeable for various places within the locality) in 1668. The baronetcy survives, but the family have long left the locality. It became the headquarters of the Development Corporation and a new office wing added to it. By the side of the Perceton Bridge is the Emmanuel Christian Community Church, Perceton Outreach, and next to it are the ruins of the old Perceton Church in its kirkyard. The Emmanuel building was originally used as a branch church of the Perceton and Dreghorn church.

The countryside around Perceton was at one time home to many coal mines. A series of mineral railway lines criss-crossed the landscape, linking the pits with the main lines. Miners' rows were built to house the workers, and some of these survive. Perceton Row lies south of Muirhouses farm, between Dreghorn and Perceton. Other rows were at Sourlie and Doura. Annick Lodge is an attractive Georgian mansion standing by the side of the Annick Water. The house was erected around 1792 for Alexander Montgomerie, incorporating the older house known as Outer Peirston. Cunninghamhead is today a small village, formerly known as Dykehead, but being named after the railway station and estate. The Cunninghames owned the estate, and were granted a baronetcy in 1627. This became extinct in 1724.

East of Dreghorn, and originally part of the New Town, is Springside village. This was basically untouched by the more radical developments of the New Town, being further from the centre of Irvine. If the original scheme had been as successful as proposed, Springside would have been developed the same as the rest. The village as we see it is relatively modern, most of the buildings dating from the twentieth century. There are few old buildings. Springside's claim to fame is that it was the birthplace of boxer Jackie Paterson (although one Paterson biographer claims he was actually born in Dreghorn, in 1920). Paterson became British, Empire and then world flyweight champion when he knocked out Englishman Peter Kane at Hampden Park in 1943. Many boxing aficionados argue that he was Scotland's greatest-ever boxer, ahead even of such luminaries

Jackie Paterson, right (1920–66)

as Benny Lynch and Ken Buchanan. Tragically, Paterson died in violent circumstances in South Africa in 1966. He was in the first group of fifty sportsmen and women to be inducted into the Scottish Sports Hall of Fame in 2002.

South of the Corsehill Roundabout at Dreghorn is the Holmsford Bridge Crematorium. The Caledonian Crematoria Investment Company erected this in 1997, the architects being Anthony Ward Partnership. The crematorium takes its name from the bridge across the river Irvine, of which it has a view. This bridge was erected in 1880, the work of Charles Reid. Near the bridge, on the north side of the river, was an old mound known as Maid Morville's Mount.

Drybridge is a small village lying on the south side of the river Irvine. The name comes from the fact that here one of the first railway bridges was erected, and thus was dry, as opposed to bridges that crossed water. Although there are a few modern houses around the village, it is still a small community. An ancient standing stone can be seen in the field west of the village, near to the railway line. Shewalton Road leads westward from Drybridge into another major industrial area of Irvine. Here is the factory owned by GlaxoSmithKline that in 2000 employed over 680 people on a 135-acre site. The Beecham company established this in 1973 to manufacture antibiotics and other medicinal products. Beecham merged with SmithKline Beckman in 1989 to form SmithKline Beecham. This company in turn merged with Glaxo Wellcome in 2000 to form the present company.

This area is known as Shewalton, and Shewalton House formerly stood on an elevated site north-west of Drybridge, overlooking the river Irvine. The mansion was a plain Georgian building, erected in 1806 for Colonel John Boyle. It was demolished in the early twentieth century and a bearing factory erected on the site.

The Caledonian Paper Mill stands on the western edge of Shewalton Moss, the large pulp mill turning softwood logs into glossy paper suitable for magazines and other publications. This factory was erected in the late 1980s and officially opened in 1989 by the Duke of Edinburgh.

# 5

# Kilbirnie, Dalry and Beith

THE RIVER GARNOCK RISES in the North Ayrshire Heights. On the southern slopes of the Hill of Stake – the highest summit in these parts at 1,711 feet – the river begins its life as a small stream, issuing from a boggy piece of land. On its journey southward it soon collects the waters from numerous other small streams and within a mile becomes a sizeable burn. About a mile and a half from its birth the stream arrives in a rocky gully, and here the waters are left to tumble over a waterfall, known as the Garnock Spout. This fall is about forty feet in height, and is one of the most spectacular in the north of the county.

Other waterfalls can be seen nearby. The Murchan Spout is where the Murchan Burn tumbles over the rocks into a narrow ravine. The Surge Burn has an unnamed fall on it below the Red Craigs, and the King's Burn has another series of falls in its rocky bed. The Garnock itself tumbles over the Grip Linn and other falls on its way to the more level valley bottom. This area of countryside is home to a number of grouse moors, where the heather is burned and game birds are encouraged to breed. The Ladyland Moor is home to one of the sporting moors.

Some of the place names hereabouts have names that make one keen to find out more. Who is the king referred to in King's Burn? What does the name Plump Jordan in the Garnock mean? What does the obviously Gaelic based hill-name Auchenbourach mean? One of the summits here is known as Standingstone Hill; its derivation is more obvious but there is no standing stone to be seen nowadays. Just below Standingstone Hill is the Pundeavon Reservoir, or Plan Dam, formed by damming the Pundeavon Burn. This stores water that was used to supply Kilbirnie, the reservoir created by Ayr County Council. The river Garnock passes through a deep and narrow defile here, known as Glen Garnock, and at its foot, near Blackbarn farm, tumbles over its final waterfall.

Glengarnock Castle ruins stand in a promontory formed by the river. The castle is one of the oldest in the area, perhaps dating from 1400–52, according to the castle experts, MacGibbon and Ross, but with an addition of 1627. It was built by the Cunninghame family, and remained one of their principal seats until 1757 when it was destroyed by fire. It lay in ruins thereafter, and in January 1839, during a violent storm, one of the walls of the main tower collapsed. The castle comprised a main keep structure, some of which still stands to a considerable height, and a courtyard wall, within which were various buildings. The kitchens occupied one of these buildings, the vaulted roof surviving. Entrance to the castle was via a gateway in the east wall of the barmkin, and fragments of the gatehouse survive. A postern gateway existed on the north side of the castle, allowing an exit down to the riverside. The Ridel family anciently owned Glengarnock, but the male line died out and the heiress married Harvey Cunninghame, who was a hero at the Battle of Largs. Galfridus Cunninghame, his second son, was given the barony of Glengarnock and his descendants held it for many centuries.

Fragmentary remains of a second castle can be found nearby at Ladyland House. Ladyland Castle was a standard square tower house, rising through a number of floors to a continuously corbelled parapet. In 1669 the tower was remodelled and made more suitable for domestic living, with the addition of a fore stair to the first floor doorway, the door surround remodelled and decorated with a pediment. This pediment with the date is now built into the gateway to the walled garden.

Ladyland House dates from 1817–21 when it was built to plans by David Hamilton for William Cochran. Hamilton's designs are quite unique, for the house has unusual glazing bars on the windows and bold corner quoins. James Houston of Kilbirnie designed a wing of 1925. The stable block is contemporary with the house, but may incorporate seventeenth century buildings in the wings. A sundial in the grounds is dated 1821, perhaps erected to celebrate the completion of the buildings. An older dial in front of the mansion is dated 1673. Ladyland's policies are attractive, being richly wooded along the side of the Maich Water. The watercourse was dammed by Renfrew County Council (for the river forms the county boundary) to store water. The Maich Water, like the Garnock, has a series of waterfalls on its descent from Mistylaw Muir. Below Ladyland House, by the side of the water, is the Smuggler's Cave. In a field next to the mansion is a large boulder known as the De'il's Chuckie Stane.

The Maich Water empties itself into the Kilbirnie Loch, the surface of which is ninety-nine feet above the level of the sea. This loch forms one of a chain through the valley, with Barr Loch and Castle Semple Loch, which at one time were thought ideal for cutting a canal. Although near to the Garnock Water, Kilbirnie Loch empties itself into the Dubbs Water, which flows north into the Barr Loch and thence the Black Cart Water that reaches the Clyde at Renfrew. At one time the loch was known as Loch Thankart. The southern shores of the loch formerly extended quite a distance to the south, but the loch was partially filled in over the years. In this former part of the loch was found an old canoe in 1886. It was eighteen feet long, and within it were found a lion-shaped ewer and a three-legged bronze pot. The canoe was found with the remains of a crannog, but this has long-since been buried beneath the ever extending slag-bing. A second canoe was found in 1930.

Kilbirnie today is a sizeable town, but as late as 1742 there were only three houses here, and even by 1792 there were only around eighty. In 1788 Knox's Mill had been erected, and the town grew around it. The old part of the town was built to either side of the Garnock Bridge. The town is centre of a parish of 10,641 acres.

The Auld Kirk is one of the most interesting buildings in the town. It was built on or near the site of a sixth century Christian site dedicated to St Brendan of Clonfert, who was an uncle of St Columba. Brendan may have established a cell here sometime prior to his death in AD 578, hence the present name of the town, from the Gaelic *cille Brendan*. The present building dates from the fifteenth century, making it one of the few pre-Reformation churches in the county. The nave dates from 1470 and the low tower was added in 1590. Sir James Cunninghame added the Glengarnock burial aisle in 1597. Sir John Crawfurd of Place erected a second aisle in 1642. The Crawfurd laird's loft has some acclaimed wood carving of that time and armorial panels of 1705, commemorating John Crawfurd, the 1st Viscount Garnock, and his ancestors. The carvings are thought to have been the work of Italian craftsmen. The pulpit is of around 1620, constructed of Norwegian pine. The Ladyland pew has initials commemorating Captain William Hamilton of Ladyland and Janet Brisbane his wife, along with the date 1671. The north transept was added to the church in 1903–5, designed by Charles Johnston of Edinburgh. The carved panels on the front of this aisle were donated by local families and depict local trades and industries. The organ dates from 1911, the bell from 1753. John Milne of Edinburgh cast it. Stained glass includes work by Guthrie & Wells. The church received its present name of Auld Kirk in 1978 when it was united with the Glengarnock Parish Church, previously being known as the Barony Old Parish Church. The church is open to the public during weekday afternoons in July and August. In the kirkyard can be seen the rather fine Crawfurd Mausoleum of 1594. This commemorates Thomas Crawfurd of Jordanhill (d. 1603), who was an MP, Provost of Glasgow and captain of the Protestant armies at the time of Mary Queen of Scots. He led a successful attack on Dumbarton Castle and retook it from English hands in 1571. A copy of the original armorial panel and inscription can be seen within the church.

Kilbirnie was at one time home to various large mill buildings, some of which have been demolished. The Stoneyholm mills survive, dating from 1831, and are famous for the manufacture of fishing nets. The Dennyholm mills were erected around the same time but were demolished in the 1970s. The Nether Mill was erected in 1792, and during the construction work a stone cist, or coffin, was discovered in the ground.

The Knox family, who over the years have contributed much to the town, owned most of the local mills. Robert Knox, who was succeeded by his two sons, William and James, established the firm in 1778. Grandson James was knighted. One of the main gifts to the town was the Knox Institute, on the south side of the Cross, which was opened in Main Street on 19 November 1892 to give the residents a place to relax, read books and enjoy themselves. The architect of the building was Robert Snodgrass. The steel sculpture at the Cross was the work of John Henry White and was donated by the British Steel Corporation. In front of the institute is a statue of Hygeia sculpted by D. W. Stevenson in 1894. This was erected to commemorate Dr William Walker (1807–85) who, for fifty-two years was devoted to the well being of the people. Dr Walker is interred in the parish cemetery, his grave marked by a tall obelisk. His son, also William, was a doctor in Buenos Aires and donated £2,000 with which the Walker Halls were built, opening on 9 September 1916.

The Eglinton Inn is one of the older buildings to survive; it is dated 1835. The Masonic Lodge Royal Blues was founded in 1859 and erected a hall in 1904. The Fire Station was opened on 19 December 1989. The health centre building at the road junction was erected in 1994 on the site of the old Central School. This had been erected between 1914 and 1921, and had carvings on the rainwater heads depicting children. Moorpark Primary School was opened in 1978, a modern education establishment, built to replace the old Ladyland School. This had been established in 1869 and extended in 1937.

One of the finest twentieth century buildings in Kilbirnie has been poorly maintained. The former Radio City cinema (and later the George cinema and then bingo hall) was designed by James Houston and opened in 1938. For its time it was one of the most modern buildings of its kind in the country. On 16 May 1943 Sir Harry Lauder entertained there as part of a wartime fundraising variety concert. St Columba's Church is located in Glasgow Street. It was built as the East Church in 1843, when it was a Free Church. The building was restored in 1875 and 1903. The West Church was erected in 1824, when it was a Reformed Presbyterian place of worship, remaining thus until 1876. At the uniting of the West and East churches to form St Columba's, it was converted into a hall. St Bridget's RC Church was opened on 11 May 1862, and was extended in 1957 to plans by James Houston. A St Bridget's School was established in 1894 (demolished and replaced by Garnock Court) and replaced by the present primary school in 1963.

At the southern end of the town, in Dalry Road and to the east of it, is the Garden City. This development of council houses was erected in 1916 to plans by J. Walker Smith to house the workers employed in the steelworks at Glengarnock. Two hundred and fifty dwellings were erected on a plan that incorporates a Central Avenue, oval and circle. This was one of the first, and most successful, examples of town planning in the district, made all the more remarkable considering that the estate was built during the First World War.

Access to the public park is made through the war memorial gateway, unveiled on 8 October 1922. The neo-classical archway was the work of James Houston. The panels list 159 men who sacrificed their lives. Within the seventeen-acre park is Garnock pool, opened on 29 March 1969, and designed by James Houston & Son. Extensions were added in 1990 and 1992 creating a complete leisure centre, with pool, sauna, fitness suite and other facilities. The new library building dates from 1975. Kilbirnie Ladeside Junior Football Club was founded in 1901, and plays at Thistle Valefield, at one time the park of Glengarnock Thistle, which folded during the war.

Dipple Road leads north from the town up the east side of the Garnock towards Ladyland. On the way it passes Redheugh House, built around 1840 by Hugh Knox. His son extended it in 1890 in a baronial style drawn up by Clarke & Bell, and again in 1905–8 to plans by John Snodgrass in a similar style, imitating an old tower house with corbelled parapet. The extensions incorporated a dining room, drawing room, billiard room and bedrooms. The house was for a number of years used as a residential school for deprived children, run by the Salvation Army, but in the 1990s was restored into a number of flatted dwellings.

Another minor road passes by Garnock Academy (opened 1972) on its way towards the Smallburn reservoir and various farms. On this route is Moorpark House, dating from around 1848. This is a substantial mansion of two storeys, in which the windows are distinguished by their arches. The house was erected for Robert William Knox who was a local mill owner, but was later sold to the council who have now converted it into offices.

Following Largs Road from Kilbirnie one soon passes Kilbirnie Place golf club, a par 69, 18-hole course of 5,543 yards. This was laid out in 1925 as a nine-hole course, the second nine being added in 1977, and the present clubhouse in 1978. Beyond it stood Kilbirnie Place, or Place House, a fine mansion designed by Henry Lord of Manchester and erected in 1892–4. As with most of the country houses around Kilbirnie, the house was built for the Knox family, in this case Sir James Knox, formerly of Redheugh. On the opposite side of the road is the ruined Kilbirnie House, or Place of Kilbirnie, standing behind Place Farm. The Crawfurds erected the house around 1470 and to this a large wing of around 1627 was added. In 1638 the Crawfurd-Polloks of Pollok and Kilbirnie were granted a Baronetcy, but this became extinct in 1885. The castle suffered a fire in 1757 whereupon the family moved to Bourtreehill, near Irvine.

On the farm of Auchencloigh was a lime works. The lands of Coldgreen, surrounding the Gowkhouse Burn, have been afforested. At one time a public road ran from Kilbirnie this way, heading for Largs. The old route climbed past Moorpark House to Wattieston farm before striking across the hillside to Coldgreen and rejoining the present road at Whitehill.

The southern extremity of Kilbirnie parish, on the farms of Lintseedridge, Mossend, East and West Mains and Tennox, can be found a number of former bings, left behind when the mines associated with them had gone. This area was an important source of ironstone, limestone, coal and sandstone. The natural ores were taken to the Glengarnock Iron Works, which formerly stood at the southern end of Kilbirnie Loch. Merry & Cunninghame, who erected eight blast furnaces there, established the works in 1843. These were used to produce pig iron from local blackband ironstone and splint coal. In 1884 four Bessemer converters, a cogging mill and a plate mill were added. The works were taken over by the Glengarnock Iron & Steel Company in 1890 and in 1916 by David Colville & Sons. In later years iron ore was imported to the site, and the works became part of British Steel. However, the works were closed in 1985 and the whole site flattened and landscaped. The Glengarnock and Lochshore industrial estates occupy part of the ironworks site whereas the recreation ground is located on the former slagheap.

Glengarnock village is today a string of houses and other buildings along the B777 from Kilbirnie almost to Beith. The village owes its origin to the foundation of the ironworks, and soon a sizeable community lived here. The old school had been erected in 1887–1903 but was closed in May 1992 when pupils transferred to the new building, officially opened on 23 March 1993.

Glengarnock Church was erected in 1870 as a United Presbyterian place of worship, but it later became a United Free Church before becoming part of the Church of Scotland in 1929. The church continued in use until 1978 and the church was demolished in 1989. The bell tower from the church was saved, and erected in 1992 in a small garden area in the village. The bell itself was sent to Zambia where it hangs in a mission church. The former hall of 1931 was converted into the Valley arts centre.

Kilbirnie and the Garnock valley were well served by railways. The Lanarkshire & Ayrshire Railway built a branch from their Barrmill to Kilwinning line into Kilbirnie, passing through the Brackenhills station. This branch was opened on 1 November 1889 for goods and on 2 December the same year for passengers. Later taken over by the Caledonian railway, Kilbirnie station was closed in 1964 and Montgomerie Court, erected in 1977, now occupies the site. The Glasgow, Paisley, Kilmarnock & Ayr Railway (later part of Glasgow & South Western Railway) was opened through Glengarnock and Beith on 10 July 1840, a station being established at Glengarnock. The Glasgow, Paisley, Kilmarnock & Ayr line passed through Glengarnock, the station there opening on 10 July 1840, and is still in use, serving Kilbirnie, Beith and surrounding areas.

The parish of Dalry lies to the south and west of Kilbirnie, extending to 19,361 acres. The northernmost extremity of the parish is at Slaty Law (1,584 feet), where the parishes of Dalry, Largs and Kilbirnie meet. There is a sizeable track of moorland here which is almost separated from the rest of the parish, the lands of Knockside, which fall within Largs parish, virtually isolating the lands of Blairpark, which in turn might have been better located with Largs parish.

There are a number of small but prominent hills in this part of the parish, including Irish Law (1,584 feet), Feuside Hill (1,399 feet), and Rigging Hill (1,269 feet). This last-named summit is the least distinct summit, comprising a series of knolls and rock outcrops, each of which has its own name. Hence here we have Jock's Castle, Mount Stewart, Paton's Hill, Jamieson's Hill, Cochrane's Craigs and the Thief's Craigs. Who these folk were is unknown. On the lower slopes of the Irish Law is the Yean Stane, a large boulder that marks one of the corners of the parish boundary. On the west side of Irish Law the Rye Water has its source, here known as Rye Water Head. It soon drops into the valley and enters the Muirhead Reservoir, the uppermost of two man-made lochs hereabouts. Above the reservoir rise the Knockside Hills, which rise to over 1,400 feet. The southernmost summit is marked by two pre-historic burial cairns.

Below the Muirhead Reservoir is the Camphill Reservoir, constructed by Paisley Corporation Water Works. The filter houses and water works are located by the side of the Rye below South Camphill Farm. One of the streams that falls into the reservoir is known as Routdane Burn, said to commemorate the Battle of Largs. The name Camp Hill is derived from where the Scots forces spent the night before the battle.

The B784 leaves the A760 at the former Hourat Toll and strikes south to Dalry. Above South Hourat is the Castle Hill, its name indicative of an ancient fortification. Above Swinlees is Carwinning Hill, the summit of the little steep knoll being crowned by an ancient fort. This affords fine views of the surrounding valley and would have been an ideal site for defence. The name, Car-, or Caer-, winning, connects the hill with St Winning, who is also commemorated by a well in the parish. The fort comprises of a central enclosure measuring 300 feet in diameter. Circling this is a second wall, around 500 feet in diameter. A smaller enclosure within the centre, measuring about 100 feet in diameter, may be the remnants of an old dun. All the ramparts and stone walls have long-since tumbled and are in a poor condition.

The Rye Water takes a more remote route from Camphill to Dalry, passing down through a narrow valley. The South Burn at Brodoclea tumbles over a fine waterfall in the deep and rocky Raven's Craig Glen. Access to here is possible by following a minor road from Dalry past Windyedge Farm. The Rye drops through the gorge-like Hindog Glen before entering Dalry at Doggartland. Above the deep chasm are the remains of an ancient dun.

The massive Roche Vitamins Ltd chemical works dominates the north end of Dalry. The factory was built in 1950 to produce ascorbic acid (Vitamin C) and other vitamins. Extensions to the factory were erected in 1970 and 1983. North of the Roche factory is the pleasant Georgian house of Pitcon, built on a low knoll in what would have at one time been a marshy valley, where the Rye, Garnock and Mains Burn join. The present house dates from around 1787, when James Robertson bought the estate from George MacRae, an Ayr merchant. A wing of the 1920s was added to plans by James Houston. Within the grounds is an old laundry building, on which an old stone with a date from the 1660s has been incorporated. No doubt this came from an older building that stood here.

Dalry is a pleasant self-contained town occupying the raised ground between the Caaf and Rye tributaries of the Garnock. Its parish extends to 19,361 acres but, like Kilbirnie, the village was slow to come to fruition. In 1700 there were only six houses in the village, but it extended considerably after 1845 with the arrival of the Blair Ironworks. These works operated until 1871.

The town centre has a number of distinguished old buildings, of which St Margaret's Church must be regarded as one of the most impressive. The spire dominates the town, rising 159 feet above the level of the street. The church was erected in a cruciform pattern in 1871–3 to plans by David Thomson. The stone came from Auchenskeith and the building cost £4,500 to erect. The clock was donated by Gavin Fullarton of Kerelaw and lit from 1882. The pipe organ dates from 1899, and was made by Blackett & Howden; originally installed in the St Matthew's Highlanders Memorial Church in Glasgow, it was brought to Dalry in 1954. The church suffered from a fire in 1951 after which the interior had to be refitted. The stained glass is particularly fine, with work by C. L. Davidson, Guthrie & Wells, Rona Moody, Charles Payne, and Gordon Webster. Inside can be seen an old stone of 1608 that is inscribed 'Remember Lot's Wife'. There are also preserved two silver communion chalices, dating from 1618, made in Edinburgh by Gilbert Kirkwood. In the porch two old armorial stones have been built into the present wall. One is dated 1604 and bears the arms of Daniel Ker of Kersland and Annabella Campbell of Loudoun, his wife. The other has the arms of John Blair of that Ilk and his wife, Grizel Sempil. An oak panel within the church bears the arms of Blair of that Ilk impaled with that of Boyd of Pitcon. The church has a bell of 1872, cast in Glasgow, and one of 1661, which came from Amsterdam in the Netherlands. It was cast by the famous bellmaker, Francis Hemony, and is the only one of its kind in the United Kingdom. In the churchyard is a large sundial with metal gnomon of around five feet in height. Here also can be seen a number of old stones with interesting carvings and death symbolism. A fragment of the original manse wall survives here.

The first church in the parish may have been established early in the thirteenth century, when the church here is referred to as a 'chapel of Ardrossan'. It was replaced around 1604 on the present site, after which the kirktoun of Dalry appeared around it. In 1771 a third church was erected, a simple building 'devoid nearly of every external ornament as the humblest dwelling-house'.

The Cross in the centre of Dalry has some fine old buildings around it. Here can be seen the old town hall, which was erected in 1853. It is adorned with a belfry and Ionic columns. This building is now the public library. On the opposite side of the square from the parish church is the Trinity Church, erected in 1857 as the Courthill United Presbyterian Church to plans by Robert Snodgrass of Beith.

New Street extends south from the Cross. Here are the King's Arms Hotel and Royal Hotel, two fine old buildings that date from coaching days. New Street was created with the arrival of the railway in 1840, Dalry station being established across the Garnock where it is to this day. The station was rebuilt at the beginning of the twentieth century, when platforms 765 feet in length were built. In 1864, during excavations south of the station a stone axe was found. The south side of the Garnock was

Dalry: the Square showing the library

the location of a number of mines and associated bings, pit heads and miners' rows. The old Stoopshill, Furnace and Peesweep rows have now been demolished and replaced by more modern council housing.

The former St Andrew's United Free Church was located in Townend Street, its foundation stone laid on 10 September 1844 and the church opening in 1846. St Andrews and the West Parish churches merged in 1945 to form the St Andrews and West Church. This congregation merged in 1962 with the Courthill church to form the Trinity Church. Near to St Andrew's Church was the public hall, opened on 25 April 1884.

The Bridgend Mills were erected from 1876 onward, established by Thomas Biggart & Co. to carry out wool-combing and spinning. They are long out of production and the buildings demolished. The Tofts Mill stood on the north side of the Garnock. At the Tofts is St Peter's Episcopal Church, established in 1888.

North Street strikes out of the Cross at its north-west corner. There are a few old buildings here. Beyond it is the extensive public park, dropping down to the Rye Water. John Blair presented this to the residents in 1893. Here can be found the long-established bowling green and, on the slopes above, the war memorial, unveiled on 5 June 1927, a massive cross designed by Kellock Brown. Main Street in Dalry is now bypassed somewhat. The street links North Street with the modern relief road

(Roche Way) that was cut through the town. Within Main Street is the Auld Hoose Bar, perhaps dating from around 1790.

East from the Cross, next to the Trinity Church, runs Courthill Street. The name comes from the ancient hill of justice, which stands nearby. In the winter of 1872 excavations here revealed large deposits of human bones and ashes. In the street is the Mission Halls, a fine Tudoresque building of 1876 designed by William Railton of Kilmarnock. Beyond is Parkhill House which dates from the early nineteenth century but which incorporates an old lintel of 1732. The wings date from 1900, designed by Leadbetter and Fairley. Nearby is Easterhill House.

At the south end of the town the Saltcoats road crosses the Caaf Water at Lynn Bridge. A plaque here commemorates 'Hughie's Field', erected by a sister in memory of her brother. At the junction of Saltcoats Road with Kilwinning Road was an ancient mound known as the Green Knowe. The Lynn Spout is a notable local waterfall, its name something of a tautological hybrid. Within the glen is a stone cliff known as Peden's Pulpit, or Point, where the Covenanting minister, Revd Alexander Peden, is thought to have held conventicles during the years of struggle. This rocky promontory is shown on some maps as Pinnoch Point.

Lynn House has now been demolished, but it was an interesting building dating from the first half of the nineteenth century. It was built for the Crichtons who purchased the lands in 1812. In 1960, another family, the Neilsons, sold the house and it was eventually demolished and the lands developed for housing. West Lynn was the home of George Houston (1869–1947), a notable local artist. He was a prolific painter, producing many landscapes in oil and watercolour. Most of his scenes were of Ayrshire or Argyll landscapes, and he also produced some etchings. Broadlie House survives, standing north west of the town. It was erected in 1891–7 to plans by T. G. Abercrombie of Paisley for John Fulton. The house is not huge, but it is an attractive building. The Baidland Burn flows past the house, dropping over a small waterfall within the woods. Baidland Manor is a small laird's house of the seventeenth century, still occupied. Ryefield House stands on the north side of the town, perched on top of a low hill. The building probably dates from the 1850s, but incorporates an old date stone of 1786. Following a fire at the end of the First World War, the house was restored and extended, a ballroom being added at this time and a walled garden rebuilt, the latter dated 1924. The house has been subdivided in recent years, and the former stable block has also been converted into dwellings.

The Caaf Water drains a sizeable stretch of countryside west of Dalry. The watercourse rises on the slopes of the Green Hill, not too far from

Fairlie, though still within Dalry parish. From its high moorland source the infant stream drops over a couple of waterfalls into the valley below, before joining the waters of the Knockendon Reservoir, created in 1938–47. Below the dam the Caaf tumbles over falls in a rocky gorge and soon enters a second reservoir, the Caaf Reservoir. This was built for Irvine and District Water Board in 1906. Ayr County Council created a third reservoir at Auldmuir. At Auldmuir Farm is an ancient mound of unknown provenance, located across the Auldmuir burn from the farm steading. Some maps denote this as a motte. Across the Garnock from the centre of Dalry can be found the railway station and a further housing estate. Here also is the present St Margaret's manse, erected in 1893 at a cost of £1,500. A number of old collieries were located hereabouts, and a brickworks by the side of the Garnock.

The estate of Blair lies to the east, at one time the seat of the Blairs of that Ilk. The family has owned the estate since time immemorial, at least from the time of King William the Lion, though it passed down through the female line in recent years so that today the family surname is Borwick. At one time the Blairs of Dalry disputed with the Blairs of Blair Castle in Fife over which family was the oldest, and thus who held the chiefship of the family. Eventually it was decided by the Lord Lyon that whichever Blair head of the household was older, then they would be chief. Thus the chiefship usually alternated between the two. Today both families have died out in the male line, so this unusual arrangement no longer applies.

Blair House or Castle, as it is sometimes known, is one of the finest old houses in the county. Over the original entrance doorway in the re-entrant angle is an armorial panel and the date 1203, though this probably only refers to the earliest known reference to the existence of the Blairs, rather than an original date stone from an early building. The oldest part has walls fourteen feet thick in places and rises over four storeys. The house is rather fine within. The grounds around the house are often open to the public, and walks can be made through the extensive policies of Blair Park. The little Bombo Burn passes by the house, and drops over a small waterfall beyond it. The stable block is adorned with the Blair arms – a saltire on which are nine lozenges. The Blair policies and woodlands extend south to the Dusk Water, the name coming from the Gaelic *Dubh Uisge*, meaning black water. In the Dusk Glen is a deep gorge with a series of caves known as Cleeves Cove. These were partially excavated in 1883 to reveal that prehistoric man made use of them. At Auchenskeith and Jameston are former stone quarries from where stone used for construction was excavated.

Pencot Farm has a mound behind it known as Castle Hill, perhaps the site of an early fortification. Giffen House stands in a wooded hillock above the infant Dusk. The house is a rather fine neo-baronial mansion, erected in 1869 for Henry Gardiner Patrick to plans by Andrew Heiton Jr. North-west of here are the tell-tale bings from old mines, and depressions from old quarries.

The countryside is reverting back to nature, and among the fields can be found a few interesting buildings. Here is Maulside House, built for a Glasgow Writer to the Signet, Andrew Mitchell. It dates from sometime in the 1830s or thereabouts, and occupies the site of an earlier mansion. By the side of the Powgree Burn is Kersland, an old seat of the Ker family. A date stone of 1604 with the name Daniel Ker is built into the present farmhouse, and remains of the old tower and barmkin wall survive.

The A737 from Dalry to Beith passes through a couple of roadside communities. Nearer Dalry is Highfield, at a busy junction. Further east is Crossroads and The Den, where Kersland Barony School was located. The school was used as a church on Sundays, the belfry over the front gable being sufficiently ecclesiastical looking. The school, like the village store and most of the other cottages, no longer exist. Further east again is Brackenhills, which at one time had a railway station on the branch from Barrmill to Kilbirnie.

The town of Beith lies on the slopes to the east of Kilbirnie Loch. Numerous warehouses and the Willowyard Industrial Estate occupy the land between the loch and the town. Beith is also centre of a parish of 11,222 acres. The main road bypasses the centre of the town, which has a number of narrow streets at its centre. However, a lesser bypass road within the middle of the town has divided the main shopping areas into two distinct halves. Many of the buildings in the centre of Beith are old traditional structures, some of which have seen better days. Others have been well restored or replaced by suitable infill building. Other developments have left the centre of town rather open, or else replaced old buildings with unsuitable regular blocks of modern housing.

The eastern half of the town centre consists of Main Street and Mitchell Street. The narrow Main Street is lined with some old buildings, occupied by local businesses including the long established butcher, James T. Blackwood, founded in 1775, and the Smugglers' Tavern of around 1750. The library building is one of the best modern replacements, opened in 1987. From the east end of Main Street, King's Road drops down to the United Reformed Church, formerly the Evangelical Union Church, opened on 20 November 1864. The building is a simple Gothic structure and cost £200 to erect. Along Laigh Road is the small but modern brick-

Beith: the narrow Main Street

built Church of Latter Day Saints, distinguished by its small spire on the roof. It was erected in 1997.

From the crossroads at the north end of Main Street can be seen the Trinity Church, located at the north end of Wilson Street. This Gothic church was erected in 1883 but was damaged in a fire in 1917 and not rebuilt until 1926. It contains some fine woodwork and stained glass by W. Meikle & Sons and John C. Hall & Co. The organ is of 1937, by Hill, Norman & Beard. The church has a rather thin steeple, but dominates the road junction at the north end of the older part of the town. Robert Baldie designed it.

Mitchell Street climbs past the Roman Catholic Church of Our Lady of Perpetual Succour. This church was erected in 1816 as the Mitchell Street United Presbyterian Church, and is distinguished by its small spirelet on the gable. In the garden alongside are two memorials, including one to Revd Dr James Meikle, minister of the UP church for fifty-eight years. In Head Street is the former United Presbyterian Church, erected in 1784, and now a hall used by the Boys' Brigade. There is an old graveyard at the southern side of the building.

The Auld Kirk of Beith is located in its old kirkyard at the foot of the hill at the west end of Main Street. The building dates in part from 1593 but has been rebuilt to create a clock tower and burial vault. It has an attractive belfry containing a bell. Within the yard is a memorial to John Speir, formerly located in Speir's School but refurbished and placed in the old churchyard in March 1985. John Speir was the son of a Beith solicitor and banker. He died at the age of 28, and left £12,000 with which the Speir's School was erected in Barrmill Road, east of the town. The school was designed by Campbell Douglas & Sellers and was erected in 1887, the building dominated by its 100-feet-tall clock tower. The school was used to educate boys and girls under the Scotch Education Endowment Scheme. The school closed in June 1972 and the buildings were demolished in 1984.

Extending west from the Auld Kirk is The Cross. Some old buildings at the corner have been acquired by North Ayrshire Council and the St Vincent Crescent Preservation Trust for restoration, being rather fine examples of local building styles. One of the buildings in this group (30–32 The Cross) was the home at one time of Revd John Witherspoon (1722–1794). He was born at Gifford in East Lothian and became minister of Beith parish church in 1744. In 1756 he moved to Paisley where he became minister at the Town Church. In 1768 Witherspoon emigrated to the United States where he became President of Princeton University, which at that time was known as the College of New Jersey. During his time at Princeton – one of America's prestigious Ivy League universities – Witherspoon was influential in the formative years of many future leaders of the country. He was instrumental in drawing up the United States Declaration of Independence and he was one of the signatories. Witherspoon is also credited with having invented the term, 'Americanism'. A statue to Witherspoon can be seen in Paisley and a plaque marks his birthplace in Gifford.

Eglinton Street is Beith's second main shopping area, extending west from The Cross. Here is the late eighteenth century Saracen's Head Inn, the former post office (now Royal Mail depot) of 1897, and numerous traditional buildings, mostly well kept in this part of town. The Strand strikes south from Eglinton Street, forming a rather fine open square. At the corner is the Council House, a simple yet distinguished building of 1817 complete with a small belfry and painted representation of a flag. This was used until 1884 as the local court. At the top end of the Strand is a former granite fountain, the gift of John Gilmour, Mount Vernon, in 1876. The Clydesdale Bank dates from 1902–6 and was built in the baronial style from Ballochmyle sandstone. The bank's turret is one of its more ornamental features. Townhead Street can be followed further south and a turn made into Kirk Road, at the end of which is the prominent High Church, its tall five-stage tower visible for miles around.

The High Church is a Gothic T-plan building that dates from 1807–10. The church was extended in 1885 and an extensive group of halls stand alongside. Internally is a Harrison & Harrison pipe organ of 1885 and some fine stained glass by G. Maile and Gordon Webster. Behind the church, on a pathway back to the town centre, is the former Beith Primary School, closed in 1999 when the new school opened in Glebe Road. The school had been opened on 15 March 1875 as Beith Academy, the architect being Robert Snodgrass. Beith Town Station was opened on 26 June 1873, the terminus of a branch line of the Glasgow, Barrhead & Kilmarnock Junction railway, leaving Lugton and passing through Barrmill. The station was closed in 1962 and the site is now occupied by housing.

North of Beith is the Woodside estate, the house a rather fine baronial tower which at first glance looks as though it is an ancient tower house. The house in fact only dates from 1890 in its present form, for previously it was a Georgian mansion of two storeys, created in 1759. The mansion itself was a reworking of an even earlier building incorporating work of 1551 and 1640, and thus the old tower built by Hew Ralston has virtually come full circle as taste for defensive features came and went. Charles S. S. Johnston was the architect responsible for returning the house to its present baronial form. It is now divided into flats.

Grangehill House stands in woodland north-east of Beith, the much-altered structure perched on its low hill. Originally built in 1804 for John Fulton, the house has been altered over the years, and is now distinguished by its bay windows and three-storey tower next to the entrance front.

Behind Grangehill, Threepwood Road climbs up onto a low range of hills, the highest of which is known as Lochlands Hill, 689 feet above sea level. The north side of the hill is home to Loanhead Quarry. On the hill top is Beith golf course, a par 68, 18-hole parkland course 5,641 yards in length. On Lochlands Hill can be found St Inan's Chair, a large boulder associated with St Inan. The stone chair has a high back and a place to put your feet. On the lower slopes, next to Cauldhame cottage, is St Inan's Well. The traditional St Inan's Fair was held in this vicinity on 18 February, the saint's day. This was Beith's main fair, though the name was often distorted to Tenant's Fair.

A minor road drops down to the disused Mill of Beith, its power originally coming from the dammed Roebank Burn. The eastern shoulder of Lochlands Hill has the name Cuff Hill, and on its slopes are three notable antiquities. Within a small circular wood is the Rocking Stone, a large boulder of about eleven tons in weight that at one time had an ability to move slightly. A series of prehistoric standing stones lie to the south-west of the Rocking Stone. They are known locally as the Four

Stanes. On the eastern slopes of Cuff Hill can be found the remains of a chambered cairn known as the Long Cairn. This has been robbed of much of its covering to reveal cists. It formerly measured 165 feet in length by 58 feet wide and 12 feet in height.

The lands north of Lochside and Cuff hills have a number of smallish reservoirs in the hollows, adding to the attractiveness of the area. The two smaller ones surrounding Cuff Hill are known as Kirkleegreen and Cuffhill reservoirs. Further north, beyond the former Threepwood estate, is the larger Barrcraigs reservoir, established by Paisley Corporation Water Works. The reservoir here was also known as Rowbank reservoir. It forms the boundary between Ayrshire and Renfrewshire at this point. Threepwood is no longer a landed estate of any extent, but at one time it was the seat of the Love family in the north of the county, held by them since 1633. At one time there was a small tower house of sorts here.

Another road heading east from Beith is Wardrop Street (B777), which links the town with Lugton, an important road junction and former railway junction. It passes an entrance to Geilsland School on the right. This establishment was opened in 1964, taking over Geilsland House, which was built around 1870 by William Fulton Love. It is now a Church of Scotland school where boys with behavioural problems or young offenders are educated. In 1976 staff and pupils erected a small chapel building, named Millport. Further east the road soon reaches the small village of Gateside, where can be found the Gateside Inn. The village hall dates from 1897 and may well be the work of Charles Johnston. It is a distinguished Tudor building. South of here is Broadstone where a number of former quarries were used to excavate stone. Just north of Gateside, near Bog Hall Farm, is the ancient Court Hill, a small mound next to a small burn.

The Lugton Road continues, passing the site of Trearne House, which is now occupied by the large Trearne limestone quarry. The house was probably erected in the mid-nineteenth century on the site of an older building. The house was Gothic in style, and a four storey battlemented tower over the entrance doorway was its main feature. William Ralston Patrick of Trearne, Hessilhead and Roughwood, a noted antiquarian, owned the house. Although Trearne was refurbished internally in the 1930s, the house was demolished in 1954 to allow the creation of the present quarry.

William Patrick also owned Hessilhead Castle, which was the estate lying immediately east of Trearne. Hessilhead has also succumbed to the demolisher, and its policies too are home to an extensive limestone quarry. The castle was demolished in the 1960s or 1970s and little of it remains. Alexander Montgomerie (c1550 – c1602), the poet who wrote *The Cherry and the Slae*, is thought to have lived here. Hessilhead was a fine old tower house with a vaulted ground floor. A kitchen wing and new staircase were added to the tower in the 1680s when Francis Montgomerie of Giffen Castle owned the estate. It was his intention that his son and heir, John, would live there. The tower roof was removed around 1776 since when the castle began to decay, in the nineteenth century being a romantic ruin within the extensive grounds of Trearne House. Some of the grounds now form a nature reserve.

At Coldstream Farm, between Gateside and Lugton, is an old mill, the mill dam surviving above it, creating a small loch. A natural loch is the Blae Loch, lying in a marshy hollow. South of the loch are other lochs, but these are man-made, left behind when old quarries were abandoned and filled with water.

Just before the B777 reaches Lugton it passes the woods of Caldwell estate. At the recent redrawing of the county boundaries the Caldwell policies were transferred to Renfrewshire, but historically the lands were part of Ayrshire and in Beith parish. Caldwell House, or Castle Caldwell as it is also known, is a Robert and James Adam mansion of 1773. Adam, who is famous for grand designs such as Culzean Castle, was limited to what he could do here, and the resultant castellated mansion is little more than a simple block with the addition of tiny bartizans and a crenellated parapet. The semi-circular rendered faces are typical of Adam, but the house is not his finest work. Caldwell was originally an ancient castle owned by the Mure family. The Mures acquired the estate by marrying the Caldwell of that Ilk heiress in the mid-fourteenth century. A lesser branch, the Caldwells of Wester Caldwell, survived until the end of the seventeenth century, when John Caldwell died. Caldwell became a hospital in 1927, and for many years was used to house geriatrics until it was closed in April 1985. It was later sold as a nursing home.

From Lugton the A736 strikes south towards Irvine. A number of minor roads can be taken from it westwards back to Beith. The first of these strikes west just before the main road crosses the railway siding. Passing Wester Highgate Farm, the road soon reaches the Balgray bonded warehouses, belonging to Chivas Brothers, whisky blenders, where a large number of buildings straddle either side of the infant Dusk Water. Further south past the three Gree farms a second railway (long disused) is crossed, and a second road strikes west. This passes Brownhills Farm and makes its way through the Balgray bonded warehouses.

The next road to Beith leaves the A736 at Burnhouse, where the B706 forms a crossroads. Burnhouse is a small community with cottages erected along the roadside. Burnhouse Manor is a small country house that is now used as a hotel. The Patricks of Hessilhead and Trearne at one time owned it, and William Patrick lived here while Trearne was being built. The original part of the house is a distinguished double-storey building, constructed of fine ashlar and ornamented with Tudoresque hood moulds and a gablet over the central window.

Half a mile from Burnhouse, on the way to Beith, Mains of Giffen is passed. Giffen Castle at one time stood here, owned by the Montgomeries until 1722. Soon after they relinquished ownership of the tower it fell into ruins and became a quarry for stone. Some of this found its way into Mains of Giffen where an ornate stone or two can still be seen, built into the walls. On 12 April 1838 the remaining tower, by which time it was little more than a U-shaped collection of walls, collapsed during the night. Near to Giffen Castle is Borestone cottage, named after a large boulder known as the Bore Stone. Another old quarry, filled with water, lies beyond the cottages at Greenhill, which today is a small hamlet comprising a few cottages.

Beyond Greenhills is Barrmill, a small community that owes much of its origin to the fact that here were a couple of railway junctions, and a railway station that operated from 1873 until 1962. The name comes from the mill that was at one time noted for the manufacture of threads. The mill was closed when the business was transferred to Kilbirnie. On the hill to the south stood Nettlehirst House, erected in 1844 by W. and E. Burns. The family was not especially wealthy, but was able to create a distinguished castellated building, the main tower rising through five storeys to a flagpole. Being built on a low hill meant that it was visible for miles around. Nettlehirst was consumed by a fire in the early 1930s and subsequently demolished. The grounds were later used for the quarrying and refining of limestone, but the lime works closed in 1972. Remains of the industrial heritage can still be seen, including the two kilns.

Between Barrmill and Beith is the large Royal Navy armament depot, occupying extensive grounds south of the B706 and as far south at the Bankhead Moss. Here are many stores and other buildings located over a wide stretch of countryside, used for the storage of munitions and army equipment.

# 6

# Dunlop, Stewarton and Fenwick

THE VILLAGE OF DUNLOP lies by the side of the tiny Glazert Burn, five miles or so from Beith. The village is the centre of a parish of 7,181 acres, extending from near Uplawmoor on the Renfrewshire border, south towards Stewarton. At one time 1,101 acres of Dunlop parish was located within Renfrewshire, until the Boundary Commissioners redrew the county boundary in 1891 to include this within Ayrshire. Dunlop village is a fine little community. The A735 passes through it on a north-south axis, but one of the finest streets is Main Street, the B706 towards Beith. At the foot of the street is the parish church, erected in 1835 but incorporating the Dunlop Aisle of 1641. The present building has a battle-mented tower adjoining a relatively simple block. Windows include work by Powell of London and Alfred & Gordon Webster.

The old churchyard has some interesting old gravestones and fune-real architecture. Here can be found a fine mausoleum to Revd Hans Hamilton (d. 1608), built of stone and having a stone-flagged roof and corbie-stepped gables. It was erected in 1641. Within are marble effigies of both Hamilton and his wife. Hans (or Johannes or John) Hamilton was the son of Hamilton of Raploch and served the parish for forty-five years. Hans Hamilton was the first Protestant minister in Dunlop. His eldest son, James Hamilton, was sent to Ireland in 1587 by James VI to gather intelligence as to what the Irish planned to do on the death of Elizabeth I of England. For his work, the King created him Viscount Clandeboyes and Baron Hamilton in 1622. The titles became extinct on the death of his grandson, also Earl of Clanbrassil. Hans Hamilton had five other sons who emigrated to Ireland and became so prominent that they established the noble houses of Clanbrassil, Roden, Massareene and Dufferin.

The former manse building is now known as Kirkland. This is a tra-ditional Scots-style building of around 1514–25, built on the L-plan with a turreted stairway in the re-entrant. Revd Gabriel Cunningham, the Covenanting minister, held conventicles within the house during the years of struggle. James Chalmers designed extensions to the house in 1910, keeping the traditional style. Another manse was erected in Main Street in 1781, replacing Kirkland, which then became a farmhouse. The Clandeboyes School building dates from 1641, a traditional double-storey schoolhouse, and the first in the village. An inscription reads, 'This school is erected and endowed by James, Viscount Clandeboyes, in love to his parish, in which his father, Hans Hamilton, was pastor 45 years, in King James the Sixt, his raigne.' It was extended in 1925 and was later converted into a hall.

Main Street strikes east from here, a traditional streetscape comprising single-storey cottages that are well kept and maintained. Here can be found the post office and the present primary school, erected in 1876 and extended in 1931. At the junction with Stewarton Road stands the former Free Church of 1845, now the parish-church hall. The public hall was opened on 8 December 1891, built at the corner of Kirkland Road with Main Street. It contained a reading room and main hall, and was extended in the 1920s. The open belfry is a distinguishing feature. The war memorial was at one time located at the hall before being moved to the kirkyard.

The railway passes through Dunlop, the station being opened on 27 March 1871 on what was the Glasgow, Barrhead & Kilmarnock Joint Railway. The station was closed for a number of years, but has reopened and still serves passengers on the line from Kilmarnock to Glasgow. On the opposite side of the railway from the old town is an extensive sawmill and other works, the property of Robert Howie & Sons, which was founded in 1850. By the side of the Glazert Burn was the Hapland Mill, originally a woollen mill. It was closed in the early 1980s.

The name Dunlop is known beyond the locality as a type of cheese. Barbara Gilmour first produced cheese using whole milk sometime around 1690, previously it having been universally made from skimmed milk. Barbara had spent the previous years in exile in Ireland, avoiding the struggle of the time of the Covenanters, and some folk reckon that she obtained the recipe there. However, this is unlikely, as Ireland was not particularly noted for its cheeses, and certainly not of this quality. The new cheese was considerably superior to other cheeses and soon this became the normal method of production in the south-west of Scotland. It was quite significant that on the Dunlop estate, rents were payable in cheeses, as opposed to pounds, which was regarded as being most satisfactory to the tenants. William Cobbett described Dunlop cheese as 'equal in quality to any cheese from Cheshire, Gloucestershire or Wiltshire.' Gilmour died in 1731 and is buried in Dunlop kirkyard.

Dunlop is also the home of one of Scotland's most recent sporting heroines: Rhona Martin. At the 2002 Winter Olympics in Salt Lake City, Martin was the skip of the all-Scottish team that won the gold medal in the women's curling event. The team beat Switzerland 4–3 in the final to secure the first gold for Britain at the Winter Olympics for eighteen years. Despite the fact that England, Wales and Ireland have virtually no tradition of participation in curling, the final was watched avidly by viewers across the United Kingdom.

The landscape around Dunlop is one of small hills and rolling country-side. Some of the hills are quite steep on their sides, among them Dunlop Hill, which rises to the west of the village. Although just over 400 feet in height, the hill is a significant landmark. The summit is thought to have been the site of an ancient castle, from which the name *Dun-luib*, Gaelic for fort by the winding stream, is thought to be derived. To the east of the village is another low hill, the summit of which is crowned by a large boulder known as the Carlin's Stone.

At Mains Farm is an old quarry, the hole now filled with water. Other disused limestone quarries are located at Laigh Gameshill, also south of the village. All around here are small farms and cottages, many becoming homes for Glasgow commuters.

At the foot of another small but prominent hill is Aiket Castle, a distinctive building in the locality. The castle dates in part from the fifteenth century, having been built by the Cunninghames. That family was granted a charter to these lands around 1479. Alexander Cunninghame of Aiket was implicated in the murder of Hugh, 4th Earl of Eglinton, in 1586 and was himself shot nearby. Others occupied the castle thereafter, but the Cunninghames were later restored to their lands. The castle passed to other hands in 1700 and around 1734 the new owners reduced the original tower and tarted the building up to look like a 'modern' Georgian house. The castle remained in occupation until 1957, when a fire destroyed it. In 1976–9 the ruins were purchased by the architect Robert Clow, who set about restoring it to its former glory. This has been fully achieved and the present building is one of the finest tower houses in Ayrshire. The restoration received a Europa Nostra award in 1987. Next to the castle is the old Aiket Mill, used for grinding corn. Millhouse of Aiket nearby was a simple cottage that was extended in 1982 to plans by Robert Clow, forming an attractive small house.

The A735 heading north from Dunlop soon arrives at a historical site. By the side of the road, in the field below another wooded hillock, is the Chapel Well, indicative of an old religious site. Hereabouts stood the Chapel of the Virgin Mary, but it has long since disappeared, the last ruins of it being removed sometime in the early nineteenth century. Some accounts claim this as the original church of Dunlop, whereas others state that it was distinct from the parish church. On the hill above the well, located in the middle of a field, is 'Thougritstane', or 'Thugartstane', a large boulder that traditionally was associated with the chapel.

Lochridgehills Farm recollects the former Halket Loch, which at one time extended to around ten acres, but which was drained in the 1830s. East Halket House is a plain country house of modest proportions, erected in the early nineteenth century, probably 1847 as appears on a nearby date stone.

The main road heads north to an important junction at Lugton. The village here is tiny, but its importance as a meeting of roads, and formerly as a meeting place of railways, has resulted in its name being better known beyond the area than its size would suggest. This little village at one time had two railway stations, for the Glasgow & Kilmarnock and Caledonian railway companies both passed this way on their route to the Ayrshire coast. The High station was a 'Caley' station, and opened in 1903. It continued in operation until 14 December 1964. The Glasgow and Kilmarnock Joint Railway operated the Low station, opened in 1873. A junction here allowed services to go either to Kilmarnock or Beith. Although this line is still operational, the station closed in 1964.

Lugton was noted for its inn, which was erected sometime around 1830, for the *New Statistical Account* states, 'a very respectable inn has been built at Lugton bridge.' Here also was the Lugton Brewery, a small-scale operation that produced a variety of real ales for a time in the late twentieth century. A large house in the village (erected in 1877) has been converted to a second inn, known as the Paraffin Lamp. There was at one time a church in the village, but it has long closed. South and west of the village are former lime works and limekilns. Lime smelting was an important industry in Lugton, but the local sources have proved to be uneconomical. A lime works owned by Robert Howie & Sons of Dunlop still operates, however.

The A735 joins the A736 at Lugton, which continues northwards and soon reaches Renfrewshire just short of Uplawmoor village. On the way it passes a large nursery complex near Caldwell House, and beyond it the Caldwell golf course, which lies across the infant Lugton Water and hence in Renfrewshire.

South of Uplawmoor a series of minor roads criss-cross the rolling countryside, where even more small hills rise suddenly out of the farmland. Summits like Craighead Law rise quite abruptly, Craignaught Hill is home to a large quarry, and a road passing the quarry can be followed back towards Dunlop. En route it passes the community at Newmill, where Newmill House stands alongside the large New Mill. Here for many years was a sawmill.

Before reaching Dunlop a private drive heads through the wooded policies of Dunlop House. The house itself is a fine building of 1831-4, designed by David Hamilton. The penultimate Dunlop built it, Sir John Dunlop of that Ilk, Baronet (1806–39), and MP for Ayrshire who was created a baronet in 1838. The Dunlops had lived here for centuries. The previous castle to occupy the site was either erected or extended in 1599 and 1601, for date stones from this time are incorporated within the present building. This castle was also known as Hunthall, a name that survives for the buildings next to the large walled garden. The house became a home for children with learning disabilities in 1933 but this was closed and the house placed on the market.

The Dunlops of that Ilk were a notable family in the district, and on the wider stage of Scotland. They can be traced back to 1260 when a charter mentions William de Dunlop. Neill FitzRobert de Dunlop signed the Ragman Roll in 1296. Mrs Frances Dunlop was a friend of Robert Burns, and he stayed at Dunlop at least five times and corresponded regularly with her. The last Dunlop of that Ilk was Sir John's son, Sir James Dunlop, who was a notable soldier, holding the rank of Lieutenant General. On his death in 1858 the baronetcy became extinct. The estate was let to various occupiers, of which the Henderson family was the most notable. They were the proprietors of the Anchor shipping line.

Stewarton parish lies to the south of Dunlop, the two communities being just two miles apart. Stewarton is the larger by a considerable margin, and today is a prosperous small town within commuting distance of Glasgow. As a result there are quite a few housing estates being erected around the core of the old town, enlarging the population considerably. The town has been a Police Burgh since 1868. The parish extends to 13,667 acres, most of which is good arable or grazing land, though to the north east of the parish the lands degenerates into moorland (Glenouther Moor is the largest), much of which is now afforested. The old town of Stewarton lies on the slopes north of the Annick Water. Main Street and High Street form a fine thoroughfare, the main artery through the town. Here are a variety of traditional buildings, most of which have been unaffected by modern shop fronts, creating an unspoilt shopping street. The Royal Bank of Scotland dates from 1860.

St Columba's Church is a fine old building, one that has been adapted and altered over the years. It is located off Lainshaw Street, and can be accessed down the narrow vennels that run either from Lainshaw Street, or else from Vennel Street. The oldest part dates from 1696, distinguishable by its corbie-steps. Extensions were added in 1775 and 1825, creating the present Greek-cross-shaped plan. The small belfry is quite peculiar, having on it a spirelet, bell housing, clock, the Cunningham shakefork and an unusual triangular window. Within the church is the Lainshaw

Loft, originally associated with the local lairds, but now used for smaller services. In 1996, to celebrate the church's tercentenary, new windows were installed, and some of the older ones restored. Around the church is the old kirkyard of Stewarton, filled with a number of interesting old tombstones. The modern cemetery is located on Dalry Road. Among the graves in the kirkyard one should look out for the obelisk commemorating Robert Burns, uncle of Robert Burns. Here also lies the mother of the noted industrialist and philanthropist, David Dale (1739–1806). A memorial stone commemorates two workers who were killed during the construction of the Lainshaw Viaduct.

John Knox Church dates from 1841 and stands in the High Street, its steeple a local landmark. The church played an important part in Scottish ecclesiastical history, for it was the Stewarton Case that resulted in the Disruption, when many ministers left the Church of Scotland to form the Free Church. The congregation in Stewarton had built a new church in Avenue Street (now the United Reformed Church) but lost the right to worship there. They bought land in the High Street where the present building was erected, but not without opposition from the local laird, William Cunninghame. He took the case as far as the House of Lords, resulting in the Disruption. Cunninghame was something of a religious fanatic, and spent much of his life anticipating the Second Coming. He even spent time on the roof of Lainshaw House awaiting this.

Further along the street was the Cairns Church, also boasting of a spire. This church was erected in 1854 as a United Presbyterian place of worship, and in 1900 became a United Free Church named in honour of Revd Peter Cairns. It became a Church of Scotland and was united with the parish church in 1961, the building being demolished a few years later. At the west end of Lainshaw Street, just below the railway viaduct, is Our Lady and St John's RC Church. This was erected in 1974 and within are stations of the cross by a local art teacher.

Avenue Square and Avenue Street are two of the finest streets in the town. The local laird, Cunninghame of Lainshaw House, laid out the streets in an attempt at improving the centre of the town. Here can be found the Cunninghame Institute, a simple classical building with arched windows on the first floor and a circular clock on the apex of the pediment. At one time used as a school, in 1877 it was taken over by the town council as a public hall, renamed the Institute Hall. Up Avenue Street is the small Congregational Church, now the United Reformed Church, which dates from 1828. Within is a memorial to Lord Handyside.

Vennel Street heads south from the cross towards Kirkford, at one time a distinct village on the other side of the Annick. The Kirkford Bridge

Stewarton: Avenue Square

replaced the Kirk Ford itself, so called from it being the way across the water to the church from most points south. Further south the Brides Bridge crosses the Brides Burn. Kirkford has a number of traditional houses and buildings within it, creating an attractive group.

North from the cross Rig Street passes by the railway station and on passing under the bridge becomes Dunlop Road. Within Rig Street, but no one knows exactly where, David Dale (1739–1806) was born. He founded the famous watermills at New Lanark in 1785, and is renowned today for his enlightened social principles, looking after his workforce and introducing many beneficial schemes. Another notable son was Robert Watt (1774–1819) compiler of the *Bibliotheca Britannica*.

On a low hill to the east of Dunlop Road stands a tall tower of masonry, all that remains of Corsehill Castle. Remnants of the old earthworks and ditches around the castle can still be seen. The castle was a seat of the Cuninghames, but has long been in ruins. In 1672 the family was granted a Baronetcy of Corsehill. In the second quarter of the eighteenth century Sir David Cuninghame of Corsehill abandoned the castle in favour of a new house he built at the Doura in Kilwinning parish. An old engraving dated 1791 shows Corsehill Castle as having a vaulted ground floor and only one more above, but it was by that time in considerably decay.

Stewarton's signposts designate it 'The Bonnet Toun', for here bonnets have been made for centuries. The earliest reference to bonnet making in the village dates back to the sixteenth century. Competition from inferior manufacturers resulted in the formation of the Bonnet Guild of Corsehill in 1666 to ensure that standards were met, and to develop the marketing strategy of the makers. The traditional hand-knitted bonnets were replaced in the nineteenth century with machine-knitted ones. The manufacture of bonnets continues at the Bridgend Mills, for many years the property of Thomas Mackie & Sons. Indeed, when Sherpa Tenzing Nordgay reached the summit of Everest with Sir Edmund Hillary in 1953 he was wearing a Stewarton-made balaclava. The railway reached Stewarton in 1871, the station opening on 27 March. To cross the valley of the Annick George Cunninghame designed the fine Lainshaw Viaduct of ten arches, opened on 3 August 1868.

A number of large villas and houses around the centre of Stewarton were home to local businessmen and mill owners. Cragston was erected in 1902 to the plans of H. E. Clifford for a Mr Cuningham, a local mill owner. It is a fine building in the Arts and Crafts style, constructed from Ballochmyle sandstone and extended in the 1920s or 1930s. Woodland House dates from around 1840. Braehead House from 1809.

West of the town, but slowly being encroached by it, is the mansion house of Lainshaw. The house is quite simple, but extensive, having been extended over the years from an old core. It was a seat of the Cunninghame family, later Montgomery-Cuninghame. One of the daughters of the house, Margaret Montgomerie, married James Boswell of Auchinleck (1740–95). Lainshaw latterly became an old people's home. The estate was at one time something of a showpiece, for a massive octagonal lantern tower rising out of a classical house with wings adorned by arched windows distinguishes Lainshaw Mains. Within the former policies can be found a chalybeate spring.

West of Lainshaw are two small estates with country houses. The first – lying within woodland off Kilwinning Road – is Kennox House, at one time the seat of the MacAllister of the Loup, chief of the clan. The main building dates from 1820, but behind it is a smaller and older block, bearing the date 1761. Other work was added in 1831 and in 1911, the latter by James Morris of Ayr. Within the wall of the garden is a dovecote. The other is Chapeltoun House, which stands on a slope above the Annick Water. The house dates from 1908–10, having been erected to plans by Alexander Cullen of Hamilton for Hugh Neilson, owner of the Summerlee Iron Company. The gatehouse was added in 1918, again designed by Cullen, Lochead & Brown. An older mansion of the same name stood at Chapeltoun, but it was demolished to make way for the present house. As it was being pulled down it was discovered that it had incorporated much earlier work. Chapeltoun gets its name from an ancient chapel that formerly stood here. Still to be found are the old Chapel Hill, located across the minor road from Chapeltoun House, and the Monk's Well, lying in the haugh by the side of the Annick. Near to Bonshaw Farm, which itself lies south of Kennox House, is the Hutt Knowe, an ancient earthwork.

As the Kilwinning Road nears Torranyard, there are a number of farms bearing the name Auchenharvie. Here stand the ruins of Auchenharvie Castle at Auchenharvie Farm itself. This castle was a simple rectangular tower, perhaps dating from the fifteenth century. The ground floor was vaulted, and an external stair originally reached the vaulted great hall. The upper floors were then reached by a small spiral staircase built into the north-west corner. Auchenharvie was another Cuninghame property but it was abandoned when they built a new Auchenharvie House on the coast at Stevenston. The family was granted a baronetcy in 1633, but this became extinct in 1715. Girgenti Farm to the south of here is quite a distinguished building, built out of the remains of Girgenti House. There survives a tall tower with an octagonal roof, on the walls of which are clock faces. Girgenti House was erected around 1828 for Captain John Cheape. The house was demolished in the 1940s, and the remains rebuilt to create the present farm steading. Two former Italianate gatehouses survive.

From Torranyard the A736 passes through the west end of Stewarton parish for a mile and a half before leaving it as it crosses the Lugton Water. At a cottage named the Old School the B778 heads east for Stewarton again. This part of the parish seems to be lacking in antiquities, being home instead to a number of farms. The farms of Kilbride, however, hint at a former church that stood here, the Kirk Hill being located east of South Kilbride. Further east is Kirkmuir Farm, again indicative of an ecclesiastical settlement.

East of Stewarton, Old Glasgow Road gradually enters the open countryside, firstly having to pass the linear settlement on the east side of the Darlington Bridge. A gatehouse marks the entrance to Robertland House, which was erected around 1804 to plans by David Hamilton. The house is noted for its pilasters and small pediment, creating a simple and smallish country house. The estate was for centuries the seat of the Cuninghams, but became a Kerr property, that family erecting the house. In March 1914 the house was destroyed by fire, set off by the Suffragettes as part of their campaign.

The remains of Robertland Castle can be found in the field to the south of the Swinzie Burn. In 1630 Sir William Cuningham was created a Baronet of Robertland. He was Master of Works to James VI. Of the castle only an old doorway survives. A carved stone, bearing a coat of arms and a 1590s date stone, was taken from the castle and incorporated in the walled garden of the present house. The Fairlie-Cuninghame family now holds the baronetcy. Further on is Lower Williamshaw, where a track strikes uphill to High Williamshaw, a rather fine small laird's house of 1771. It is adorned by a pediment and was for many years a seat of the Donaldson family. The house gradually fell into ruin but in the 1980s it was acquired and restored by Stuart Ingram.

The small clachan of Kingsford lies astride the tiny Kingsland Burn. Here was the Kingsford School. The schoolhouse was designed by Thomas Leverton Donaldson (1795–1885), who was born at Williamshaw. He later became professor of architecture at London University, and wrote many books on architecture.

The B769 continues to meander beyond Kingsford through the Whitelee and Blacklaw areas before leaving the county at Windy Yett. On the north side of the road can be seen the small but prominent Black Law, which rises to 797 feet above sea level. Part of the hill has been quarried, but there still survives remains of an ancient mound on its summit. On the south side of this moorland road lies the Corsehouse Reservoir, which extends into Renfrewshire.

South of Stewarton, beyond Kirkford, is the Cutstraw area, where a variety of houses lie alongside the roads heading for Fenwick area. The remains of a prehistoric burial cairn can be found on Cairnduff Hill, which overlooks the town. Lochridge House stands on a low hill above the Lochridge Burn. The old part of the house dates from the seventeenth century, but around 1856 the house was extended in a Victorian style with the addition of a tall tower at the entrance, topped by a French-style roof. The B769 heads south from Stewarton towards Irvine. Within Stewarton parish it passes the Castleton farms, High and Laigh. On a low hill above High Castleton is the Law Mount, an old earthwork.

Loudoun Street leaves the Kirkford part of Stewarton and crosses country to Fenwick. The village has for decades been bypassed by the busy A77, which links Glasgow with Ayrshire. Fenwick as a community is historically divided into two, Laigh Fenwick, which lies nearer Kilmarnock, and High Fenwick, or the Kirkton of Fenwick, which lies to the north. Laigh Fenwick was traditionally home to a weaving community, whereas High Fenwick had a large concentration of shoemakers.

The village is centre of a parish of 18,161 acres, stretching north to

Floak and the Renfrewshire border, and eastward over the Craigendunton and Craigends moors to Eaglesham parish. Fenwick parish was originally part of Kilmarnock parish, but in 1642 it was disjoined to create a separate parish. Initially it went by the name of New Kilmarnock until the name Fenwick was adopted from the Fenwick Hill that lies west of the village. Weaving was at one time the most important trade in the village. The last of the weavers was Matthew Fowlds, who died in 1907 at the age of 101. He had a number of sons, including Sir George Fowlds (1859–1934), a distinguished man in New Zealand.

Fenwick village has a fine selection of old cottages along the main street, many of which have been restored over the years. Some of these bear date stones, indicating when they were first erected. Surrounding the old heart of the village are some more modern housing developments, home to the growing number of commuters who travel either to Glasgow or Kilmarnock to work.

Fenwick: the old church with the jougs on the wall

The old parish church at Fenwick is one of the most interesting places to visit in the village. The church lies off the main road, down Kirkton Road. The church is a simple traditional Scots style of building, complete with small belfry. The church was erected in 1643, in a cruciform plan, each of the gables terminating with corbie steps. The windows are simple and

101

on one of the walls can be seen the original jougs that were used to lock up malefactors. The belfry was an addition of 1660, the work of John Smith of Kilmaurs. The church was renovated in 1889–90 at the cost of £600. The church suffered a severe fire in 1929 but was restored under the direction of Gabriel Steel. An external stairway leads to the Rowallan Loft, where the family of Mure of Rowallan worshipped. The doorway here is dated 1649 and bears the Mure arms. Inside the church can be seen an hourglass by the side of the pulpit, originally turned over at the start of the sermon. Here also hangs the Fenwick Covenanting standard. The graveyard around the church is of considerable interest. Here can be found a good selection of Covenanting martyrs' graves, as well as memorials to others associated with the Covenanters. Also in the grave-yard are two sentry boxes, bearing the date 1828, which were erected at a time when body snatching was rife.

The manse of Fenwick was built in 1645, once work on the church was completed. This was replaced in 1783 with a new manse, into which the lintel bearing the 1645 date stone was incorporated. The manse was again rebuilt and extended in 1830. The minister at the time of the building of the church and manse was Revd William Guthrie (1620–65). Born the heir of the laird of Pitforthy in Angus, he gave this up to join the ministry. At Fenwick he became so popular that the church could not hold all who had come to hear him, and many had to listen intently from outside. He refused to accept the king as head of the church and so was ejected from his charge on 24 July 1664. On that day he preached from four in the morning until nine o'clock, when the soldiers came to eject him. He held many house meetings thereafter, some of these within Rowallan Castle which was home of two other zealous Covenanters, father and son, of the name Sir William Mure. On his death Guthrie was buried in the Guthrie of Pitforthy burial vault at Brechin Cathedral.

Fenwick formerly had two other churches, both of which are now disused. These were the Free Church and the United Presbyterian Church. The Free Church was a result of the Disruption of 1843. In the following year the dissenters erected the Guthrie Memorial Free Church. It merged with the Orr Memorial United Free Church in 1913. The UP church started as a Secession Church in 1784 but in 1832 a new church was erected. This continued in use until 1933 after which it united with the parish church. The building was demolished in 1947.

In Main Road can be seen the John Fulton Memorial Hall, which was created from the old Guthrie Memorial Free Church. John Fulton (1800–53) was a local shoemaker who had considerable skill in the manufacture of fine machinery. He lived in the Kirkton Brae but his cottage has been demolished, leaving behind a massive yew tree that grew in the garden. He was also a keen astronomer, and was able to construct a very fine orrery in 1832. This was displayed all over Britain and the Society of Arts of Scotland calculated that it was the most perfect ever constructed to that time. Glasgow's museum authorities now preserve it. His gravestone can be seen in the old churchyard. Hugh Wilson, who penned the tune 'Martyrdom', which became one of the most popular tunes for singing psalms, occupied another of the former Kirkton cottages. He died in 1824 and was buried in Old Kilpatrick churchyard. The Fenwick Weavers' Society is claimed to be the first co-operative society ever established. The weavers joined together and in 1769 formed a retail system that was adopted by later societies. The society thus predates the Rochdale Co-operative Society, which was the earliest of the modern co-operative movement.

The A77, which will be replaced by a new motorway (the M77) in the next few years, passes through Fenwick parish, allowing travellers to pass from Ayrshire across the Fenwick Moor to Glasgow and back. From the Meiklewood interchange at the north end of Kilmarnock the drivers speed past a few places of interest, but so busy is the road that it is virtually impossible to stop and explore. Once the new motorway is built the old road will become quieter, and dawdling along will become the norm.

The road continues past the popular Fenwick Hotel, which has as its origins an old coaching inn. The village lies east of the main road, bypassed since the 1930s, which has really been to its benefit. Beyond Gardrum a minor road strikes off to the north, crossing the open country-side towards Stewarton. Off this road is another minor roadway, heading west towards Pokelly and Meikle Cutstraw at Stewarton. From this road a farm track drops down to Balgray Mill and thence to Pokelly Hall. On the south side of the stream from Pokelly Hall stood Pokelly Castle, a seat of the Cochranes. Old accounts name it Pathelly Hall.

South from Pokelly Hall lies the Burnfoot Reservoir, created by Kilmarnock Corporation Water Works. At East Pokelly is a date stone bearing the year 1837, along with a carving showing a scythe and other agricultural implements. A group of farms bearing the name Gree lies to the north of here. Beyond Laigh Clunch the road crosses the Swinzie Burn and returns to Stewarton parish.

At the junction of the A77 with the B764 (better known as the Eaglesham Moor road) stands a large memorial cross at the edge of a forestry plantation. The cross marks the spot where Alice Corbett was buried. She was the wife of Archibald Corbett, 1st Lord Rowallan. Sir

Robert Lorimer, who was engaged on building Rowallan at the time, designed the monument. The main road continues north passing South and North Drumboy farms before leaving the county at the Floak Bridge, where the main road crosses the infant Earn Water. Much of this moorland is now afforested.

On the Eaglesham Moor road is the farm of Kingswell, or Kingswells on older maps. This was at one time an inn, much used by coaching traffic. Originally the main Glasgow road passed by the inn, taking a route east of Drumboy Hill, now just a minor road. Kingswell gets its name from the day when King James V was making his way from Glasgow south to Sorn Castle in order to attend the wedding of the daughter of his Lord Treasurer. His horse became stuck in a peat bog, and the King was forced to continue on foot until a suitable replacement horse could be found. On arrival at Sorn he was asked how his journey was, to which he responded, 'If I wished to play a trick on the Devil, I would send him to a bridal at Sorn in mid-winter.' Another version has it that the King was going to Pokelly Castle when this incident happened, and that the spot where the horse sank was known thereafter as the King's Stable.

The moor road continues, through the forest from Kingswell, passing Moor Farm and leaving the county at the Soame Bridge. Just beyond the bridge, a farm track strikes southwards and after nearly a mile returns to Ayrshire. Further on, on top of the hill, can be seen the tall obelisk commemorating John Howie and the Covenanters. This was erected in 1896 to plans by Thomas Lyon.

Lochgoin (or Lochgoyne) Farm lies just over the summit of the hill to the south-east. The farm is a typical moorland steading, rebuilt in 1858, but it is unique in the fact that it is home to a small museum of artefacts associated with the Covenanting struggle. The farm was for centuries tenanted by the Howie family, which seems to have arrived here in 1178 as Waldensian refugees from France. During the Covenanting period the farm was tenanted by James Howie, who welcomed Covenanters into his home. This placed his own life in jeopardy, indeed the house was pillaged twelve times by the enemy, but he survived until 1691 and was buried in Fenwick churchyard. John Howie of Lochgoin (1735–93) compiled a massive book entitled *The Scots Worthies*, which was published in 1775. In it he details the life story of the Covenanters known to him and of the privations and tortures they had to endure. It was reprinted many times. The Lochgoin museum has on display a sword and Bible owned by Captain John Paton, the Covenanters' standard belonging to Fenwick (or 'Phinigk') parish, and a drum used at the

Battle of Drumclog. The farm belongs to the Lochgoin and Fenwick Covenanters Trust, established by Lord Rowallan.

A track crosses the Dunwan Moss towards the dam that creates Lochgoin Reservoir. The original Loch Goyne was much smaller, but in 1910 Kilmarnock Corporation Water Works dammed the valley head and created a sizeable reservoir, most of which actually extends into Renfrewshire. The dam was at one time known as Blackwoodhill Dam.

The A719 leaves the A77 at Laighmuir, crossing the infant Fenwick Water by the Glassock Bridge. At Amlaird are the water filters associated with the reservoirs on the moorland. Soon the village of Waterside is reached, a small community in a little valley created by the Dunton Water. The village grew around an eighteenth-century wool mill.

At Hareshaw Farm, on the south side of Waterside, a minor road strikes uphill, passing East and West Collary farms, before arriving at Hareshawmuir Lodge. From Hareshawmuir a track climbs up to Airtnoch Farm before crossing the moor towards the Dunton Water. Where the track crosses the Calf Fauld Burn a descent can be made to the Dunton side, where the Dunton Cove can be found. This is a significant cave on the cliff face that was in great demand as a hiding place for Covenanters. The Dunton water passes through some rocky gorges on its way towards Waterside, at two points tumbling over small waterfalls, one of which is known as the Head Linn. The track here continues past Craigendunton before arriving at Craigendunton Reservoir, created by Kilmarnock Corporation Water Works and opened in 1901. It is now a popular spot for fishing.

The minor road past Hareshawmuir continues eastward to almost Craigends from where a track through the forest leads to Whiteleehill, perched high on the hill of that name. Meadowhead Farm was the birthplace of the Covenanting martyr, Captain John Paton. All of the surrounding moorland has been planted to create the extensive Whitelee Forest. Near Craigends can be found the Carlin Stane, a huge boulder by the side of the Hareshawmuir Water. South of here is Cameron's Moss, associated with the Covenanter, Revd Richard Cameron. Langdyke Farm lies east of the A719, just south of Waterside. Near the farm, by the side of the Hareshawmuir Water, is a man-made mound on the slopes of the valley. This is a prehistoric dun, built as a place of defence.

Below the disused Hareshaw Mill the Hareshawmuir Water meets the Dunton Water to create the Craufurdland Water. A minor road passing Horsehill Farm drops steeply to the Bruntland Bridge, before climbing steeply once more to the road linking Fenwick and Waterside. Further down the Craufurdland glen is Dalsraith Bridge, giving access to Dalsraith Farm.

# 7

# Kilmarnock and Kilmaurs

KILMARNOCK IS THE SECOND biggest town in Ayrshire, with a population of around 50,000. It grew up around an old church erected at a river crossing, and has expanded considerably over the years. Created a Burgh of Barony in 1591, Kilmarnock became a Police Burgh in 1832. The parish extends to 9,552 acres, but prior to 1642 the parish of Fenwick was part of Kilmarnock. The town became a major industrial centre in the nineteenth century and was renowned for its many world-class companies in such diverse fields as whisky, carpets, locomotives and shoes. The town centre today is a busy hub for shopping and business. Most of the central streets have now been pedestrianised, creating a pleasant place to walk and browse. Here also are some interesting places to visit, including old churches, graveyards, theatre, museum, and memorials.

The town centre is located at what is known as the Cross. This was at one time a very busy junction, but it has been pedestrianised for many years, and today forms an open piazza. Here can be seen the statue commemorating both Robert Burns and his printer, John Wilson, who lived in Kilmarnock. The very first edition of *Poems, Chiefly in the Scottish Dialect* by Robert Burns, was issued from the press of Wilson on 31 July 1786. The site of his workshop was located in what was the Star Inn Close, later widened to become Waterloo Street, but this is now incorporated within the Burns Mall Shopping Centre. In the mall can be seen a plaque marking the site of the print works. Also within the mall, at the round entrance-feature, is a stone slab on the floor marking the spot where the Covenanter, John Nisbet of the Glen, was executed on 4 April 1683.

The buildings facing the cross are all relatively modern. The former Royal Bank building (now Ladbrokes) was erected between 1937–9 to plans by W. K. Walker Todd, its round frontage and dome being a distinctive feature. The Burns Mall dates from various periods, the first segment being opened in 1976. The bus station had been erected in 1974, but the mall was added in three stages, including modern retail outlets facing onto King Street.

The Foregate is a pedestrianised lane striking off the Cross. This used to be the main road north, known as Fore Street, but it was bypassed when Portland Street was created in 1805. Foregate comprises of modern concrete blocks, the shops on the west side erected in 1972 to plans by Percy Johnson-Marshall and Partners. The east side is occupied by a multi-storey car park. At the north end is the brash Clydesdale Bank, erected in 1975 but seemingly isolated somewhat at the periphery of the commercial centre. Portland Street (also pedestrianised) links the Cross with George Street and routes north. The street was one of the first improvements made to the town centre, creating a fine thoroughfare through the town, avoiding the old narrow lanes. Most of the street has been rebuilt in the 1990s, in particular the east and top end of the street.

King Street strikes south from the Cross. This was the first of the new streets created in the centre of town, work beginning in 1803. Previously the little Sandbed Street that survives behind the modern shops was the main route south, and King Street was built through the back lanes and yards. The buildings here are almost all modern, erected from the last world war onward. Few old buildings survive, but of interest is the former Lauder's Emporium, dating from 1923 and a fine example of the modern style. The street is closed to vehicles, and today is paved with granite cobbles and setts. Within the streetscape are some interesting sculptures, the most amusing being the men who look as though they are swimming in the sea of stone. On the ground the names of the streets and lanes have been carved into granite slabs, a useful addition to the signs on the walls.

King Street merges into Titchfield Street and continues south. The Earl of Glencairn built the new street here in 1765. The street then becomes High Glencairn Street, but is still lined with shops and commercial premises. In Titchfield Street is the former fire station, now divided into flats and shops. It was erected in 1937 to plans of Gabriel Steel. The former cinema was built in 1904 as the King's Theatre, but closed shortly after the present Odeon opened in Welbeck Street. Here also can be found the Galleon Centre, a large leisure centre containing swimming pool, ice rinks and other facilities. This was erected in 1986 to plans of Crichton Lang Willis & Galloway.

In Douglas Street, which lies to the south of the Galleon, is a small cairn commemorating Alexander Smith (1830–67). He became a lace pattern designer, like his father, moving to Glasgow and Paisley. Smith spent much of his time writing poetry and books. These include *Life Drama* (1851), *City Poems* (1857) and *Dreamthorp* (1863). The general reader has long-since forgotten most of these, but his *A Summer in Skye* (1865) has been reprinted in recent years and still entertains those interested in that Hebridean island.

Titchfield Street joins the Armour Street bypass road. The road continues southwards, as North Glencairn Street. This reaches a busy crossroads at Glencairn Square, three sides of which are still built up, the fourth being left rather open with the formation of a supermarket and its car park. The Hunting Lodge Hotel on the south-east corner is a fine Tudor-style building of the late 1800s. It adjoins a fine sandstone building erected in 1892, complete with public clock. South Glencairn Street is lined with small industrial premises and businesses. At the southern end, just as it crosses the river Irvine, are the Scottish Power buildings. This was originally part of the Kilmarnock power station, which at one time stood here. Originally erected in 1903–4, the station produced electricity until the 1960s, the two prominent cooling towers being demolished in June 1976.

The power station was vital in the development of the Kilmarnock tram service, which opened for business on 10 December 1904. The depot was located at Greenholm Street, next to the power station, and lines ran from there south to a terminus at Riccarton. The lines also ran north up Glencairn and Titchfield streets to the Cross, and up Portland, Wellington and Dean streets to the northern terminus at Beansburn – Burns Avenue. From the Cross a branch made its way along London Road as far as Hurlford Cross, in total just over four miles. The architects for the scheme and associated sheds were C. S. Peach and Charles Fairweather. Services to Hurlford were withdrawn on 15 December 1924 and the rest of the service closed on 3 May 1926, during the General Strike. Part of the former tram depot survives, rebuilt for use by the electricity board. The Greenholm Street council offices were erected in 1929 of red brick with blonde sandstone dressings.

Much of this area was home to Kilmarnock's major employers. Here, where the Galleon centre now stands, was the Saxone shoe factory, famous for its high quality footwear. The factory had a tall tower with 'Saxone Shoes' in huge letters around it, a landmark in the Netherton area of town. The company was founded in 1908 when two local businesses, Clark & Co. and Abbot's, merged. The name has been claimed to originate from 6–1, a good score at football, or else from 61, the street number of the company's offices! The company grew to employ a thousand staff in the 1950s, but since then cheap imports have decimated the industry.

The manufacture of carpets has long been carried out in Kilmarnock – some claim that Maria Gardner who came from Dalkeith introduced the skill to the town in 1728. One of the more famous names was BMK, which stands for Blackwood & Morton, Kilmarnock. This was founded in 1908 when William Blackwood formed a partnership with Gavin Morton. From Glencairn Square East, Shaw Street heads into another commercial area, where numerous small businesses operate. Here also is a variety of old mill buildings, used by woollen manufacturers and other businesses. At the sharp bend in the road stands St Andrews

Church, with its churchyard behind it. The church was erected as a Free Church in 1844 at a cost of £1,200.

This area was at one time home to the large valve-manufacturer, Glenfield & Kennedy. Thomas Kennedy, who was originally a gunsmith, patented a water meter in 1852 and set up the Kennedy Patent Water Meter Company to produce them. The Glenfield Iron Company was also founded by him, in 1865, and in 1899 the two businesses were merged. Glenfield and Kennedy valves became synonymous with quality, and they were in demand all over the world. The company also produced many other engineering items at its premises in Low Glencairn Street, including the country's first wave-making machine for a municipal pool, included in the old Kilmarnock baths in 1938–40. Indeed, such was the 'Glen's' success that it had more than 2,500 staff at its peak, making it Kilmarnock's biggest employer. Hit hard by the recession of the 1970s Glenfield and Kennedy has since had a number of owners, but still produces valves in its Queens Drive works, albeit on a more modest scale than in the glory days.

Armour Street leads to Old Mill Road and Fowlds Street, which is one of the main roads into the centre of town. At the crossroads stand two Baptist churches, the Kilmarnock Baptist Church of 1869–70, and the Sovereign Grace Baptist Church of 1857. The former is a simple building, the foundation stone being laid by Thomas Coats of Ferguslie. The latter is a small, more domestic looking building, erected as the Original Secession Church at a cost of £500. A Free Church was located further west in Fowlds Street, the site now occupied by a supermarket.

A couple of roads strike north from Old Mill Road, leading over a hill before dropping down to London Road. Most of this area is residential, traditional stone buildings lining the gridded streets. Here, however, can be found a few notable buildings, including St Columba's Primary School, Loanhead Primary School, Kilmarnock Academy and the Dick Institute.

Kilmarnock Academy was originally located in the vicinity of the Grand Hall, having been erected there in 1808 to replace the older parish schools. In 1876 it moved to North Hamilton Street (architect, William Railton) where Woodstock School occupies its site. The hilltop site at Elmbank became available after Elmbank House and its grounds were acquired to create the Dick Institute. The first building, the Queen Anne block, was opened in 1898, having been designed by Robert Ingram. The eighty-feet tall tower is a local landmark. Kilmarnock Technical School was added alongside in 1909 (Gabriel Andrew), later merged into the Academy. The technical block was extended in 1928 but in

2002 was converted into flats. A modern wing with games complex was added to the Academy proper in 1968. Opposite the Academy in Elmbank Drive is St Columba's Primary School, the work of Alan Crombie in 1902. In Loanhead Street is Loanhead Primary, another Robert Ingram building of 1904–5. The great Scottish industrialist, Andrew Carnegie, laid the foundation stone.

The Dick Institute is one of the finest buildings in Kilmarnock, and stands at the north end of Elmbank Avenue, just off London Road. Designed in the classical style, the institute was erected in 1897–1901 to plans by Robert Ingram. The cost was met by James Dick (1823–1902), who had made his fortune out of rubber. He had in 1886 gifted the Cathkin Park to the citizens of Glasgow. He and his elder brother, Robert (1820–91), realised that gutta percha could be used to create rubber soles for shoes, and they established a factory to produce these. When Robert died, James decided to gift the funds for building a museum and library in his memory. The institute suffered a fire in 1909 but it was subsequently rebuilt. Today the Dick Institute still serves as a library, art gallery and museum and is a fitting monument to Victorian enterprise and philanthropy.

On the other side of the road from the institute is the war memorial. This takes the form of a Grecian temple, and was erected in 1927 to plans of James Miller. Within are plaques listing those who died, as well as a statue of The Victor. Within a grassy area next to the war memorial is a statue commemorating Sir James Shaw, Bart. (1764–1843). This originally stood at Kilmarnock Cross but was moved here in 1929 when it became too much of an obstacle for traffic. Ironically, when the street was redeveloped in 1994, it was cheaper to commission a new statue to take the same spot than to move Shaw back to where he had come! The statue was unveiled on 4 August 1848 and is the work of James Fillans, using Carrara marble. Shaw was born at Mosshead Farm, in Riccarton parish. At the age of seventeen he emigrated to the United States where he worked in commerce. He then moved to London, where he worked with his brother, becoming a partner. He was to become the first Scot to hold the office of Lord Mayor of London, being appointed in 1805. He had an interest in politics and was elected MP for the City of London in 1806. He was given a baronetcy in 1809 and in 1831 was elected Chamberlain of London. Shaw never forgot his Kilmarnock roots, and often supported needy causes back home.

London Road used to strike east from Kilmarnock Cross towards Hurlford and thence Dumfries or Edinburgh. The section at the Cross is no longer in existence, but pedestrians can follow the original route through the Burns Mall and beneath the ring road. Today the road begins at the Palace Theatre, a massive red-sandstone building lining the street corner. The building was erected in 1862–3 as the Corn Exchange, and the tall tower at the corner is known as the Albert Tower in honour of the Prince Regent. The architect was James Ingram. The exchange was converted into a theatre in 1903 and is still used for shows of all types throughout the year. Adjoining the theatre is the Grand Hall, erected in 1886 by James Ingram's son, Robert. This was built as the burgh Art Gallery, but in 1947 was converted into the hall.

London Road crosses the Kilmarnock Water by the Green Bridge. On the north-east side of the bridge stands the imposing Henderson Church, with its massive tower. The church was erected in 1907 to plans of Thomas Smellie (1860–1938), a local architect and book illustrator. The style of the church is quite unique; it has Gothic features, but here and there the Arts & Crafts style shines through, and the turret on the tower is reminiscent of work by Mackintosh or Lorimer. The fine carillon of bells dates from 1950. Internally there is an organ by Norman & Beard, stained glass windows by Stephen Adam, Gordon Webster of 1907 and Wendy Robertson of 1987. Probably the most famous minister was Revd David Landsborough, minister of the previous church from 1851. He was a noted naturalist and died in 1912. Landsborough's son, also David, became a medical missionary in what is now Taiwan.

On the south side of the street, near Braeside Street, a plaque commemorates Tam Samson, who lived here and operated a long-established seed-merchant business. London Road is lined with many large buildings that were originally houses, but which today tend to be offices, dental surgeries or hotels. A few survive as domestic buildings, often sub-divided, however. The Masonic Hall by William Valentine (1923) lies south of the road. Only a few of the London Road villas have details of their architectural provenance known. Deanmont was by James Ingram. Numbers 45–47 were by Thomas Smellie.

Kilmarnock College lies north of London Road, reached from Holehouse Road. The college was erected in 1966 as a replacement for the old Kilmarnock Technical School and further education centre. The East Ayrshire Council headquarters lies on the south side of London Road, near its eastern end. The offices were established after the creation of the present local authorities in 1996. Previously the building was used as educational offices, the building originally having been erected in 1933 as James Hamilton Academy.

The Laigh Kirk is one of the oldest churches in the town. It stands off the main town centre, still surrounded by an old graveyard. The church itself has a distinctive tower, the base of which is particularly old. One only has to look at the masonry to appreciate this. The tower is said to have been erected in 1410, but only the lower courses can be as old as this. The upper part of the tower probably dates from the sixteenth century. The weathercock was added in 1721 and a bell installed in 1853. The present church was erected in 1802 to plans by Robert Johnstone. It replaced an earlier building that was the scene of a major disaster. During a sermon on 18 October 1801 some plasterwork fell in, and the congregation feared that the whole building was about to collapse. They tried to escape as quickly as possible, but the exits were narrow and twenty-nine people were crushed to death in the rush. As a result, the present building was designed with seven possible exit doors. Inside the church can be seen a number of old memorials, including one to Sir Thomas Boyd (d. 1432) and Robert, fourth Lord Boyd (d. 1590), who was a supporter of Mary Queen of Scots. The graveyard around the church is home to a number of interesting old gravestones. Here can be seen three stones commemorating Covenanters. The graveyard is also home to memorials to a couple of Burns's companions. One of the better known is that to Tam Samson (1723–95), who for many years was a seed merchant in the burgh. His grave includes the misspelled named 'Kilmarnockock'. Here also lies Revd James MacKinlay and Revd John Robertson, mentioned in his poems.

The little streets around the Laigh Kirk have some traditional Scots-style buildings in them, and this makes a pleasant place to stroll. Croft Street is home to the rebuilt Wheatsheaf Inn, originally dating from the eighteenth century and one of the old coaching inns of the town. On the opposite side of the street are the strange buildings with no, or few, windows. These were erected in 1897 to plans by Gabriel Andrew for Johnnie Walker, who used them as bonded warehouses.

John Walker was born at Todrigg Farm in 1805. In 1820 he decided to give up his farm and moved into Kilmarnock where he established himself as a grocer in King Street. At that time most grocers blended and sold their own brand of whisky, and Johnnie Walker's Kilmarnock Whisky became one of the best. The business thrived under his son Alexander, who was a marketing genius, and by 1910 when John's grandson, Alexander, had taken over, the business had mushroomed into a national then international concern. It was Alexander Walker who introduced the striding dandy figure, now recognised the world over, and the distinctive square bottles with the angled label. The uniquely shaped bottles even merited a W. Heath Robinson cartoon, which depicted in his usual inimitable style how the bottles were squared off. Johnnie Walker's business remained in Strand Street until 1955 when the headquarters were moved to a forty-acre site at Hill Street, north of the railway. Today Johnnie Walker whisky is part of the giant multi-national conglomerate Diageo, which promotes it as a world brand. The brands produced under the Johnnie Walker umbrella include Red Label, Black Label and Blue Label, as well as a Johnnie Walker malt. There is a statue of Johnnie Walker in the shadow of the Laigh Kirk.

Bank Street is home to a number of traditional buildings, among them the distinctive corner turret at the junction with Bank Place. Opposite this is the classical façade of the Bank of Scotland, which was erected as two houses. In front of the bank is one of the many sculptures that now ornament the centre of town, a seated figure named 'Stan Reid', erected in 1996. This one depicts a man reading a newspaper. At the north end of Bank Street is a lane leading to the Town Bridge, now hidden to some extent from passing traffic. This was at one time the main bridge across the river in town, and the present structure dates from 1762. Opposite the Bank of Scotland is the back of the modern Royal Bank of Scotland building, standing rather incongruously on three streets. It was erected in 1976 by Henry Dawes. Minor roads continue to the west here, leading out onto John Dickie Street.

John Finnie Street is one of Kilmarnock's main thoroughfares, built on a north–south axis and still busy with traffic. The street is named after its Kilmarnock-born developer, John Finnie, who bought up various properties hereabouts and slapped this wide street through them. Finnie had made his fortune as a merchant in Manchester. Work began in 1864, and much of the plan was provided by William Railton, architect, and Robert Blackwood, surveyor. The south end of John Finnie Street is the least distinguished, for here the buildings are of inferior quality, being simple commercial premises. As the road makes its way north the buildings become grander, and include the main Post Office of 1907. Here also are the former banking premises of the Halifax (1968–70, Hay Steel MacFarlane and Associates). The Oddfellows Hall was erected in 1889 to plans of Gabriel Andrew. Further north are the East Ayrshire Council buildings, originally erected in 1879 by Gabriel Andrew for the Co-op. On the right (number 12) is the former Opera House, designed by James Ingram in 1874. This was later converted to a church, saleroom and latterly a nightclub, but it was badly damaged in a fire and the building demolished apart from the façade, which was retained. The northern end terminates below the railway station. The Glasgow, Paisley, Kilmarnock & Ayr Railway Company opened this in 1843. The present buildings were erected in 1850 to plans by Hugh MacLure and extended in 1878.

The style is a mix of Italianate and castellated Gothic, and makes an interesting scene on its hilltop. East of the station the railway takes an elevated route through the town centre, crossing viaducts and bridges before reaching the higher ground once more on the other side of the Kilmarnock Water.

West of John Finnie Street are a number of minor streets passing through industrial and residential areas. Within this area can be found Grange Church, a massive Early English-style building with a spire measuring 160 feet. This church was erected in 1877–9 of Ballochmyle sandstone at a cost of £8,000, to plans of Robert Ingram. In Grange Street is the former home of the Tannock brothers, James (1784–1863) and William (1794–1879), who were notable artists in their day. James was the more successful, having his work displayed in the National Gallery. The house is noted for its bas-relief of an artist painting at his easel, and for the large Venetian window that lit his studio and gallery.

In West Langlands Street is the factory of Hunslet-Barclay, better known in the district by its original name of Barclay's. Andrew Barclay established his business in 1840 and made his first complete locomotive in 1859. In 1921 the firm took over the old locomotive works of the Glasgow & South Western Railway and in 1989 became Hunslet-Barclay. Some of the older buildings hereabouts are fine examples of industrial architecture.

Bonnyton Road continues westward, passing below the Troon branch line of the railway and entering the residential area of Bonnyton. In Warwickhill Road can be found the small twentieth century Church of God and a bowling green.

The south end of John Finnie Street is located at a busy crossroads. Here stand three major ecclesiastical buildings. St Marnock's Parish Church is located on the south-east corner. This was erected in 1836 to plans by James Ingram. A Perpendicular Gothic revival building, the church has a tall tower that contains a fine carillon of bells. Within is a three-manual pipe organ of 1872. Just off the north-west corner is the Howard St Andrews Parish Church, a modern concrete edifice erected in 1970–1.

Two church buildings, Holy Trinity Episcopal Church and Winton Place Congregational Church, occupy the south-west corner of the crossroads. Holy Trinity dates from 1857, a considerable Gothic structure by James Wallace, costing £1,400. In 1876 the church was extended by Sir George Gilbert Scott who added the chancel, but its proposed tower was never built, leaving a forlorn stump. The interior of the church is very fine. It has stained glass by William Aikman, Clayton & Bell and Powell & Sons, and marble mosaic work by the same artists. The walls and timbers are painted by Burlison & Grylls. Winton Place Congregational Church was erected in 1860 to plans of James Ingram, again Gothic in style.

St Marnock Street is also home to Kilmarnock's law and order centre. Here can be found the large police station of the 1970s, the modern Sheriff Court of 1985–6 (David M. Gregory of PSA architects), and the Procurator Fiscal's office, which was erected in 1852 (William Railton) as the Sheriff Court. On the wall is a plaque marking the approximate site of the first railway in Scotland, which ran from Kilmarnock to Troon. The car park here occupies the site of Kilmarnock House, the replacement for Dean Castle. The house was erected sometime in the late seventeenth century, extended in the eighteenth century, but demolished in 1935.

The road west from the crossroads is Portland Road, lined with a number of large terraced homes, many of which have either been subdivided or converted into offices. Springhill House of around 1840 was built for the Finnie's, owners of local coalmines. It was converted into an old-folks' home in 1945. Beyond the railway bridge is the Grange area, with Grange Academy located off the main road to the south. Beyond, the road leaves the built up area of the town and on the left are the grounds of Annanhill. Most of this is now occupied by a municipal golf course, opened in 1957. The course has 18 holes, is a par 71 and 6,198 yards in length. Annanhill House still stands within the woods, now divided into smaller units. The house was erected in 1796 by William Dunlop, commander of an East India merchant ship, and extended by his son, James. Within the grounds is the modern development known as the Courtyard, erected to plans by Nicholas Groves-Raines, who also carried out the restoration of the big house as well. The courtyard comprises a semi-circular terrace of houses. Beyond Annanhill is the former Annandale brick works, now home to lesser industries, and the Ellerslie Hotel. This gets its name from the fact that it is claimed that William Wallace was born near here, but more of that later.

Dundonald Road (A759) strikes south from the bottom end of John Dickie Street. The street is lined with large villas at the start, erected from 1860 onwards, but as the road makes its way further from the town centre the size of the dwellings diminish, until at the end, next to the bypass, the street is lined with modern private housing.

Lying east of Dundonald Road is the Howard Park, originally known as Barbadoes Green. This was part of the grounds of Kilmarnock House, which stood in St Marnock Street. Baroness Howard de Walden granted the lands to the burgh in 1894. The park is a pleasant quiet spot in the centre of the town, with tree-lined avenues and pathways. Within the park are two memorials, one in memory of Dr Alexander Marshall

(1827–94), who was a respected doctor for more than forty years. This was erected in 1896 in an Early English style.

The second memorial is located behind some bushes and commemorates the residents of Kilmarnock who died from the cholera epidemic in 1832. The number of deaths in the town was so great that the old kirkyards could not cope with the numbers and a mass grave had to be dug in this corner of the park. Over 250 corpses were interred here between July and October that year.

Off Dundonald Road, in Rugby Road, are the highly impressive stands of Rugby Park, home to Kilmarnock Football Club. The club was founded in 1869 and is the second oldest surviving football club in Scotland. When founded, the club participated in a wide variety of sports, including rugby and cricket, and the park was mainly used for the former, hence its name. In 1873 the club was one of the eight founder members of the Scottish Football Association. The team has always enjoyed the enthusiastic support of local people and boasts a record attendance at Rugby Park of 35,995 for a game with Rangers in 1962. Among their successes, Killie were league champions in season 1964/65 and lifted the Scottish Cup in 1920, 1929 and 1997. The ground has been substantially upgraded in recent years and is now the finest in Scotland outwith Glasgow and Edinburgh. In 2002, to enhance its revenues, the club built a hotel and conference centre next to the stadium.

Holmes Road strikes off Dundonald Road, leading to a bridge across the river Irvine. Here stands the former Dairy School for Scotland, at one time part of the West of Scotland Agricultural College. The school occupied the former Holmes Farm and was opened in 1899, being extended considerably in 1903–4 at a cost of £5,500. It was closed in 1937, when the college moved to Auchincruive near Ayr, and the buildings were converted into Kilmarnock Maternity Home, which operated until 1989. It is now the Strathlea Centre, operated by the health board.

Kilmarnock extends quite considerably to the north of the railway. The line was constructed in 1843 and forced its way through the centre of town, causing a number of buildings to be demolished. Across the Kilmarnock Water and west to the station the line is supported on a long viaduct. Just north of the railway, standing in Portland Street, is the West High Church, its tall tower dominating the streetscape. Originally erected in 1844 to plans of Cousin & Gale, it was extended in 1881 by Gabriel Andrew. The opposite side of the street has long-since been demolished and is now occupied by a car park. Beyond this is the historic High Kirk of Kilmarnock, still standing in its kirkyard. The church is a simple classical building, erected in 1732–40 at a cost of £850 and now the oldest church building in Kilmarnock. The builders were the Hunter brothers, who adopted a design based on St Martin's in the Fields in London. The tower dates from 1740, rising through a clock to a campanile and cupola. Inside the glasswork is by W. & J. J. Kier, dating from the 1860s, one window commemorating the 4th Earl of Kilmarnock who gifted the land to the church at a rental of one penny Scots, 'if asked'. The Kiers were born in Irvine but worked in Glasgow.

The High Kirkyard has a few interesting old gravestones that are worth looking for. Here lies John Wilson, printer of the Kilmarnock edition of Burns's poems, Thomas Kennedy, inventor of the water meter, James and William Tannock, artists, and Thomas Morton, an engineer who built an observatory in Kilmarnock. At the eastern end of the kirkyard, built into the external wall, is the Soulis Cross. This is a fluted column within an arched niche, restored in 1825. The origin of the cross is no longer known, but it is said to commemorate Lord Soulis who was killed here in 1444 during a feud with the Boyds of Dean Castle (the Soulis's had been earlier owners of the castle, and they may have been trying to win it back). This causes something of a puzzle, however, for there was no Lord Soulis in 1444.

The hill above the West High Church is known as Mount Pleasant, and on the summit can be seen the former Kilmarnock Infirmary. This was erected in 1867 to plans of William Railton, but was extended and adapted over its century of treating patients. The hospital was closed when the new Crosshouse Hospital was opened in 1982. In among this area is St Joseph's RC Church, a Gothic structure of 1847, built at a cost of £3,000.

The town extends north from here by some distance, the schemes of Hillhead, Longpark, Onthank and Southcraig having been built over the years. There is little of any antiquity or interest here, but among the houses are one or two distinguished buildings. Our Lady of Mount Carmel RC Church was built in 1963 and contains some fine stained glass as well as a sculpture depicting Christ Crucified. At Knockinlaw Mount, which was destroyed when the houses were built, an ancient urn was discovered in a Bronze Age cairn. Near to it was an old well, known locally as the Roman Well. Rowallan Creamery lies to the east of Glasgow Road, near the Howard Park Hotel of 1975. The creamery was established in 1888 and specialised in margarine, the 'Banquet' and 'Sunflower' trade names being popular products, but closed in 2002.

East of the Kilmarnock Water and north of the railway line lies the extensive housing estate known as New Farm Loch. The council erected most of the houses here between 1960 until 1972. Within the estate are

St Joseph's Academy, the newer James Hamilton Academy and a few primary schools. Here also are the modern St Kentigern's Parish Church, designed by Stewart Hunter and erected in 1969, and St Matthew's RC Church, dedicated by the Bishop of Galloway on 24 April 1977. The cemetery here was opened in 1876, and extended in 1893, bringing it up to fourteen acres in size. It is reached through a baronial gateway.

New Farm Loch butts on to the cemetery, and the Kay Park, one of Kilmarnock's main public open areas. The council purchased the park in 1866 using funds left to it by Alexander Kay, who had made his fortune in the Glasgow insurance business. Within the park are the following features: a large pond, grass areas, bowling green and various walks. Here also stands the local Burns Monument, erected in 1879 to plans by Robert Ingram. This is probably the largest Burns memorial ever erected, for it stands eighty feet in height and contains exhibition rooms. These formerly held museum displays, but sadly the memorial costs too much to maintain and has been neglected in recent years. The statue of Burns by W. Grant Stevenson stares forlornly out over the parkland, wondering why he merits such disdain.

A second large memorial in the park was erected in memory of the Reformers in 1885, also the work of Robert Ingram. In December 1816 a number of Kilmarnock citizens were involved in the campaign for parliamentary reform. At a meeting in December that year 6,000 people turned up to listen to Alexander MacLaren (1785–1822) address the crowd. He claimed that parliament was unjust, for a town of Kilmarnock, which had 13,000 residents at that time, had only one person eligible to vote. Thomas Baird (1777–1826) subsequently printed the speeches. The two men were later arrested and at the High Court in Edinburgh were found guilty of sedition. They received exacting fines and a prison term of six months. The monument formerly had a statue of liberty by Charles Grasby perched on top of it. Unfortunately it was blown off in a storm in 1936 and never replaced, leaving the Corinthian pillar rather bare.

Between the housing estates of New Farm Loch and Beansburn lies the Dean Castle Country Park. Lord Howard de Walden, who later gifted the castle in 1975, gifted thirteen acres of this to the citizens of Kilmarnock in 1974. The council bought the rest of the policies in 1977. The Dean Castle, or Kilmarnock Castle as it was also known, stands right in the middle of the park, near to the junction of the Craufurdland and Fenwick waters, which merge to form the Kilmarnock Water. The castle is one of the oldest in the area, the old tower having been erected in the fifteenth century. A palace block was erected to the east of the tower in the sixteenth century, and further courtyard buildings were erected within the barmkin wall.

Dean Castle, with old keep on left and 'palace' block on right

Dean Castle was anciently a Lockhart then Soulis seat, but on 3 May 1316 it passed to the Boyds. Charles II created William, 9th Lord Boyd, the Earl of Kilmarnock in 1661, but in 1746 the 4th Earl was executed for his part in the Jacobite rising. The title was confiscated, so his son was simple James Boyd. He sold the estate in 1748 and it passed through the Earls of Glencairn and Dukes of Portland to the Howard de Walden family in 1879. Dean Castle suffered a fire in 1735, which left it in a ruinous condition. The family moved to Kilmarnock House, leaving the old buildings to the mercy of the elements. The 8th Lord Howard de Walden (who inherited in 1899) decided to commence restoration. This was done to traditional styles, hence the unusual existence of the timber walkway on the courtyard walls. The new gateway was erected in 1935–6 to plans by J. S. Richardson, basing it on the gateway at Tolquhon Castle in Aberdeenshire. The interior of the castle was also restored. The rooms were either filled with Lord Howard de Walden's unique collection of arms, tapestries and musical instruments, or else filled with antique furniture and objects.

The castle is regularly open to the public and forms a popular tourist attraction. Entrance is made to the first floor hall by means of an external flight of steps. This hall measures thirty-eight feet by twenty-two feet, the vault rising to twenty-six feet. A small minstrel's gallery overlooks it. Within are preserved armoury and musical instruments, collected by Lord Howard de Walden. The palace block contains the old kitchen. The dower house, which was erected alongside the castle, is now an exhibition area, with information on the history of the estate and of the Boyds. There seems to have been a building here for many years, the current mansion created in the late nineteenth century with the merging of two dwellings. Near the park entrance from Dean Road is a modern visitor centre complete with café and gift shop. In the grounds are various walks, a children's menagerie and countryside centre.

The grounds of Dean Castle have many interesting features. West of the castle, up the hillside, can be found the old burial enclosure of the family. Across the Fenwick Water rises Judas Hill, named from the fact that here the Boyds had their seat of justice. Here also are the old Dean quarries, where white sandstone was excavated for building work from around 1790 until 1872. Most of central Kilmarnock, which was being redeveloped during this period, was built with stone from this quarry.

The part of Kilmarnock that lies south of the river Irvine, and cut off to some extent by the A71, is in fact in a separate parish. This is Riccarton, which to most folk is now part of the larger town, but for centuries was a separate community with its own identity. Riccarton parish extends to 7,598 acres (which includes a formerly detached area), and includes the communities of Riccarton and Hurlford, but today there is little to connect them. Roads have destroyed the old hub of Riccarton, so that there is little of a 'village' centre. Probably the most significant survivor is the parish church, which stands proudly, if somewhat bemused by its present surroundings, on top of a low hill. This hill was anciently the Judgment Hill, but the church was erected on its summit in 1823 to plans of John Richmond. The church is a most distinguished feature, visible to many as they make their way along the busy A71. Classical in style, it has a unique pediment from which rises a steeple containing a clock. The kirkyard has a number of old stones of interest. South of New Street is the older kirkyard, and here a number of old memorial stones still occupy the burial ground.

In front of the modern Kilmarnock Fire Station is an inscribed stone noting that this was the site of Riccarton Castle, which was anciently a property of the Wallace family. In the thirteenth century Richard Wallace owned the castle. His nephew was William, the great Scots freedom fighter. The castle was later abandoned and subsequently cleared away, so that nothing of it now remains. Wallace was reputedly born at Ellerslie, which was to the west of Kilmarnock, in the approximate area where Crosshouse Hospital now stands. Locals claim that the name was misrepresented as Elderslie, and from this the Renfrewshire village of that name claimed Wallace as its son. The debate between the two will probably never be settled. William Wallace is claimed to have had one of his encounters with some Englishmen near Riccarton. West of Maxholm Road was an old tree known as the Bickering Bush, and tradition claims that it was here Wallace was accosted by some English soldiers who asked him to hand over fish that he had caught in the river. Not one to give things up lightly, Wallace fought the soldiers over the fish and, of course, won.

Bellfield and Shortlees are two extensive housing schemes that lie south of Riccarton. Bellfield was built on the lands of Bellfield House, which stood in the surviving Bellfield Park until 1970. A memorial stone in Hurlford Road records a Civic Trust award granted in 1960 for the development. The former Riccarton School of 1908, located in Campbell Place, is now a nursery school.

The Caprington housing estate lies next to the Caprington Golf Course, an 18-hole course established in 1909 and laid out by David Kilpatrick, green-keeper at Barassie. This is 5,810 yards in length and is a par 68. Within the course stands the Blacksyke Tower which, from a distance, looks like an old Scots tower house. This is not the case however, for the tower was only erected in the early nineteenth century. It was formerly a pumping station for the Newhouse and Blacksyke Colliery, and was designed to look traditional because it was located within the ornamental grounds of Caprington Castle, from where it was visible.

Caprington Castle is a fascinating old building perched on a low hill above the river Irvine. The core of the castle is ancient, perhaps dating from the late fifteenth century, but in 1829 the whole castle was restored and the external facades recased in dressed stone to create a Gothic-style building. The architect of this was Patrick Wilson. The castle is still occupied by the Cunninghame family, who have lived here since before 1462, the earliest reference to them. The family were granted a baronetcy of Caprington in 1669, but this became extinct in 1829. Within the castle are a number of ancient treasures, including the hunting horn traditionally used by Old King Coil, who is supposed to have lived around 325 BC. The horn is claimed to be around two thousand years old, and thus Scotland's oldest musical instrument. Here also is preserved the whistle that was kept as the trophy in the drinking competition described by Burns in his poem 'The Whistle'. The grounds of Caprington are extensive and boast a large walled garden and various pathways through the woods. The tiny village of Earlston lies south of Caprington Castle. Here are the kennels associated with the Eglinton Hunt.

Abutting the south end of Shortlees is the former estate of Treesbank House. The estate was of some antiquity, the original house dating from around 1770. This was demolished and replaced by the present Treesbank, a fine mansion of 1926 designed by James K. Hunter for Gavin Morton, one of the owners of the BMK carpet factory. For many years this was used as a trade union education and recreation centre. The house was sold and is now in private hands once more. Within the immediate grounds of Treesbank can be found an old dovecot, dating from 1771, and a stone stable block of a similar date.

Craigie Road is a minor route that strikes south from Shortlees, passing beneath the bypass before climbing up the slopes of Craigie Hill. Another country road from Bellfield is the Treeswoodhead Road, which heads towards Carnell. Trees Farm lies west of this road, and in a field there can be seen the remains of a circular earthwork. Dallars House stands on a low hill by the Cessnock Water. The house is a Georgian building, erected in 1779. It is still occupied and one wing is sub-let. The stable cottages date in part from 1635.

The hamlet of Crossroads lies at the junction of the A76 with the A719. The larger building at the junction was at one time an inn, positioned where it would benefit from passing trade. Crossroads Primary School lies behind, a small rural school but one that is popular. Cessnock Mill lies near to the Cessnock Water. The water was dammed and a lade drove the mill. On the opposite side of the river, upstream a bit, lies Shaws Mill, another old mill.

The large Kilmarnock Prison occupies a site east of the A76, north of Crossroads. The prison received its first inmates on 25 March 1999 and is large enough to accommodate 500 prisoners. Built using the Private Finance Initiative, the building only took just over one year to erect, the cost being around £32 million. Day-to-day operations at the prison are conducted by Premier Prison Services Ltd. Kilmarnock Prison occupies the site of a former ordnance factory that was built during the First World War. Here explosives were made within semi-subterranean buildings. The factory was abandoned after the war, and for many years lay disused, gradually crumbling away.

From the prison entrance the B7073 (at one time the A76) leads into Hurlford. En route it passes the large bonded warehouses and bottling plant where Johnnie Walker Scotch whisky is produced. The distillery employs many people, and produces over three million bottles of whisky and other spirits per week. The distillery was built on the site of the former railway works, which had its own Barleith Station on the Kilmarnock to Edinburgh railway line. There was also a community of workers' houses here, known as 'The Blocks', which at one time had a population of 600.

The signs for Hurlford list some of the earlier spellings of the community, which include 'Hurdleford and Whirlford.' The ford was across the river Irvine, which marks the village's northern boundary, and this was at one time one of the most important fords in the area, for the routes to Edinburgh and south from Kilmarnock came this way. Most of the old part of Hurlford has gone, leaving only a few traditional buildings here and there. Most of the community comprises later local authority housing, built to replace old miners' rows and workers houses.

In Mauchline Road is the former United Presbyterian church, closed in 1938, but the Gothic building survives and is used for other purposes. The church was designed by Gabriel Andrew and was erected in 1898. Its spire rises above the village. The church was used as a hostel during the war, and latterly was acquired by the Co-operative Association, which used it for leisure activities.

At the roundabout in the centre of the village can be seen a large propeller, which is quite an unusual feature for an inland village. This came from the Blair Foundry, founded in 1864, which made propellers and other castings for many years. David Chapman, George Burns and three other partners established the Portland ironworks in 1846 on land owned by the Duke of Portland. The company did not prosper, and the ironworks were sold to English proprietors in 1852, sold on in 1857 and acquired by the Bairds in 1864. The works were closed in 1890. In later years Hurlford was an important producer of drain covers and other road furniture, and the name Hurlford can be seen on roadways all over Ayrshire and beyond.

Few other interesting buildings survive in Hurlford. The primary school in Academy Street dates from 1905, the work of Andrew & Newlands. In Galston Road is St Paul's RC Church, a yellow-brick Gothic building of the mid nineteenth-century. St Paul's Primary School is in Union Street and in Blair Road is Blair Park, home since 1912 of Hurlford United Football Club, which was founded in 1874. Riccarton Road has a few older buildings in it, among these the former co-operative building and the Masonic lodge.

Much of old Hurlford has been demolished. Among the lost buildings we can mention only a few, including Galloway's Miners' Institute, which stood at the cross. This was erected with funds donated by John Galloway (d. 1889), of the Barleith and Dallars coal company, and opened in October 1888. A second Galloway Institute was erected around the same time at New Street in Riccarton. Shawhill House lies by the side of the Irvine, just to the north of Hurlford. Erected in 1820, the main front is a five-bay classical box, the simple façade enlivened by the porch and chimneys on the pediment.

From Hurlford two roads lead into Kilmarnock. Riccarton Road keeps to the south of the river Irvine, passing Kaimshill House en route to the large Bellfield interchange on the Kilmarnock bypass. South of this road is Torrance Lodge nursing home, the Riccarton cemetery, and a service area for travellers. Kirklandside Hospital is located south of the A76.

From Hurlford Cross the B7073 bridges the river Irvine and enters the community of Crookedholm. Although located in Kilmarnock parish, Crookedholm has more of an affinity with Hurlford, for here stands the present Hurlford parish church. This was erected in 1875 to plans of J. & R. S. Ingram, its Early English style tower being a local eye-catcher. Among the stained glass is a modern window of 1981 by Sadie MacLellan. Further along Crookedholm's Main Road is the Reid Memorial Church, built in 1857. Crookedholm was a mining village, for here stood a number of miner's rows. They were eventually demolished and replaced with more modern housing, creating the scheme up Grougar Road. West of Crookedholm, located on the east side of Kilmarnock bypass, is Struthers Farm. This was the birthplace of James Paterson (1805–76), the noted Ayrshire historian, and a plaque on the wall commemorates this.

There is a sizeable part of Kilmarnock parish located between Fenwick and the river Irvine, extending east towards Moscow. Most of this is rural countryside, with one or two small estates. The former Templetonburn House lies on a low hill above the Irvine. The house was erected in 1901 to plans of James K. Hunter and was one of his finest works. The house was sadly destroyed by fire. Nearby is Grougar Mains Farm, the name recalling the long-lost Grougar estate. Grougarbank House is a smallish country house of around 1860, erected of blonde sandstone. The eastern extremity of Kilmarnock parish is marked by the Polbaith Burn, which rises within the Whitelee Forest and tumbles down to the Irvine. Within the Castlehill Glen are a couple of minor waterfalls.

Grassyards Road extends from Kilmarnock in a north-easterly direction towards the village of Moscow. The name has nothing to do with the Russian capital, although locals take great delight in informing visitors that the little stream that passes through the village has been named the Volga Burn.

Kilmarnock seems to have more than its fair share of castles, for within the parish stand three significant castles and the remains of a fourth smaller tower. Craufurdland Castle is still inhabited, for it was extended considerably to create a rather fine Gothic mansion. The old tower, which survives intact at the western end, dates from the late fifteenth century. It was built by the Craufurd family as their seat. An addition was made to this tower in 1648, and this survives within the present complex. In 1810 the house became too small for the tastes and lifestyle of the landowners, so they added a large Gothic building alongside. This is one of the finest Gothic houses in the country. The main doorway is a richly moulded structure, over which are the Craufurd arms. The windows are tall lancet-style, and the main tower is topped with crenellations and turrets in a style reminiscent of Adam's Culzean Castle. The castle remains the seat of the Houison-Craufurd family. Within the policies is the Craufurdland Loch, a sizeable stretch of water now used as a fishery.

The remains of Assloss Tower are incorporated in the present Assloss Farm. Only the ground floor of a traditional Scots tower house survives, but this has the distinction of being vaulted and with a shot hole. Assloss was originally the seat of the Assloss of that Ilk family, but they died out in the late seventeenth century and the lands later became part of the Kilmarnock estate. A later Assloss House was built nearer the Dean Castle in the early eighteenth for William Parker.

Kilmarnock's fourth castle is Rowallan Castle, which stands at the northern extremity of the parish, between Kilmaurs and Fenwick. The old castle dates from the middle of the sixteenth century and contains a rather fine forestair to the main entrance, which lies between two round turrets. These form the main feature of the old castle, and are purely ornamental. This part of the castle was erected around 1562. Over the doorway are the Royal Arms. A pend leads into the courtyard, from where the rest of the castle is accessed. The ground floor is vaulted, and the main apartments are located on the first floor. The rest of the castle is quite a simple structure, forming an L-shaped block around a courtyard. In the grounds can be found King William's Well. Rowallan was anciently a Comyn seat, but in the thirteenth century an heiress married a Mure, who had been active at the Battle of Largs. A later daughter, Elizabeth Mure, became King Robert II's queen. The Mures were granted a baronetcy in 1662, but died out in 1700, and the heiress took the castle and estate to the Campbells of Lawers.

The Corbett family acquired Rowallan estate in 1901. Archibald Cameron Corbett had made his fortune in the development of Glasgow and then London. He bought various properties, including Rouken Glen, around Glasgow, but decided to move further from the city as it gradually encroached onto his lands. He actually gifted the lands of Rouken Glen to the city in 1906 to form a public park. Another gift the same year was the extensive peninsula in Argyll known as 'Argyll's Bowling Green'. Archibald Corbett decided to build a brand new country house on the Rowallan lands. He engaged the noted Scots architect, William Lorimer, to design a new mansion in the traditional Scots-castle style. Work began in 1901, but unfortunately his wife, Alice, died and so the plans were reduced somewhat. The castle that was built, however, is still a considerable building. Archibald Cameron Corbett (1856–1933) was created Baron Rowallan in 1911. He was a noted MP for Glasgow Tradeston. Thomas, second Lord Rowallan, was Chief Scout 1945–59 and Governor of Tasmania 1959–63. The Corbetts remained at Rowallan until 1989, when the castle and immediate policies were sold. Lord Rowallan now lives at Meikle Mosside, nearby.

The village of Kilmaurs lies two and a half miles north-west of Kilmarnock town centre. The village is the centre of its own parish of 5,940 acres, but today most of this is associated with an ever-expanding Kilmarnock. Kilmaurs remains a separate village, however, with just over half a mile of open countryside between itself and the Altonhill estate of Kilmarnock. It was created a Burgh of Barony in 1527 for Cuthbert, 3rd Earl of Glencairn. Kilmaurs gets its name from St Maurs, who is thought to have lived in the fifth or ninth century, depending on which account is read.

Kilmaurs village centre is an attractive and traditional one. It is fortunate not to be on the main road to anywhere, so a number of old buildings survive. The most notable is that known locally as the Jougs, though this really only refers to the iron neck-ring that is attached to the gable of the building. These were padlocked around the neck of miscreants, much in the same way as the English used their stocks. The actual building was the tolbooth, a double storey building with a vaulted ground floor. The vaults were used as cells, the upper floor a courtroom. This was erected sometime between 1527 and 1600. At one end a stone clock-tower was added at a later date, with stone forestairs leading to the upper floor. At the end of the Jougs is the old market cross, a simple structure topped with a ball finial. The curved main street has a number of interesting old buildings along it. The former Public Hall of 1892 (erected at a cost of £1,400) has been demolished and replaced by modern buildings.

At one time there was a Secession Church in the village, established in 1740, and it became the Mother Church of the Secession in Ayrshire. A new church was erected in 1865 at a cost of £1,311 and a hall added in 1895. This church later became a United Secession Church, United Presbyterian, United Free and in 1929 the Glencairn Church of Scotland. The congregation was linked with the Kilmaurs parish church in 1963, and after a time the church and hall were sold off, the church being used by Susan Bradbury and Paul Lucky for the manufacture of stained glass windows.

In Crosshouse Road is the Maxwell United Free Church, erected in 1844. A simple building with an empty belfry, the church was named after one of its most distinguished ministers, Revd James Maxwell, who served from 1848 until 1885. The library and local museum is located on the site of the former primary school of 1876, situated in Irvine Road. Further on is the former Kilmaurs Creamery, established in 1903 by the Kilmaurs Farmers' Association. This was later operated by other groups, before closing in 1975, the manufacture of cheese being transferred to Lockerbie. A lane leads to Kilmaurs station, originally opened on 27 March 1871. The station was closed in November 1965, but in 1984 it was reopened and remains in use.

John Boyd Orr (1880–1971) was born at Holland Green in Kilmaurs. He trained at Glasgow University and served in the First World War, where he was awarded the Distinguished Service Cross and Military Cross. In 1929 he founded the Imperial Bureau of Animal Nutrition and later became Director of the Rowett Research Institute and a Professor of Agriculture at Aberdeen University. When the United Nations Food and Agricultural Organization was established in 1945, Boyd Orr was appointed its first director. He won the Nobel Prize in 1949 for his part in improving agricultural standards worldwide and in the same year was created a Baron.

Between the Jougs of Kilmaurs and Kilmarnock is the Kirktoun of Kilmaurs, where the old parish church of St Maur's Glencairn is still located. The first church was connected with Kelso Abbey as early as 1170 and in 1413 Sir William Cunninghame established a collegiate church here. The building as it stands today was the work of Robert Ingram in 1888, who created a cruciform building with tower. Michael Burgerhuys made the old bell in 1618. Adjoining the church is the Glencairn Aisle, where the Cunninghame Earls of Glencairn were buried. James, 7th Earl, erected this in 1600. Within are effigies representing the 8th Earl, his countess and children. The sculptor was David Scougal from Crail in Fife.

Behind the church is the former manse building, now known as Kirkfauld. This was erected in the eighteenth century but has been altered in recent years. Within the grounds are the foundations of the ancient 'Tour' of Kilmaurs. Here also survives an old dovecot of 1636. In the wood nearby is the Lady's Well, with a stone-built canopy. This was probably used by nuns to get water for the old settlement that stood nearby. The Cunninghames of Kilmaurs were created Earls of Glencairn in 1488, their secondary title being Viscount Kilmaurs. The first Earl was given his title for his services at Blackness.

Nearer the larger Kilmaurs, and standing above the Carmel Water, is Kilmaurs Place, an old domestic building of around 1620. This is a T-shaped laird's house of two storeys, rising to corbie-stepped gables. Within the grounds are the remains of Kilmaurs Castle. The surrounding land is now a public park, where can be seen the war memorial of 1921, a pillar by the side of which is a statue of a soldier. George Morton of Lochgreen House, Troon, a native of the village, gifted the park of eleven acres to the village in 1921. Tour House stands within its walled policies east of the Kilmarnock road. The house was erected in 1841 to plans of James Ingram for a Glasgow merchant.

North of Kilmaurs, at Buiston, was a loch, only recognisable today by the flat piece of ground south of Lochside Farm. A crannog was discovered here and excavated in 1989–90, the archaeologists unearthing a canoe, two ovens and a fourth century hanging bowl, a particularly rare discovery. Earlier excavations had been carried out here in 1880–1. By the side of the Carmel Water is a circular earthwork known as the Bailie Hill. This probably dates from the Norman period. Another old earthwork can be found at Greenhill Farm, the farm obviously taking its name from the mound located on a low hillock.

From Kilmaurs the B751 takes one to the little village of Knockentiber. This had its origins as a mining community, for a number of coalmines existed round about. Remains of some of the pit bings and other structures can still be found in the local countryside. A Roman Catholic school, known as St Mary's, existed here, serving the parish of Kilmaurs from 1891 until the 1960s. At Knockentiber stood Busbie Castle, demolished in 1952. This tower house was erected around 1600 by the Mowats and was three storeys in height. The tower was virtually entire to the wall-heads when MacGibbon and Ross visited, but it was latterly a shattered ruin before being cleared away.

Crosshouse village was also something of a mining centre, but any association with coal has long since ceased. The old houses were mostly demolished and replaced by council houses in the 1950s and 1960s. These, together with some modern private estates, act as a dormitory for Kilmarnock. The red sandstone Early Perpendicular parish church stands in Kilmarnock Road. The foundation stone was laid on 29 December 1881 and the church opened on 19 March 1882. The architects were Bruce & Sturrock of Glasgow, the proposals by Robert Ingram not being used. The church contains windows by Meikle & Son. A Roman Catholic chapel was erected in Crosshouse in 1891, but this is now closed.

At the road junction is an open space where the Carmel Water passes by. Here can be found a memorial commemorating Andrew Fisher (1862–1928). Fisher was born nearby and entered the pits at the age of twelve. At the age of twenty-three he emigrated to Australia to work in the mines there. He became active in the trade union movement and entered politics in Queensland. By 1907 he was the leader of the Australian

Labour Party, which he led to victory in the election of 1908. He was to hold the Prime Minister's office three times in total, in 1908–9, 1910–13, and 1914–15. In 1916 he was appointed Australian High Commissioner in London. Andrew Law (1873–1967), a noted portrait painter and artist, was also born in Crosshouse, coincidentally in the same house as Fisher. Many of his works are on display in the Dick Institute.

On the east side of Crosshouse is the large Crosshouse Hospital, which serves most of north Ayrshire. The hospital was built in 1973–82 to replace the old Kilmarnock Infirmary. The architects were Boissevain & Osmond, who created a horizontal sandwich of pan bread, broken by two white towers. The flat roof of the hospital proved troublesome and was replaced with the present pitched roof in the 1990s. George Younger, secretary of state for Scotland, opened the hospital on 2 June 1984.

Thorntoun House stood in its woodlands west of Crosshouse. A simple Georgian building erected in the eighteenth century for the Cuninghame family, the house was demolished in 1968 and replaced by a school operated by Dr Barnardo's charity. Milton Road strikes south from Thorntoun towards Craig House and Laigh Milton Mill. Craig House was erected around 1788 by the Morrice family following a fire in the 1780s building. The architect was James Ingram, who used a massive Ionic portico to adorn the main frontage. A winter garden designed by John Burnet was added in 1902. The house was later used by the council, but was abandoned by them in 1989 after which it became roofless and fell into ruins.

Laigh Milton Mill was erected in the nineteenth century on the site of a much older mill. The weir across the river Irvine is still in existence. The mill was later converted into a hotel. From the mill a pathway heads up the right bank of the river Irvine towards the Laigh Milton Viaduct. This has the distinction of being the oldest railway viaduct in Scotland, for it was erected in 1807 as part of the Kilmarnock to Troon railway. William Jessop provided the drawings, and the railway was carried across the river on three arches. The railway had followed a rather sharp bend across the river, so a newer bridge was erected upstream in the 1850s and the old viaduct was abandoned. In 1992 its importance was realised and conservation work commenced.

Gatehead village lies on either side of the railway line to the north of the bridge over the Irvine. The village at one time had a railway station of its own. From here the road back into Kilmarnock passes the Moorfield Industrial estate. This was formed when the Massey Ferguson tractor factory, which formerly occupied the buildings, was closed in 1980. Massey Ferguson came to Kilmarnock in 1949.

# 8

# Galston, Newmilns and Darvel

TO THE LOCALS, THE three villages or small towns of Galston, Newmilns and Darvel are the 'valley towns'. They are strung out along the road that makes its way through the rather narrow Irvine valley, on what is still one of the main routes out of Ayrshire heading east. Galston, which used to be a problem for travellers due to the many sharp bends and junctions, has fortunately been bypassed since 1978, but the traffic still thunders through Newmilns and Darvel,

Galston claims itself to be the 'heart' of Ayrshire. The town is small and compact, built around the mouth of the strangely named Burn Anne, pronounced and sometimes written, Burn Awn. It was created a Police Burgh in 1864. Galston was a mining village for many years. The pits were located around the parish, but unlike many other Ayrshire mining communities, there is little left to hint at this former industry, which died out in 1933 with the closure of Maxwood Pit. In 1839 the Cessnock Ironworks were established, but this proved to be a fruitless venture and the furnaces were closed down after five years. Weaving was also a main industry in the town, with blankets the main product.

The parish church is perhaps the centre of town, occupying a site on which a church has stood since 1252. The church stands in its old kirkyard, the spire rising above the rest of the roofs; it dates from 1808–9 and was the work of John Brash of Glasgow. The wright was a local man, John Stewart of Galston, but the mason was Peter Menzies of Auchterarder. A simple preaching box of two 'storeys', externally the church is Georgian in style, adorned by arched windows and pedimented gables. The steeple rises 120 feet from the eastern end. A chancel was added in 1912. Inside can be seen a J. J. Binns organ of 1913, and stained glass by Oscar Paterson. Within the kirkyard can be found some Covenanters' graves. One of the most interesting commemorates Andrew Richmond, who was shot by John Graham of Claverhouse in June 1679, and the stone depicts Graham taking aim at Richmond with his gun. Another stone commemorates Revd Dr George Smith, great-grandfather of Robert Louis Stevenson, who is also mentioned in Burns's 'Holy Fair', 'The Twa Herds' and 'The Kirk's Alarm'.

One of the ministers of Galston from 1824–78 was Revd Robert Stirling (1790–1878). Born at Cloag, Perthshire, he had a deep interest in engineering, making scientific instruments and inventing what became known as the Stirling engine. This was a heated-air engine that could produce forty horsepower. Modern mechanics have taken another look at Stirling's engine and have discovered that it might form some sort of replacement for the internal combustion engine due to its non-polluting properties. Stirling's grave is in the kirkyard and a plaque adorns the church vestibule.

In Wallace Street is a second church, Romanesque in style, erected in 1859 to plans of J. Dick Peddie. This later became the Erskine Hall. The church merged with the Trinity Church in 1949, the Trinity building, which was distinguished by its tall spire, being demolished in 1963. The Trinity Church was a Free Church, erected in 1888 to replace the original Free Church of 1843 that had been erected at Kilnknowe, now Barrmill Road. Also in Wallace Street is the former Picture House erected in 1912 and now a veterinary surgery. In Station Road is the war memorial, a tall cross on a base containing 128 Great War names and 46 from the Second World War. The memorial was unveiled in December 1922. The railway station opened in 1848 and closed in August 1966.

St Sophia's RC Church stands on an elevated part of the town. This church is quite unique in its architecture, and was actually based on the Hagia Sophia in Istanbul. The 3rd Marquis of Bute paid for the erection of the church, which was built in 1885–6. Robert Rowand Anderson, and perhaps his successor, R. Weir Schultz, supplied the plans for the red-brick church, cruciform in plan with a circular tower rising from the centre. It was said that the Marquis had hoped to have a church like this erected in Troon, but the local Catholic adherents were unimpressed with his preference for Byzantine architecture.

Galston's Town House stands at The Cross. The building was only erected in 1925 to plans of Hay & Steel, but it has a traditional baronial style in red sandstone. Brown's Institute was erected in 1874 to plans of James Stark. It is now used as a woollen factory with mill shop. Next to the institute is the Muckle Brig, completed in 1839.

The primary school in Galston was erected in 1875 by William Railton. It was extended in 1909 when Galston Academy was built to the plans of J. & J. Armour. This was closed and the whole building converted in to a primary school in 1971 when Loudoun Academy was built across the river.

Some of the buildings around the centre of town are quite old and traditional in style. Others are Victorian structures erected by the Co-operative movement, which was quite strong in the valley. Galston Co-operative Society was founded in 1852. One of the main buildings, in Brewland Street, stood four storeys in height and was erected around 1901. It is now converted to flats.

The old square tower of Barr Castle stands in the centre of town, its extant garden wall enclosing an area occupied by modern bungalows. The tower dates from the fifteenth century and was erected by the Lockhart family. In 1545 George Wishart preached here, followed in 1556 by John Knox. The Lockharts sold Barr to the Campbells of Cessnock in 1670. Around 1899 the tower was altered slightly, a porch was added and the rather unfortunate hipped roof replaced the original parapets and gabled upperworks. The Masonic Lodge acquired the tower, and still uses it as a temple. Fiercely proud of the building, the lodge has created a small museum of artefacts within and this is open at irregular intervals. Against the wall of the tower the traditional game of Hand Ba' was played.

Galston has a second castle within its parish. Cessnock Castle is a fine tower house that has been extended a number of times over its life. Still inhabited, the castle stands on a knoll overlooking the Burn Anne. The oldest part dates from the fifteenth century, perhaps as early as the thirteenth, to which a number of additions have been made. These include the stair tower of 1665. The walls are as thick as eighteen feet in places. The Campbells owned the castle for centuries, but an heiress took the castle to Sir Alexander Home, who was created Lord Cessnock at the bench in 1704. The castle has been owned by a number of families since, including Baron de Fresnes. It is now divided into two dwellings.

The Burn Anne rises on the Mean Muir, a high tract of moorland on the Sorn border. Here also is the Monk Muir, a name recollecting the association with the monks of Fail Monastery. South of Middlefield farm is a fairly straight road heading for the Sorn boundary known as the Monk Road. Below Hillhouse farm the Burn Anne drops over a series of waterfalls. Further downstream, below Middle Third, is the Holy Well, dedicated to the Virgin Mary. Burn Anne is also celebrated for its agates, which used to be avidly gathered by collectors from all over Scotland. This was because the stone was one of the finest examples of its type, with a beautiful variety of colours ranging from yellow to purple.

South of Cessnock is the little roadside hamlet of Sornhill. Comprising of a row of single storey cottages, old photographs depict these as thatched. There was even an inn here at one time. Sornhill Farm stands nearby, on the southern slopes of the Sorn Hill. The original farmhouse, which is sadly abandoned, was a simple Scots tower house of 1660. Rising through three floors, the L-plan building has a watchtower in the re-entrant. This was long a seat of the Shaw family.

West of Sornhill is Milrig, a small estate whose mansion was demolished around 1960. Built in the late eighteenth century, Milrig had a variety of owners over its life. The house was a Gothic structure, with an unusual central tower. Due south of Milrig is Bruntwood, a former laird's house of the late seventeenth century. The old house still has its corbie-stepped gables, and over the doorway is the Moor coat-of-arms, but that family probably had to sell off sometime in the late eighteenth century.

South-east of Galston are the Maxwood Smallholdings, a number of small agricultural units. On the hilltop above, known as the Gallow Law, can be found the remains of a prehistoric cairn. Here also is a modern cairn erected by unemployed miners during the General Strike of 1926. The cairn was built to commemorate the Covenanters, who had many local associations. The Smith family, for example, tenanted Threepwood Farm, and James Smith was persecuted for his religious adherences.

The extensive Lanfine estate occupies the northern slope of this hill. Lanfine House is a very grand mansion of 1912–20, designed by James K. Hunter, but incorporating an older Georgian house of 1769–72. James Armour, Burns's father-in-law, worked on this earlier part. It occupies a promontory of land between two burns, and overlooks the Irvine valley. Within the policies can be found an old cylindrical doocot, of the eighteenth century, and a fine bridge of 1828, spanning the gorge of the Newlands Burn on the drive from the Ranoldcoup Bridge at Darvel.

The countryside east of Lanfine is more usually associated with Darvel than Galston, even although it still falls within the parish of the latter. The higher ground is used for sport, for here is a number of grouse moors, in particular the Barr Moor. This moor is drained by a number of smallish watercourses, including the Gower Water, which is formed by the merging of the Glenoul, Logan, Changue, Tulloch and Dubs burns, many of which carve a deep glen through the moor. By the side of the Tulloch Burn can be found the remains of the Long Cairn, a Bronze Age burial. Adjacent to it is another burial cairn, one of which has had a chamber within it. In the gully below these cairns the Tulloch Burn has to negotiate a waterfall known as the Ladystone Linn.

The parish of Galston, and consequently the county of Ayrshire, finds its eastern extremity here at the Avon Water, which flows north-eastwards toward Strathaven and ultimately the river Clyde. The Avon rises at a point known as Avon Head, where the Avonhead Well is a natural spring, just within Ayrshire. The infant stream flows past Avon Moss towards the Kaims of Avon, near which is an ancient earthwork, known as Main Castle. This comprises a circular mound constructed on top of a promontory above the stream. West of here the moor is known as the King's Moss, perhaps in reference King Robert the Bruce, but no one is really sure. A low hill rises north of the moss, known as Cairnsaigh Hill. This was the site of another ancient cairn, long robbed of its stone for building material. The Avon passes beneath the Avon Bridge on a minor road, and shortly after this leaves any Ayrshire connection for good. The land between Cairnsaigh Hill and the distinctive Loudoun Hill on the north of the valley is composed of sand overlain with soil or peat. The sand is in big demand for construction work, and various sandpits exist, or have existed in this area.

The river Irvine is just an infant stream hereabouts. The river rises in what is now the forest at Hareshawhill, north of Loudoun Hill. The river forms the boundary between Galston and Loudoun parish, the latter being located to the north, although at Hareshawhill and Mosside it forms the boundary between Loudoun and Lanarkshire. To the east of Loudoun Hill can be found an earthwork that is known as Wallace's Knowe. This is said to have had connections with Sir William Wallace, who passed this way in 1297 and defeated the English force under Sir John Fenwick. The knowe may be the spot where the dead were buried. Another possible burial spot was Wallace's Cairn, which stood at Allantonplains, but which has been lost to sand and gravel extraction.

The Romans were active in the vicinity of Loudoun Hill, for a fort dating to around 200 AD existed here. It is reckoned that 500 soldiers were based here. A Roman road linked it with other sites in Avon and Clydesdales, and no doubt also headed west towards a port at Hunterston. The site of the fort was on the south side of the A71, at Allantonplains.

Loudoun Hill

Loudoun Hill is a wonderfully strange sight in Ayrshire. It rises suddenly out of the landscape, looking most unnatural. And yet is one of the finest natural features to be seen in the county. The hill owes it origin to the time when volcanoes were active in what was to become Scotland. The remains of the centre of the volcano, or plug, created the present hill. From the south the hill rises through a sheer cliff face to the summit, which is 1,036 feet above sea level. Naturally this summit is a prominent viewpoint, for there is little so high within a wide radius. Rock climbers frequent the cliffs, but those who wish to make a gentler ascent of this notable summit will do it from the north. Near the summit of the hill can be found two memorials. One of these commemorates the Battle of Loudoun Hill, which took place on 10 May 1307. Robert the Bruce and his 1,200 men defeated an English force of 3,000 under the Earl of Pembroke, near to Allantonbeg, although the exact place of battle is not known. Tradition claims that Bruce's men were able to defeat the English troops by his use of trenches to prevent their cavalry from advancing. The memorial comprises a large pink granite slab that was hauled up the hill on 8 May 1983. The second memorial was erected to commemorate John Robin Jackson (1948–68) who was killed climbing in the Italian Alps. A native of Strathaven, his grave is located in the cemetery there.

The dismantled Caledonian railway snaked its way through the Irvine valley, and below Loudoun Hill crossed the upper reaches of the glen by the Loudounhill Viaduct. This was a thirteen-arch structure, erected in 1905 but demolished in 1986 against much protest from the locals. Near Allanton is the Loudoun Hill Inn, looking over the valley towards Underlaw and Glaister farms. On the summits of the low hills above the farms are three prehistoric cairns, one above Henryton, one above Glaister and the third above Underlaw. The cairn at Henryton was excavated to reveal stone axes and bronze implements. At Bankhead Farm an ancient Castle Hill occupies a knoll high above the Glen Water. North of here is the Calder Moss, a marshy area of moorland, now surrounded by forestry plantations and part of the extensive Whitelee Forest.

The Glen Water rises high in the moorlands between Darvel and Eaglesham. The headwaters are in Renfrewshire, but the stream soon makes its way into Ayrshire and cuts a deep glen for itself as it tumbles towards Darvel and the river Irvine. An old roadway made its way across the moor here, often used in the past by weavers taking their product to Glasgow markets. The roadway can be followed by existing minor roads and tracks for most of its way, but at the highest point, where it crosses the county boundary at the Crook of the Lench, it is indistinguishable on the ground.

One of the more remote farms in this glen is Lochfield, which lies on the east side of the Glen Water. It was here that Sir Alexander Fleming (1881–1955) was born and a memorial stone by the side of the farmhouse commemorates him. He was educated in Darvel and at Kilmarnock Academy before entering St Mary's Hospital Medical School in London, where he qualified as both a surgeon and physician. Fleming then served with distinction in the First World War before returning to the study of infections. He made his first major finding in 1921 in quite extraordinary circumstances: a drip from his nose fell on a plate of agar, in which contaminants were growing, and Fleming noticed that the contaminants were quickly killed. He had discovered lysozyme, which was not only useful in its own right but would also pave the way for his discovery of penicillin. Fleming made his most important breakthrough in 1928:

Sir Alexander Fleming with the Queen Mother

when he was clearing out old cultures he noticed that on one of the dishes the mould had destroyed the staphylococci culture. Realising that he had found an antibiotic that could attack infection, Fleming isolated the mould and grew more of it; he had, in fact, discovered penicillin. Although his research paper on the subject was met with little interest at the time, in the early 1940s a team at Oxford University led by Ernst Chain and

Howard Florey solved the problems involved in the mass production of penicillin. It was a development that would save millions of lives. Fleming's crucial work in this field was recognised throughout the world and he was showered with honours, including a knighthood in 1944 and the Nobel Prize for Medicine in 1945 (shared with Chain and Florey). The prestigious *Time* magazine put him on its front cover in 1944, and described him as one of the greatest men of the twentieth century. In any list of the greatest Scots of all time Fleming is invariably close to the top. On his death he was honoured with burial in St Paul's Cathedral in London, and thousands turned up to pay their last respects.

The Glen Water passes under the Braidley Bridge, which carries a minor road from one side of the glen to the other. On the west side, near Gateside farm, is an old earthwork known locally as Carnals Castle. This may have been a Norman motte hill, but there is little of its history known. The Mucks Water flows past the old earthwork, draining the Darvel Moss. Here also is the Wallace Gill, a tiny stream rising on Wallacegill Muir, which is supposed to have connections with William Wallace. The Blood Moss nearby hints at some struggle or other.

The Glen Water flows through the centre of Darvel and meets the river Irvine on the south side of the small town. Darvel is a planned village, built with a grid pattern in the narrow valley of the Irvine. The Campbells of Loudoun laid out the village in 1752, when twelve feus were granted around what became Hastings Square. The village soon grew as a centre of excellence in the weaving trade and in 1873 was granted burgh status. The town was, and still is to some extent, famous for its lace products. Alexander Morton first introduced the production of lace into the valley in 1876 and soon Darvel and Newmilns became the heart of lace production in Scotland.

The hub of Darvel is Hastings Square, where stands the Central parish church with its 130 feet tall spire. Designed by Robert Ingram and erected in 1887–8, the church is Early English in style. The church contains a stained glass window by Douglas Strachan, commemorating the diamond wedding of Alexander and Jeanie Morton in 1923. The window was originally erected in Gowanbank House, but was moved to the church in 1958. In the middle of the square are a few memorials, as well as the ancient Dagon Stone. The Dagon Stone is traditionally thought to be a standing stone, which newly-wed couples would walk round thrice in order to bring good luck. It has moved around the village a number of times, formerly being located at the top of Ranoldcoup Road, then at Brown's Institute, before being erected in the square. At some point in its life a round boulder was added to its top. The parish war memorial stands in the centre of the square, a thirty-feet-tall white-granite obelisk with bronze plaques on the base. General Sir Aylmer Hunter-Weston of Hunterston unveiled it. Here also is the memorial bust to Sir Alexander Fleming, originally erected in a memorial garden on 23 April 1960, but moved to the square following subsidence at its original site. The bust was the work of E. R. Bevan.

On the north side of the Square is the Black Bull Inn of 1840. Near to it is the town hall, a façade of windows and balustrades, designed by T. H. Smith of London and erected at a cost of £15,000. This was defrayed by public subscription and William Morton opened the hall on 30 June 1905. The Turf Hotel in West Main Street occupies a house that dates from 1781. Around 1850 it was converted into a coaching inn. In East Main Street is a former co-operative building of 1890.

A number of former church buildings can be seen in Darvel's town centre. The former Easton Memorial Free Church was erected in 1885 to plans by Baldie & Tennant. The Evangelical Union Church dates from 1889, the building designed by Robert Boyd. The Roman Catholic church of Our Lady of the Valley in West Donington Street was originally erected in 1874 as the Original Secession Church. The church closed in 1927 but the building was acquired by the parish church for use as a hall in 1951, remaining as such until 1983. The building was then sold to the Diocese of Galloway, which converted it into a place of worship, the chapel being officially opened on 25 November 1984 by Bishop Maurice Taylor.

Ranoldcoup Road leads from the centre of town south towards the Ranoldcoup Bridge and the gatehouse for Lanfine. The former co-operative buildings were the work of George Sinclair in 1900. In the street can be seen the former Mair's Free School of 1863, designed by William Railton, and now used as a nursery school. Brown's Institute was erected in 1872, perhaps the work of James Stark. It is now converted into houses. At the southern end of the road is Morton Park, the burgh's public park, gifted to the town in 1892 by Alexander Morton. Down Irvinebank Road is Recreation Park, home since 1919 of Darvel Juniors Football Club. This team was formed in 1889 when they played at Kirkland Park.

Darvel Primary School is a fine sandstone-building, opened on 5 January 1904 by Loudoun School Board, the architect being Henry Higgins of Glasgow. It stands on the high ground up Jamieson Road, which climbs from the town centre towards Knevocklaw. Built of Ballochmyle sandstone, the school cost £10,000 to build and can accommodate 700 pupils. The railway reached Darvel in 1896 and the railway station operated until 1964.

At the east end of Darvel, on the opposite side of the Tongue Burn, is the small community of Priestland, which retained its independence from the larger burgh from being in a different parish; Galston as opposed to Loudoun. Priestland was also an older community. Although now virtually linked with Darvel, the village likes to keep its own identity and is fiercely proud of its own road signs.

The A71 makes its busy way westward from Darvel, heading towards the sister community of Newmilns. Shortly after crossing the old railway-bridge, Gowanbank House is located on the north side of the road, built on the steep hillside. Alexander and Robert Morton, who made their fortune in the lace mills, built the house in 1880. By the roadside is a memorial commemorating Alexander Morton, designed by the renowned Scots architect, Sir Robert Lorimer, and erected in 1927. The memorial comprises a sculptured wall, with panels depicting lace workers, along with a memorial to Morton at the centre. Alexander Morton (1844–1927) was a weaving agent in Darvel who studied the lace machines at Nottingham and decided to invest in one for himself. In February 1876 the new machine was installed in the old Clipping Mill and work began. So successful was the business that within a few years Morton had to erect a number of lace mills in the town, and eventually he was joined by a number of other manufacturers, keen to employ the former weavers. By 1887 there were fifteen mills in the valley, and business boomed.

Above Gowanbank is a salubrious suburb of Newmilns at Alston-papple. Here are a number of fine villas erected by local mill owners and others. Among them are the fine Lisden and Everton, the work of Eric Hurcomb in 1928 and 1935 respectively. Here also is Westlands, a large suburban house. North of here is another old Castle Hill, occupying a tongue of high ground between two streams.

The 'New' in Newmilns is quite misleading now, but was a relevant description of the mills established here in the fifteenth century by the Loudoun family. One of these, the Loudoun Meal Mill, still survives, being used until the 1960s. It is now converted into a house. James IV created the village a Free Burgh of Barony in 1490, the first burgh to be created in the county that did not lie by the coast. In 1566 Mary Queen of Scots granted a charter allowing the burgh the right to hold courts and in 1707 the village became a Burgh of Regality. All of this was mainly as a result of the influence of the Campbells of Loudoun, who were Hereditary Sheriffs of Ayrshire.

There are many old buildings in the centre of Newmilns, and fortunately some of them have been restored in recent years. Probably the oldest is the tower, or keep, known as Newmilns Tower or Castle. This is located in a side street behind the Loudoun Arms Inn. The keep is a simple square-planned building, rising through three storeys to a lost parapet.

The turnpike stair is located in the south-east corner. The Campbells of Loudoun probably erected the tower around 1530, perhaps as a temporary home after the Kennedys destroyed Loudoun Castle in an attack. The keep was abandoned to some extent for many years, but in 1991 the Strathclyde Building Preservation Trust acquired it and the whole building was restored over the next eight years. This included reharling the exterior and replacing much rotten timberwork. The finished building is now used as a house that can be rented by interested parties.

The churchyard here has a good selection of Covenanter memorials, including one to John Law. The parish church was constructed in 1844 to replace an older building of 1738. The church is a typical Scots 'preaching box', though it has a fine tower with clock and steeple. James Ingram may have been the architect, but this is unconfirmed. The graveyard, apart from the martyrs' graves, has a few other interesting old headstones. In the High Street stood the former West Church, erected in 1833 to replace an older building of 1773. The church was founded as a United Presbyterian place of worship, but in 1961 the West Church was closed. The former East Church was built in 1847 as the Free Kirk, but it was closed in 1980 and demolished in 1986.

Newmilns: the Council House

The Loudon Arms Inn probably dates from the early eighteenth century, and is a rather fine example of the traditional Scots architecture, with its corbie-stepped gable and pedimented windows at eaves level. The Loudoun Kilwinning Newmilns Masonic Lodge used the inn and Robert Burns came here on 17 March 1786 to be installed as an honorary member. Another old inn, the Black Bull, was erected in 1829 but was later converted for banking purposes and is now occupied by the Clydesdale Bank. On the opposite side of the street is Brown's Institute, the gift of Miss Martha Brown of Lanfine to the burgh in 1870.

The former Council House of Newmilns is a small, but attractive building overlooking a widening of the street, erected by the 4th Earl of Loudoun. The building dates from 1739 and is quite ornamental for a small Scots burgh, being adorned with arched windows on the first floor (reached by a double forestair), corbie-steps on the gable, and an attractive belfry with its bell of 1547. As with most townhouses of the period, the ground floor contains vaults that were used as the burgh gaol. It was used until 1898.

Newmilns was one of the villages that took to the co-operative movement with zeal. There are no co-operative shops in operation there today, but the legacy of the period survives in some fine buildings. The best of these is the large sandstone shop occupying the corner of Main Street and Doitburn Road. This was erected in 1900 to plans of Andrew & Newlands, the corner tower being a distinctive feature on the arrival at the town centre. In June 1908 the shop was gutted by fire. The building was restored, and is now occupied by flats.

Lady Flora's Institute was erected in 1875–7 as a school for young girls, but latterly was used as a public hall. F. T. Pilkington designed the institute, this was eventually closed in 1981, but the building was restored as a nursing home. In front of the institute, in the attractive garden area, stands the burgh war memorial, a marble base with a statue of a soldier, erected in 1922 and commemorating 138 dead from the Great War and 40 from the Second World War.

Lady Flora Hastings was born in 1806, daughter of the 1st Marquis of Hastings and Lady Flora Mure Campbell, Countess of Loudoun. Lady Flora was a Lady of the Bedchamber to the Duchess of Kent, Queen Victoria's mother. A rumour was started that she was pregnant, causing a scandal in the Royal household, which rocked the early reign of Victoria. She died in Buckingham Palace on 5 July 1839 and was brought back to Loudoun Castle where her corpse lay for a week before being interred in the vault at Loudoun Kirk. It turned out that she suffered from an infected liver, which resulted in her swollen stomach. Lady Flora's poems were published, raising £700, and her sister, the Marchioness of Bute, gifted £12,000, allowing the institute to be erected in her memory. Nearby is the Morton Hall, erected with red sandstone in 1896–8 to plans by Arthur Harrison of Birmingham. This was the gift of William Morton, who was the senior partner in a local lace manufacturer.

The west end of Newmilns extends along the side of the main road, the old houses being typical examples of weavers' dwellings. One or two have quite early date stones. Beyond the Huggin Craig Burn bridge are a number of larger villas, including the old manse of the town, located on

St Margaret's Hill. This was erected in the eighteenth century and is a good example of the traditional style. The manse has associations with Robert Burns, who visited Revd Dr George Lawrie (1729–1878) here. A window inscribed by Burns still survives in the Dick Institute, but was unfortunately broken in 1949. In the manse kitchen Eleanor Allan Moore, one of the Glasgow school, painted a self-portrait, known as 'Marmalade'. The more modern houses at the western extremity of Newmilns, known as Gilfoot, were laid out on Garden City principles in the 1940s. The last buildings in the town are the primary school of 1964 (built to replace the public school of 1894, which was burned down in 1960) and the fire station.

The vagaries of parish boundaries has meant that the part of Newmilns that lies on the south side of the river Irvine is officially known as Greenholm, and was never really part of the old burgh. It was only in 1872 that the two communities were united as the Police Burgh of Newmilns and Greenholm. Greenholm has a few streets of houses in it, but is more industrial in nature, and is home to the Vesuvius Crucible Company. The Royal Bank building is one of the southern community's finest buildings, erected in the Victorian period and incorporating a three-storey tower. This building was originally erected around 1890 for the Mitchell family, owners of Johnstone Shields Ltd. The house was modelled on Brodick Castle and the windows contain stained glass depicting the writers Burns, Scott, Ramsay, Tannahill and Hogg. Newmilns railway station was located at Greenholm, even although the railway did actually cross the river by a twenty-six arch viaduct that still survives, dissecting Newmilns village green. The railway came this way in 1860, the station serving the community from then until 1964.

The extensive Loudoun Castle estate lies north of Galston and west of Newmilns. The estate is no longer the grand affair it once was, for the castle has been in ruins since 1941 when it was destroyed by fire, and much of the land has been sold off. Part of the former castle grounds now form the Loudoun Gowf Club, which retains the older spelling of golf. The eighteen-hole golf course dates from 1908 but occupies the flat land north of the main road that was for centuries known as the Gowf Field. The course is 6,016 yards in length, a par 68. Within the course, at its eastern end, are the remnants of a Neolithic burial cairn.

Loudoun Castle is an ancient structure that has been extended over the years. The oldest part is probably fifteenth century work, now located at the east end of the present structure, on top of which the highest tower was erected, rising through seven storeys. King David I granted a charter to James de Loudoun in 1190 of the lands forming the parish. His

Loudoun Castle ruins

daughter married a Crawford, taking the estate to that family, but simultaneously acquiring the hereditary sheriffdom of Ayr. The lands passed to the Campbells in 1303 and remained their possession for centuries thereafter. The hereditary sheriffdom was abolished in 1747. In 1804 the Countess of Loudoun and her husband, the 2nd Earl of Moira, commissioned Archibald Elliot to rebuild the castle, and he enclosed the old tower in a massive Gothic pile that became known as the Windsor of the North. Within were ninety rooms, the entrance hall being seventy feet by thirty feet in size, open to the roof. The Earl of Moira was later to become the Marquis of Hastings. The immediate area around the castle is now the Loudoun Castle theme park, which attracts children and their parents from all over the country. Here can be found the adventure rides associated with theme parks, as well as a tearoom and shop, located in the stable block of 1764, and a children's pet area. The walled gardens of 1801 are being restored. In the grounds is the 800-year old Loudoun yew tree.

The woodlands around Loudoun Castle are home to a number of other antiquities. The ancient Norman motte hill rises above the Bowhill Burn. Here stood Arclowdun Castle, Loudoun's predecessor. Further up the same stream is another mound known as the Judge's Hill. The Loudoun Yew is reputedly the site of the signing of the Article of Union between Scotland and England in 1707. The 3rd Earl of Loudoun was instrumental in drawing up the document. Among the farms at the north-west end of Loudoun parish can be found the old Castle Hill of Redding, and another Castle Hill at Alton.

The Alton Burn flows past the Castle Hill on its way towards the river Irvine. Just short of the river it passes the tiny hamlet of Loudoun Kirk, named after the old parish church of Loudoun, which stands in ruins within the old graveyard. Alicia Campbell established the church in 1451 in memory of her husband, Sir John. The surviving building is the

Loudoun burial vault, which probably dates from the sixteenth century, and restored by the Marquis of Bute in 1898. Here lie the Earls of Loudoun and their families for many generations. Also buried in the vault is Lady Flora Hastings. In the graveyard can be found a martyr's grave, commemorating Thomas Fleming, killed at the Battle of Drumclog in 1679, and a memorial to Janet Little, the 'Scottish Milkmaid', a poet and contemporary of Burns.

# 9

# Mauchline, Catrine, Sorn and Muirkirk

THE ANCIENT PARISH OF Mauchline or Kylesmuir was divided to create smaller parishes of Mauchline, Sorn and Muirkirk. Muirkirk was separated in 1626 and Sorn was detached in 1792. Each of these parishes has a village at its centre, although the parish of Sorn has one other village within it, Catrine, which is actually larger than the mother village.

Mauchline is an ancient village. It stands on the western slopes of Mauchline Hill, a fairly high piece of ground north of the river Ayr. Why a village should grow there is a mystery, for water has been a problem for the community for many years. Indeed, the oldest artesian well in Ayrshire was sunk here to allow water to spout from the sandstone basin below. In recent years the village has been connected to a supply that originates from Glen Afton at New Cumnock. The early church had a strong hold on the community, for the Abbots of Melrose Abbey had a base here. The village was created a Burgh of Barony in 1510 for the abbots and in 1707 became a Burgh of Regality for the Earl of Loudoun.

The old castle of Mauchline is also known as Abbot Hunter's Tower, and still stands somewhat hidden in the centre of town. The tower dates from around 1450 and rises through two vaulted storeys to a lost parapet. Some of the stonework is quite ecclesiastical in style, for here can be found ribbed vaults, and a bracket and niche over the original doorway, which probably held a statue of a saint. Mauchline Castle was owned by the Cistercians of Melrose Abbey as an outpost to guard their extensive estates in the west. In 1606 they passed to Hugh, Lord Loudoun. The tower was used as a prison during the years of the Covenant. The adjoining wing was added at various times, but some of it may be as old as the tower, for here can be found a vaulted ground floor, indicative of great age. In the eighteenth century the tower and adjoining house was home to Gavin Hamilton, a lawyer and factor on the Loudoun estates. He was associated with Robert Burns, being a patron and friend, and to whom Burns dedicated the Kilmarnock Edition. Burns's wedding is thought to have taken place in Hamilton's office, which was located somewhere around Castle Street, though others think it took place in the castle's dining room. The tower is still roofed and being attached to the adjoining house is still relatively well cared for.

The old church of Mauchline stands on an ancient site, where the thirteenth century chapel of St Michael stood. The present church is a fine sandstone structure, opened in August 1829, and designed by William Annan of Southbar, who, although an amateur, has created a most distinctive Gothic edifice. It has a tall foursquare tower that contains a public clock and is topped by four slender tourelles. Inside can be seen the old Covenanters' flag of Mauchline, flown at the battles of Mauchline Muir, Drumclog and Bothwell Bridge. The church has a Willis pipe organ of 1888 (formerly in Strathbungo Church, Glasgow), and a bell cast in 1742. A stained glass window of 1903 commemorates Sir Claud Alexander of Ballochmyle.

In the graveyard can be seen many headstones and memorials associated with Robert Burns's time in the village. Here lie, among others, Revd William 'Daddy' Auld (1708–91), Gavin Hamilton, James Hamilton, Mary Morrison, Robert Wilson, William Fisher, Nance Tannock, James Bryan, Poosie Nansie and four infant children of Burns and Jean Armour. A plaque on the church wall contains a plan indicating their whereabouts. Here also lie the Alexanders of Ballochmyle, founders of Catrine, and William and Andrew Smith, box makers. An old stone with the dates 1796 and 1885 was rescued from the now demolished North Church. A small headstone commemorates James Smith, Covenanter. The Battle of Mauchline Muir took place in 1648 when the opposing forces of Scots Royalists and Covenanters met. General Middleton's Royalist army prevailed, and something in the order of thirty to forty men were killed. Around sixty Covenanters were captured and held for trial, but they were eventually pardoned. The site of the battle is located south of the railway, in the field behind the present cemetery in Barskimming Road.

There is today only one church in Mauchline, a surprisingly low figure considering how the village has grown in recent years to become a desirable location for commuters. There were, however, two other church buildings at one time. The Abbey Free Church, erected in 1884, stood behind Loudoun Street in Horwood Place. In 1925 it merged with the Walker Memorial Church and was latterly a cinema before being demolished. The Walker Memorial Church was located at the Knowe and had been erected in 1884–5, replacing the old box kirk of the Burgher Congregation, which itself had been erected in 1796. Baldie & Tennant of Glasgow designed the Walker building and it was erected at a cost of £2,300. After the merger with the Abbey Church it became known as Mauchline North Church, but was united with the parish church in 1975 and subsequently demolished in 1983.

The original town centre of Mauchline has changed considerably from the early nineteenth century. In 1820 a new roadway was built through the town centre, replacing the old and narrow streets, which then became back lanes. Thus Earl Grey Street was created, each building having to be erected to a similar style. Here can be found the old Black Bull Inn, perhaps of 1776, with its arched pend that formerly led to stables. On the north side of the Cross, New Road was built, allowing traffic to avoid the narrow lane of Castle Street.

Cumnock Road is the continuation of Earl Grey Street. The roadway is lined by some substantial houses, including Beechgrove at the end of Cowgate, Haplan with its Baronial round tower, Viewfield of around 1800, probably an old farmhouse rebuilt and a rather fine sandstone double-villa (St Elmo and Estcourt). The war memorial at the Catrine road junction was unveiled on 20 May 1927 by Sir Hugh Trenchard, and built to plans of A. C. Thomson, a massive Ballochmyle sandstone base supporting a cylindrical column. This stands at a point known as the Brackenstanes.

Mauchline: Robert Burns's house in Castle Street

Castle Street leaves Mauchline Cross and heads for the back of the churchyard and the church hall. It is lined with some old buildings, including the important Burns House, a sandstone double-storey house where Robert Burns set up home after his marriage to Jean Armour. The house is now a museum, open throughout the summer months. It has the original room in which Burns lived, but the rest of the building has been altered inside. Here can be seen a number of original Burns artefacts, including a few manuscripts, a silver watch, razors and a walking stick.

The museum also has a splendid selection of local historical items, including a fine collection of Mauchline Ware (small wooden treen that was made locally). Most of this was decorated with a highly polished finish, and could incorporate transfers depicting scenes, or else tartan finishes. Here also are examples of curling stones made locally. The firm of Andrew Kay has been making stones in Mauchline since 1864 and is today the only manufacturer of curling stones in Great Britain. Granite from Ailsa Craig is still used for the base of the stones, the bulk of which is composed of Welsh granite. On the wall of the museum is a bronze relief of C. R. Cowie who gifted the house to the Glasgow and District Burns Association. The plaque was the work of G. H. Paulin. On the opposite side of Castle Street is the old house that was Nanse Tinnock's Inn, perhaps dating from 1712, and now part of the museum complex, and next to it is the former shop occupied by 'the divine' Jean Markland.

Mauchline strengthened its links to the Bard still further in December 2002 when a statute to Jean Armour – the first anywhere in the world – was unveiled at the Cross. Designed by Ruaraig Maciver it was cast in bronze by Beltane Studios in Peebles. The statue depicts the young Jean, aged 23, and the idea to erect it came from the Mauchline Burns Club. It is only yards from where she and Burns lived.

The main street of Mauchline is Loudoun Street, which extends west from the Cross. The street is quite narrow for modern traffic, being lined with a fine selection of traditional buildings. One of these is Poosie Nansie's Inn, which dates from 1700. This will forever be associated with Burns, for here he set his fine poem, 'The Jolly Beggars'. On the opposite side of the Cowgate, which was at one time the main road south, a plaque marks the site of the Whitefoord Arms Inn, where Burns himself drank. Further on, on the opposite side of the road, is the entrance gateway to Mauchline Castle. Nearby is the Loudoun Arms Hotel, again connected with Burns. In his day this was MacLelland's Inn, where Burns took part in a reading society. The Loudoun Spout flows freely from the ground here, the marble surround erected in 2000 to commemorate the millennium. This is Ayrshire's earliest artesian well, sunk in 1763. The old arched gateway at one time led to Netherplace House, seat of the Campbell, then Hamilton-Campbell family. An old Scots mansion of around 1620, it was considerably extended in the Tudor style, the foundation stone of the newer work being laid on 4 April 1827. The house developed dry rot and was demolished in 1956. A small memorial affixed to the gateway commemorates the Hamilton Campbell family that owned it.

New Road has a few old buildings at its southern end, but it soon leaves the old village behind. One of the shops has a plaque on it marking the original showroom associated with the Smith brothers, box makers. The old factory was located immediately to the north of this, but it was burned down and the present fire station of 1963 by Ian McGill was erected on the site. The practice of making boxes in Mauchline dates back to the 1820s. The older boxes were made to hold hones, but latterly small fancy boxes were made from sycamore, and sold as gifts. In New Road stood Mauchline's Temperance Hall, of around 1870, used for local meetings and events. It was demolished in 1965.

Mauchline's High Street is the original main road to Edinburgh. It climbs gradually to the top of Mauchline Hill, which is a fine viewpoint. On the way the street is lined with some interesting old buildings, including a listed little summer-house at Springfield House, decorated with Gothic features. On the Loan is a memorial erected in 1830 marking the spot where five Covenanters were hanged in 1685. Two other memorials commemorating this event can be found built into the wall of the primary school. The sandstone building of the school itself dates from 1889, though it has been extended a number of times.

On the east side of Kilmarnock Road is the 1930s housing scheme of Beechwood and Jean Armour Drive. At the top of the hill, where the Tarbolton Road strikes west, stands the tall National Burns Memorial. This is a fine baronial tower built of red sandstone and rising over three floors to a viewing platform. The foundation stone was laid on 23 July 1896 and it was opened on 17 May 1898. The architect was William Fraser of Glasgow, winner of a competition in which a dozen architects entered. The tower, which rises sixty-seven feet in height, cost £1,515 to erect. North of the tower, in the gusset between the roads, are the National Cottage Homes, the first six of which were erected in 1897 to house deserving pensioners rent-free. The estate of James Dick paid for another ten in 1911. Five more cottages were added in 1931 (including Bulloch), and the last one was gifted in 1938. Beyond the original houses, which were erected in sandstone in a distinctive Scots Renaissance style, are the Jean Armour Homes, less impressive externally, but just as welcoming to their tenants.

Tarbolton Road from the Burns monument strikes north-west. The first farm on the right is East Mossgiel, the farm that Burns tenanted from 1784–8. It was here that he wrote some of his finest work; the field to the south-east of the steading is where he turned up the field mouse celebrated in his poem, 'To a Mouse', and that behind the steading is where he turned over a 'Mountain Daisy' with the plough. Near the farm road-end is a memorial cairn commemorating a large horse-drawn ploughing match held here in 1996. The event was attended by almost

10,000 people on one day, gathered to watch Clydesdale horses pull ploughs in the way that they would have been in Burns's time.

Beyond West Mossgiel is the Mossgiel or Skeoch Tunnel, where the Kilmarnock to Dumfries railway line passes below Skeoch Hill. The tunnel is over 650 yards in length, one of the longest in the county. The round stone walls protect ventilation shafts, important when the trains were pulled by steam engines. The tunnel was excavated in 1848.

To the east of the A76, beyond Knowehead Farm, is the former Mauchline Colliery. The Caprington & Auchlochan Coal Company, the manager of which lived at Beechgrove House in Mauchline, sank this pit in 1925. By the 1950s, the mine was part of the National Coal Board and employed 800 men. The mine operated for forty-one years until it was eventually closed on 26 August 1966. Today, only the flattened bing remains to mark the site, even the railway siding having been filled in.

The A76 and the B744 make a crossroads at a small clachan known as Crosshands. The junction was quite a busy one in years past, and the older buildings here formed an inn for stagecoaches and other travellers. Woodholm was a school from 1848 until the 1940s. North of here stands Rodinghead House, perched on a low hill above the road. The house was probably erected in the late eighteenth century as a factor's house for Loudoun estates and was used latterly as a dower house for Carnell Castle, but in 1964 it was acquired by Lord Weir and remains his family home. The northern extremity of Mauchline parish is here marked by the Cessnock Water, which makes a sinuous route through a deep glen, here and there tumbling over waterfalls.

East of the A76, within Mauchline parish, is a stretch of farmland criss-crossed by minor roads on which it is quite easy to get lost. These roads meander back and forth, up and down the rolling countryside, seemingly linking farmsteads in no particular order. There is nothing of any great significance hereabouts, other perhaps than the site of the birthplace of the poet and author, Adam Brown Todd, which was located at Craighall. This croft stood west of South Auchenbrain Farm. Auchmillan was the site of an old mill, and here today is a long-established joinery and building contractor.

The countryside south of Mauchline, beyond the railway line, drops to the river Ayr valley. The river carves for itself a deep glen hereabouts, and at various places takes on the form of a rocky gorge. The Barskimming estate straddles the gorge, part of it being in Stair parish to the south. The stable block lies on the north side of the river, with Old Barskimming House located to the south, reached by crossing the rather grand bridge of 1788. The house is three storeys plus an attic tall, a fine classical box erected in 1883 to replace an older house of 1771 that was destroyed by fire in 1882. The stable block is a rather grand structure of 1774, comprising archways, Venetian windows, and a central tower. The stables have been converted into dwellings. Drives and walks permeate the wooded policies, the Sand Walk extending westward from Barskimming Bridge to the bridge at Barskimming House. Further west, at the top of Netheraird Holm, is a cave carved from the rock. Another can be more readily visited on the north side of the Barskimming Bridge, opposite Mauchline sewage works. Here stood an old cottage that was occupied by Kate Kemp, a young woman Burns admired.

The deep red sandstone for which Mauchline (or Ballochmyle) is famous lies beneath the surface of the ground here, and a number of quarries formerly hewed the rock from the ground. Remains of these can be found at Mosshead (established 1891), now filled with water, or at Haugh Road, now filled with domestic refuse! The sandstone was of a fine quality, much in demand for building, and most deep red sandstone buildings in Ayrshire owe their origin to the Mauchline quarries. The last quarry closed in the 1950s.

On the hillside above the sewage works is Mauchline Creamery, built in 1938 by the Scottish Milk Marketing Board to convert locally produced milk into milk powder. The architect was Alex Mair, though the distinctive 1930s style of architecture has been stripped back and lost over the years. It was later used for the processing and packaging of cheese. On the same road can be found Mauchline's new cemetery, where grave of Marcus Bain, local quarry-master, can be seen.

From the war memorial Station Road drops to the former railway station, opened on 9 August 1848 and closed on 6 December 1965. There have been many campaigns to have the station reopened, but none of these has come to fruition. A road leaves Station Road at an angle and heads south to the Haugh, which lies by the side of the River Ayr. Here is the rather unusual Swiss-style building, the Ballochmyle Creamery, latterly used as an optical works. The mill was opened around 1900. Robert McCrone was the proprietor and one of his sons was Guy McCrone (1898–1977), author of many novels including the *Wax Fruit* trilogy, which is still in print.

East of the Haugh is Kingencleugh, access to which is made from the A76. The present Kingencleugh House was erected around 1765 but rebuilt in 1957 to plans of Mervyn Noad. It was a dower house for Ballochmyle estate and is still the residence of the Alexander of Ballochmyle baronets. Over the doorway is an elephant, crest of the family. Claud Alexander (1753–1809) acquired Ballochmyle estate in 1785, having made his fortune in India, where he was involved with the East India Company. In the field behind Kingencleugh House are the ruins of Kingencleugh Castle, an L-plan tower house erected around 1600. The house was built by the Campbells to replace an older building in which John Knox preached in 1556. The tower itself was abandoned when the present Kingencleugh House was erected.

The main road and railway have to cross the deep Ayr valley to the south of Mauchline, and both require large bridges to do so. The old roadway snaked its way down to the valley bottom and back up again, crossing the river by the old Howford Bridge. This was erected in the early eighteenth century and has a parapet with mortise and tenoned masonry to give it extra strength. Robert Burns' father-in-law, James Armour, is reputed to have been involved in its erection. Unfortunately the bridge is no longer strong enough to support traffic, and it is only open to pedestrians. The bridge was bypassed on 28 October 1962 when the present Howford Bridge was opened, spanning the glen in one huge 300 feet crossing. The bridge, which is made from pre-stressed concrete, was engineered by F. A. MacDonald & Partners and cost £294,000 to build.

The railway crosses the gorge by the Ballochmyle viaduct. This was erected between 8 April 1847 (when the foundation stone was laid) and 12 March 1848 (when the last stone was put in place) from sandstone quarried locally. Crossing the gorge in seven arches, the central span, which is 180 feet in length, is one of the wonders of Victorian engineering, and is still listed in the *Guinness Book of World Records* as the longest masonry arch in Britain. The bridge was the scene of some unusual attempts at driving a golf ball over it from a nearby promontory in 1860 by 'Old' Tom Morris (1821–1908). Morris could only hit the balls onto the pathway, 400 feet above him, which in itself was a remarkable feat with the old gutta ball. In the gorge between the road and railway, by the side of a small stream, is a sandstone rock-face on which is carved Bronze Age cup and ring markings. These were only discovered in 1986 when a plantation was being felled, but is probably the largest single collection of such markings in Ayrshire.

Ballochmyle House is one of the most important old mansions in Ayrshire, but unfortunately has lain derelict for many years. A tower house, home of the Reid family in the late seventeenth century, originally occupied the site. In 1760 Allan Whitefoord built a new house on the same site, the plans for which were furnished by John Adam, brother of the more famous Robert. Sir John Whitefoord lost a considerable amount of money in the Ayr Bank Crash of 1772 and was forced to sell the estate to the Alexanders in 1785. In 1886–90 Sir Claud Alexander extended the house considerably by adding a new sandstone block in front, in a Jacobean style, almost doubling its size. The architect was Hew Montgomerie Wardrop. The front doorway of this house is distinctive for its large armorial panel. Ballochmyle was latterly the seat of the Alexander family, of which Sir Claud Alexander MP (1832–99) was created a Baronet of Ballochmyle in 1886. Ballochmyle House was taken over during the Second World War and the grounds in front of the house were laid out with temporary hospital wards. The house was originally used for staff accommodation, but due to dry rot it was eventually abandoned in 1969. The very first case of plastic surgery was carried out here during the war. The 'temporary' hospital remained in use until August 2000 when it was closed and replaced by a community hospital in Cumnock. The wards were demolished and the whole site is now being redeveloped. Ballochmyle has associations with Burns. At the time when he lived in Mauchline, Miss Wilhelmina Alexander lived at Ballochmyle. Burns referred to her as 'The Lass of Ballochmyle'. She is buried somewhere below Glasgow Airport! The Ballochmyle Golf Course was laid out on the lands of Ballochmyle House in 1937. An 18-hole course, 5,972 yards in length and par 70, the clubhouse stands by the roadside at the former gate to Ballochmyle House.

*

The village of Catrine lies in a pleasant hollow formed by the river Ayr. The valley opens out between the Sorn Hill gorge and the Braes of Ballochmyle, and the old part of the village was laid out on the level ground by the side of the river. In more recent years the Shawwood housing scheme was built on the higher ground to the south east of the old part of the community.

Catrine was a planned village, established to take advantage of the river Ayr, which was strong enough to drive the massive mill wheels that at one time existed here. In 1787 Claud Alexander built a massive mill building right in the centre of the community, so central in fact that the main road through the village had to make four right angles in order to pass around it. In style the mill was similar to the old mill building at New Lanark, with Venetian windows and pediment containing a belfry. The mill stood until 1963 when it was destroyed in a fire, and it was subsequently pulled down. The roadway was then able to make a direct route through the centre of Catrine, and the former site of the mill became Mill Square. Claud Alexander set up a partnership with David Dale (of New Lanark fame) in 1786 to ensure that the works were on a sure financial footing. Catrine mill was used to spin cotton, which was bleached elsewhere until a bleachworks was established at Catrine in

1826. The water to power the mill was taken from the river Ayr, which was dammed near Daldorch House, and channelled through tunnels to the top of the mill wheels. These were fifty feet in diameter, making them one of the largest in the country and collectively the largest water-powered unit in the world. They were finished in 1827 and worked for 120 years thereafter, being replaced by a power station built alongside the river. The pair of wheels produced 240 horsepower each.

Mill Square has traditional buildings around the southern side of it, but the northern side is rather open, destroying the effect that could be achieved if it were complete. Within the Square is a sculpture in sandstone, depicting a mill wheel, and bearing carvings representing Catrine's past. The grassy area on the south side of Mill Street was occupied by a modern mill building, erected between 1945–50, worked until 1968, and was demolished in 1987. It was latterly used as a furniture showroom, the largest in the country for a time.

West of the Square are some traditional Ayrshire buildings, including the Old Mill Inn. Ayrbank House was the mill manager's house. On the hillside above this street stands the most attractive parish church. This was erected as a chapel of ease in 1792. Paid for by Sir Claud Alexander of Ballochmyle, the church was built of pink sandstone. Paired lancet windows and a low belfry adorn the church. Overlooking the village is a smart pediment, with carved swag and round window. Inside is a Harrison & Harrison pipe organ of 1874, installed during a restoration of the building. The steep graveyard around the church has few stones of any great interest, but there can be seen some commemorating folk employed in the local mills. The Chapel Brae climbs steadily behind the church. At the foot of the brac is a single storey house dating from 1808 when it was built as a toll cottage. The road continues beyond the church to the village war memorial. This is perched on a promontory overlooking the village beneath.

The Congregational Church building dates from 1845. This church began as a Free Church, but in 1960 was taken over by the Congregational Church. The church was closed in 2002. Next door to the Congregational Church, but hidden behind a fine sandstone presbytery, is the Roman Catholic Church of St Joseph. This is a timber building, opened in May 1962. At the corner of Ballochmyle Street and Mauchline Road is the parish church hall, erected in 1836 to plans by James Ingram. This was originally the United Presbyterian, or West UF Church, but it was later used as a Masonic Hall.

On the opposite side of the road is a former gatehouse to Ballochmyle estate. From here a pathway and a steep set of steps, known as Jacob's

Ladder, made its way up to Ballochmyle House, which is perched on the hillside above, affording a fine view over the village. The street on the east side of the Square is known as St Germain Street, after the patron saint of weavers. Here is the Royal Bank building of 1874, designed by Peddie & Kinnear. There are a number of traditional buildings here, as well as a number of modern infill buildings designed in a congruous manner. The building that occupies the corner site to the north of here, along Wood and Ayr streets, is totally out of place, with its brick and steel façade.

Ayr Street leads alongside the river Ayr to one of Catrine's most pleasant spots. St Cuthbert's Street is a row of double-storey terraces overlooking the Catrine Voes, the reservoirs where water was held for the mill. The voes are now preserved by a trust, and the wetlands attract a variety of wildlife. Also in the meander of the Ayr are the Glen Catrine bonded warehouses, where a variety of whiskies and other spirits are blended and bottled. The bowling green occupies the site of an ancient chapel dedicated to St Cuthbert.

Across the river Ayr, occupying a meander of the river, is Daldorch House, now extended to form a school for autistic children. Archibald Buchanan, a director in the mill company, built the original house in 1812. An extension was added in the Victorian period, more than doubling the size. For a time the house was known as Catrinebank.

That part of Catrine located on the south side of the Ayr is known as Newton. Nether Catrine House still stands in a terrace of modern houses at the road junction. The house was erected in 1682 and was the home of Professor Dugald Stewart at the time of Burns. It was here that Burns dined in the company of Lord Daer, heir of the Earl of Selkirk, in 1786, leading to his later verses recalling when he 'dinner't wi' a lord'. The house is a traditional Scots small mansion, with crow-stepped gables, but from the south east it takes on a more Georgian appearance, with it pediment and urns. Behind here was Catrine railway station, built as the terminus of a short branch line from the Brackenhill Junction on the main Kilmarnock to Dumfries railway. The station opened on 31 August 1903 but closed to passenger traffic on 3 May 1943. The line remained in use for a number of years thereafter for goods, but the line was closed completely in 1957 and the rails lifted. Today the station site is occupied by Catrine Games Hall.

Just off Newton Street, down by the river, is the Brown Institute. This was erected in 1898 following a gift of £1,500 to build it and £500 to fit it out from A. M. Brown, a director with the firm of Finlay & Company which owned the mills from 1801 until they were eventually closed in 1968. Robert Ingram designed the building, and even although it has an attractive corner tower with clock, the location of the building means that few passers-by actually see it. Today the Institute is the village library and community centre. Within can be seen a bust of Alexander Marshall Brown of Gryffe Castle himself.

The Wilson Hall in Bridge Street, opened on 4 January 1882 to plans by Robert Ingram, is now demolished and the site occupied by old peoples' homes. The old primary school in Newton Street, erected in 1860–1 and extended in 1897, has also been demolished, replaced by a new school at Shawwood. Part of the old school complex is still used as a nursery school.

Newton Street continues past Whiteflat Farm to the A76 at the southern end of the Howford Bridge. Here stood the newer Catrine House, erected in 1819–20 for Lieutenant-Colonel Matthew Stewart, but demolished shortly after the Second World War. Only the former stable block and gardens survive, now used as a nursery and small caravan site. Beyond here are the Low and High Clews, now a small community of houses.

Catrine falls within Sorn parish, the southern boundary of which is delineated by the Dippol Burn, beyond which is Auchinleck parish. The road from Catrine to Auchinleck passes by the Logan farms, perhaps one of the places where the ancient Logans of that Ilk lived. Beyond South Logan is Glenshamrock Farm and Gilmilnscroft cottages, located in an area that formerly was home to a number of coal mines. A few old bings still survive, and the moors hereabouts are criss-crossed by the trackways of old mineral lines.

Gilmilnscroft House is an ancient building that has been extended and stripped back over the years. It was anciently a seat of the Farquhar family, but it passed into other hands for a time, before being repurchased by descendants of the family, and is today the seat of the Earl of Lindsey, descended from the Farquhars through the female line. The oldest part of the house perhaps dates from 1682, with an extension of 1708, but the building was extended considerably in the 1830s and 1888 to create a sizeable mansion. This was used as a school for a time. Many of the Victorian additions were removed in 1968 to create a more manageable house, one that retains the traditional block with its conically roofed towers, but with some 1830s work.

North east of Gilmilnscroft, lying in the valley of the Ayr, is Glenlogan House, another old mansion that dates from the mid-eighteenth century. Hugh Logan of that Ilk was an owner in the late eighteenth century. J. G. Stephen, who owned a shipyard at Linthouse in Glasgow, at one time owned the house and he established an experimental model ship tank here. In the woods above the house is an old tree associated with

Revd Alexander Peden, the famous Covenanting minister, who probably hid in it at one time.

The minor road along the south side of the Ayr peters out by the three Heilar farms. Between Upper and Mid Heilar the river Ayr makes its way over a series of small waterfalls. These can be quite impressive after heavy rain. At Shiel Farm are remnants of mines, and at one time there were miners' rows here, now long gone.

The B713 drops down into Sorn, reaching the village across the New Bridge of 1871, built by G. Reid of Catrine, a building firm that only went bankrupt in 2000. Main Street is more open than it was in past years, for the older roadside buildings have been demolished in many cases and the replacements erected back behind gardens. There are a few old buildings surviving, however, such as the old woollen mill, near Dalgain. The Dalgain Bridge is inscribed, 'Jean Smith Mahon 1778'. The Sorn Inn was established in the eighteenth century to satisfy the needs of travellers between Ayr and Edinburgh. Another old inn, the Greyhound, which was established in 1700, has in recent years been converted into houses. The village school, with its Venetian windows and clock tower, was erected in 1850 and extended in 1874–5. Next to it is the village hall, a building of 1954.

At the west end of Sorn is the most interesting part of the village. Here can be found the old parish church, which dates from 1658, making it a church of the Commonwealth. It stands in an attractive graveyard, which is full of interesting old stones. Here can be found the grave of George Wood, the last, and youngest (at sixteen years of age), martyr to die for the Covenant. The graveyard is also the resting place of a number of local landowners, including the owners of Sorn Castle. The church itself is a fine building, little more than a single storey T-plan building built in the local pink sandstone. The church was rebuilt in 1826 and restored in 1910 to plans of Harry E. Clifford. External stairways lead to the lairds' lofts, and inside can be seen some fine stained glass commemorating local families. On an external wall is a memorial to Revd Lewis Balfour, who was the uncle of Robert Louis Stevenson, and from whom RLS is said to have received his middle name of Louis, despite the difference in spelling. On the southern gable hangs a set of jougs, used to lock up malefactors. Across from the church can be found Sorn's Old Bridge. This is a high humpbacked bridge with a narrow roadway across it. The bridge dates from 1710 and is still in use by traffic. Next to the bridge is the former Dalgain Mill, now converted into the church hall. Adjoining this is a small area of garden, scene of one of BBC television's *Beechgrove Garden* projects.

The B743 leaves the west end of Sorn and snakes its way alongside the river. Where the Cleuch Burn is bridged, next to an attractive baronial gate house, the traveller can get a glimpse downstream to the impressive location of Sorn Castle, perched on its rock above the dammed river. A minor drive leads to the castle from here, but the main entrance is located further along the B743, opposite the junction with the Galston Road. The gatehouse at Sorn is a fine baronial building, incorporating a large arched pend, through which vehicles can pass. It was erected in 1865 to plans by David Bryce. The garden's gateway was erected in 1913 to plans by Henry Clifford & Lunan. The drive leads to the front of the castle, which has a large porte cochère. This was added in the 1907 extensions, the work of Clifford & Lunan.

Sorn Castle

Sorn Castle is one of Ayrshire's architectural and historical gems. The grounds are regularly open to the public, pathways leading through the woods from a parking area at the old saw mill. The castle itself is open during the summer, and visitors are shown the main rooms on the principal floor. These include the large entrance hall, dining room, drawing room, library and billiard room. The rooms are finely furnished, and within can be seen the Sorn parish Covenanters' banner and a drum associated with the period. The oldest part of the castle is the foursquare tower located at the back of the present building, occupying the rock high above the river. This probably dates from the fourteenth century though it was rebuilt around 1490. In 1793 this was extended to the north-east to plans by William Railton, increasing the size considerably. Further additions were made in 1864–5 to plans of David Bryce, and again in 1908–10 when the new entrance and billiard room were added to plans of Henry E. Clifford. The castle was anciently a seat of the Keith family. It passed to the Hamiltons of Cadzow and then to the Setons of Winton. The 2nd Earl of Winton sold the estate to the Earl of Loudoun around 1680, and in the eighteenth century it was home to the improving dowager Countess of Loudoun, who lived here for fifty years and died just short of her one hundredth birthday. In 1903 the MacIntyre family, who remain in possession, acquired the castle.

Sorn parish extends considerably to the north-east of the village, but the good agricultural land soon peters out as the land rises to the moors and hills. The Auchmannoch, Grange and Weitshaw muirs are used for shooting grouse. Auchmannoch House dates from the seventeenth century, and is a fine Scots mansion, sporting corbie-stepped gables. Over the door-way is a Campbell coat of arms. North of here is Auchencloigh Farm where, in 1626, the Covenanting minister, Alexander Peden, was born. The actual house in which he was born still survives, but has been super-seded as the farmhouse.

The moors rise to the hills of Distinkhorn, the summit of which lies just beyond the Sorn boundary, and Blackside, the highest in the vicinity. Blackside is a large composite hill, with a number of summits, the highest of which is known as Wedder Hill, 1,411 feet above sea level. The summits known as Glen Garr and Blacksidend are topped by Bronze Age burial cairns. At Reoch Hill, on Auchmannoch Muir, can be found a prehistoric enclosure, occupying a low eminence on the moor. The road from Sorn to Muirkirk leaves the river Ayr behind at Sorn, and keeps a respectable distance for the remainder of the journey. Tincorn Hill is now a major quarry. On the southern side of the road, on a promontory between the Wyndy Burn and the river Ayr, is a major earthwork that formed a motte and bailey.

*

Muirkirk parish lies east of Sorn parish. It was separated from Mauchline in 1631 and a new church planted on the moors, known originally as the Muir Kirk of Kyle. The parish was for many years a poor one, struggling to survive on the wild moors that were little more than peat bogs and rough ground. Things changed considerably in the late eighteenth century with the development of ironstone and coal reserves, resulting in the foundation of ironworks at Glenbuck in 1794 and Muirkirk itself in 1787. The village of Muirkirk is today in decline, for the mines that once supported the population have long gone, and most residents have to travel some distance to find work. Some of the houses have been demolished, and parts of the community are much more open than they once were. The older part of the village is located at the east end, where the ancient clachan of Garan, or Garron, was located. The parish church stands in its graveyard at the east end of the village, at the top end of the Kirkgreen. The church dates from 1812–14, and is one of the few surviving works by the architect, William Stark. It is distinguished by its squat tower and heavy buttresses, and cost £1,876 to build. It includes a stained glass window by Stephen Adam, formerly located in a church at Kames that was erected in 1903–4 and demolished in December 1952.

The churchyard has a number of old stones, including the grave of the Covenanting martyr, John Smith. Here also lies the poetess, Isobel, or 'Tibby', Pagan (1741–1821) who wrote the original verses of 'Ca' the Yowes' that were later improved by Burns. Pagan was born at New Cumnock but moved to Muirkirk where she ran a small inn, or drinking shop, by the side of the Garpel Water, serving the miners. An old bridge across the Garpel is known locally as Tibbie's Brig, and there are remains of a memorial to her at its southern end. Another stone commemorates John Lapraik (1727–1807), a minor poet who corresponded in verse with Burns. An obelisk stands in memory of John Finlayson (1778–1826) who invented Finlayson's Plough and Harrow; and a memorial has a representation of a wildcat that is claimed to have killed the two young children commemorated here. West of the parish church stands the Roman Catholic Church of St Thomas. This was erected in 1906 using materials transported from Belgium. A Catholic primary school had been erected in 1882. The new St Thomas's RC primary school, opened in 1973 at Stitt Place, was closed in June 1996.

Main Street, Muirkirk, is lined with houses old and new, a mixture of buildings in this remote village. The former Post Office was opened on 1 July 1931. Here also is the Clydesdale Bank building, and former school. Main Street school had been erected in 1815 and closed in 1970. The United Presbyterian Church formerly stood at the west end of the street, opened in 1824. It closed in 1915 and was converted into a cinema but was eventually demolished.

Glasgow Street leaves the village centre, climbing gradually on its way towards the Strathaven Moor. A memorial stone commemorating the martyrs of the parish lies in the memorial garden at the corner of Glasgow Street. This was originally built into the front wall of Glenbuck church, but moved here when that building was eventually demolished. The old church hall on the left dates from 1845. It was opened on 13 April 1845 as the Chalmers Free Church, but later became known as the UF and then Wellwood Church, before being closed and used as the church hall. On the opposite side of the road stands the disused Congregational Church, erected in 1893–4 and closed on 11 December 1966. The church replaced an older building, still standing further down the street. It was latterly used as a gospel hall, but is now converted into a house. The present Muirkirk cemetery lies at the north end of the village. Within the older part of it is an obelisk commemorating all of the Covenanting martyrs of the parish, which Charles Howatson of Glenbuck erected in 1887 as part of Queen Victoria's Golden Jubilee celebrations.

West of the Glasgow Road junction the old buildings of the village begin to reduce in number and the modern Smallburn housing scheme comes into view, built on the hillside north of the main road. These houses date from the 1930s and were erected to replace the old miners' rows that were being demolished at that time. The post-war prefabs that stood here have long disappeared. One old cottage surviving is the Toll Cottage. The war memorial for Muirkirk takes the form of an ornamental gateway leading to the public park. The Glenbuck war memorial was also located here after that village succumbed to opencast workings. Here also can be seen an old millstone, found by the side of the Garpel Water.

Furnace Road strikes south from the A70, heading for Muirkirk's 'Southside'. At the corner stands the Black Bull Hotel, originally known as the Eglinton Arms. This was a coaching inn established in the eighteenth century. An older coaching inn was the 'Great Inn' of 1790, erected opposite the junction of Furnace Road. A fine three-storey block, the inn closed around 1875 and was converted to a house for the manager of the ironworks. The building was demolished in the 1950s and the site used for the present primary school, which opened on 3 November 1970. Furnace Road School was erected around 1810, though it was considerably extended later in the century. It was closed in 1968 due to subsidence. Furnace Road continues towards the former community of Kames, which had numerous miners' rows spread about the moor. Most of these have been demolished, leaving only the former institute of 1903–4 and the Ironworks Cottages alongside. Muirkirk station existed to the east of Furnace Road, on the Ayr to Lanark line. The station opened in 1848 but was closed to passengers in 1964.

The Muirkirk ironworks were located to the east of Furnace Road. Building of the works commenced in August 1787 and James Ewing & Co erected three furnaces. The first such works established in Ayrshire, they produced iron that was rolled and forged. There were also ammonia, oil and pitch works associated with the complex. The strange tower, known locally as the 'Castle', distinguished the ironworks, which was more ecclesiastical in appearance. The works remained in production until 1923 and the 'Castle' was demolished in 1968. The gasworks at Muirkirk were the last ones still operating in Scotland, producing town gas before the arrival of natural gas. The works, which had been established in 1859, and gave Muirkirk the distinction of having the first public gas lights, closed in 1979.

The 'Old Sanquhar Road' continues south from Kames, originally part of a coach road linking Glasgow with Carlisle. The roadway was constructed in 1793 but was later abandoned in favour of more suitable routes to the west and east. Today the section between Muirkirk and Sanquhar disintegrates to a mere footpath in places. Here can be found Muirkirk Golf Club, a 9-hole, 5,383 yard, par 67 course. Kaimeshill House stood nearby, another large house occupied by a colliery manager. It was erected in 1790 and demolished in 1956.

Beyond Springhill cottage can be found a cairn commemorating the road maker, John Loudoun McAdam. The cairn was erected on the site of the tar kilns, which he managed for the 9th Earl of Dundonald (1749–1831). The works operated from 1786 until around 1825. The British Tar Company, as it was called, proved to be unsuccessful, and McAdam had to abandon the project.

From near Kames a footpath makes its way to the summit of Cairn Table, the highest hill in the locality at 1,945 feet. The summit is crowned by a number of Bronze Age burial cairns, but these have been rebuilt over the centuries by visitors. Volunteers erected the large cairn on the summit from 17 July until August 1920 to commemorate those who suffered in the Great War. Revd John Henderson dedicated it on 23 August 1920.

Wardlaw Hill to the west of here is also crowned by a couple of Bronze Age burial cairns, in one of which was found a bronze finger-ring. Like Cairn Table, Wardlaw Hill has a later memorial cairn marking its summit. This was erected in memory of John George Alexander Baird of Wellwood (1854–1917). Baird was a local landowner and manager in the steelworks. He was MP for Central Glasgow from 1886–1906, and in 1910 wrote a small book entitled *Muirkirk in Bygone Days*. He was munificent to the parish of Muirkirk, donating the kirk organ in 1884, adding to the minister's stipend in 1910 and donating the Baird Institute to the village in 1888. This stood next to the war memorial gates, but was demolished in 1957.

An extensive grouse moor occupies the northern slopes of Wardlaw

Hill. Among the heather and heath can be found a number of other burial cairns, as well as six prehistoric enclosures where cremations were found. Also on the moor can be found some old shielings. Upper Wellwood Farm (which has a marriage stone of 1606 rebuilt in the wall) has a martyr's grave lying by the side of the Proscribe Burn, commemorating Covenanter William Adam. The Wellwood estate no longer has a mansion at its centre, for this was demolished in 1926. The old house was erected in 1600 for the Campbells and extended in 1740. It was sold to Keith Stewart in 1785 and was considerably extended in the Gothic style in 1878. The house was latterly home to the Bairds. Within the wood at Kineknowe are the remnants of another Bronze Age cairn.

The Sorn Road leaves the A70 at Entryhead, passing the Dalfram and Greenock farms. Between West Dalfram and Townhead of Greenock (dated 1885) the river Ayr is observed from the road to make a large meander. In the middle of it can be seen a small cairn, marking the site of the home of John Lapraik. He lost money in the Ayr Bank crash and had to give up his farm. He then set up a post office at Muirkirk, in a cottage that still stands next to the kirk gates. He corresponded with Burns in verse, and the bard wrote a number of epistles back to him.

The Greenock Water passes below the B743 before joining the river Ayr. The older bridge, which is now bypassed, lies alongside. Upstream from here can be found a small ruin known as Chapelhouse, which is supposed to either have been a chapel itself, or else occupy the site of one. Whether or not a castle occupied the low knoll of Castle Hill is not known – perhaps it was just a fortified site. The nearby Scaffold Wood and Battle Craigs also hint at a troubled past. A minor road strikes north, passing Garpel Farm and heading for the Whitehaugh farms. The Garpel Linn is a small waterfall in the glen above the farm. Heath Cottage is a modern shooting-lodge, constructed of timber, with a grass-covered roof. Up the Pennel Burn from here was a spot where haematite was quarried and used at Tarrioch ironworks.

Limestone was quarried by the side of the Harwood Burn, a tributary of the Greenock, and smelted in kilns that existed here. Forkings is another shooting lodge, located on what is known as the Muirkirk estate. Above the lodge rises Middlefield Law, reaching 1,527 feet above sea level. The summit is crowned with a cairn commemorating the wedding of R. L. Angus of Ladykirk in 1928. He was a manager in the Muirkirk Ironworks. The Greenock Water drains the countryside around here, the headwaters rising on the Lanarkshire boundary. At Linburn can be found two other prehistoric cairns, one at the head of the Lamonburn Plantation, the other in the field west of the farm steading.

Near the shepherd's cottage of Waterhead can be found a group of antiquities dating back from prehistoric times. A few enclosures are located on the slopes of Brown Hill, and an unidentified mound lies by the side of the little stream that flows past. Almost due east of here is the Weatherhill Cairn, another Bronze Age burial site. From Blackside a trackway crosses the moor to Priesthill Farm, located high on the moor on the slopes of Priesthill Height. About three-quarters of a mile east of the steading can be found the grave of John Brown, one of the most famous Covenanting martyrs.

The A70 heads east from Muirkirk towards Lanarkshire, terminating in Edinburgh. On the edge of the village is Kerlstone House, an old house. At Lightshaw farm a solitary standing stone can be seen in a field by the side of the road. Whether or not it had any other stones associated with it is unknown. On the south side of the river Ayr, here in its infancy and little more than a moorland stream, are two old farms, Auldhouseburn and Crossflat. It is claimed that Mary Queen of Scots visited Auldhouseburn. The present house dates from 1866, perhaps incorporating some of the older 1610 work of the Campbell owners. A secret tunnel formerly existed from the house to a nearby stream, allowing Covenanters to escape in times of trouble.

Opencast mines have disfigured much of the countryside around here, or in the case of those that have excavated the site of old mines and their spoilheaps, it could be claimed that the landscape had been restored. These opencasts exist or existed at Tardoes, Lightshaw, Airdsgreen, Glenbuck and other places. Previously, coal mines were sunk to win the coal for use in the local ironworks, and latterly for use in coal-fired power stations or for domestic use. Numerous pits were sunk on the moors here, and in many places the remains of mineral lines, coal bings, water features and other derelict remains can be seen. There were numerous pits in the immediate area around Muirkirk, such as Kames, Lightshaw, Bankhead and the Viaduct Mine. A number of fatalities occurred at the pits, including the Kames pit disaster of 1958 when an explosion killed nineteen workers. The last of the large pits to close was Kames, which ceased production in June 1968. The Viaduct Mine worked as a private concern for some years afterward before closing.

The 'lost' village of Glenbuck formerly existed in the little glen north of the A70. The village was founded with the establishment of the iron-works in 1790 and at one time there were 1,750 residents living in the numerous rows, most employed as miners in the many pits in the area. The village even had at one time its own church, co-operative store, rail-way station and a famous football team, the splendidly named Glenbuck

Cherrypickers. Ironstone was discovered in a survey of 1786 and in 1790 John Rumney obtained a ninety-nine year lease of the Newmains Farm. Furnaces were erected and these came into production in 1794. Ownership changed in 1805 but the works fell into financial difficulties resulting in their closure in late 1813. Attempts in 1845 by John Wilson of Dundyvan to revive the works failed.

Glenbuck Church was built at a cost of £2,000 to plans by Robert Ingram in 1881–2. Opened on 16 July, it had a memorial to the local Covenanters on the front wall, but when the church was demolished this was relocated to Muirkirk. The church was closed on 25 May 1954. The public school at Glenbuck was opened on 13 March 1876 and closed on 1 August 1951. The former Glenbuck House was demolished in May 1948, and today little remains to remind folk that it once existed. The neo-baronial house was erected in 1879–80 to plans by John Murdoch for Charles Howatson (1833–1918), who made his fortune from black-face sheep. The home farm survives.

The Glenbuck Cherrypickers club was founded sometime in the 1870s but sadly the team, like the village itself, no longer exists. Glenbuck competed at junior level for a number of years and, though it did not win any major trophies, the number of players who later went on to greater things has conferred a degree of distinction on the club. Indeed, it is estimated that more than fifty men from the village played league football in both Scotland and England, while seven Glenbuck players were capped for Scotland. The most famous of these was Bill Shankly (1913–81), who was born in the village and worked down the local pit as soon as he left school. But he had a driving ambition to better himself and, at the age of 18, signed for Carlisle United. An excellent wing half, he later played for Preston North End and was subsequently capped five times by Scotland. But he is best remembered today as one of the finest managers in British football history. He became manager of Liverpool Football Club in 1960 and, under his charismatic leadership, the team won many trophies at home and abroad, paving the way for the team's later domination of English football in the 1980s. He retired in 1974 and was awarded the OBE in the same year. He is also fondly remembered for his many pithy sayings – known as 'Shanklyisms' – such as 'Football isn't a matter of life and death. It's much more important than that.' A memorial was erected in his memory at Glenbuck in 1997. And, in 2002, Shankly received still greater recognition when he was one of the first fifty sportsmen and women to be inducted into the Scottish Sports Hall of Fame

Glenbuck Loch is a man-made water feature, created in 1802 to store water for the Catrine mill. The sluices were released at night and the water reached Catrine by the following morning when it was time to start work. Today the loch is a pleasant spot, hemmed in between steep hills. The county border passes through the middle of the loch, and locals claim that the little cottage at the roadside is in fact split between two counties. Not only is the loch split by the county boundary, the Edinburgh railway line also passed through part of the loch, giving travellers on the old line a weird sensation of passing through water.

# 10

# Auchinleck and the Cumnocks

DIVIDING THE LARGER PARISH and barony of Cumnock in 1650 created the two parishes of Old and New Cumnock. The Earl of Dumfries disputed this and the division was rescinded in 1667, but the parishes were divided again in 1691 and have remained separate ever since. The boundary between Old Cumnock and Auchinleck parishes, although distinctly marked, has become blurred in recent years. Although the Holmhead part of Cumnock lies within Auchinleck parish, Dumfries House estate west of the town straddles both parishes, and east of the town, at Lugar and Logan, the two villages are linked in many ways, despite lying in different parishes.

Auchinleck parish lies to the north of Old Cumnock. The parish is one that is long and thin, extending from the remains of Auchinleck Castle in the west to the high moors of Wardlaw Hill and Stony Hill on the boundary with Lanarkshire. In total it extends to 24,273 acres, most of which is moorland. The west end of the parish is occupied by Auchinleck estate, where the name *Achadh na leac* probably comes from, descriptive of the field of flagstones. The ancient Auchinleck Castle occupies a high rock between the Lugar Water and the Dippol Burn. Little of it remains, but it is quite easy to see how it was a major place of defence. The castle was the seat of the Auchinlecks of that Ilk, who held the barony until 1499 when the male line died out.

The Boswells were given a grant confirming their ownership of Auchinleck in 1504 and in 1507 received a charter founding the burgh of Auchinleck. This was probably never acted upon, and the present Auchinleck village was erected much later. A second Auchinleck Castle, also known as the Old Place of Auchinleck, was erected in 1612, the ruins of which survive further east. This, in turn, was abandoned when Alexander Boswell, Lord Auchinleck, a distinguished law lord, erected the present Auchinleck House over a number of years around 1760. So slowly and prudently did he build the house, it is said that he didn't really notice the expense. Although thought to be the work of the Adam brothers, it is in all probability an artisan house built by master craftsmen to the plans of Lord Auchinleck himself. Designed in a neo-classical style that reflects the growing importance of the Scottish Enlightenment, and Lord Auchinleck's love of Greek and Roman culture, the house is beautifully proportioned and has a particularly elegant façade. Other highlights include a fine dining room and a forty-foot library to house Auchinleck's splendid book collection. Another notable feature is a Latin epigram by Horace carved into the pediment, which translates as 'What you seek is here in this remote place if you can only keep a balanced disposition.' Lord Auchinleck was also a very active laird and considerably developed the estate, established the present village and laid out a number of roads.

Although there has been a number of distinguished members of the Boswell clan, there is one whose achievements and renown now completely overshadow those of his kinsmen – Lord Auchinleck's son, James Boswell (1740–95). Boswell trained – with great reluctance – as a lawyer and was admitted to the Scottish Bar in 1766, but his real passions were

James Boswell (1740–95)

for literature, politics and the glittering attractions to be found in London. He met the eminent writer Dr Samuel Johnson for the first time in 1763 at the age of 22 and was heavily influenced by him; from then on their lives would be inextricably linked. Boswell persuaded Johnson to tour Scotland and the Hebrides with him in 1774 and, on their way home, the pair stopped off at Auchinleck House, which greatly impressed the notoriously hard to please Johnson, although he was 'greatly incommoded by very frequent rain'. Both men subsequently published brilliant and insightful accounts of their journeys. The Boswell book – *Journal of a Tour to the Hebrides* – is generally thought superior to the work produced by his mentor. Boswell later wrote *The Life of Samuel Johnson*, which appeared in 1791, and it is justly recognised as the greatest biography in the annals of English literature. He also won acclaim for his sparkling journals and diaries, particularly *Boswell's London Journal* and *Boswell on the Grand Tour*. Although he inherited Auchinleck House on the death of his father in 1782, Boswell's last years were spent pursuing a dissolute lifestyle in London, where he died in 1795. His international fame did not grow until the mid-twentieth century when his diaries were discovered and republished over the following decades. Indeed, such has been their impact that many critics now place him alongside Samuel Pepys as a chronicler of British culture and society.

The Boswells sold Auchinleck House in 1987 – by which time it was derelict and badly affected by rot – to the Scottish Historic Buildings Trust and it passed in 1999 to the Landmark Trust, which painstakingly restored it at a cost of £2 million. To complement the restoration work Georgian furniture, pictures and various editions of Boswell's books have been acquired. In addition an excellent collection of Boswell memorabilia is on display in the morning room. It is now an upmarket holiday house, but some of the rooms are open to the public on occasion. The estate remains in Boswell hands, and among the interesting items to be found are the man-made caves carved from the solid sandstone. These include Wallace's Cave, the Deer Cave, and Lord Auchinleck's summer house, which he reckoned was built at less cost than he would have incurred building an equivalent-sized structure above ground.

The Barony Road leads from Auchinleck House to Auchinleck village. It passes the large chipboard factory that was built on the site of Barony Colliery. The chipboard factory takes timber from all over Scotland and chips it into pieces that are then glued and pressed into large sheets used for the manufacture of kitchen units and other furniture. Barony Colliery operated from 1906 until 1989, the old head frame being kept as a memorial to the mining industry. A small memorial stone by the roadside commemorates those miners who lost their lives in the pit, including the terrible Barony disaster of 1962 when four men were killed, their bodies remaining underground to this day. Just west of the colliery was the Barony Power Station, built in 1956–7 to burn coal slurry from the washing plants of local pits. The station was quite unique in this respect, and a number of local pit bings were removed to supply it. Unfortunately, the large Barony bing that was supposed to have been used was found to be unsuitable. The power station was closed in 1982 and the buildings demolished between 1983–6.

Lord Auchinleck laid out Auchinleck as a planned village. The old community that stood around the ancient church was cleared away and a new streetscape on a right-angled grid was laid out. Among the older properties surviving is the Boswell Arms Inn, erected in 1766. Most of the other buildings have been rebuilt over the years, but Main Street retains much of its original appearance. The present parish church dates from 1838, having been erected to replace the older church that was by this time too small. The architect was James Ingram. In 1894 the church was extended to plans by his son, Robert, the tower dating from that time. It includes stained glass by Stephen Adam commemorating Lady Jessie Boswell, widow of Sir James Boswell. There are windows depicting the Ten Commandments, but for some reason two of them are numbered 'VI'.

The old church of 1683 was left to fall into ruins, but was re-roofed and in 1978 opened as the Boswell Museum. Here are a collection of artefacts associated with James Boswell and his family. Also on display are items associated with Auchinleck's past, as well as with William Murdoch, inventor. Adjoining the old church is the Boswell Mausoleum of 1754, where many of the Boswells of Auchinleck lie. The square sandstone building, with its flagged roof, is one of the finest mausoleums in the area, and the external wall is adorned with a fine carving of the Boswell arms. Inside, the ground floor has a partitioned-off area in which lie a couple of coffins. A trap door lifts and steps lead down to the vault below the church. This was carved from the solid rock, and on one side are chambers in which lie a number of Boswell family members. They include the great writer, James. A tablet also recalls later members of the family, including Sir Alexander Boswell, who was created a Baronet in 1821. Sir Alexander was a minor poet, MP and Lieutenant Colonel in the Ayrshire Yeomanry. He wrote a sarcastic poem against James Stuart, younger of Dunearn, which was published in a Glasgow newspaper. This resulted in Boswell being challenged to a duel, which took place at Auchtertool in Fife, in which Boswell was killed.

The churchyard that adjoins the museum has a number of interesting old stones. The parish war memorial is located here, and near to it is an obelisk commemorating a number of sons of the parish. Most of these are Covenanters who suffered elsewhere, such as Peden and the Airds Moss martyrs. Another side commemorates William Murdoch, and a fourth commemorates William MacGavin (1773–1832), author of *The Protestant* and other works. He was born at Darnlaw Farm, at the west end of the village, and became a manager in a cotton works at Paisley before becoming a bank agent. He was buried in Glasgow's Wellington Street Chapel, but in the Necropolis a major memorial was erected to his memory, second only to John Knox in importance. He has been virtually forgotten otherwise.

The first stretch of Barony Road is now occupied by small industrial units, but here stood the Highhouse Colliery, which operated from 1894 until 1983. The winding frame of the pit survives, giving this part of the village a feeling of some connection with its coal-mining past. Much of this area was occupied by old miners' rows, one or two of which still exist, converted into small units. When built, they had to have their doors facing away from the Barony Road, in case the miners felt inclined to stand and watch the Boswells as they made their way to the church. The Barony Road was Lord Auchinleck's *Via Sacra*, and was one of his improvements to the estate. Previously the roadways in the parish were ill defined and passed closer to the Lugar Water. When originally laid out, the road was lined with trees, the B and O of beech and oak representing the first two letters of Boswell. Further along Barony Road from Highhouse are a number of private houses, in one of which lived Robert Samson Ingram (1840–1915), a prolific Ayrshire architect.

Main Street, Auchinleck, extends for almost one mile from the Boswell Arms to the crossroads at the foot of Sorn Road. The street is lined with older buildings along most of its length, few of which are of any major architectural merit, but which together form a typical Ayrshire street scene. Near the bottom end is the former Secession Church, now a plastics warehouse. This was erected around 1780. Some of the street frontages are made up of terraces, including Shiloh and Searle terraces, which date from 1900–5. These tend to be at the upper end of Main Street, on the other side of the railway bridge. Here also is the Railway Hotel, built around 1850. The railway reached Auchinleck in 1848 and the station was opened on 17 July. It was closed in 1965 but was reopened in 1984.

To the south side of Mauchline Road is the Merlin Park, which occupies the site of the Merlin Loch, created at a time when curling was more popular than it is today. The far west-end of this street, just where it joins the roundabout at the bypass, was known as Templeton, and claimed to be an independent village, appearing as such on some censes.

Sorn Road climbs from the Toll at Auchinleck, where Market Place recalls the markets that were once held here. The village's Lamb Fair was a notable event, but the last fair was held in 1902 and no lambs were offered for sale that year! Only a street name survives to remind the community of its earlier past. School Road leaves Sorn Road on the right, obviously named after the former primary school that still stands there. This was built in 1914 to plans of A. C. Thomson, but was closed in 2000 when the new Auchinleck Primary and Nursery School was built on the site of the old Dalsalloch miners' rows. Further up Sorn Road is St Patrick's RC Church. The hall was erected first, in 1940, with the presbytery and chapel added in 1964. St Patrick's Primary School is located off Quarry Road. Auchinleck Academy occupies the hilltop of Auchinleck, a massive bulk visible for miles around. This was opened on 31 March 1971.

East of Sorn Road, and north of the railway, is the Backrogerton housing scheme. Most of the houses date from the 1950s onward and were built to accommodate miners moved from the old rows that existed both in Auchinleck and on the moors to the east. Within the scheme is the former Peden Church of 1951, designed by J. A. Carrick, now used as the parish church hall. The southern end of the scheme abuts onto Coal Road, which makes its way from the cross out onto the moors where the mines were. Just off Coal Road, near its start, is Beechwood Park, home to the Junior football team known as Auchinleck Talbot (founded 1909). Coal Road crosses the main railway line, as well as a former branch line, before emerging into the country. The branch line was opened in 1848 to link Auchinleck with Muirkirk, and there were stations at Commondyke, Lugar and Cronberry.

Lochnoran House occupies the site of St Patrick's convent, which was demolished in 1992. In this small area also stood the Catholic primary school and the Chapel of Our Lady and St Patrick. The chapel had been erected in 1867 by the Roman Catholic mineworkers of the area, who had no real place of worship at that time. At first it served the Cumnock and Catrine areas, but when chapels were erected to cover both those parishes, Birnieknowe was left to serve Auchinleck. In the field opposite the gates of Lochnoran House can be seen a sandstone cross. This marks the spot where a train killed the Revd Sister Laurienne Cusack as she made her way across the mineral branch-line. She had been suffering from an ear infection and did not hear the train reversing into the former mine. She died on 7 August 1888. The school at Birnieknowe was closed in 1966 when a replacement school was opened in Auchinleck. The only real memory of this community is the cross in the field.

There are three 'lost' villages in the vicinity. Commondyke village consisted of a number of rows in the field around the cross, as well as a few more on the road towards Lugar. It had a railway station and co-operative store, and there were even enough men to form a Junior football club, Common Thistle, playing on a field behind the pit bing. The road continues further to the north-east, towards Common Farm, from where Darnconner Farm can be seen out on the moor. Here was another former village, Darnconner, complete with church, co-operative and school. The church was originally a temporary building but, in 1897, a sandstone structure was erected at a cost of £3,000 to plans by Robert Ingram and survived until 1979. The community has virtually disappeared, apart from the former schoolhouse and manse, now private dwellings. Other miners' rows existed on the moors hereabouts. The Ballochmyle Rows, yet another lost village, were so named because they were erected on part of Ballochmyle estate.

The bottom end of Auchinleck's long Main Street makes its way down to Bridgend Garage, which occupies the site of an old mill. Here also were the old gasworks and Currie's lemonade factory, which operated for many years. The new cemetery lies on the west side of the road. Within it can be found a number of stones commemorating the Polish Resettlement Corps, which was active in the district during the war. Behind the cemetery is Auchinleck's old manse, a fair sized house. Here lived A.K.H.B. who wrote numerous articles and over thirty books. Andrew Kennedy Hutchison Boyd (1825–99) became a minister but was renowned in Britain and America for his *Recreations of a Country Parson* and other works.

*

The B7083 (formerly the A76) leads one into Cumnock from Auchinleck. The gap between the two communities is quite short, but the gap culturally is quite large, and there is a friendly rivalry between the two towns. On the way one passes a small former tollhouse, known as Rigg Toll, one of the least altered cottages of its type. The Rigg is a small group of houses built at the western end of the Rigg Road. At one time there was a small church here, connected with the Secession church, but two separate congregations in Cumnock and Auchinleck replaced this when the group split.

Cumnock is an old community, shown on older maps as Cumnock Kirk. In 1509 it was created a Burgh of Barony for the Dunbar family, and by 1866 became a Police Burgh. The parish of Old Cumnock extends to 14,209 acres. The part of Cumnock built north of the Lugar Water is more or less all in Auchinleck parish, though the original burgh of Cumnock and Holmhead boundary included this area. Holmhead is today a modern private-housing-development, extending up the hillside. In its midst is Holmhead Hospital, erected in 1898 as a fever hospital but it is now a geriatric hospital. Some older buildings are located along Auchinleck Road, including Cumnock Rugby Club, occupying the former Broomfield farmhouse. The lands were converted into playing fields in 1962. The former St Conval's High School (now St Joseph's Academy Cumnock Annexe) was erected in 1961. A fine selection of villas line the street from here to the Lugar Bridge, including the former UP manse of 1868, Lochnorris of 1891, and Stepends House.

Lochnorris was the home of the founder of the Labour Party, James Keir Hardie (1856–1915). Hardie was born out of wedlock, and into grinding poverty, at Legbranock in Lanarkshire. His family moved to Glasgow where he started work as an errand boy at the age of seven. By the age of ten he was working down a pit. He moved to Cumnock in 1879 – which would remain the family home for the rest of his life –

James Keir Hardie (1856–1915)

where he married a miner's daughter. He was active in the Ayrshire Miners' Association, became secretary of the Ayrshire Miners' Union and wrote extensively on trade union issues and socialism for the radical press. In 1888 he founded the Scottish Labour Party and in 1892 was elected Labour MP for West Ham (until 1895) followed by Merthyr Tydfil (1900–15). He was the founder of the Independent Labour Party in 1893 and in 1900 helped form the Labour Representation Committee, which then became the Labour Party. Always down to earth, Hardie caused a sensation in the House of Commons when he turned up in a cloth cap and tweeds. He later campaigned vigorously against Britain's involvement in the First World War. Today Hardie is widely recognised as the father of working-class representation in Parliament and, arguably, as the seminal figure in the history of British socialism.

The Congregational Church occupies a site at the foot of the Wood Road. The church as a congregation dates from 1838 but built the present place of worship at a cost of £1,600 in 1882–3, to plans of John Murdoch of Ayr. The windows are simple leaded glass and there is an open belfry on the gable. It was this church that James Keir Hardie attended.

The Woodroad Park occupies an attractive valley of the Lugar. Here can be found the outdoor swimming pool, constructed in 1937. At the head of the park can be seen the Bank Viaduct, a tall thirteen-arch structure erected in 1848–50 to plans by the engineer John Miller. The highest arch is 175 feet above the Lugar Water.

On crossing Lugar Bridge, Lugar Street takes one to the centre of Cumnock, at the Square. The Old Church occupies the middle of the Square, the third building to occupy the site. The second church was erected in 1754 to plans by Robert Adam, one of his earliest works. This church became too small for the parish, and in 1866–7 the present building was erected to plans of James Maitland Wardrop of Edinburgh,

Cumnock: Old Church in the Square

costing £6,227. The blonde sandstone gives the church a light appearance, its bulk being constrained by the site. The clock tower was supposed to rise much further into a spire, but cost prevented this from being completed. The church contains some interesting stained-glass, with windows by James Ballantine and A. L. Moore. Here also can be seen the old parish church bell, dated 1697 and cast by Quirinus de Vesscher of Rotterdam. A number of memorials on the walls commemorate local lairds and ministers, and to the rear of the church is the Bute Hall, where a number of members of the Crichton Stuarts are interred. There is a gallery originally used by the Marquis of Bute but, shortly after erecting this church, he converted to Catholicism and paid for the erection of a chapel as well. The organ is a modern one of 1966 and on the wall behind the pulpit is a mosaic of Jesus walking on the water by James Harrigan. The Old Church is open to the public during the summer months, or by arrangement with the Words of Wisdom tearoom and bookshop in the Square.

The buildings surrounding the Square date in the main from the eighteenth or nineteenth centuries. The Mercat and Royal hotels occupy the east side. The south side has a former bank at its east end, followed by some fine eighteenth-century buildings. The west side of the Square has the old Sun Inn occupying half its length, with other old buildings alongside. The north side of the Square is the shortest (for it is not a true square) and here can be found the Clydesdale Bank (John Murdoch, 1882–4) and one other building. In the Square are two memorials, one a boulder with a plaque commemorating some renovation work done in the vicinity, the other a dry fountain commemorating Queen Victoria's Diamond Jubilee in 1898. Here also is the old Market Cross, a simple shaft on top of a set of steps. The finial comprises a cube and ball, the cube containing the arms of the Earl of Dumfries, a sundial, and the dates, 1703 and 1778.

In Lugar Street is the Baird Institute, now a district history centre and museum. The building was erected with money left by local draper and architect, John Baird (1812–88), in 1891, the design being by Robert Ingram. Inside are various museum rooms, one containing a collection of artefacts associated with Keir Hardie, another having a changing exhibition, and two others having local-history research material. Here can be seen the ancient Cumnock Covenanters' banner, as well as several other Covenanting relics.

The rest of the street is occupied by some older properties, including the Post Office. The west end of the street was destroyed considerably when the Tanyard was widened and latterly when the link road to the bottom of the Barrhill was created. Barrhill Road is the A70, the main route to Edinburgh. At its foot are the parish church hall of 1900 and Greenmill Primary School of 1926–39. The old cemetery occupies the site of the ancient Gallows Knowe, where local malefactors were hanged. Within the enclosure are two hawthorn trees, which, tradition claims, will result in a disaster for the town if their branches ever entwine. This spot was used for burying Covenanters, and around 1750, when it was decided to do away with the old churchyard in the Square, this spot was deemed suitable for the new cemetery. The cemetery has long been disused, but it still contains a number of interesting stones and, in an enclosure by the gate, four Covenanters are buried.

The Covenanting tradition has deep roots in Scottish church history and the movement took its name from the notion that a special contract, or covenant, exists between God and the people, without the need for interference of a king or bishops. The concept was affirmed by Scottish Presbyterians in both 1557 and 1581 and again by the National Covenant of 1638, a move provoked by Charles I's attempt to introduce the *Book of Common Prayer* without the involvement of the General Assembly of the Church of Scotland. Such was the popular support for the movement that 300,000 Scots were thought to have signed copies of the Covenant. The Covenanters allied themselves with Cromwell during the English Civil War, and Charles I even surrendered to a Covenanting army in 1646. However, Scots were appalled by the execution of the King in 1649 and his son, Charles II, was crowned at Scone in 1650, but only after agreeing to sign the Covenant. After the Restoration of the monarchy in 1660 Charles went back on his word and restored episcopacy, provoking open rebellion from many Covenanters. Forced out of the established churches Covenanters preached in the open air in gatherings known as Conventicles. Inevitably there were many armed encounters with government forces, which were led by John Graham of Claverhouse, later Viscount Dundee. These were particularly prevalent in the 1680s, which became known as the 'killing times' and they created many Covenanter martyrs. Ayrshire was a particularly strong Covenanting redoubt and several battles took place in the county.

Ayrshire was also the birthplace of the most famous Covenanter of all, Alexander Peden, who was born at Auchencloigh, in the parish of Sorn, in 1626. He became schoolmaster at Tarbolton but in 1659 was ordained as minister of New Luce in Wigtownshire. In 1662 he was ejected from his charge and by 1666 was pronounced a rebel by the Privy Council. He was imprisoned on the Bass Rock between 1673 and 1678, whence he was to be transported to Virginia to work as a slave. However, he escaped and spent the rest of his life hiding in northern England, southern Scotland and Northern Ireland. He died on Auchinleck estate in January 1686 and was secretly buried at Auchinleck. However, forty days later this was discovered and his body was disinterred. Soldiers took his corpse to Cumnock, with the intention of hanging him on the gallows tree. This was disallowed and the soldiers buried him at the foot of the tree 'out of contempt', according to one of the headstones. The large white memorial to him was erected in 1891 to plans of Robert Ingram.

Within the graveyard are buried William Simpson (1758–1815), and Anne Rankine, associates of Burns. 'Winsome' Willie was a schoolmaster firstly at Ochiltree and then in Cumnock, and was also a poet of sorts. Anne Rankin is claimed to be the original of Annie in *The Rigs of Barley*. She later married John Merry, keeper of an inn in the town. Here also can be found the grave of James Taylor (1753–1825), whose stone notes that he was the 'Inventor of Steam Navigation'. Taylor was born at Leadhills but moved to Cumnock to manage the 6th Earl of Dumfries's Cumnock Pottery, which was established in 1791. He was active in developing a paddleboat and later added a steam engine to create a self-propelled vessel. This was sailed successfully on Dalswinton Loch, in Dumfriesshire, the first in the world.

On the opposite side of Barrhill Road from the cemetery is the Baptist Church of 1887. The road climbs gradually up the hill towards the site of the railway station, opened on 20 May 1850 and closed on 6 December 1965. South of the Barrhill are the housing estates of Drumbrochan and Barshare, the latter the work of Sir Robert H. Matthew. Barshare won a Saltire Society award for the best housing design in Scotland for 1963. Townhead Street can be followed back towards the town centre. Here can be found Townhead Park, home to Cumnock Juniors Football Club, which was founded in 1913. Most of this street has been rebuilt in modern times, but originally it was lined with single-storey thatched cottages, occupied in the main by weavers. The former Townhead Smithy is now a hardware shop, and the site of the market cross is marked in the roadway by a cross of cobbles.

Ayr Road heads west from the town centre. In it stands Crichton West church, its tall spire being a local landmark. The church was erected in 1899 to plans of David Menzies of Edinburgh. The church occupied the site of the old Free Church of 1843, but in 1896 Miss Crichton gifted money with which the present building was erected as a memorial to her father, Hew, and brother, Sheriff James Crichton, both of whom died in 1892. The church contains some fine stained glass, as well as memorials to former ministers. Originally known as the Crichton Memorial Church, it was renamed Crichton West in 1949 when the former West Church was abandoned. This building survives in the Tanyard, and is a fine example of a box kirk, dating from 1831, and thus the oldest church building in Cumnock. It is now used as a youth café. Ayr Road continues further west, passing the former Bankend woollen mill, Cumnock Academy and the East Ayrshire Community Hospital of 2000, designed by Maclachlan Monaghan architects.

Glaisnock Street is one of the town's main thoroughfares. It starts at the Square, squeezing its way out between the Royal Hotel and a former bank. The Craighead Inn is an old building of 1722, the original lease of which required payment of £21 plus two hens and two loads of coal in rent. The Gorbals Bridge crosses the Glaisnock Water. The Glaisnock Shopping Centre is a modern carbuncle of 1975, replacing older shops that occupied the narrow space between the road and the water. The west side of the street retains the old buildings, including the Dagmar Inn, formerly the Bucks Head Inn, where David Reid was shot in a riot concerning poaching in 1833. The street rises to the Dumfries Arms Hotel, the oldest surviving coaching inn in Ayrshire. The Earl of Dumfries erected this in 1717. Burns visited the inn on many occasions, and the hotel has been host to many other important guests over the years, including Sir Walter Scott, who wrote one of his sonnets here: 'To Old Cumnock, where beds are as hard as a plank, sir.'

The town hall was erected in 1885 to plans of Robert Ingram. It is a Free Renaissance building, built of red sandstone. Inside are the main hall, lesser hall, and former council chambers. In front of the hall is a bust of James Keir Hardie, the work of Benno Schotz. The statue was unveiled in August 1939. On the other side of the street from the town hall stood Cumnock Pottery. This was founded by the Earl of Dumfries to bring employment to the area. The pottery worked until around 1907, by which time finer china imports from England and abroad were more in demand. Examples of Cumnock Pottery survive. It was distinctive for its natural brown and cream colours, but was unique for its 'Scotch Motto Ware'. This included everyday pieces such as egg cups, butter dishes, milk jugs, and so forth which were adorned with couthy mottoes such as 'Rax furrit and help yersel'' (on a bowl), or 'Help yersel an' dinnae be blate' (on a dish).

Further up the street is the small United Free Church of 1939, named St Andrews. Breezyhill was the home of author and poet, Adam Brown Todd. Further on is St John's RC Church. This fine building was erected in 1882 from funds supplied by the 3rd Marquis of Bute. He employed the notable architect William Burges (1827–81) to build the church. Burges was noted for his work at Cardiff Castle and Cork Cathedral. He created an Early Decorated style church, but unfortunately this building also had to forgo its intended spire. Nevertheless, internally it is rather fine, with glass by N. J. Westlake and painted murals by J. F. Bentley. When built, it was the first church in the country to be lit by electricity.

Glaisnock Street begins to drop again, crossing the Glaisnock Water at the Caponacre Bridge. On the way down the fire station of 1964 is passed, as well as the newer cemetery. Here also was the Cumnock railway station, on the Ayr and Cumnock line. The station opened in 1872 and served the town until 1964. Of the line, nothing remains in the immediate area, but beyond the flats of Patrick Finn Court can be seen the thirteen arched Glaisnock Viaduct. This is now used as a footpath to link two parts of the town. In the cemetery can be found the grave of James Keir Hardie and Emrys Hughes (1894–1969), his son-in-law, also an MP, and political author. Here also is buried Adam Brown Todd (1822–1915), poet and author of some books on the Covenanters.

Beyond the small Murray Park is Netherthird, a post-war housing scheme built to rehouse miners from their rows. Within it can be found St Ninian's Church of 1955. Craigens is another scheme erected to rehouse miners.

The A70 leaves Cumnock on passing below the railway and heads for Muirkirk. On the right is a road leading to Logan, a housing estate created to rehouse miners from the old rows at Lugar and Cronberry. The village was erected on the former Logan estate, the old mansion house being demolished. This had been the home of Hugh Logan (1739–1802), the celebrated 'Laird of Logan', who was known to Burns and to a wider audience for his wit. Hugh Logan inherited the estate in 1759, despite being the third son, but he made little of it and was forced to sell it in 1798. He later lived at Wellwood, near Muirkirk. Hugh Logan was renowned for his humour, and as a result was a sought-after guest at many society parties. Trying to pay back these invitations by holding his own parties left him destitute. A book of humorous anecdotes, many of which were attributed to Logan, was published in 1854 and went through many editions. When he died he was buried in Cumnock Square. The Logan one sees today has little history before 1948, for the school was erected in 1963, the church hall in 1959 and the Logangate Arms in 1955.

Logan has affiliations with the village of Lugar, which lies on the other side of the Lugar Water, and consequently is in Auchinleck parish once more. The old stone Logan Bridge is bypassed by the steel girder Holmhead Bridge. Lugar has some later miners' rows, the houses in Park Terrace being more modern examples of the traditional row. The bowling green splits the terrace. Peesweep Brae leads up past Craigston House (c. 1820 on the site of an older house owned by the Boswells) to the site of the old ironworks. John Wilson of Dundyvan founded these in 1845. Four original furnaces operated down in the valley but in 1864 Bairds erected a new works at the top of the hill, with five new furnaces. The works produced pig iron on and off until they were finally quenched in November 1928. The National Coal Board later used the site as work-shops, and today lesser factory units and offices occupy the site. A few older buildings can be seen off the brae, including the former primary school of 1859 with extension of 1889–90.

Craigston Square is another group of attractive rows, at one end of which is Lugar church. This was created in 1867 out of a former furnace house. The church is a simple low building, adorned only by a small belfry. In the yard is the war memorial, which is quite distinct in that it not only lists those who died for their country, but also those who served and returned from the Great War of 1914–18. A group of modern houses is followed by Rosebank Park, home to Lugar Boswell Thistle Football Club, which was founded in 1878 and still plays in the junior leagues. On the opposite side of the road is the Lugar Spout, an old spring from which most of the villagers drew their fresh water. Beyond Rosebank is Bello Mill, where the ruins of the old mill and millwheel can still be found. The present mill house contains a plaque commemorating William Murdoch (1754–1839), inventor of gas lighting. Murdoch was born here and educated in Cumnock before he moved to London then Cornwall. He found employment with Boulton and Watt, and became their works manager at Soho in Birmingham. Murdoch invented many things, including an underwater paint, parts of the steam engine and the 'D' valve. He was buried in Handsworth Church, Birmingham, beside Matthew Boulton and James Watt.

Behind the mill house is the former weir, now washed away, and an old cave where Murdoch is said to have carried out many of his early experiments. This cave is a simple square cavern carved from the rock. To the east of Bello Mill, in the field next to the cottage, is an old stone circle or burial mound, known locally as the Rocking Stone. The boulder has long since ceased to rock, but it still lies there.

The narrow defile where the A70 passes between two steep banks and the river is known as the Bello Path, or Pass. In the seventeenth century this spot was used by the local Covenanters to spring the release of Revd David Houston from the hands of the dragoons. The countryside turns to moorland quickly beyond the Bello Path. On the moor is the village of Cronberry, a relic of old miners' houses that were left behind. There were many other old rows here, but these were demolished as the occupants were rehoused in Logan, but the houses of Riverside Terrace were more modern and were left. They have been rebuilt in recent years as private flats. Cronberry at one time had its own railway station, school, church, co-operative shop and football team.

The moor of Airds Moss is blighted by former pit bings and old mineral lines, recalling the many coal and ironstone mines that once worked here. Today there are a number of opencasts, or sites of these. Up the Gass Water valley can be found the remains of mining of a different sort. Barytes was mined here from 1917 until 1965 at three main mines, the mineral being transported down the glen by means of a mineral line, track or aerial ropeway, to a plant at Cairnhill. The works were owned by the Hedworth Barium Company but were taken over by the Wrentnall Baryta Company in 1923 followed by Anglo-Austral Mines, and over the years the barytes produced here was regarded as some of the purest in Britain. Beyond Boghead, Airds Moss becomes more of a peat bog. Out on the moor can be seen a squat obelisk, erected around 1840. This marks the site of a battle between the Covenanters and the soldiers under Andrew Bruce of Earlshall, which took place on 20 July 1680. Within a few hundred yards of the memorial is a Bronze Age burial cairn, little of which can be made out on the ground.

To the south of Airds Moss is a high stretch of countryside, mainly used for grouse shooting and rearing sheep. The moors stretch south over the Gass Water valley to the Glenmuir valley, the Glenmuir Water being another tributary of the Lugar. Glenmuir is a long valley striking east of Cumnock, access to which is made by minor roads from either Logan, or else from Wallaceton at the east end of Lugar. The latter road passes Laigh Glenmuir cottage, formerly a rural school of 1876 (closed 1916) by Robert Ingram. In the immediate area stood Hallglenmuir, perhaps an old tower house, but long since gone. The Glenmuir Burn is a tributary of the Glenmuir Water. Up the burn, beyond High Glenmuir, are old lime-workings and remains of a kiln.

On Glenmuir Water Road from Logan lies Darmalloch Farm, birth-place of the Latta brothers who were to make their fortune in shipping, and of which Sir John Latta (1867–1946) was given a baronetcy in 1920. Dornal Farm lies to the side of a massive earthwork known as Dornal Moat. This comprises a large circular ditch 450 feet in diameter. At the southern end of this rises a motte hill. Nether Guelt Farm contains an old mill.

Dalblair, a small community located five miles east of Cumnock by the side of Glenmuir Water, was originally the location of a hunting lodge, owned for a time by James Boswell, but sold by him to repay debts. The lodge has long gone, but here is an attractive group of houses by the riverside. One of the houses was built as a school (operated from 1937–50), but it has been disused for many years.

Beyond Dalblair Farm is a gate, with a track leading to Kyle Farm. On the hillside to the north stand the hoary remains of Kyle Castle, little more than a finger of masonry pointing at the sky. Little of the castle's history is known, other than the Farquhars of Gilmilnscroft owned it in 1445. Beyond Kyle Farm there is little more than grouse moors reached by a track up the valley of the Guelt Water. A track climbs from Dalblair Farm and follows the north side of the Glenmuir Water, or Shaw Water as this part is sometimes known, eastwards for three and a half miles to Glenmuirshaw. Beyond here the track terminates, and only foot passengers can continue to climb to High Shaw or Penbreck and rejoin the Old Sanquhar Road that links Muirkirk and Sanquhar. The headwaters of the Glenmuir Water tumble over the Deil's Back Door waterfall, known also as Connor Linn. Connor Hill above it has an ancient enclosure on the ground near the March Burn.

The lands of Penbreck are now afforested. Here stood Penbreck Farm, which also had a small school attached to it. Limestone was mined locally, and remains of the workings can still be found. The parish of

Auchinleck, and therefore the county of Ayr, extends eastwards to the summit of a low hill known as the Threeshire Hill, for here Ayrshire, Dumfriesshire and Lanarkshire meet. A boulder marks the spot.

West of Cumnock lies Dumfries House estate, an extensive property owned by the Marquis of Bute, whose heir takes the title Earl of Dumfries. Dumfries House is a very fine Adam mansion, erected between 1754–9 to plans of John and Robert Adam, their first real commission. The 4th Earl of Dumfries, who built the house, had originally intended Robert's father, William Adam, to be the architect, but he died before the work could commence. After some persuasion, he agreed that the younger Adams were capable of the work. The original estimate that Robert Adam provided was for £7,979 11s 2d, and the final cost was only out by a few pennies. The house is a magnificent Palladian mansion, the central block rising through three storeys, with the main rooms on the piano nobile. A wide stair at the front reaches this, beneath which is the gun room. To either side of the main block are wings, linked by corridors. The original wings were part of Adam's plan, but in 1895–9 these were extended and rebuilt to plans by Robert Weir Schultz. Internally the house is rather fine, with a fine selection of public rooms and private bedrooms. The west wing contains the library and tapestry room, whereas the east wing contains the dining room.

The policies around the estate contain a number of important items. Before Dumfries House was built there stood a castle here, known as Leifnoreis or Lochnorris. This was anciently a Craufurd seat, but in 1635 the Crichton-Stuarts, who had in 1633 been created Earls of Dumfries, acquired the lands. Previously their seat was Sanquhar Castle. Nothing of Leifnoreis remains today, but its foundations lie below the lawns north of the present house. The only building as old as the castle to survive is the old dovecot, which is located next to the tennis courts. This is a simple rectangular building, with crow-stepped gables and an armorial panel over the door. This contains the arms of MacDowall of Freugh and the date 1671.

North from the dovecot the drive makes its way over the Avenue Bridge, a fine triple-arched bridge that was designed by Robert Adam. The bridge contains some fine balustrades and obelisks, but unfortunately the Lugar Water is too small in scale for the bridge. The drive on the north side of the river makes its way to the Barony Road at Auchinleck. In the woods can be found the Temple, latterly a folly within the estate. The Temple gates and adjoining houses were erected by the Earl of Dumfries to form a main entrance to his property. North of the gates the land was owned by the Boswells, but Lord Dumfries hoped they would allow him to build a drive from the Mauchline road directly to the gates. When the Boswells refused to allow this, the drive had to take a sharp turn on the 'outside' of the gates, thereby linking the drive with the existing drive through the Boswell property. The gatehouses were occupied for some years, but latterly mining subsidence meant that they had to be abandoned. A track and various pathways make their way through Dumfries House's policies to the east. On the way they pass the Crucifix, a statue of Christ on the cross that was erected near to the spot where John, third Marquis of Bute, was converted to Roman Catholicism in 1900. This was regarded as a major coup for Rome, and inspired Benjamin Disraeli to write *Lothair*. Now separated from the rest of the estate by the bypass, Terringzean, Taringzean, or 'Tringan' as it is pronounced, castle stands on a knoll above the Lugar Water. The remaining tower is probably the oldest part of the castle, built with walls ten feet thick, and perhaps dating from the fourteenth century. North and west of the tower are lower foundations marking out an extensive courtyard, part of which is built over what is probably a very ancient hall castle. The castle was anciently a seat of the Boyds, Craufurds then Campbells, but it fell into ruins in the seventeenth century. The Earl of Loudoun takes a secondary title, Lord Taringzean from this castle, even although it has long been in the hands of the Dumfries and then Bute families.

The A76 and A70 meet at the Dettingen roundabout, named after the circular wood here that is called the Dettingen Wood. This was planted as part of an eighteenth century scheme to commemorate the Battle of Dettingen (1743), at which the local laird, William, 5th Earl of Dumfries, took part. The battle, which took place in Germany during the War of the Austrian Succession, was particularly notable as it was the last occasion in which a British king – George II – fought in person. Further to the southwest are two other circular woods, Stair Mount and Blackwood Mount, commemorating the position of the British troops.

Near Orchardton Farm a minor road strikes south from the A70 and climbs uphill towards the village of Skares. On its way it passes the former Skares railway station, which opened in 1872 and served the mining village until 1964. Further south is the site of Whitehill Pit, now marked by a large spoil heap. Skares village itself stands at the crossroads of the minor roads with the B7046. There used to be a number of miners' rows here, but these were demolished and replaced by a pine plantation. The remaining part of the village comprises older cottages and some new bungalows. One of these was built on the site of the village school, which operated from around 1900 until 1966.

The B7046 can be followed back towards Cumnock. At Garrallan is another former school, this one dating from 1876, and still retaining its wind vane. It became a special school in 1954 but was closed in 1972. Garrallan House survives, an old building that has been extended over the years. On it are datestones with arms varying from 1660 to 1868. At one time it was the seat of a branch of the Boswells of Auchinleck, but today it belongs to the Stevenson family. Various old mines existed round about here, most of which have been obliterated from the surface of the ground. Similarly, the old Glengyron rows have disappeared, as has the former Dumfries House Station, a private station on the Ayr and Edinburgh line that was used by the Marquis of Bute and his family.

From near Garrallan a minor road strikes south-east, heading for New Cumnock. It passes Greenfields Farm, for a time used as a centre for rare breeds. At Benston Smithy are remains of old limeworkings. Benston Road can be followed north to Cumnock, passing en route the gates to Glaisnock House. This house was built in two main stages, firstly in 1833 by James Ingram for James Allason and again later that century. The estate has been owned by a number of families, notably the Campbells whose arms are over the door. It was a rural school from 1952 until 1973, and latterly the house was used as an outdoor centre, but is currently disused.

From the southern end of Cumnock is the Dumfries road, the A76, making its way to New Cumnock. Shortly after crossing the railway line the disused Borland reservoirs are passed, originally formed in 1868 to supply Cumnock with drinking water. These are now used for fishing. By the side of the railway here stood Borland Castle, an ancient seat associated with the Hamilton family. Nothing of it remains, but a stone from the castle, containing the initials 'HM, MH and 1677', was built into the old smithy building at Borland Farm. Between the reservoirs and Watston Farm can be seen the ruin of Chapelhouse, which occupies the ancient site of Borland Chapel. An old stone coffin lid, from the grave of an infant, is built into the walls. Above Watston, and reaching 1084 feet, is Avisyard Hill, topped by a radio mast. On the lower slopes, at Coila Hill, was an ancient stone circle, perhaps a relic from some form of prehistoric enclosure.

*

The A76 leaves Old Cumnock parish at Calton Farm and enters New Cumnock. In the past both parishes were one, but it was decided to divide them, and as New Cumnock had the poorer ground, it was given the larger area. Between the two Cumnocks are the three lochs of Black Loch, Creoch Loch and Loch o' th' Lowes, the latter also known locally as Lochside Loch. Tradition claims that the Black Loch drains in two directions, north to the Ayr and south to the Nith. Thus, many old guidebooks describe a fish making its way up the Nith, into the Lowes, Creoch and then Black Loch, before leaving by the Blackloch Burn and joining the Glaisnock, Lugar, and river Ayr before returning to the sea! The most southerly of the three lochs is the largest, by the side of which stands the Lochside House Hotel. The Marquis of Bute originally built this as a shooting lodge, but it passed into other hands and has been a hotel for a number of years now. Between Loch o' th' Lowes and the A76 is New Cumnock's 9-hole golf course. This is 5,176 yards in length, par 68.

The A76 soon enters New Cumnock at Pathhead, as that part of the village north of the river Nith is known. There are few buildings of any great architectural merit, just traditional cottages built by the side of the road. The main road swings to the south to cross the railway and soon after the river Nith. The station at New Cumnock was originally opened in May 1850 but was closed in the Beeching cuts on 6 December 1965. After some years of campaigning it was reopened on 27 May 1991.

On crossing the Nith, one is in the older part of New Cumnock, for here stood a castle, known as Cumnock Castle, but also from its location as Black Bog Castle. No fragments of the castle remain, the last of these disappearing in the eighteenth century, but remnants of its moat can still be made out on the ground. The original tower may have stood roughly where the Arthur Memorial Church now stands. Cumnock Castle anciently stood in the middle of a loch, known as Loch Cumnock, which extended from North Boig Farm eastwards for almost four miles to the foot of Corsencon Hill. The castle could only be reached by either a causeway or else by boat, and tradition claims that the stones used to build it were rolled down hill from Cairnscadden Hill and ferried across the water.

The Arthur Memorial Church was erected in 1912 to plans of the Cardiff architect, W. Beddoes Rees, as the UF church in the village. It served until September 1972 when it was closed. On the other side of the lane that passes the church can be found the old parish churchyard, in which stand the remains of the old church. This was erected in 1657, according to the date on the lintel, making it one of only two Commonwealth churches in Ayrshire. In the graveyard are a number of old stones, including the grave of Revd Thomas Hunter, minister at New Cumnock for fifty years until his death in 1760.

The main street of New Cumnock is known as the Castle, and here can be found the parish church, town hall, and most of the village's main services. The parish church is a fine building of 1833, designed by James Ingram. It rises to a square tower, with clock and spirelets, not unlike

Mauchline. Within is a fine pulpit with sounding board, and stained glass windows. The town hall is quite a distinguished building, though it lies back somewhat and does not stand proud like most other municipal buildings. The architect was Allan Stevenson, and the hall was erected in 1888 at a cost of £852. At the north end of the Castle is Loch Park, home to Glenafton Football Club, which was founded in 1930. On the other side of the street from here is the running track and beyond it the confluence of the Afton Water and the river Nith. Further along the street can be found the Miners' Memorial. This comprises a carved Davey lamp on a granite base, erected in 1985 to commemorate the local mineworkers who lost their lives in the pits. The sculptor was Hugh MacLachlan of Ayr. There is an outdoor heated-swimming-pool next to a leisure centre and nearby is the community centre, opened in 1958.

New Cumnock has many connections with Robert Burns, who seems to have stopped here on many occasions on his travels between Ayrshire and Dumfriesshire. A number of plaques mark sites of interest, and these include the Castle Hotel, where Burns is thought to have spent a few nights whilst passing through the village. At the southern end of the Castle is Mossmark of Oldmill, an old mill dating from the seventeenth century, but rebuilt in 1902. It was here Burns wrote an 'Ode, Sacred to the Memory of Mrs Oswald of Auchincruive'. To commemorate Burns and other associations from the parish's past, Pamela Ramage painted a large mural on the south wall of the Castle Hotel in 2000. The adjoining area was named the Mary Morrison Memorial Garden.

At the Castle Primary School (erected in 1873) the main road strikes east, heading for the Afton Bridge. It passes the Evangelical Church, founded in 1988 and now located in what was a former public house. On the east side of the bridge are some old cottages, the original Afton Bridgend. This name applies to a much larger scheme of houses, built to rehouse miners from their rows. Most of the houses here date from the 1950s and 1960s, and there is little of interest. Within the scheme can be found Cairnhill Primary School, opened in 1960, St Margaret's RC Church and New Cumnock Baptist Church of 1965–6. At one time there was a Reformed Presbyterian Church (later Free and United Free) at Afton Bridgend. The church was erected in 1868 with a manse along-side, but only the former manse survives.

The A76 heads east from New Cumnock down Nithsdale. There are various farms here, their lands extending uphill to the south. At Meikle Westland the Garepool Burn can be followed southward on foot to find an old slurry mill, the former steel waterwheel of which lies in ruins. Archibald Brown of Liverpool made this. This wheel was used to drive shafts that operated paddles used to churn up clay and water into slurry that was pumped down to the Nithsdale Tileworks at Westland.

Further south, at Fountainhead, high on the slopes of The Knipe, or Hare Hill as it is also known, can be found the fragmentary remains of an old antimony or stibnite mine, little of which remains other than some small spoil heaps. It operated between 1838 and 1860. The ore was used in England, but when a source closer to the demand was found, the New Cumnock mine was abandoned. The mine consisted of little more than a level driven into the hillside, working the practically vertical vein of around twelve to eighteen inches in thickness. The summit of The Knipe is disfigured by the erection of a number of wind turbines, used for the creation of electricity.

Above Waistland Farm can be seen a martyrs' memorial, standing out on the horizon next to a stone dike. To the east of Over Cairn farm the A76 leaves Ayrshire just short of the March Burn. The river Nith continues to flow down Nithsdale, though now it is no longer an Ayrshire river, and is perhaps more at home in Dumfriesshire. A minor road from the main A76 road strikes down to the river and crosses it by the March Bridge. It climbs up again on the opposite side of the valley, passing below the railway and then makes its way along the southern slopes of Corsencon Hill. This hill is one of the most prominent in the area, and was probably used as a beacon hill in the past.

A minor road, also off the A76, climbs between Corsencon and Craigdullyeart hills, leading to the forest plantations around Craigshiel and the Lethans. The road passes eighteenth-century limeworkings, with mines below Craigdullyeart and an old double limekiln at the head of the Limekiln Burn, this dated from 1837. This minor road, which passes around the north of Corsencon and back down to Kirkconnel, used to be the main route down Nithsdale hereabouts, the crossing over the river and valley bottom being too wet and marshy in early times.

Mansfield House no longer stands; it had been erected around 1850 and was home to the Stuart-Menteth family, who also owned Closeburn Castle in Nithsdale. This family was granted a Baronetcy of both places in 1838. The house was demolished in 1957. By the side of the burn the old Mansfield Mill still survives, though has long since been disused. More former limeworkings can be found at Hall of Mansfield, with the remains of a three-draw kiln. The Mansfield Road returns to New Cumnock at Pathhead. On the way it passes through the formerly separate village of Mansfield, now part of the larger community, and site of some more modern cottages.

*

Glen Afton strikes south from New Cumnock, the Afton Water draining a large area of hill country to the south of the village. The road up the glen starts at Mossmark, and at first is lined on one side by a row of cottages. Soon the new cemetery (of 1901) is passed, where New Cumnock war memorial is located, as well as various headstones commemorating folk who died in the mines. At the southern end of the cemetery are footpaths eastward, across the Afton Water to West Park and into the Cairnhill housing scheme, and westward, across Knockshinnoch Moss to Knockshinnoch and Connel Park.

The west-heading pathway passes a memorial cairn that was erected to commemorate those miners who lost their lives in the Knockshinnoch Castle Colliery disaster of 7 September 1950. As the men were digging below ground, the roof of the pit caved in and the rain-soaked peaty moss above rushed in to fill the void. Thirteen men were killed, and another 116 were trapped below ground. A major rescue operation, with teams from all over Scotland taking part, managed to free the men while thousands watched on from the surface. The story of the disaster was later recounted in a film, *The Brave Don't Cry*.

Laight Farm is next to be reached up the glen. At the time of Burns this was home to John Logan and Burns often paid a call. For many years a window existed in the farmhouse that Burns had inscribed by a diamond stylus, but this was broken and lost. Near Laight Farm, on the side of the roadway, is a memorial cairn commemorating Burns's connections with the glen. One of his most famous songs is called 'Afton Water', and at this spot one can see why he was keen to immortalise the river in song. New Cumnock Burns Club erected the cairn in 1972. A small parking area and picnic site can be found adjoining it. There used to be a prehistoric burial cairn on the west side of the road, known as Buchanny Cairn, but all sight of it has long since been lost. There is also a local tradition that claims that there was a secret tunnel linking Little Dalhanna (now in ruins) with Dalhanna Farm, used at the time of the Covenanters.

The Glenafton Leisure Park occupies the site of the old Glenafton Sanatorium. The hospital was erected in 1905–6 as a local tuberculosis hospital, and served as such until the 1950s before being converted into a geriatric hospital. It was eventually closed in the 1960s. Today it is home to holiday lodges and caravans. Glen Afton gets wilder beyond the caravan site, the hills becoming higher and the side of the glen steeper. Blackcraig Hill is the highest in the area, rising to 2,298 feet above sea level. On its western slopes is a depression in the rocks known as the Giant's Cave, and local tradition claims that William Wallace hid here at one time. More tangible is the coin hoard found at Blackcraig in 1882 by Peter Murdoch. This contained 141 silver and 40 gold coins, some as old as the reign of Robert II. One was discovered to be a forgery.

The Afton Reservoir was constructed in 1929–35, at a cost of £270,000. An earth dam was erected across the valley, impounding a large reservoir. The water was then piped down to a filter works where the water was cleaned ready for drinking. A former fountain at the foot of the dam has inscribed on it words from Burns' song, 'Flow gently sweet Afton'. In 1989–91 a new filter works was erected.

A circle of high hills surrounds the Afton headwaters. To the south of Blackcraig is Blacklorg Hill (2,232 feet). On its north-eastern slopes is the Cold Well, the source of the Kello Water, a tributary of the Nith. To the west of Blacklorg is a long arm comprising two hills, Cannock Hill and Craigbraneoch Hill. The latter is a prominent summit in the glen, 1,887 feet above sea level. The locals tend to call it Stayamrie, but that name is more accurate in describing the vertical rock face on its western flanks. South of Blacklorg is the Meikledodd Hill, the summit of which is 2,110 high, but which is a few hundred yards across the boundary into Kirkcudbrightshire. West of here is Alwhat (2,064 feet) and Alhang (2,106 feet). Between the two is the source of the Afton.

The hills on the west side of Glen Afton are not as high as those on the east. Millaneoch Hill is the tallest, at 1,991 feet, but it is really only a shoulder of the larger Windy Standard (2,290 feet), which is located in Kirkcudbrightshire. Windy Standard, Jedburgh Knees, Trostan Hill and Polwhat Rig have been disfigured by thirty-seven large wind turbines. Between Millaneoch and Alhang is a pass 1,595 feet above sea level. At one time there was a public road through here, linking New Cumnock with Dalry and the rest of Galloway, but there has been no sign of a road for many years. Much of the west side of Glen Afton has been afforested, the higher lands of Lochingerroch and Pencloe being planted with pine trees, as has the former lands around Glenlee, Monquhill, Lochmeharb and Hillend, all former shepherd's cottages.

The B741 strikes west from New Cumnock, linking it with Dalmellington. The first few miles of the road has a number of cottages and old buildings lining it, relics of mining communities that have reduced in size. The first village reached is the Legate, where a number of cottages line the road. Connel Park, the old mining village built at the junction of the Boig Road, follows. Here stood the Connel Park Baptist Church, erected in 1900 to replace a tin building of 1873. South of the village stood Knockshinnoch Castle Colliery, where the disaster took place in 1950. The mine took its name from an old castle that stood near to Knockshinnoch House. The Boig Road strikes north-west from

Connel Park. The site of Ardnith House is no longer obvious, other than the trees on the low hill on which the house stood. The house was home to the manager of the Lanemark coal company. T. M. Brown of Ardnith was tried for murdering a woman by poisoning in 1906, but he was found to be insane. The former Afton Brickworks are located to the west of the Boig Road, reached by a minor road past Fordmouth. The brickwork was built to use some of the spoil from the coal works, as well as clay quarried in the vicinity. The Boig Road crosses the Nith at the Nith Bridge and climbs uphill towards Benston and Cumnock. At Meikle Creoch is a small knoll known as the Mote Knowe, perhaps indicative of an Iron Age settlement.

Bank Glen is the third mining village west of New Cumnock. This village had a school, which was erected in 1873. It was later converted into a school for pupils with special education needs, but was closed in the 1980s and demolished. The village war memorial still stands here, recalling the names of those who suffered for their country. The Bank UF Church was erected in 1898 and stood until 1961. Bank House was erected in the nineteenth century in an Italianate style, but the house was demolished in the 1960s. The Hyslops of Bank, who were major shareholders in the New Cumnock Coal Company, occupied the house. The fourth mining village was Burnside, known also as Burnfoot. The older part was Burnfoot, but the rows there were demolished and newer houses erected at Burnside. Most of these have also been taken down and the residents re-housed in New Cumnock.

Between Burnfoot and Bank Glen was the Bank Colliery (No. 1) and the Bank Brick Works, closed in 1969. The site of it has been totally obliterated, like much of the countryside south of the road here, by the Roughhill opencast workings that have only in recent years been filled in again. West of Burnfoot Rows was Lanemark Colliery, also gone. A fifth small community survives at Dalleagles, where there is a single row of houses and a few others further west at the road junction. There are no public buildings at Dalleagles, but at one time it boasted an inn and school. The countryside south of here rises to Enoch Hill, the highest of the local group at 1,866 feet. All this is sheep rearing countryside, although part of it has been given over to forestry. North of the hamlet, at Whitehill, a number of silver coins were discovered in an earthenware jar in 1834.

The B741 begins to climb to the west of Dalleagles, making its way across country towards Dalmellington. At Craighouse are the remains of more limeworkings. The infant Nith is crossed once more by another Nith Bridge, at Nith Lodge Farm. The river is but a mountain stream here, and its source can be found among the forests to the south, 1,416 feet above sea level. Beyond Nith Lodge the road climbs to the top of Knockenlee Hill, where can be found the remains of a Bronze Age burial cairn. From Knockenlee a track descends to the stream known as the Beoch Lane, much of this area being former opencast workings. At one time there was a coalmine here, as well as miners' rows. The Beoch Lane drops down to join the Nith. North of the lane is the Martyrs' Moss, named after the Covenanters who crossed this way and were to be captured on Carsgailoch Hill. In the midst of the moss is the Whig Hole, one of the places where the hunted men were wont to hide.

At Waterhead Farm can be found the remains of Waterhead Castle. This was an ancient tower measuring fifty feet by thirty feet, owned by the Chalmers family, but which has been ruinous for many centuries and only the foundations survive. Some of the stones were incorporated in the nearby Waterhead Farm. At Craigman the public road can be rejoined and followed along the north side of the Nith towards Benston. Craigman used to have a small coalmine, and at Tappet Hill was a quarry. At Dalgig Farm a forest track can be followed north into the Kyle Forest and up the slopes of Carsgailoch Hill. Near the summit is a martyrs' grave, marking the spot where Highland soldiers caught up with a group of Covenanters, returning from a Conventicle at Glenmuck. The present memorial was erected in 1827 to replace a simple stone, perhaps erected by Old Mortality. North of Fardenreoch Farm can be found a Bronze Age burial cairn. The site of another is commemorated by the name Cairn Knowe at Rigghead Farm. At Hall of Auchincross stood a castle for many years, but nothing of it can now be seen. Nearby was a knoll known as the Court Knowe. Part of the countryside has been subject to opencast working here.

# 11

# Coylton, Ochiltree, Stair and Drongan

THE A70 BETWEEN CUMNOCK and Ayr passes through two villages: Coylton and Ochiltree. Coylton is the further west, a growing community that has found itself something of a dormitory town for commuters to Ayr and other places of work. The village is linear, built along the A70, but with modern housing estates springing up it is becoming more compact in relation to its size. The village was at one time so long and spread out that its constituent parts had different names, and these survive to some extent. The west end is known as Joppa, the middle part New Coylton, and the eastern part Hillhead.

Coylton is the main village of a parish of 11,590 acres, which extends south from the river Ayr to the moors above Dalmellington. The old parish church is now in ruins, left somewhat isolated at the old community of Laigh or Low Coylton. The church dated from the pre-Reformation period, was rebuilt in 1776, but in 1836 was abandoned when the present parish church was finished. The graveyard around the old church has a few interesting old stones, including one in memory of a boy who drowned in Loch Martnaham in 1960. Another commemorates a man and wife drowned in the Coyle in 1866. There is also a stone for a railway guard, killed at Hurlford in the discharge of his duty in 1878. Other memorials commemorate mining victims. A small window high on the gable of a neighbouring house was used at the time of the body snatchers to guard the corpses.

Next to the kirkyard is the Coylton Arms Hotel, an old country pub dating from the late eighteenth century. Little more can be found in Laigh Coylton, other than a few industrial workshops and a farm. In a field south of the hamlet is an ancient mound, its origins unknown. The former manse is now known as Low Coylton House. It dates from 1839. At Millmannoch Farm stands a tree known as the 'Trysting Thorn', associated with Robert Burns, and where he composed 'The Soldier's Return'.

Hillhead is where the parish church of 1832–6 was built, the designs by the notable Scots architect, David Bryce. The T-shaped church is Gothic in style. Although it has a tower sixty feet tall, being located back from the street the church is not as prominent as it could be. Inside are three galleries, the Sundrum gallery containing a bronze plaque by Robert Bryden, commemorating John Claud Campbell Hamilton. The church was extended to the rear in 1996 to plans of Robert Potter & Partners.

At the east end of Hillhead is the parish war memorial, a cross of white granite, designed by Robert Bryden. East of here is Duchray House, sitting in the trees, owned by the Montgomerie family.

Robert A. Bryden (1865–1939) was one of Hillhead's most prominent sons. He was born in Coylton parish, educated at Ayr Academy and apprenticed to a firm of architects – Morris and Hunter – in Ayr before going on to study in London, where he lived for fifteen years. On his return from London, Bryden settled in Ayr and became an elder in St Leonard's Church. He was an accomplished sculptor, producing a number of fine works. In 1896 he designed a series of etchings on Burns subjects to celebrate the bard's centenary. In 1899 he was appointed as Royal Engraver. Examples of his work can be found in Ayr: he fashioned the plaque on the McAdam Memorial in Wellington Square; and his plaque in the Auld Kirk commemorates a former minister, Dr Dykes. There are also several of his etchings in the Carnegie Library. Bryden was buried in Ayr cemetery.

The Claud Hamilton Memorial Hall dates from 1909, designed by A. C. Thomson, and was erected in memory of a son of Sundrum Castle. A semi-circular porch, enriched by the arms of Hamilton, adorns the front of the hall. Apart from the Finlayson Arms Hotel and a shop, there are few other commercial buildings at Hillhead.

Despite its name, New Coylton is in fact quite an old community, built along the side of the main road. Here can be found the present primary school, erected in the 1960s, the post office, Kyle Hotel, library and Masonic Lodge Coila St Andrew No. 1334. Within the school are bronzes to the writer George Douglas Brown (whose career is covered later in this chapter) and John Smith, Brown's schoolmaster, the latter by Bryden. There are a number of traditional cottages lining the road, but there has also been quite a bit of modern infilling. Joppa is now quite an extensive community of houses, and here most of the facilities have been located, including the leisure centre.

The former Sundrum Castle estate lies to the north of Coylton, the castle itself now divided into lesser dwellings, and other houses built alongside. The castle incorporates an ancient tower of the around 1360, known as the Wallace Tower after Sir Duncan Wallace, who was responsible for its construction. The castle passed to the Cathcart family and was sold by them to the Hamiltons in 1750. It was rebuilt in 1792 and various wings were added over the years, resulting in quite a long façade extending east to west. The clock tower was erected in 1877 to commemorate the marriage of Claud and Marion Hamilton. Within the castle were a number of secret passages, constructed within the thickness of the walls. Behind

Sundrum Castle

Sundrum Castle the Water of Coyle meanders past in its deep gully, at one point dropping over the Ness Waterfall. At one time this was used to drive an electricity turbine. In the policies can be seen Cushats House, a cottage-orne-style building dating from around 1880, formerly the dower house, but now a private dwelling.

The river Ayr forms the northern boundary of Coylton Parish, here occupied by Gadgirth. The Old Ha' is a ruin by the side of the river, little more than fragments of masonry on a promontory of land. Of Gadgirth House itself nothing survives. This was a fine house on a higher headland, built in 1808 for the Chalmers family on the site of an old castle. The council acquired the house as a children's home in 1949 but it was demolished in 1968. A few good estate buildings still exist however, including Gadgirth Mains of around 1840, which has a pend and doocot in the gable, and Gadgirth Holm, an Arts & Crafts group of cottages of 1906. An old obelisk on the hill above Gadgirth Mains has no inscription.

To the north-east of Broadwood Farm was the site of a small village known as Woodside. This comprised of a row of thatched cottages, but these were cleared away in 1954 and nothing of the community survives.

A large projection of Coylton parish lies within a pronounced meander of the river Ayr. This land is occupied by numerous farms and smallholdings, and at one time was part of Auchincruive estate. Here can be found the Auchincruive Holdings. North of here, in the bend of the river, are woods planted to commemorate a battle, the names Mount Scarburgh, Mount Stair and Mount Loudoun recalling the leaders of the armies. By the side of the Ayr, next to the Leglen Bridge, is a large memorial cairn, erected in 1929 to mark the spot where Robert Burns spent some time musing on his idol, Sir William Wallace. Wallace himself is known to have hidden in the woods of Auchincruive, and various spots alongside the river are said to have been his hideout.

Carbieston House dates from 1894, built of red brick for Claud Hamilton. The tower has a French-style roof, and the house is still occupied. At Westpark and Highpark farms can be found a couple of ancient earthworks. That at Westpark is a circular knoll, visible from the main road, and known as the Witch Knowe. The earthwork at Highpark is larger, but has no name.

Loch Martnaham is divided between Dalrymple and Coylton parishes. The loch is one of the largest in the immediate area, and is over twenty feet deep in places. Martnaham Lodge dates from the nineteenth century, having been built by the Earl of Cassillis as a fishing lodge. Between 1900 and 1912 the house was the home of James Edward Shaw, author of *Ayrshire 1745-1950: A Social and Industrial History*. Shaw was the county clerk and treasurer, a deputy lieutenant, justice of the peace and solicitor.

South-east of Martnaham the land rises gradually, becoming rougher to the south when it reaches the heights known as the Craigs of Kyle. On the northern slopes of the Craigs can be found the spring known as St Bride's Well, an ancient waterhole associated with the saint. It is sometimes known as the Chapel Well, and it is claimed that there used to be a small chapel here, used up to the Reformation. The Craigs of Kyle are composed of a strange granitic rock that has been given the name 'Kylite'. The South Craig Quarry on the slopes of the hill at one time extracted the stone.

The villages of Littlemill and Rankinston fall within Coylton parish. Littlemill is a small community, consisting of only a farm, a few cottages and a school. Rankinston is larger, though it is little more than a street of houses built up the hillside, located on either side of a dead-end road. Most of the houses are of the same date, and were originally built to house mineworkers.

West of Rankinston was the Littlemill Colliery, worked until 1974. A number of other smaller mines were located in the near locality, including the Bowhill and Kerse ironstone pits. From Rankinston, where a branch of the railway line linked Cumnock with the Doon valley, mineral lines snaked their way up Ewe Hill to reach the pits. The Water of Coyle passes to the east of Rankinston. The watercourse drains the afforested moors to the south east, rising on the eastern slopes of Benquhat Hill. In its infancy, the Coyle drops over a few waterfalls in the vicinity of Rankinston Farm.

Much of the high forest ground around here lies within Ochiltree parish. The Kyle Forest extends from the Doon valley eastwards towards Cumnock, and covers many thousands of acres. Around the periphery there are still some moorlands, used for grazing sheep. Some of this area is being worked by opencast means for coal, large sites either existing or having been reinstated at Piperhill and Auchlin. This countryside was riddled with old mine workings, pits having existed at Polquhairn, Auchlin, Old Polquhairn, Drumsmodden, Kayshill and elsewhere.

The small communities of Hayhill and Sinclairston owe their origins to the mines. Hayhill is a simple row of houses on one side of the road, with no other facilities other than a small play-park. Sinclairston was the older and larger of the communities. Here was the local school, later used as St Clair's RC School for the Drongan area. It was erected in 1909–10, the design by A. C. Thomson, but closed in June 1996. By the side of the road is an old water pump, made by Glenfield & Kennedy of Kilmarnock. Belston Loch lies to the east of Sinclairston, a kettle-hole lochan used by fishermen. Of the Plaid Loch, which lay further to the north-east, little remains other than a small marshy area within woodland.

Drumsmodden Farm, less than a mile from Sinclairston, was the home of the father of George Douglas Brown (1869–1902), author of *The House with the Green Shutters*. Brown was the natural son of the farmer, by the maid Sarah Gemmell, who later moved to live in Ochiltree. She later moved to Kayshill, in Stair parish. Brown was educated in Ochiltree, Coylton then at Ayr Academy, from where he won scholarships to Glasgow University. There Brown won the Snell Exhibition, allowing him to study at Balliol College, Oxford. Brown worked as a journalist in London, but spent much of his free time writing books, including *Love and a Sword*, a boys' adventure story (published in 1899), and *Green Shutters*, which made his name. The book was an immediate success, ending decisively the 'Kailyard School' of writing, and was compared favourably to the work of Thomas Hardy. The novel examines the life of the Gourlay family in a small Ayrshire village and its quality clearly indicates that Brown could have gone onto great things. Sadly, his death from pneumonia at the age of only 33 prevented the completion of two novels that he had been working on. He never forgot his roots and set up the George Douglas Brown Trust to benefit the poor of the parish of Coylton. There is a headstone to his memory in Ayr cemetery.

At Auchencloigh Farm are the scanty remains of Auchencloigh Castle.

This building appears to be quite old but has long been in ruins, and little of it remains today. The Burnock Water rises in the Kyle Forest and flows north towards Ochiltree, meeting the Lugar Water just east of the village. The headwater of the Burnock is known as the Black Water, from the deep peaty colour it has at this point. Shortly after passing beneath the Burnock Bridge, which carries the B7046, it passes Burnock Mill, an old mill that still has its weir upstream. Further on the stream flows below the Burnock Viaduct, which carries the railway line between Ayr and Cumnock.

On the west of the Burnock is Glenconner Farm. The Tennant family, who were known to Burns in the eighteenth century, at one time owned this. John Tennant was land factor to the Duchess of Glencairn and advised Burns to take the lease of Ellisland Farm near Dumfries. One of the sons, Charles Tennant, patented a method used for bleaching linen. He moved to Glasgow where he set up a major chemical works at St Rollox. There he made his fortune, and was able to buy the Glen estate near Innerleithen in Peeblesshire. In 1885 Charles Tennant was created a Baronet and in 1911 his son, Edward, was created Baron Glenconner. The family became one of the richest in Scotland and even owned the island of Mustique in the Caribbean. There have been various books written about the family, including *Tennant's Stalk* by Nancy, Lady Crathorne (nee Tennant), published in 1973, and *Broken Blood*, by Simon Blow (1987).

*

The village of Ochiltree lies above the confluence of the Burnock with the Lugar. The village has grown slowly over the years, but used to be well known for the manufacture of toddy ladles and sickles. The older part of the village is located at the eastern end, and Main Street comprises of a line of old cottages climbing up the hillside to the west. Down near the dam across the Lugar (built to hold water used for cooling the Barony Power Station) can be found the old churchyard, any remnants of the old church having long since disappeared. There are a few old and interesting gravestones, however, including a memorial to the Simpson brothers, one of whom was the 'Winsome Willie' of Robert Burns. Also buried here is Robert Johnstone (1831–92), founder of the Robert Johnstone Bursary.

Of Ochiltree House nothing survives. This was an old Scots tower house of the seventeenth century that was owned by the Colville, Stewart then Cochrane families. The Stewarts held the title Baron Ochiltree from 1543 until 1675. The house latterly passed through a couple of hands, including the Boswells of Auchinleck, but was demolished in 1952 and a new building erected on its site. Access to the house was from Mill Street, which extends from the cross eastwards to the modern bridge across the Lugar (erected 1961). The older bridge of around 1830 lies further north. Most of the older houses in Mill Street were built in 1789. Ochiltree Mill was erected in 1859.

Burnock Street makes its way south-east from the cross, heading for Cumnock. The houses here are slightly more modern, one of them containing an old mural sundial, dated 1787. Here also can be found a stone bearing the arms of the Cunninghames of Glencairn, with their distinctive shake fork, and the motto 'Over Fork Over'. This building is known as the Noble House and dates from 1807, perhaps being erected as a coaching inn. Burnockholm House is quite simple-looking from the street, but to the rear is a fine three-and-a-half storey building of some charm. This house lies on the opposite side of the Burnock Bridge (1838) from the village, and within a small garden area alongside can be seen the ruins of the old bridge, the road passing to the other side of the house at that time.

Ochiltree Cross is a simple stone shaft, located in the middle of the road junction. The shaft may date from the sixteenth or seventeenth century, but the cross has unfortunately been knocked over on a number of occasions by vehicles and has had to be rebuilt. It was restored to commemorate Victoria's Diamond Jubilee in 1897 and Queen Elizabeth's Silver Jubilee in 1977. Facing the cross are two inns, the Commercial Inn, which still functions, and the former Head Inn.

Main Street climbs from the Cross. There is a fine selection of traditional buildings along the roadside but, unfortunately, here and there some have been demolished and buildings out of character have been put in their place. An old Glenfield & Kennedy pump can be seen. The old church dates from 1789, a simple building with little in the way of ornament. It contains two stained glass windows by Stephen Adam. On the other side of the street was the old smithy, now rebuilt as a private house. A bronze plaque sculpted by Robert Bryden, on the wall of the British Legion, marks the birthplace of George Douglas Brown. This house has green shutters on it, to recall the name of his famous novel.

The Community Centre is a modern building of 1971, costing £28,000 to build. The older primary school was erected in 1909, designed by A. C. Thomson, the present primary school dating from 1976. At the west end of the older part of Main Street is a cottage that was erected as a convalescent home for patients of Ayr Fever Hospital in 1881. Main Street was too steep for many vehicles and it was decided to create a newer road contouring round the hill to the south. The village war memorial

Ochiltree: Main Street showing the 'House with the Green Shutters'

stands in a triangular garden here, recalling the names of those who perished in battle. The cross formerly stood at the side of the smithy, for this garden was occupied by the Free Church, erected in 1846 and demolished in 1967.

Mauchline Road leaves the Cross by a narrow exit and makes its way along the west side of the Lugar Water towards Crosshill, from where Mauchline can be reached by way of Barskimming. The old manse of Ochiltree is found on this road, as well as a number of modern houses. These extend as far as the new cemetery. Between the cemetery and Carston Farm can be found the Witch Knowe, perhaps an old motte hill dating from the Norman period.

Ochiltree Castle stood on a headland above the Lugar Water, on the opposite side from Auchinleck Castle. No remnant of the castle can be seen, for Ochiltree House or a predecessor probably replaced it. The castle was a seat of the Colville family, which feuded with the Auchinlecks of that Ilk in the 1440s. The Auchinlecks burned Ochiltree Castle, and it may have been at that time it was abandoned. Robert Colville was killed at New Cumnock in 1449 as part of this feud. Another Robert Colville was killed at Flodden in 1513. The lands later passed to the Cochranes and Stewarts. Below Auchinbay Farm, by the side of the Lugar Water, can be found Peden's Cave. This was a hideout used by the famous Covenanter, Alexander Peden, in particular during his dying days. His brother farmed Tenshillingside on the other side of the river at that time.

Barskimming Estate lies along the side of the river Ayr and comprises some finely wooded farms. Old Barskimming House stands on a rock above the river, facing upstream to the bridge. The house dates from 1883 and is owned by Lord Strathclyde. The Miller family, who erected the previous house in 1771 on the site of an even older structure, originally owned the estate. In 1946 Thomas Galbraith, who in 1955 was created Baron Strathclyde, acquired it. On the south, or Stair parish side of the river, are a few notable houses, including Burnbrae Lodge, and Stairaird. Burnbrae Lodge was erected as a gatehouse to Barskimming, but it was extended and turned into a small country house. Stairaird was likewise a Barskimming farmhouse of around 1775, but this was rebuilt as a small country house. For a time it was owned by Lord Glenarthur.

\*

West of here is Stair village, a tiny place with little more than a few scattered cottages, a pub and a church. Stair House stands nearby, a rather fine seventeenth century building erected by the Dalrymples on an ancient site. The Dalrymple family acquired Stair by marrying the Kennedy heiress and James Dalrymple, eighth laird, was created Viscount Stair in 1689. His son, Sir John, was created Earl of Stair in 1703. He was infamous as the man who signed the orders resulting in the Massacre of Glencoe in 1692. The house was later leased by various families, but no longer remains the property of the Stair family.

Stair church lies nearby. It owes its origins to the Dalrymple family who felt that it was too inconvenient to travel to the parish church in Ochiltree. They campaigned with the king and in 1669 he agreed that Stair could be separated into a parish of its own. The old church is a rather fine Gothic building, dating from 1864 and built to plans of William Alexander. The kirkyard contains some fine memorials, including some commemorating local lairds. The former manse, now known as Stairwood House, was erected in 1807.

The Stair Inn lies on the southern end of Stair Bridge. The inn perhaps dates from 1820 and was a popular resting-place when coaches used the B730 as a main thoroughfare. A predecessor may have been here since 1700. Stair Bridge itself dates from 1745, a rather fine single-arched bridge that spans the Ayr. At one time it was the first bridge upstream from the Auld Brig in Ayr.

Dalmore House was an elegant building completed in 1880–1 by the Heron family, using John and Robert Ingram as architects. The house was a mix of styles, incorporating Tudor, Elizabethan and Gothic elements. Dalmore House was destroyed by fire in April 1969, leaving only the stone walls standing. In the vicinity were a couple of small mines, where stone used for sharpening hones was dug from the ground. More will be mentioned of this in the following chapter. At Laigh Dalmore plumbago was mined between 1808 and 1815.

South of Stair is the old mining village of Trabboch. Most of the buildings associated with the village have gone, in particular the miners' rows, but one or two still survive. The former school stands by the side of Trabboch Loch. A Free Church used to exist here, known as Stair Free Church and latterly as the Schaw Kirk. This building was erected in 1843–4 following the Disruption and used until 1956 when a modern church in Drongan, where most of the congregation were rehoused when the miners' rows were flattened, replaced it.

Trabboch Castle stands in hoary ruins to the east, next to Trabboch Mains Farm. The Boyds built the L-plan castle sometime in the fourteenth century, whom tradition claims was given the lands by Bruce for their part at Bannockburn. The castle was later owned by the Douglases, Arthurs, Lord Ochiltree and Campbell of Loudoun. Trabboch Mains is quite a fine steading, typical of the eighteenth century when much improvement was being carried out to agricultural property.

The B730 joins the A70 at Coalhall, a modern community of private houses attached to an old set of buildings. Here is the Gateside Inn, a traditional roadside public house. There was at one time a police station here, as well as a coal mine at North Barbeth.

The buildings to the east side of the railway bridge were built around what was known as Drongan Pottery. This was established in the eighteenth century, and in 1790 the potter, Peter Moir, was given a contract to make water pipes for use at Muirkirk ironworks. The works also produced general domestic ware, and many items were stored in a small cottage on the opposite side of the road. The pottery seems to have closed around 1878 and the cottages converted into miners' houses.

Drongan House is a fine farmhouse of 1775, classical in style and adorned by pediments on the main fronts. It is said that James Armour, the father-in-law of Robert Burns, was employed in its construction. An older, crow-stepped house known as Lochmark is attached to the rear. The Smith family, who did much to develop their estates, owned the house. An old tile works existed at Joppa, established in 1833 at the expense of Robert Boyle of Drongan Pottery. Bricks and tiles were produced here until 1866, when Boyle went bankrupt.

Drongan village is a modern community, established in 1946 when it was hoped to create a complete new town here. This did not come to fruition, and instead only the two main estates on either side of the

Taiglum Burn were completed. The old miners' rows at Taiglum, lining the B730, were demolished. Drongan today is mainly a dormitory for Ayr, the large-scale employment at Killoch Pit being a thing of the past. The village has two churches, the Schaw Kirk of 1956 and St Clare's Catholic church of 1967. Here also is a post office, library, shops and primary school (the last of 1959). At Drongan Mains stood Drongan Castle, all sign of which has virtually gone, other than a few fragments of masonry. The castle dated from the fifteenth century and was owned by the Craufurds. On the other side of the Water of Coyle was Drumsuie, or Drumsoy, Castle, also a seat of the Craufurds, the tower being dismantled in the nineteenth century.

The Killoch Colliery, located on the A70 between Coylton and Ochiltree, was opened in 1953 by the National Coal Board and was the most modern coal mine of its time. Production of coal started in 1960 but the mine suffered from geological faults. Local miners claimed that it should have been built on the other side of the road, for had it been located further south, then it would not have suffered so many faults. The pit formerly had two large glazed towers, visible for miles around, but when the pit closed these were demolished. The remaining surface buildings are now used as offices by a local construction and engineering company. The west end of the Killoch site has a large bing, covering many acres, and here is still a coal preparation plant, coal being brought here for screening and washing before being loaded onto trains.

# 12

# Tarbolton, Craigie and Symington

THE PARISH OF TARBOLTON extends to 12,141 acres, lying on the north side of the river Ayr. The villages of Annbank and Mossblown, both owing their origin to mining, occupy the western end and at the east it is bounded by the parish of Mauchline. Tarbolton village lies off the main roads, so that it does not really enjoy any passing traffic, and anyone heading for the village needs to leave the main roads behind. Tarbolton was erected into a Free Burgh of Barony in 1671, a unique creation, and one that was not officially removed when burghs were abolished in 1975.

The parish church is the most significant building in Tarbolton. It stands in its old churchyard, which contains a number of interesting stones. Here can be found the gravestone of William Shillilaw, a Covenanter, and also buried in the kirkyard is Dr Patrick Wodrow, mentioned in the Burns poem 'The Twa Herds'. A number of stones commemorate victims of mining accidents. The church building is a large foursquare edifice, with projecting front, topped by a ninety feet spire containing a clock and weathercock. This was hit by lightning in 1909 but rebuilt. The church was built in 1820–1 to plans of Robert Johnston at a cost of £2,500. The church hall is located in the former Erskine Church, a box kirk that was erected in 1830. The Erskine Church continued in use until 1943.

Any tourists who do head for Tarbolton are usually followers of Burns and are heading for the Bachelors' Club, one of the most significant buildings in the county associated with the poet. It occupies a seventeenth-century building in the Sandgate, one that still has a thatched roof. In 1780 Robert Burns, his brother Gilbert and five friends formed the Bachelors' Club. This was a literary and debating society, but members had to 'be a professed lover of one or more of the female sex'. The Bachelors' Club was acquired by the National Trust for Scotland in 1938 and is open to the public during the summer months. There are essentially two rooms that visitors can view: the lower and upper, though one has to go outside to visit the other. The lower room contains furniture from the period. The upper room was where the club met, and here can be seen a number of relics associated with the bard.

The main thoroughfare in Tarbolton, which is named Montgomerie Street, heads south from this area. Here can be found a few buildings of interest, including the Lorimer Library, erected in 1879 with funds gifted by John Lorimer, a businessman in Kilmarnock and Glasgow. It is an

Tarbolton: Bachelors' Club and parish church

architectural oddity, the work of Gabriel Andrew. Here also is the Masonic Lodge, erected in 1889, and extended in 1925. The old Black Bull Hotel was built around 1822, and is a slightly classical building with a pediment. Daisybank House is a rather fine classical structure, probably dating from around 1800. Parliament Close is an arched pend, so called from the fact that the local men were wont to meet here to discuss village business and world affairs. The parish war memorial is located at the southern end of the village, unveiled in November 1920 by James Brown MP. In Burns Street stands Tarbolton's Town House, erected in 1832. A plaque by the side of the road marks the site of Manson's Inn, where Burns joined Lodge St James in 1781. In 1784 he was elected Depute Master. The inn is named after John Manson, who is mentioned in 'To Doctor MacKenzie' and who is buried in Tarbolton kirkyard.

Garden Street in Tarbolton has to make a detour around a green mound that had as its origin a motte and bailey. At one time a wooden Norman castle or fort occupied the hilltop. Further along this road, almost hidden in the hedge, is a small memorial marking the spot where Burns is reputed to have encountered 'Death', which resulted in his 'Death and Dr Hornbook'. Tarbolton Mill lies further on. When Burns's partner, Jean Armour, was thrown out by her parents for becoming pregnant to the bard a second time, she was taken in by Willie Muir, miller here.

Three roads strike south from Tarbolton, all joining the B743 Ayr to

Mauchline road. The furthest east road passes the modern cemetery, as well as Middlemuir Caravan Park. This occupies the former gardens of Montgomerie Castle, or Coilsfield, as the house was also known. Coilsfield was an ancient house or castle that was demolished and replaced by Montgomerie House in 1798–1804, the work of John Paterson. Montgomerie was a magnificent mansion built on two floors, but with a basement floor to the rear. The house had a rather fine projecting circular portico, with a fine dome overhead. The house was built for Hugh Montgomerie, who became the 12th Earl of Eglinton. In later years the house was owned by the Patersons, and then was a hotel, but in 1969 the house went on fire and was subsequently demolished. There is little left to indicate where it once stood.

The former policies of Montgomerie Castle have been virtually eradicated from sight, only a small gatehouse near Outmains surviving. In the field at Coilsfield Mains can be seen an ancient Bronze Age cairn, better known locally as Old King Cole's Grave. Old King Cole or Coil (of the 'merry old soul' nursery rhyme) was a local king who is said to have lived in the immediate post-Roman period. He was king of the former land of Strathclyde. Tradition claims that he was slain here by Fergus, King of Scots. The Dead-men's Holm nearby commemorates the battle. The cairn was opened in 1837 and within it was found several urns containing bones. Old King Coil's Well existed nearer to Failford. The Water of Fail flows past the site of Montgomerie towards the village of Failford. On the opposite side of the water, which is little more than a large burn, were the Roman trenches. There has been much speculation about these, some folk claiming that they are purely natural.

The Water of Fail flows into the river Ayr at Failford, a tiny village located in a hollow. There is a single line of older cottages between the road and the river, one of which is the Failford Inn. More modern bungalows occupy the other side of the road. A pathway leads to a sandstone column that marks the traditional spot where Robert Burns and his sweetheart, 'Highland' Mary Campbell, parted for the last time in 1786. Burns had decided to emigrate to Jamaica, but Mary went home to Greenock, where she died in 1786. Some say that Mary died in attempting to give birth. It is said that as Burns and Mary swapped Bibles at this parting, they were really carrying out a simple wedding ceremony. The monument was built of Ballochmyle sandstone and was erected in 1921 by the Burns Federation, the cost being met by Harland and Wolff, shipbuilders in Greenock.

There is a pathway from Failford alongside the river Ayr, leading into the Ayr Gorge wildlife reserve. The Scottish Wildlife Trust protects this. Extending to 113 acres, the reserve is home to a fine selection of broadleaf trees, as well as wild animals, birds and flowers.

To the east of Failford, by the side of the Mauchline road, are a number of fine houses located in the woods to the north. Old Auchenfail Hall is the oldest, a rather fine Georgian mansion of 1786. The house was built for William Cooper, a successful businessman from Glasgow, and at that time the house was known as Smithston. The former gate lodge is now located on the 'wrong' side of the main road from the entrance gates, due to the realignment of the B743. West of Failford, the B743 passes below the railway at what is known as the 'Fancy Bridge'. This railway passes to the south of Tarbolton, and the former Tarbolton station was located at Benston, one and a half miles from the village. The station opened on 1 September 1870 but was closed to passengers in 1943.

The B730 drops down from the heights of Carngillan to the river Ayr, reaching the small community of Milton and the Stair Bridge. On the way it passes the Yett and Wellflat smallholdings, a group of small agricultural units. The Tam o' Shanter Hone works (a hone is a sharpening stone) are mainly located on the north side of the Stair Bridge, but the complex at one time extended over both sides of the river. A suspension bridge of around 1900 links the two halves. A minor road strikes west from the Milton, a community on the north side of Stair Bridge, towards Annbank. Between Pierhill and Burn farms is a wood formerly protected by the Scottish Wildlife Trust, but the agreement behind this has been relinquished. Just south of the wood, within the wooded Holm Bank, is an ancient tumulus, its origin unknown.

The lands hereabouts form part of Enterkine estate. Enterkine House is a small mansion of 1939, erected to plans by John Fairweather & Sons. It is currently operated as a country hotel and restaurant. The house was built on the site of an earlier mansion of the late Georgian period. This proved to be too large and damp for the owners, who demolished it and erected the present building. It was three storeys in height and had Venetian windows on the ground floor.

The village of Annbank is of modern origin. In the middle of the nineteenth century miners' rows were erected to house workers in the Annbank and Enterkine pits. Others were employed in the Annbank Brickworks. A granite memorial at Weston Avenue commemorates James Brown (1862–1939). Brown was born at Annbank and was educated in the village school. He was an active campaigner for miners' rights, and was elected to Parliament in 1918, serving until 1931. Re-elected in 1935, he served until his death. He was appointed a Privy

Councillor and was three times elected as Lord High Commissioner to the General Assembly of the Church of Scotland. He lived most of his life at 51 Weston Avenue in the village.

Annbank United Football Club, which now plays in the Scottish Junior leagues, is based at the park west of Weston Avenue. The club was founded in 1879 at which time it played at senior level. The former Annbank House no longer exists, having been demolished sometime in the 1970s. The house occupied a prominent location high above the river Ayr and had been erected in the eighteenth century. The Cunninghams of Enterkine owned the estate, but the house was latterly occupied by a coalmaster.

The B744 leaves Annbank at the south-west end and drops gradually to the Tarholm Bridge, which crosses the river Ayr, entering Coylton parish. Off the road to the south is Privick Mill, the dam for which is below the former Annbank House, the lade running alongside the river to the old mill.

North of Annbank is the neighbouring village of Mossblown, again a fairly modern community but with one or two older buildings scattered through it. The village was originally known as Annbank Station, for here the passenger station for Annbank was located, one mile or so from Annbank itself. The names caused some confusion over the years, and once the station itself was closed it was decided formally to name the village Mossblown, after Mossblown Farm on which much of it was built. Another name used locally is Drumley, for here is Drumley House, Drumley Farm and the Drumley Inn. Mossblown is the location, to add to the confusion, of Annbank Parish Church, erected in 1871 as a chapel of ease. Annbank School was also here, but it was renamed Mossblown Primary School in recent years. A second church, the brick-built Catholic church, also exists.

Drumley House was erected around 1800 for Captain Robert Davidson, a merchant from Ayr, who bought the property from the Montgomeries of Coilsfield. It was later a private school, then merged with Wellington School in Ayr and is now the nursery and primary department. Nearby is Neilshill House, now part of a caravan site, and Templehouse, now extended and used as a nursing home.

Further east is Afton Lodge, a fine building dating from around 1790. The house was built for Mrs Catherine Stewart, who named it after the Afton estates her father, James Gordon, owned in New Cumnock parish. She was one of Burns's patrons and the collection of poems he sent her in 1791 is now known as the 'Afton Manuscript'. The house was extended in 1905 and 1919 to plans of Allan Stevenson. Today the house is subdivided.

To the north of Tarbolton, the Water of Fail passes over some low lying ground that was formerly a loch, known as Tarbolton Loch. The west side of the loch has been developed as a fishery, with a number of lagoons created in the marshy ground. The north-east side of the loch, where Mosside Farm once was, is used as a landfill site.

The clachan of Fail lies at the junction of the B730 with the A719. There is little to the hamlet today, other than a farm, a few cottages and the former Fail Mill. Yet Fail has a lengthy and important history, for here stood the Monastery of Fail, which was dedicated to St Mary. Andrew Bruce established the monastery in 1252 for the Red or Trinity friars. They were also known as Mathurines, from St Mathurine's monastery in Paris. As an old poem notes:

> The friars of Fail drank berry-brown ale,
> The best that ever was tasted;
> The monks of Melrose made guid kail,
> On Fridays, when they fasted.

A different version runs:

> The Friars of Fail
> Gat never owre hard eggs, or owre thin kale;
> For they made their eggs thin wi' butter,
> And their kale thick wi' bread;
> And the Friars of Fail they made gude kail
> On Fridays when they fasted,
> And they never wanted gear enough
> As long as their neighbours lasted.

In the middle of the fourteenth century there was a dispute between the friars of Fail and the monks of Melrose over the monastery lands. As part of this dispute Brother John of Fail gifted a white horse to John Graham of Tarbolton in payment of the right of patronage to the church of Tarbolton. However, Brother John later stole the horse back. The monastery was demolished by order of the lords of council at the Reformation in 1561 and the lands acquired by the Wallace family.

From the monastery an old monk's road made its way along the ridge of high ground towards Mauchline, where the abbots of Melrose Abbey had their local headquarters. The roadway passed by Redwrae and the Long Wood (still used as a minor road) then across country to Mossbog and thence by way of the minor road passing Ladyyard and Skeoch to the top end of Mauchline.

North of Fail is the former Fail Loch, again virtually drained and leaving only a stretch of low-lying marshy ground. One of the streams, which flows into Fail Loch, rises near Lochlea Farm. Robert Burns tenanted this between 1777 and 1784. In a thatched cottage that formerly existed around one mile away, James Thom (1799–1850) was born. He was a stonemason who became renowned for his sculptures of Burns and his contemporaries. In 1832 he moved to London and two years later moved to New York, where he was much in demand. His son, James Crawford Thom (1835–98) became a noted artist, painting portraits and landscapes. Old surface buildings of the former Lochlea coal mine can still be seen north of the farm. It was never a large complex.

The parish of Craigie lies to the north of Tarbolton. It is not a very large parish, extending to 6,579 acres, nor is it very populous, for the only centre of population within it is the tiny village of Craigie itself. Prior to 1647 the parish was attached to that of Riccarton.

The former Underwood estate, owned by the Kennedys since 1785, occupies the south-west end of the parish. The mansion house dates from around 1790 (but was divided in 1984) and stands by the side of the little Underwood Burn. This has a number of footpaths alongside, extending south across the public road into Underwood Glen. William Roxburgh (1759–1815), a noted physician and botanist, was born here. Nether Underwood is a largish country house erected by the last Kennedy of Underwood in the 1930s.

The Wallace Monument on Barnweil Hill

East of Underwood the land rises considerably to Barnweil Hill which, although only 503 feet above sea level, is a prominent local eminence. Barnweil is the location for a number of sites that are of great historical significance. The hill reputedly took its name from the time when William Wallace set the barns of Ayr on fire, killing untold number of Englishmen. He retired to this hill from where he looked back and remarked, 'The barns o' Ayr burn weel'. The tale may be apocryphal, but in 1855 it was deemed sufficiently accurate for a number of locals to put up a large memorial in memory of Wallace. The monument takes the form of a foursquare Gothic tower, rising eighty feet above the summit of the hill. A door on the ground floor gives access to a winding cantilever stairway that leads up to the viewing platform above. From here many local landmarks can be seen, as well as a number of distant mountains including Ben Lomond, Merrick, Paps of Jura and Goat Fell on Arran. William Patrick of Roughwood paid for the construction of the monument and employed the architect, Robert Snodgrass, to design it. The ground was the gift of James Smith Neil of Barnweil. The tower was given to the people of Ayr and is maintained from the Common Good Fund administered by South Ayrshire Council. Access is available to those who wish to collect the key from the council offices in Ayr, but at the time of writing the tower was closed for reasons relating to health and safety.

The slopes of Barnweil Hill were also used by the Romans who established some sort of fort here, though the remains of this can only be seen using aerial photography. What can be seen on the ground is an old motte hill, dating from the Norman period. This is located on a lower eminence to the north, the north-west slopes of which are naturally steep. Some maps simply depict this as an earthwork. Between the motte and the Wallace monument can be found the ruins of Barnweil Church, still surrounded by an ancient kirkyard. The church is said to date from pre-Reformation times, but was abandoned in 1653 when Barnweil parish was divided between Craigie and Tarbolton. Of the church little remains other than some ruinous gables, and there are few stones to be seen in the graveyard. Access to the churchyard is made along an old trackway from the public road near the motte. Barnweil House lies on the north-east slopes of Barnweil Hill. The house was erected in the late eighteenth century but was restored to the plans of Ronald Alexander for himself. The gardens around the house are sometimes open as part of Scotland's Gardens Scheme.

The B730 separates the Barnweil area from Craigie Hill. The ruins of Craigie Castle can be seen near to Craigie Mains. The castle seems to occupy a poorly defended site, considering the number of eminences in the vicinity. However, the low-lying ground around the castle was at one time marshy and this would have greatly assisted the defence effort. Traces of old ditches and earthworks indicate that the outer courtyard was of a considerable size, indicative of the castle's importance. Craigie was a Wallace seat, the castle dating from the fifteenth century. The actual ruins one sees today contain fine examples of masonry work, with quality ashlar and ribs from the old vaulted great hall. The castle seems to have been abandoned around 1600, when the Wallaces moved to Newton Castle in Ayr, which must have been quite a comedown from such elegance. Perhaps the marshy surroundings had resulted in a damp building.

A minor road leaves the B730 behind and climbs up Craigie Hill to the village itself. A quaint and invariably bypassed community, Craigie nevertheless has considerable charm. Here can be found the Craigie Inn, an eighteenth-century hostelry. It stands next to the parish church, which dates from 1776. The church is T-shaped in plan, with a small belfry at the north-east end. The old kirkyard around the church has a number of interesting old gravestones within it, as well as the remains of the 1580 church. Here can be found a stone commemorating Thomas Allan (1833–1901), which is proud to note, 'He crossed the Atlantic Ocean twenty-four times.' The village also has a village hall and a former school, the latter dated 1874. The House of Craigie dates from 1808; it was originally the parish manse.

The actual summit of Craigie Hill, which was 508 feet above sea level, has been taken away by the massive Craigie Quarry, which lies west of Craigie Road. To the east of this road the hill survives, and here can be found a selection of antiquities. At the foot of one of the knolls that forms the summit of the hill can be found Peden's Cave, used by Alexander Peden at the time of the persecution of the Covenanters. Immediately behind Craigie's street an ancient fort occupies the summit of the hillock, the circular ramparts surrounding the summit. Just north of here is the more interesting Camp Castle, another fortified earthwork. This was originally thought to have been a dun, but more recent work on the site has proved that there was also a broch here, a rather strange location for this type of fortified tower, more commonly associated with the highlands. The broch was excavated in 1961, unearthing a central courtyard thirty feet in diameter, surrounded by a wall fifteen feet thick. Within this was found part of a mural chamber. Quarrying has destroyed much of the broch.

Craigie parish drops to the east, reaching the Cessnock Water at Carnell. Carnell is a very fine mansion house that was built onto an old tower house. Some older accounts of the castle name it Cairnhill. The tower is still visible to the west side, its masonry different in colour to the rich red sandstone of the more modern house. The old tower dates from the late fifteenth century and was built by the Wallace family. A stair tower was added in 1576. William Wallace of Carnell was killed at the Battle of Flodden. The estate passed to the Cathcarts and was acquired by the Hamiltons, who built the present house, employing William Burn as architect. The result is a Jacobean house, with square turrets, crow-stepped gables and shaped dormer heads. Further additions were made in 1871. Today the Findlay family owns the house. The gardens at Carnell are open to the public on occasion as part of Scotland's Gardens

Scheme. The walled garden is still used, and immediately south of it is a flower garden with a long rectangular pond. The gardens are noted for their herbaceous borders. The Garden House is a modern dower house. When the gardens are open, it is also possible to walk through the grounds around the castle, where teas are often served. Near Carnell's western gatehouse is the small community of Fiveways, little more than a row of modern houses, built for agricultural workers.

*

Symington Church showing Norman windows on gable

Symington village lies halfway between Prestwick and Kilmarnock, passed by the busy dual carriageway of the A77. To turn off the main road into the village is to re-enter the past, where life is lived at a slightly slower pace. Symington has the distinction of having the oldest parish church in Ayrshire still in use, dating from Norman times. It may have been built in 1160 when Symon de Loccard established a church here. The church was extended and altered over the years, and even the fine Norman windows were covered over, but in 1919 Peter MacGregor Chalmers was commissioned to undertake restoration work. Chalmers was as keen a historian as an architect, and he was responsible for allowing the windows to be uncovered once more, as well as other work. The interior has bare stone walls, and even the collar-beamed roof is open, showing some original timbers. There is some stained glass by Douglas Strachan and Gordon Webster. In the kirkyard are a number of old tombstones, including the burial place of the owners of Dankeith House, adorned with heraldry. There used to be a second church in Symington, a result of the Disruption in 1843. The church stood at the junction of Symington Road with Main Street but no longer survives.

Symington was at one time noted for its weavers, and also had people employed in quarrying and agriculture. There are a number of old cottages in Symington, most of which have been restored and well looked after. In the village is also the Wheatsheaf Inn, an old hostelry of the eighteenth century. The inn still has a tethering ring affixed to the wall, used for tying up horses. At the road junction can be seen the war memorial, commemorating the dead of two wars. The Robert Hay Boyd Memorial Hall dates from 1908.

To the north east of the old part of Symington is an extensive estate of more modern housing. The Scottish Special Housing Association started this, but in more recent years private houses have been built, extending the village out to an old avenue that led to Dankeith House. In Main Street is Townend Cottage, a dower house for Townend House, dating from around 1810 but incorporating a 1743 datestone from an earlier building. Townend House itself is a larger Italianate building of the nineteenth century with an attractive stable block, occupied at one time by the Boyds. Symington House in Kerrix Road was originally the manse, dating from 1786. In Brewlands Road is Craigowan House of 1849–50, built as the factor's house for Dankeith estate.

The parish of Symington extends to 3,736 acres, most of which is occupied by farms, a few former estates and a number of largish houses. Dankeith House is a large country house dating from 1893, although an earlier building is thought to be incorporated within the present structure. The house is Tudoresque in style, but the architect is unknown. A number of additions have been made to the house over its lifetime, most of which were the work of Ayr architects. Dankeith was damaged by fire in 1932 and during the Second World War was occupied by soldiers. In 1948 it was acquired by the Passionate Fathers as a retreat but was closed around 1968. Today caravans surround Dankeith as part of a leisure centre. The B730 passes to the east of Dankeith, from where views of the house are possible. This road has the new Symington Cemetery on it, a mile and a half from the village. Here also is Muirmill Equestrian Centre, originally the David Brown Riding School.

Coodham House lies on the east side of the B730, penned in by three roads. The house is invisible from the roads, however, for its parkland has been finely wooded. The house is currently in a sorry state; there was a proposal to divide it into flats and build other houses in the grounds, but the plans have so far failed to materialise. The desecration has resulted in the loss of a fine mansion of 1828, without doubt one of the most elegant in the county. It is Georgian in style, rising through three floors, and adorned by a large portico with four columns. At the west end of the house is a chapel of 1874, originally used for Anglican services. Coodham was originally built by Margaret Ogilvy Fairlie at a cost of £20,000 but was acquired by William Houldsworth in 1871. He was the owner of a number of local ironworks and mines and in 1887 was created a Baronet of Reddish, in Manchester, and of Coodham. During the war the house was used for military purposes, and in 1942 King George VI visited to inspect the troops. In 1948 the estate was acquired by the Passionist Fathers and used as a centre for retreats until 1987. In the grounds of Coodham is Coodham Lake, a man-made loch over-looked by the house and partly surrounded by trees. On the opposite side of the loch is a burial enclosure, used by the Houldsworth family, and including a Celtic cross.

Bogend and Bogend Toll are small communities of houses and industrial premises occupying the crossroads formed by the A77 with the B730. Here can be found a nursery, and industrial premises in a former mill. Whitelees is another roadside hamlet, the cottages having to suffer the passing traffic all day long. The Halfway Hotel occupies the other side of the road. This dates from around 1937, built to replace the old inn that went on fire in 1935. At Helentongate a minor road strikes to the south, terminating at Helenton Mains. There is a disused quarry here. Between the road and the Pow Burn is a Norman motte hill, known as Helenton Motte. Fragmentary ruins stood upon this. Danepark House is a small country house located by the roadside. The house dates from 1935–6 and was the work of James A. Carrick.

On the other side of the A77 is Hansel Village, located in the grounds of Broadmeadows House. Broadmeadows was built in 1931–4 for Percival Agnew to the plans of Noad & Wallace. The house is a fine modern mansion in the Arts and Crafts style. In 1963 Tom and Isobel Murdoch purchased the Broadmeadows estate and created Hansel Village, where disabled people could live and work in a sheltered environment. Donations resulted in the erection of Farmers House in 1966–7, followed by Fergusson and Wilson houses, where residents were accommodated. Most of the residents are employed within the village, either in the gardens, knitwear, pottery or craft shop. There is a large recreation hall, education and training workshops, and visitors are made welcome.

Rosemount Estate lies further south along the A77. The house that survives today is formed from the former service wing of a much larger house, most of which was demolished in 1948 and 1967. The original house, part of which dated from 1770, was a composite structure of different styles and dates. It was originally a Fullarton seat. A number of other large houses are located hereabouts, including Craigrethill, formed from an old farm steading, and Kersland.

# 13

# Troon and Dundonald

TROON IS A LARGE COASTAL town established on a prominent headland in 1812 by William Cavendish-Bentinck-Scott, 4th Duke of Portland
(1766–1854), who had been prime minister from 1807–9. Previously it was
just a tiny fishing hamlet within the parish of the much more important
community of Dundonald. In 1608 the Royal Burgh of Irvine was granted
permission to erect a new harbour here, the mouth of the Irvine being
unsuitable, but any works were small in scale, as were improvements made
around 1707 when the Fullarton landowners were granted a charter forming the Port of Troon. The Duke of Portland had started building a harbour
in 1808, and had built the first railway line in Scotland, linking Kilmarnock
with the port. Initially horses hauled the wagons, but later the first steam
train in the county was used, known as the 'Duke'. Troon was created a
Police Burgh in October 1896, by which time it had become a flourishing
seaport. It had grown larger than the main village of the parish at
Dundonald, and gradually the links were forgotten.

Troon is still very much an expanding town, though its spread is
hampered on a number of fronts by the surrounding golf courses. The
courses add much to the town, and attract visitors from all over the world.
Many, of course, are keen to play on the famous course used for the Open
golf championship. The housing estates have 'jumped' the green belt
created by the golf courses, and so the estates of Southwood, Darley,
Muirhead and Barassie lie at a distance from the rest of the town. Even
the independent village of Loans has extended considerably, and is virtually part of Troon now.

The name Troon comes from the Gaelic, *An t-Sron*, which means the
nose, or headland, an accurate description of the promontory that extends
westward, between two sandy beaches. The headland was used to shelter
the harbour. This has been developed over the years, so that today there
is a large east breakwater, erected in stages in 1808 and 1840, two main
basins and a lesser basin, used by fishing boats. The inner basin is home
to Troon marina, where local sailors and visitors tie up numerous yachts
and other pleasure craft. The marina was established in 1978 and is
used by Troon Cruising Club. The other basin is used for larger ships,
including a catamaran ferry that links Troon with Belfast in Northern
Ireland. This service was established in the 1990s, giving an alternative
to the Stranraer and Cairnryan services. Troon is home to a fleet of fishing

boats, a number of which were moved here from Ayr when the harbour there was being redeveloped. A fish market was built and other services associated with the trade. The lifeboat station was established in Troon in 1866, and has been responsible for saving over 500 lives since that time.

By the side of the harbour is the Ailsa shipyard. Building of boats at Troon began as soon as the harbour was developed in 1815. Troon Shipbuilding Company took over in 1843. The Shipbuilding Company was taken over by Ailsa in 1885, owned by a partnership including the Marquis of Ailsa, from whence its name. The dry dock was opened in 1899. At nationalisation British Shipbuilders took over. The large shed, which is visible from miles around, was erected in 1975. The company has waxed and waned over the years, as its products fell in and out of demand. In recent years the name has changed as different owners have come and gone. These include Ailsa-Perth (until 1996), and Ailsa-Troon (owned by Cathelco Group since 1996). Shipbuilding ceased at Troon in 2000, and the dry dock is now operated as a repair yard for vessels up to 400 feet in length.

It was from Troon harbour that the sailing yacht *Scotia* carried the Scottish National Antarctic Expedition to the polar region in November 1902. The *Scotia* was previously the *Hekla*, a Norwegian whaling ship, and had been converted by the Ailsa Shipbuilding Company. The team was led on its 33,000 miles voyage by the intrepid Dr William Spiers Bruce, who had been disappointed not to land a place on Scott's *Discovery* expedition. He decided to mount his own expedition and was provided with financial backing by the Coats family of Paisley. The venture was a great success and gathered a wealth of scientific data. There is now a Scotia Bay on Laurie Island in the Antarctic, where the expedition's first base is now a meteorological station.

There is a large timber yard at Troon, owned by Adam Wilson & Co. This company was founded in 1856 at Sorn and had a number of sawmills throughout the county. The Troon yard was opened in 1888 and was used mainly for the importation and conversion of timber from Argyll and foreign countries.

At the end of Harbour Road is a row of older cottages, now converted to offices. The roadway turns round to the left, and ends at a parking area next to a slip into the water. Here can be found an old anchor, and the start of a footpath up onto the Ballast Bank. This was formed from soil and stones used as ballast in ships returning from abroad, the ballast dumped along the west side of the peninsula. This gave the harbour the extra benefit of some shelter from the driving south-westerly winds. Port Ronnald is a small bay at the southern end of the bank. Here, in December 1894, the sailing ship *Coronella* ran aground. Men on the land managed to throw a line and rescue the crew. Another sailing vessel to run aground was the *Cleveragh*, which landed on the Black Rocks in South Bay in December 1865. Again the crew managed to land safely. These rocks were to see the demise of another vessel, the *Secret*, in February 1896. This schooner broke her mast off the Heads of Ayr and was driven north towards the Black Rocks. The crew managed to escape, but the cargo of eighteen tons of dynamite exploded, breaking the windows of buildings on the shore.

Most of Troon is formed of wide terraces or streets of substantial buildings. Many of the street names recall the town's connections with the Duke of Portland, and as such there is a similarity with Kilmarnock, where he was also a major landowner. Thus we have Portland Street and Terrace, Titchfield Road, Welbeck Crescent, Bentinck Drive and Cavendish Place. Other streets tend to be named after local areas, for example Templehill, South Beach, Dundonald Road, or are descriptive of places within the street, such as Academy Street, Church Street or St Meddans Street, the last named after St Meddans Church. Templehill is the name of the street linking Troon cross with Harbour Road. The temple after which it was named predates Portland's connections with the area. A folly, or summer house of sorts, stood here, having been erected some-time in the eighteenth century by Colonel William Fullarton as part of the Fullarton estate. It bore the inscription, *Bacho laetitiae datori, amacis et olio acrum*, which translates as 'Erected to Bacchus, the giver of happiness, for friends and for leisure'.

St Meddan is associated with Troon as well as some other locations in south-west Scotland, particularly Galloway. There is a rather fine church building of 1888–9, designed by J. B. Wilson, of this name. Located at the junction of St Meddans Street with South Beach, the large sandstone Gothic church has a tall spire, pointing skyward, on which is a public clock, acquired from the Old College buildings of Glasgow University, which stood in the city's High Street. Built as a United Presbyterian place of worship, the church has many fine features, including a large window depicting the healing of Jairus's daughter. The stained glass here is the work of John Blyth, Norman MacDonald and W. Smith.

Troon Old Parish Church stands at the corner of Ayr and Academy streets. There are really two churches here, the older church of 1837 with its spire, now used as halls, and the large sandstone mass of the neo-Gothic 1894 building, designed by Hippolyte J. Blanc. Unfortunately, the proposed tower was never erected. Inside, the church has some fine stained glass, by Morris & Co. and Gordon Webster. The ceiling is timber vaulted, and there are some fine carvings on the reredos and the pulpit.

Portland Church of Scotland in St Meddans Street dates from 1914, the work of H. E. Clifford & Lunan. Built as a United Free Church, the Perpendicular style building has some fine traceried windows. A. F. Steven donated the window in the chancel in 1920 as a war memorial. The organ is by Harrison & Harrison. Built of a yellow stone, the church has a red tiled roof. It replaced an older church of 1856. The halls were added in 1964.

The Catholic population of the town has a rather fine chapel in which to worship. The church of Our Lady of the Assumption and St Meddan was erected in Cessnock Road in 1911 to plans of Reginald Fairlie. It has a large tower at one end, more reminiscent of a tower house than an ecclesiastical building. However, there are some splendid windows, as well as a stair tower rising to an open crown. Parts of the church are based on the Holy Rude Church in Stirling. The manse associated with this church was erected in 1914.

St Ninian's Scottish Episcopal Church is located in Bentinck Drive. Proposals for a congregation in 1888 failed due to lack of support, but in 1911 members from the Ayr church started mission work and a congregation was established. The foundation stone of the new church was laid on 7 November 1912 and the nave dedicated on 18 May 1913, the architect being James A. Morris. The war held up building work and the church was not completed until 1920–1, though even then the tower was never built. Inside there is some fine woodwork, including eight items made by John Thompson, the 'Mouseman of Kilburn', bearing his unique trademark of a carved mouse.

Other churches in Troon include Seagate Evangelical Church in West Portland Street (built in 1843 as the Bethany Hall), Ailsa Road Church and the Church of the Nazarene in Union Street. A number of former churches existed in Troon, including Portland Street UF Church (erected in 1856, closed in 1914, demolished in 1926) and the Mission Hall that stood next to the sawmill at the harbour.

Troon has long been a popular holiday resort, and is well supplied with hotels. One of the more traditional is the Anchorage Hotel, located in Templehill, which dates from around 1815, when it was known as the Portland Arms. In the Victorian era a number of larger hotels were erected, and some of the town's villas were converted into hotels or guesthouses. The grand Marine Hotel in Crosbie Road was built in 1897 to plans of Salmon Son & Gillespie, a large sandstone building on five floors overlooking the golf courses and the South Bay. The former Sun Court Hotel was built in 1905–6 as a private house known as Lindisfarne, designed by Fryers & Penman, and in recent years has been converted into smaller dwellings. At one time it had one of only two real, or royal, tennis courts in Scotland, the other being at Falkland Palace in Fife. Mokoia House dates from the early twentieth century, as does Cessford House.

In more recent years other villas have been converted into hotels. These include Piersland Lodge, now known as Piersland House Hotel, and Lochgreen House Hotel, the latter probably the most exclusive hotel in the town. Piersland Lodge was erected in 1905 to plans of William Leiper for Sir Alexander Walker (1869–1950), a scion of the Johnnie Walker whisky dynasty, who was knighted in 1920. The building is mock Tudor in style, and within can be seen some excellent woodwork. The Church of England later used it before it became a hotel.

A number of fine houses can be seen throughout Troon. Welbeck House in Bentinck Drive is a magnificent Arts & Crafts building, later converted into flats. Brandon House is another fine building, also in Bentinck Drive. Wood Road links Templehill with Titchfield Road. Here stood Portland Villa, latterly the Miners' Convalescent Home, used by miners from all over Ayrshire. The building was erected around 1840 as a home by Adam Wood, manager of the shipyard, but was demolished in the 1990s.

Troon is unique in Ayrshire for its educational provision. Marr College is a state secondary school, but owes its foundation to C. K. Marr who left money with which to build and endow a school. The C. K. Marr Educational Trust operates the school, which was built in 1930 to plans of John Arthur and opened by the Marquis of Lothian on 4 September 1935. The main building is a rather distinguished structure, built of fine stonework in a distinctive classical style. The entrance is located in a projecting octagonal tower, topped by the prominent copper dome. In the grounds are the janitor's house and gate lodge, both of around 1919–20, and inspired to some extent by the work of Edwin Landseer Lutyens. Charles Kerr Marr (1855–1919) was born in Troon's Welbeck Crescent. He began working for coal agents, followed by steel merchants in Glasgow and then London. He made his fortune as a partner in the business of Hull Blyth & Company of London, and travelled the world. He is buried in Cathcart Cemetery, Glasgow.

A number of other schools exist or have existed in Troon. Portland Public School was erected in 1875 and served at various levels until 1963, when it was renamed St Patrick's RC School. Troon Fullarton Public School was built in Barassie Street and extended in 1908 to become Troon Higher Grade, designed by Robert Ingram. Muirhead School was opened in 1964 and Barassie Primary School in 1970.

The railway from Kilmarnock to Troon followed the line of the present Kilmarnock line, and headed for the harbour. The Irvine–Ayr line opened in 1840, passing through the town on a north–south axis. A loop was created to bring the railway nearer the town centre, and the new station was opened on 2 May 1892, the old station being converted to a goods station. James Miller and a Mr Melville produced the design, the latter was engineer to the Glasgow & South Western Railway. A second station exists at Barassie, at one time a busy junction. Here also were the Barassie railway workshops, closed in 1972. The direct rail link no longer passes through, the southern end being dismantled and partially built upon.

Troon town hall is located at the corner of Ayr and Academy streets. The building is rather fine, being built of brick with stone facings. In style it resembles an English country house, being neo-Georgian. The architect was James Miller and the building was opened in 1932. Inside is a model of *The Duke*, the first steam locomotive to use the Kilmarnock to Troon railway line. The concert hall dates from 1932. The adjoining Walker Halls were gifted to the burgh by Sir Alexander Walker and erected in 1974–5 to plans of Noad & Wallace. Adjacent to the town hall is the burgh war memorial, a rather fine statue of Britannia commemorating the dead of two world wars, although it was initially erected in 1924. The memorial is the work of Alfred Gilbert, and it stands on top of a large granite pedestal. Nearby, in the triangle of ground formed at the junction of West Portland Street with St Clair Terrace, is a dry fountain, presented to the town by James Dickie in 1891.

The parking area at Titchfield Road was at one time Troon's open-air swimming pool. This was opened in 1931 and boasted a large pool with areas for spectators and various pavilions. During the Second World War the commandos used the pool for training purposes. The pool was closed in 1987, when the new indoor pool was opened, and subsequently demolished. The Italian Gardens are situated adjacent to the site of the pool. They were formed in a low-lying area of ground, protected from the sea by the wall.

Troon is renowned throughout the world for its outstanding golf courses. There are six around the town, although they are not really obvious to traffic on roads, due to the courses being hidden by housing in most cases. The most famous course is Royal Troon, located at the south end of the town, a links course along the South Bay. The old course was established in 1878 with the foundation of Troon Golf Club, and has become famous after being used for the Open Championship for the first time in 1923, and subsequently in 1950, 1962, 1973, 1982, 1989 and 1997. In 1978 the club was granted the right to call itself Royal Troon. The 18-hole

The clubhouse at Royal Troon Golf Club

course is 6,640 yards in length, par 72. The clubhouse stands by the side of Craigend Road and was designed by H. E. Clifford.

On the opposite side of Crosbie Road from Royal Troon is Portland golf course, also owned by Royal Troon Golf Club, but with a smaller clubhouse. This course was established in 1894 and is located between the Old Course and the railway. The 18-hole course is 6,289 yards in length, par 71. Troon's municipal golf courses lie north of Craigend Road, and extend in a north-west direction from there to the clubhouse, which is located near to the railway station. The Fullarton is an 18-hole course, 4,869 yards in length, par 66. The Lochgreen is a par 74, 6,822 yard course. The Darley course lies east of the railway, separating Barassie and the housing estate of Muirhead. This course is 6,501 yards in length, par 71. The last course is the most northerly, and occupies the angle between the two railway lines, north of Barassie station. This course is known as Kilmarnock (Barassie) Golf Course, and was laid out in 1894. The 18-hole course is 6,400 yards in length, par 72. The Kilmarnock Ossington Golf Club, which had a nine-hole course at Kilmarnock, decided to move to Barassie in order to create a larger links course. The clubhouse was erected in 1903.

Barassie was established as holiday settlement on the coast. It was originally known as New Kilmarnock when founded in 1830, but it was slow to develop. Later adopting the name of a local farm, burn and sands, Barassie grew as a garden village scheme from 1911 onwards, the first layout being by James Chalmers, and in recent years has extended to the east side of the railway, onto the farm of Barassie itself. Most of the houses are modern, but there are a few buildings from the early period. The Tower Hotel was originally erected around 1832–6, but in 1859 it was extended considerably with its three-storey tower overlooking the beach.

Troon has a Junior football team, playing at Portland Park, which lies off Portland Street. Over the club's life it has been known as Troon Academicals, Rangers, Troon Juniors and today simply as Troon Football Club.

The Southwood area of Troon is probably the most affluent in Ayrshire. Here can be found a number of substantial villas and houses in what has become known to some as 'Millionaire's Row'. The first building in the South Wood area was probably Sandhills House, built around 1890 for the dowager Duchess of Portland. A French architect is said to have designed this house, which is built of brick with sandstone dressings. Later houses have been erected in and around the woods. Some of the more substantial buildings are almost large enough to be mansions in their own right, and most have a distinct architectural style. Dunalton House lies next to Sandhills. It was built in 1906–8 to plans of James Hay in an English manorial style. It is distinguished by its tall tower and has now been divided into smaller dwellings. Crosbie House follows; it was built in the same year to plans of H. E. Clifford. This house is a mix of styles, but the first floor windows are typically Scots. Southwood House originally followed, but today there are more buildings in between. Southwood dates from 1905, designed by John A. Campbell in a mix of Scottish and English styles.

East of Southwood Road is Monktonhall, dating from 1912, the work of H. E. Clifford & Lunan. This house was originally known as Glenholm and is English in style. Frognal House was erected in 1909 to plans by James Hay. Sporting a large tower, the house was latterly used as a respite home for children with special needs. Auchenkyle House is located within the woods. It was designed in the Queen Anne style and completed around 1905. The house is presently owned by Jan de Vries, a noted practitioner of alternative medicine. Lochgreen House follows, the work of Gardner & Millar in 1905. Silverglades dates from 1912, although at that time it was known as Deasholm, built in a Scots baronial style to plans by T. Andrew Millar.

The Fullarton area of Troon occupies the site of Fullarton House. The Fullartons of that Ilk at Fullarton near Irvine decided to move south to get away from the industrial area of the harbour and to find a more pleasant countryside on which to build a new house. Robert II had granted the old Crosbie estate to them at the same time as the Fullarton lands in 1344, but the original Crosbie House or castle was abandoned and in 1745 Colonel William Fullarton of that Ilk built a new mansion. The result was one of the finest buildings in Ayrshire, a classical building on three floors, decorated with arched windows, urns and pediment. The house had wings that were designed by Robert Adam in 1791, using his castellated style, but on a reduced scale from what he had originally proposed. Robert Burns is known to have visited the house. Prince Louis Napoleon Bonaparte stayed here when he was attending the Eglinton Tournament in 1839; he would later become Emperor Napoleon III. The Fullartons of that Ilk lost much of their wealth in raising soldiers for the Napoleonic wars and the estate was bought by the Duke of Portland in 1805. In the twentieth century the house was subdivided, but was eventually demolished in 1966. The stable courtyard of Fullarton survived, and in 1974 was converted into seventeen private houses. This had been erected in 1792 to plans of Robert Adam and displayed good examples of his use of turrets, corbels and a prominent central archway. Fragments of the old Crosbie House can still be seen. The old tower probably dated from 1673, for an old marriage stone thus inscribed, with the initials of William Fullarton and Anne Brisbane, can be found near to Lady Margaret Drive. When Fullarton House was built, the remains of the tower were adapted as an icehouse. The grounds of Fullarton have since 1928 been used as a small park, where there are a few walks and picnic areas. Within the grounds can be found two urn-topped pillars, all that remains of Fullarton House. In Isle of Pins Road are two pillars, or 'pins' that were formerly part of an entrance gateway to Fullarton.

Crosbie Church lies to the south of Fullarton, passed by Monktonhill Road. The earliest reference to a church here dates from 1229, but the present structure was erected in 1691. The church has been in ruins since the mid eighteenth century; tradition claiming that the roof blew off on the day that Robert Burns was born (January 1759). Since then the church has been abandoned, only the two gables and walls surviving. The surrounding kirkyard is no longer used, but it still contains a number of old and interesting gravestones, some bearing rather fine carvings. Here can be seen a stone commemorating David Hamilton of Bothwellhaugh (d. 1619), the son of James Hamilton, who was alleged to have been the person to slay James V's bastard son, Regent Moray, on 23 January 1570. David's sister had married David Fullarton of that Ilk.

The village of Loans lies on the A759, a road that was formerly the busy A78 road that links Ayr with Irvine, now bypassed. The village existed independently of Troon, but in recent years has lost much of its distinct identity, and is being encroached on by the housing estates of Troon, as well as obtaining a few developments of its own. There was a toll cottage at Loans, this being the original turnpike between Irvine and Ayr.

East of Loans the countryside rises to the low heights of the Dundonald Hills, the highest of which is only 477 feet above sea level. A minor road links Loans with Dundonald, and this road should be followed over the hills to obtain a fine view of the surrounding countryside. Just above Loans is Highgrove House Hotel, another popular restaurant, formerly known as Dallam Towers. The Dundonald Hills have a number of antiquities on them. Beyond Highgrove House, on the south side of the road, are the remains of an earthwork, a ditch and mound being visible in the grassy field. Further up, on the highest hill (above Clevance) and on its outlier above Harpercroft, are two hill forts. The highest hill has the larger of the two, the outermost ditch surrounding a large area of the summit. The outer ring is around 900 feet in diameter. Within this is a second circular rampart, about 300 feet in diameter, enclosing a smaller area on the summit, unfortunately disfigured by a wireless transmission mast. The fort here was probably built in the Iron Age. Above Harpercroft is the second fort, occupying the summit of what is known as Wardlaw Hill. This hill is steeper than its southerly neighbour, but the fort has not survived so well. It was much smaller in any case, measuring around 340 feet by 200 feet. The rampart survives in places to five feet in height, the remains of it spread over a large area.

On the opposite side of the hill road is the Hallyards whinstone quarry. A low promontory in the woods beyond this is known as Kemp Law, the site of an ancient dun, a fortified building. The walls of this appear to have been timber laced, and some vitrification has been discovered. The dun measures thirty-six feet internally, with a wall around fourteen feet thick. About ten feet outwith this wall are the remains of a second rampart. Hallyards Farm, which has disappeared due to quarrying, was built on the site of an ancient chapel. At Hillhouse another antiquity can be found. Maps simply describe it as a mound, and it can be found in the trees at a prominent spot overlooking the plain to the west.

At Hillhouse is a major whinstone quarry that has been worked since 1907. A considerable amount of the hillside has been taken away, and the conveyors and buildings by the side of the A759 are rather unsightly. Hillhouse itself is a mansion of 1800, owned for many years by the MacKerrell family, classed as chiefs of their own clan. Prince Louis Bonaparte is said to have stayed here in 1839. The house is now the property of the Vernon family, owners of the quarrying business. In the grounds is a point known as the Chapel Hill, for here stood an ancient chapel. Above Collenan is the Collenan Reservoir, formed in 1897 by damming the little stream that flows down the glen. This was Troon Water Works, but the town is now connected to the supply from Loch Bradan and the reservoir is used for fishing.

Another minor road skirts around the southern fringes of the Dundonald Hills. It virtually starts and finishes at the same places as the first road, but this one meanders among farms, above dale and down hill. It passes the site of Corraith House, a mansion built in 1846–7 for Captain John Deans Campbell. The architect was David Bryce, and the baronial style was typical of his work. Later owners included the Mackies. The Scottish Youth Hostels' Association used the house for a time, but in 1968 the house was abandoned and demolished. There are still a number of former buildings and gardens associated with the house in existence, including a baronial gatehouse of 1901.

Dundonald Camp, as it is often still known, or Auchengate, occupies the low-lying land below Hillhouse. The barracks were established between 1914–18 as a training centre. The military buildings have gone now, but a number of houses associated with the establishment still survive. Around the camp are a number of smallholdings. On the moor to the north of Auchengate Crescent Bronze Age urns were found in 1842.

The ruins of the old house of Auchans can be seen in the woods south of the A759, between Hillhouse Quarry and Dundonald. The house dates from 1644 and was built by Sir William Cochrane in the traditional Scots Baronial and Jacobean style. Sir William suffered during the Civil War but after the Restoration he was created Earl of Dundonald in 1669 for his services. The estate passed to the Montgomeries of Eglinton, and in 1773 James Boswell and Samuel Johnson visited Susannah, Dowager Countess of the 9th Earl of Eglinton (1690–1780) here on their return from their highland tour. In her youth she was renowned as something of a beauty, the 'Gentle Shepherd' being dedicated to her by Allan Ramsay, but in her old age it was said that she had a number of pet rats that she would allow to eat along with her. Boswell wrote that 'she had been the admiration of the gay circles of life, and the patroness of poets.' The house was still occupied by caretakers in 1890, but it was later abandoned and is now a roofless, if impressive shell.

Old Auchans House is located in the Beech Wood, south of Auchans. A new Auchans House was erected in 1819 by C. Monteaulieu Burgess of Colesfield to replace the old tower house. The architect William Wallace designed this. The house was demolished in 1970 and the grounds built on, creating the Auchans and Kilnford estate at the north-west end of Dundonald.

*

Dundonald is an ancient community, built under the lea of Dundonald Castle. The older part of the village is located at the southern end of the present community, where a number of traditional buildings line Main Street. Among these are a number of former weavers' cottages. The Montgomerie Hall dates from the nineteenth century and was built as the village school.

The parish church stands on a low knoll at the southern end of the village, its spire with clock rising above the rest of it. The church dates from 1803, the tower added in 1841, and the chancel in 1906–10. The result is a rather bulky T-plan building. Stained glass includes a unique work by Henry Dearle depicting the Last Supper. The organ dates from 1906, made by Norman & Beard. Around the church is an old kirkyard, where a number of interesting stones can be seen. Buried here is Margaret Wilson, songwriter, and Dr Robert Duncan, the 'Duncan Deep' of Burns's 'Twa Herds'. Nearby is Glenfoot House, the former manse, predating the church by around ten years. A second church existed at Dundonald, located off Main Street, near Warly Place. This was built in 1843 as the Free Church and it had a manse adjoining. Its first minister was Revd Thomas Burns, nephew of the bard. The church later became a United Free Church. Extended in 1884, it is now the parish church hall.

The primary school was located in Kilmarnock Road. The school dated from 1895 but is now demolished. The war memorial stands at the junction of Kilmarnock Road with Main Street.

Dundonald Castle

Dundonald Castle is the main attraction in the village. The castle is a ruin, but it is protected as an ancient monument by Historic Scotland. A visitor centre is located at the Winehouse Yett, operated by an organisation known as the Friends of Dundonald Castle. This was founded with the aim of promoting the castle and providing a service to tourists. The centre, which was designed by Robert Paul and erected in 1997, has a display of models of the castle, as well as information boards detailing its history. Here also is a small tearoom and gift shop. The castle originally dated from the thirteenth century, but was rebuilt during the 1370s for Robert II. A series of armorial panels bearing the Stewart arms were added to the west wall at this time. Later additions were made in the fifteenth century, and it is thought that the castle was occupied until the seventeenth century. Boswell and Johnson visited the ruins of the castle in 1773, Johnson regarding the castle as rather small for 'King Bob', as he styled him.

From the visitor centre a pathway makes its way up the slopes of the hill on which the castle was built. The remaining tower is only a fragment of a much larger castle, which soon becomes apparent when one sees the foundations of numerous walls. The tower is entered on the ground floor. A large vaulted chamber, the ceiling of which rises to thirty-seven feet above the floor level, occupies this. It formerly had wooden floors dividing its height. A modern stair leads to a platform that occupies the site of an older timber floor, half way up the vault. Stairs at the south end lead up to the Great Hall, which is unfortunately roofless, but of which there is sufficient to appreciate what a fine apartment it must have been. The bottom of some fine ribs indicates that the roof would have been vaulted also, but highly decorated, as opposed to the plain vault below. This chamber measured sixty feet by twenty-five feet. Dundonald is known as a royal castle, as it was owned by the early kings of Scotland and was Robert II's favourite home; he actually died here. The Cochrane family, who were created Earls of Dundonald, later acquired the castle. During excavation work whilst the castle was being restored to allow it to be opened to the public, it was discovered that the castle hill was first occupied in the Dark Ages. At a later date a Norman motte was created here, followed by a stone-built castle.

The B730 north from Dundonald passes Fraser's garden centre. Here is a small collection of aircraft bits and pieces, the flat fields being used as an airfield during the Second World War. The industrial estate was built in 1966 as a nylon factory, owned by Monsanto. The factory operated until 1980 and is now divided into smaller units. The lands east of the industrial estate are divided into smallholdings, the Ploughland and Harperland holdings, each with a small area of land around it.

East of Dundonald were two fine country houses, only one of which survives. Newfield was an ornamental building of the first half of the nineteenth century, perhaps incorporating an older house of around 1725, built for Captain Nugent. The estate was previously known as Galrigs, but Captain Nugent was a soldier who had been active at the Battle of Nieufeldt in Germany. The house was decorated with crow-steps, French-style tower, ogival roofs and sculpted panels. It was demolished in 1964. The former doocot survives. The other property, Fairlie House, is still occupied. It is a rather fine mansion of 1803, perhaps designed by David Hamilton for Sir William Cuninghame-Fairlie. Known locally as 'Five Lums' from its chimneys, the house is a Regency-styled building with columned porch and low parapet. The house occupies the original seat of the Fairlie of that Ilk family. Fairlie Mains nearby is a grand home-farm, the main building sporting a pediment, octagonal tower and spire. Damdyke Tollhouse sits by the Damdyke Bridge. The building dates from the early nineteenth century.

The Lady Isle, which sits in the Firth of Clyde off Troon, is part of Dundonald parish. It is said that there was an old chapel on the islet, hence its name. There is also a freshwater spring. Although the islet is rather small it has proved to be troublesome to shipping over the years. A number of vessels have either ran aground or been wrecked around it. These include the *Marjorie Seed*, which ran aground in December 1924, and the *Ahdeek*, which was being towed into Troon when it sank in December 1898. In December 1894 the *Frey* anchored off the island and fired her distress rockets. The Troon lifeboat was unable to help, due to the storm, but the Irvine boat came to the rescue. The crew of sixteen had to jump into the sea and rely on the skill of the lifeboat men to pick them up. Unfortunately, as the lifeboat headed for Troon, it capsized and threw all overboard. All but two managed to scramble back on board. The *Frey* broke from her anchor and drifted south-east towards Ayr, becoming wrecked on the Blackburn Rocks. There were two pillars on the island, erected in the seventeenth century by the magistrates of Glasgow to aid shipping. Only one of these survives, the other one being replaced by the lighthouse in 1903. At low tide the islet is almost four times as large as it is when the tide is in, with other rocks such as the Half Tide Rock and Scart Rock appearing. The islet is now a bird sanctuary, and home to a colony of grey seals.

# 14

# Monkton and Prestwick

THE COMMUNITIES OF PRESTWICK and Monkton are located in a joint parish, one that was formed around 1700 when it was felt that the two parishes were too small. Monkton and Prestwick parish, as it is known, extends to 3,971 acres, slightly bigger than the area covered by the present communities. Only at Monkton is there any open countryside, and it consists of little more than a few farms.

Monkton is now by some distance the smaller of the two communities. It has now been bypassed, but was at one time a busy junction where the Ayr to Kilmarnock, and Ayr to Irvine, roads separated. The village is quite small, but has a number of important industrial units around it. The village centre was originally the old church, in Main Street, which is now a ruin in its kirkyard. The church dates from the thirteenth century, when it was known as Prestwick Monachorum, and dedicated to St Cuthbert. The older part of the church was the main rectangle, but in the seventeenth century a northern transept and the new doorway in the south wall were added. The church still has its small belfry on the east gable. The church was used until 1837. Blind Harry, in his poem about William Wallace, claims that the freedom fighter had a dream in this church that inspired his fight. The kirkyard around the church has a number of interesting old tombstones, as well as the mausoleum of William Weir of Adamton and Kildonan, which is Doric in style, and the Angus of Ladykirk aisle. James MacRae, governor of Madras, is said to be buried here, but no stone marks his grave. A memorial commemorates a daughter of Revd Thomas Burns, himself a nephew of Robert Burns. Nearby is the old manse, erected in 1822.

The entrance gates to the British Aerospace factory are located at the foot of Main Street. This factory was founded in 1935 to build aeroplanes, originally known as Scottish Aviation Limited. The largest factory building was acquired second hand – it was first erected in Bellahouston Park in 1938 as the Palace of Engineering for the Empire Exhibition but was moved here in 1941. The architect was Thomas Tait. The factory produced the well known Prestwick Pioneer for many years. In 1966 Scottish Aviation Limited was taken over by Cammel Laird and, in 1977, became part of British Aerospace when the industry was nationalised.

Monkton Cross was where the A77 and A78 formerly split. Today it is just the village centre, although five roads still meet there. On the corner is Monkton Primary School, erected in 1877. Here stands the war memorial, a simple foursquare pillar inscribed with the names of those who died. Station Road strikes west, lined with cottages before it leaves the village and runs alongside the airport boundary. Originally this road took a route further south, heading for what was Monkton railway station on the Ayr to Irvine line. The station was located at where the bridge to St Andrews House is; it opened in 1840 but closed in the 1960s.

The Carvick Walker Memorial Hall was built in 1929 to plans by W. R. Watson who produced an Arts & Crafts style building. It has a small belfry, hinting at its former use as a Free Church. At the Cross is the Hare Stane, moved here from its original site in a field off Charles Avenue. The boulder had a long tradition of witchcraft and evil spirits associated with it, but in 2000 it was moved to its present position and a sealed 'Millennium Box' placed beneath it.

Main Street strikes north from the cross. Here is the post office and a few other shops. A former gatehouse is located at the north end of the village. This was the main entrance into Fairfield House, which has long gone. The house was built in the mid-eighteenth century, perhaps to plans by Samuel Neilson. In the grounds can still be seen a small burial enclosure, used by the Campbells of Fairfield, as well as remains of the walled garden. Most of the woodland surrounding the house has gone, the house itself being demolished around 1961 and its policies divided by the new bypass.

Beyond the bypass on this road are a few larger houses, including the White House. Monktonhill Farm is a large unit owned by the Co-operative Society. Monktonhead House lies beyond the bypass. It was built in 1910 to plans of James Miller for Kenneth Connel, a Glasgow shipbuilder. Elizabethan in style, the house is adorned with timber fronts, tall brick chimneys and herringbone brickwork. It used to be reached from Monktonhead Farm, which is on the inside of the bypass, where the former gate lodge no longer leads to the drive. Still surviving is the cylindrical doocot with a conical roof.

Kilmarnock Road leaves Monkton Cross in a north-easterly direction. It passes the Manor Park Hotel, behind which is the base of an old windmill, which probably dates from the eighteenth century. Some locals call it the doocot, hinting that it has been used for various purposes over the years. Beyond is the Dutch House caravan site, named after an old wooden building that had a mansard roof in the Dutch style. This no longer exists, but the name is well known locally.

On the low hill (151 feet above sea level) behind the Dutch House is a memorial in memory of James MacRae, which was erected around 1750 to plans of John Swan. The monument was in a state of disrepair for many years, but it has recently undergone a major renovation and is now a prominent landmark once again. MacRae (1684–1746) was born in Ochiltree parish, the son of an agricultural labourer. He later joined the Navy and moved through the ranks. He was appointed governor of Madras in India in 1725 and amassed a considerable fortune there. On his return to Scotland in 1731 he had accumulated a fortune of £100,000 and bought Monkton estate, renaming it Orangefield after William of Orange. In 1736 MacRae presented a mounted statue of the monarch to the city of Glasgow; it was originally located at Glasgow Cross, but moved to Cathedral Square in 1923.

At the Dutch House roundabout is Monktonlodge service station, erected in 1994 to plans by the Lambie Wright Partnership. The restaurant later went on fire and had to be demolished and totally rebuilt.

Tarbolton Road starts at the old church, but today the first part of it is no longer the main route east from Monkton. Here can be found some former weavers' cottages. Baird Road was built further north, leading onto Tarbolton Road. After passing the northern side of the aerospace factory, the buildings of HMS *Gannet* are passed on the north. HMS *Gannet* is a naval establishment, founded in 1942 as a United States Transport Command base named Greensite. After the war the base was taken over by Number 819 Squadron of the Royal Navy as an anti-submarine and helicopter-rescue training camp. Tarbolton Road is the B739. It passes below the A77 bypass and reaches Adamton estate. There are some modern houses here, built by the side of the bypass, but of more interest is Adamton House itself. This was erected in 1885-8 for J. G. A. Baird. A Jacobean-style building, the house has distinctive curved gables. The house was at one time a hotel, but it was later acquired by British Aerospace and converted into a school for pilots. In 1987–9 a massive extension was added behind the house to plans of Dunlop & Paige, to provide accommodation.

East of Adamton the parish extends through the lands of Bogside and Ladykirk. Bogside House is formed from the former South Bogside farmhouse. This was the home of Sir Thomas Moore, Baronet (1886–1971) MP for Ayr for no less than thirty-nine years and erstwhile Father of the Commons. His second wife was Penelope Angus, the Angus family living at Ladykirk. Ladykirk House is a rather unusual Gothic mansion, built in 1903 to the plans of Robert Ingram. The house was built for Robert Angus, who was a prominent coalmaster. In the grounds of Ladykirk can be seen the fragmentary remains of the Lady Kirk itself. The old church was built sometime in the fifteenth century and dedicated to the Virgin Mary. The ruins stand at the north side of the walled garden.

The reservoir at Raith was created in 1883 to supply Prestwick with water, but is now used for angling

Prestwick Airport separates Monkton from the larger town. It is known properly as Glasgow Prestwick International Airport, and is one of the main airports in Scotland. The airport owes its origin to the Duke of Hamilton (at that time Marquis of Clydesdale) and David F. McIntyre (1905–57), both of whom were noted for being the first men to fly over Mount Everest, in 1933. A plaque in the terminal commemorates McIntyre. In the 1930s the flat fields hereabouts were used for landing aircraft, and during the Second World War it became the base for the Flying Fortresses of the US Eighth Air Force. After the war Prestwick was designated as Britain's second major international-airport and, before the advent of the 'open skies' policy, had a monopoly on transatlantic flights from Scotland. When these routes were opened up to competition from other Scottish airports in 1989 Prestwick went into a steep decline. However, thanks to vigorous management and marketing it has been very successful in recent years in attracting low-cost airlines such as Ryanair and Buzz. Indeed, in 2002, more than 1.5 million passengers used the airport, and numbers are expected to increase still further in years to come. In addition it has become an important centre for cargo and, in the year to March 2002, handled 42,631 tons of freight. One important factor in its favour is the local climate; it is virtually fog free and very rarely affected by snow or ice. Another major boost came with the development of a dedicated rail halt for the airport on the busy Ayr to Glasgow line. These factors have encouraged the owners to invest heavily in facilities and, at the time of writing in early 2003, a sum of £4 million was being spent on the terminal building.

There are three runways at Prestwick. The main one – at 3,000 metres the longest civilian runway in Scotland – heads westward over the sea for take off, while landings come from the east. Original plans for the airport had this runway extending further west into the bay, linking up with a proposed seaplane base. The second runway is on a north-south axis, east of Prestwick itself. The third runway is a short one, running on a north-east to south-west axis. The airport terminal is a large complex, the main building erected in 1964 to plans of Joseph L. Gleave. Queen Elizabeth, the Queen Mother, officially opened the building on 22 September. At one time Orangefield House stood here, and for a number of years it was used as the airport's control tower. On 2 March 1960 Elvis Presley landed at Prestwick, the only time he ever touched British soil, and he was commemorated until quite recently by the Graceland Bar in the terminal building (now renamed the Alloway Bar).

Prestwick: the airport terminal building

Orangefield House was built for Dr Hugh Baillie, the plans provided by Samuel Neilson. Baillie had to sell up soon after the house was erected, the cost being too much for him. James MacRae then acquired the estate. The house was extended a number of times, in 1906, 1913 and in 1933 it was converted to a hotel. At the same time the roof of the house was partially removed and a weird-looking control tower for the infant airport was added. The house survived until 1966 when it was demolished. The construction of Prestwick Airport meant that the main runway crossed the road from Monkton to Prestwick. For a number of years the roadway was left intact, and traffic lights were used to stop the traffic whenever an aeroplane was taking off or landing. Eventually the traffic on both the roads and the runway was so great that this set up became untenable. The new dual-carriageway bypass road was then built, skirting the west end of the runway next to the railway.

\*

The northern end of Prestwick is bounded by the Pow Burn, a meandering stream that flows from the Craigie Hills down to the sea between Prestwick and Troon. By the side of it is the former Monkton and Prestwick parish church, built in 1837 to replace the old churches in the two communities. This remote spot halfway between the two villages was chosen to pacify both congregations. The church has a tall tower, and was designed by David Bryce in the Gothic style. The interior was rebuilt in 1925 to plans of Jeffrey Waddell. The adjoining hall dates from around 1932, the work of Alexander Mair. The church is no longer used by the Church of Scotland, having been acquired by the New Life Church. It was in this church that the Revd Thomas Burns ministered from 1830 until the Disruption in 1843. In 1843 he led a party of Free Church emigrants to New Zealand where he founded the provinces of Otago and Southland. He died in 1871.

The Towans Hotel was built as a large villa in 1897 to plans of Alexander Paterson. It has some fine panelling inside, and the exterior is in the Arts & Crafts style. At the north end of the town is a large roundabout, where the bypass rejoins Monkton Road. Shawfarm Road strikes east from here, passing Prestwick cemetery and terminating at the Shaw Farm industrial estate. The older part of the cemetery has a few stones of interest. Here can be found the grave of John Keppie (1862–1945), a partner of Charles Rennie Mackintosh, as well as his sister, Jessie Keppie (1868–1951), a noted artist and fiancée of Mackintosh for a time. Another architect, David Raeside, lies here; he was a partner with Sir John Burnet. Some stones commemorate victims of accidents, including a few air crashes and mining accidents.

In the industrial estate are a number of large factories including some involved in the aeronautical industry. Caledonian Airmotive was founded in 1980, but it has been renamed since. The industrial estate occupies much of the site of Glenburn Colliery, properly known as Auchincruive No. 4/5, a coal mine established in 1912. Its seams were worked below the sea, and at Monkton station an air shaft was constructed for ventilation. At its peak, the pit employed 700 men. The mine closed in 1973, its coal bing has been landscaped and the surface building demolished, leaving little to indicate that Prestwick had a history of coal mining. Shaw Farm itself has gone, but the Shaw monument still stands on its low knoll amid the industrial area. What the monument was has been open to speculation over the years, and theories include it being used by an eighteenth century landowner for flying his falcons. The tower is cylindrical, capped by a crown-piece top.

Monkton Road leads from the roundabout south to Prestwick Cross. The street is lined with fine housing, some of it modern flats at the northern end. On the east side of the road is Prestwick North Church, its tower dominating the vicinity. This church was established in 1843 as a Free Church, its first minister being Revd Thomas Burns, nephew of the poet. The present building was erected in 1874 to plans by James Salmon & Son, and the bell tower was added in 1896 to plans of John Keppie. There is stained glass within by James Benson. The mobile pulpit came from St Cuthbert's in Monkton.

Prestwick Cross is surrounded by traditional buildings on most sides, apart from the south west where it is open and occupied by a pleasant garden area. Here can be found the burgh war memorial, the old market cross and other memorials. The war memorial was the work of James A. Morris in 1921. The cross was rebuilt in 1777 and formerly stood in front of the Freemen's Hall until it was moved in 1963. The cross bears an early spelling of the town – 'Prestick'. A former fountain commemorates Matthew Smith. It contains a bronze plaque by Robert Bryden, dated 1903. A sundial here commemorates the fiftieth anniversary of the 14th Ayrshire (Prestwick) Scout Troop, founded in 1909, and Prestwick Academy art students erected a larger one in 1998.

Prestwick: the market cross

The Freeman's Hall stands on the north side of the Cross. The building dates from 1844 and was erected in a classical style as an office for local councillors. Here also was the burgh gaol. A Gothic spire, which was added later, decorates the roofscape. On the hall are date stones: 1600 and 1903, commemorating the charter granted by James VI in 1600 confirming Prestwick's status as a Burgh of Barony, and the election of the first town council in 1903. The later town hall was completed in 1899 to plans of James A. Morris, but was originally erected as the Unionist Hall and used as a cinema. It was taken over by the council in 1922 and converted into a hall that could seat one thousand for meetings. This stands to the east of the Cross.

Kirk Street strikes north from near the Cross. This was one of the old routes to Irvine, which tended to make their way along the shore. From Kirk Street a lane runs to the west, climbing up the low hill to where the ruined church of St Nicholas is located in its graveyard. The church was probably built in the twelfth century, but in May 1837 it was abandoned. It still has its old belfry. The surrounding kirkyard has a number of old stones within it, including some with fine carvings, and it is thought that there are Covenanters buried here, though no stone commemorates them. The Pow Burn sewage pumping station was erected in 1985.

Station Road heads west from the Cross to the railway station, established in 1840. On the other side of the bridge the street takes the name Links Road, for the road terminates at the beach. Here can be found the former Prestwick Open Air Bathing Lake, which was not only the largest swimming pool in Scotland but also renowned for being the only bathing pool in the Firth of Clyde area that was up to Olympic standard. The pool was built in 1931 to plans by William Cowie and could accommodate 1,200 bathers and 3,000 spectators. It proved immensely popular with both residents and holidaymakers and in its first year of operation attracted more than 320,000 paying customers. The swimming pool closed in 1972 and today the site is used as a play area, and the former pavilions have been demolished. North of here is a large parking area, children's play shed and, at the far end, a sewage pumping station. This was erected in 1986 and because of its rather attractive design won a Civic Trust Commendation. The former Links Hotel, by James A. Morris in 1901, is now the Malcolm Sargent Home.

On the south side of Links Road, in Ardayre Road, is Stonegarth, the RAFA building. Here can be seen a war memorial erected in memory of a number of Polish soldiers who died during the Second World War. The Poles had been based at a camp in the vicinity of St Andrews House, near the foot of the Pow Burn, where the memorial was originally located. Stonegarth was erected in 1908 to plans of J. K. Hunter.

Links Road passes by the south side of Prestwick Golf Club, which was founded in 1851. The clubhouse stands next to the railway station. It was erected in 1866 at a cost of £758 and was extended in 1893 to plans of J. A. Morris and J. K. Hunter. A cairn by the side of the road commemorates the fact that the first Open Championship was held here on 17 October 1860, and was unveiled in 1977 by Henry Cotton. For that first Open the club sent out invitations to surrounding clubs, and eight of Scotland's leading players battled it out. The winner was Willie Park, but 'Old' Tom Morris (1821–1908), who had laid out the course in the 1850s, won the event four times, in 1861, 1862, 1864 and 1866 (his son, 'Young' Tom, also won it four times). The Open was played at Prestwick Old Course on a further eleven occasions, but has not been played there since 1925, the course being unsuitable for the large numbers of spectators that turn up to watch the event. Today the 18-hole course is 6,544 yards in length, par 71.

Main Street strikes south from the Cross and heads for Ayr. The street is a popular shopping area, one that is full of traditional shops and which is not disfigured by modern shopping centres. There are many interesting buildings in Main Street. The Bute Hall dates from around 1870 and is located on the east side of the street. The hall is used for various local organisations, and was in great demand for evangelical services and when the local schools could not cope with the number of pupils. Prestwick South Church, which is located on the west side of Main Street, dates from 1879–83 and is noted for its spire. The church was built as a United Free Church, the older part to the rear by John Mercer, the newer part with its spire facing Main Street by James A. Morris, this being his first ecclesiastical commission. There is glass by W. Meikle & Sons and Oscar Paterson. The adjoining hall was erected in 1960. St Nicholas Church stands at the foot of Bellevue Road; Peter MacGregor Chalmers designed this church in a Romanesque style in 1908. The church is quite unique in that it has a slender tower rising high above the front doorway, adorned only by two small windows near the top. It also has stained glass by G. Maile and Gordon Webster.

St Quivox Road and Boyd Street strike off Main Street on the east side, and meet each other at St Quivox RC Church. This bulky Accrington-brick building was erected in 1932–3 to plans of James Carrick. Romanesque in style, the church has a Jubilee window of 2000 and a mosaic in the sanctuary. The church was extended in 1969. East of here there is a large housing estate, through which Adam Road and East Road are the main arteries, but there is little of any historical interest. Within the estate can be found Glenburn Primary School (designed by William Cowie, opened 25 October 1915) and St Ninian's RC Primary School (opened 1962). Prestwick Academy is located at the north end of the estate, in Newdykes Road. The Academy was built here in 1902 and named the High School, taking its present title in 1968. There have been numerous additions to the school, notably in 1972, making it one of the largest educational establishments in the area.

Atlantic House can be found at the end of Sherwood Road. This is the air traffic control centre for much of northern Britain. The building was erected as the National Coal Board's area offices, but was acquired by National Air Traffic Services in 1972.

Grangemuir Road strikes west from the south end of Main Street towards the shore. It passes below the 1862 steel railway-bridge, cast by the Vulcan Foundry in Kilmarnock. At the beach it meets the southern end of the Esplanade, which was formed from here north to Links Road. This is a popular spot for walkers, bathers, picnickers and sailors. Prestwick Sailing Club has its base here, and small dinghies and yachts can often be seen out in the bay. Grangemuir Road is also the location of the clubhouse for Prestwick St Nicholas Golf Club. The club was founded in 1851 as the Mechanics Golf Club, adopting the present name seven years later. The 18-hole course occupies a blunt headland between the railway and the sea. The course is 5,952 yards in length, par 69. The clubhouse is adorned by a carved golfer on the south façade, sculpted by W.G. Stevenson, though the building was designed by John Mercer and completed in 1892.

Just off the esplanade, by the side of the golf course, can be seen two small buildings. These are the Salt Pan cottages, which date from around 1760. They originally had furnaces within them to heat up seawater in order to refine it into salt. Salt making was at one time an important industry in the area. The headland here is occupied by a few cottages, some of them quite old but others modern bungalows. This little community was known as Maryborough. A pond in the golf course is all that remains of the Bellrock Quarry, which was used for quarrying coal and stone.

Maryborough Road links the headland with Ayr Road, at the southern end of the town. On the south side of the road can be found Bruce's Well, and the scanty remains of St Ninian's Chapel and Kingcase Hospital. Robert the Bruce founded the chapel in the fourteenth century. In 1913 part of the building was excavated, revealing twenty corpses. The Bruce is said to have come here in the thirteenth century to bathe in the waters as a way of relieving the leprosy-like skin complaint from which he suffered. As a consequence, he endowed the hospital. Prestwick Town Council restored the well in 1912. At the junction of Maryborough and Ayr roads is St Ninian's Episcopal Church. This building is quite small, but is attractive in its location surrounded by grass. The church was designed by James Hay and was erected in 1926 as a smaller version of St Margaret's in Newlands, Glasgow, which was by Peter MacGregor Chalmers.

Just south of here is the Centrum Arena. Glen Henderson started this in the 1980s but he had financial difficulties and the building lay incomplete for a number of years. It was eventually finished off by prominent local businessman Bill Barr and opened in the early 1990s with a view to carrying on the strong ice hockey tradition of the area. Previous local teams have included Ayr Bruins and Ayr Raiders, which played in a variety of locations including Beresford Terrace in Ayr. The Centrum became home to the Ayr Scottish Eagles, an important team that was formed in 1996 and won the Superleague title in 1998 as well as other national trophies. In 2002 the Eagles, much to the dismay of local ice-hockey supporters, relocated to the Braehead Centre near Glasgow. The move was not successful and the team later folded. At the time of writing, in early 2003, the future for the Centrum was uncertain.

In Waterloo Road are two places of worship – Kingcase Parish Church and New Prestwick Baptist Church. The former was erected in 1912 of sandstone when it was a mission hall connected with St Nicholas Church.

It achieved extension status in 1934, full status in 1950. The building was extended in 1949 and 1955–6. It has three attractive stained-glass windows and a small belfry. The Baptist Church dates from the 1920s. Kingcase Primary School dates from 1971. The building incorporates the sixteenth century bell that originally hung in St Nicholas Church and from 1882 hung in the Public School.

Prestwick Toll no longer exists as such, but the name is well known locally to describe the southern end of the town. To the outsider, who will be unable to discern where Prestwick stops and Ayr begins, it is probably easiest to state that the Carlton Hotel marks the boundary, its car park in Ayr, the hotel in Prestwick. Indeed such was the degree of integration between the two towns that, in 1933, the people of Prestwick were given the opportunity to vote in a referendum on whether it should amalgamate with its larger neighbour to the south. Clearly the good burghers of Prestwick valued their independence highly; they decided against joining with Ayr by 3,622 votes to only 170.

Prestwick has a third golf course, St Cuthbert's, though most of it extends into Ayr parish. The clubhouse is located in East Road, and the 6,470 yard, par 71, course occupies land surrounded on the west and south by housing, and to the east by the airport grounds. The 18-hole course was laid out in the 1960s to replace an older course that was located between Monkton and Prestwick but which was required for expansion of the airport. The former clubhouse, erected in 1980 to plans of J. Gibb Morton, still stands in Prestwick's Kirk Street, later converted to the Prestwick Airport Club.

Biggart Road is located west of East Road, itself a continuation of Bellevue Road. Here is the Biggart Hospital, now used for the treatment of geriatric patients. The building was opened in 1904 as a home for disabled Glasgow children but was converted to a hospital in 1966. West of here is St Ninian's Park, where can be found a race track, football field and associated pavilion, tennis and cricket grounds. Prestwick Cricket Club is based here. The park was formerly the St Ninian's (Ladies) Golf Course, but this was closed in 1953. At the north end is Prestwick Indoor Bowling Club, which has eight rinks.

# 15

# Ayr: the central town

THE COUNTY TOWN OF Ayrshire is located at the mouth of the river Ayr. The name Ayr is ancient, and probably means strong river. In 1197 King William the Lion established a castle here, but of it nothing at all remains, and there is even some doubt as to where exactly it stood. Certainly, it was in the vicinity of the south harbour, between Fort Street and the old dockyard, and was known as the 'New Castle on the Ayr'. On 21 May 1205 the king went on to establish Ayr as a Royal Burgh.

The old part of the town is based on what is now the High Street. This is a dog-legged street starting at the Sandgate and ending at the fork in the road formed by Kyle and Alloway streets, both of which are of comparatively modern vintage. The old town had a wall of sorts around it, and at the street ends were 'ports' or gateways, built for protection. Small plaques on the walls of adjoining buildings mark the sites of these. The Brig Port was located at the north end of the Auld Brig, though the ruins that can still be seen there behind the railings are no doubt of later origin. The Kyle Port was located just beyond Mill Street and the Wallace Tower. As the town extended beyond it, two new ports were created, named Cow Port, in what is now Alloway Street, and Over Port, in Kyle Street. The Sandgate was the second street to be established in Ayr, its southern end protected by the Sandgate Port, and the Kirk Port and Sea Port allowing access to the parish church and the harbour respectively.

The junction of High Street and Sandgate is Ayr's busy centre. Here stood the Malt Cross, marked by a ring of cobbles in the tar macadam. The cross was a fine structure, the base octagonal, surmounted by a shaft topped by a unicorn. John Anderson, who was given the use of the burgh quarry so long as he erected a stone cross to replace the wooden one that stood there at that time, probably erected it in 1697. The cross was removed in 1778 to aid traffic flow. It was at the cross a number of early executions took place, including that of Maggie Osborne, who was burnt as a witch.

High Street heads in a south-easterly direction from the Malt Cross. Between here and the Fish Cross the street is quite traditional in appearance, although there are a few modern shops erected on the north side. These include Woolworth's, built in 1925, and Marks & Spencer, which was completed in 1974. The south side has smaller commercial premises, less spoiled by modern trade that demands large plate-glass windows and bright fascias. The Fish Cross was probably the true town centre of Ayr, for here the High Street opened out into a triangular market-place. The Fish Cross itself has long gone (it was erected in 1539), but it marked the spot where fish and other goods were traded. In 1995 a statue of a man holding a fish was erected on the site of the old cross, the base of the statue being cruciform in plan to commemorate the cross. It is the work of Malcolm Robertson.

In a narrow gap on the north side of the Fish Cross is Old Bridge Street, at one time the most important street in Ayr for those heading

Ayr: the Auld Brig

north across the river. Old Bridge Street still has its cobbles, and the west side has a few traditional shops, looking across to the modern brick wall of Marks & Spencer. The Auld Brig itself probably dates from the fifteenth century, although when exactly it was built has long been the subject of debate. In 1491 King James IV crossed the river and gifted ten shillings to the masons working on it. Some say that this indicates that the bridge was only being built at that time, perhaps to replace an older wooden structure, whereas others claim that the bridge was simply being repaired, something that has to be carried out regularly. In any case, the Auld Brig replaced a ford across the Ayr that existed where the present New Bridge is located. The Auld Brig has a number of interesting plaques on it. Most of these commemorate the restoration of the bridge in 1907–10 at a cost of £10,000. The bridge by then had become rather the worse for wear, and there were proposals to have it demolished.

However, its saving grace was the fact that Robert Burns had written one of his great poems entitled 'The Brigs of Ayr' in which the Auld Brig argues with the New Bridge over which is best. Burns may have been something of a prophet, for he predicted that the Auld Brig would still be standing across the river when the New Bridge had tumbled into a 'shapeless cairn'. Burns enthusiasts campaigned to save the bridge, and local businessmen and dignitaries were instrumental in the formation of a fundraising committee. Eventually it was decided to save the bridge, and funds were raised for a comprehensive restoration project. On the bridge can be seen a sundial, its gnomon unfortunately broken. At the north end, two cobbles in the ground that are laid at right angles to the rest are said to mark the limit of the ground on which market stalls could be located. At one time there were two carved heads on the outside parapet of the bridge, which tradition claimed represented two sisters who lived on opposite sides of the river and who wished the bridge to be erected to save them having to pay the ferryman.

High Street continues south from the Fish Cross. Marks & Spencer has arched openings on the ground floor, reminiscent of traditional Scots arcaded commercial buildings. However, because the arches are too wide and the façade is made of brick the design is not particularly effective. An older building survives between here and British Home Stores (BHS). It was erected in the nineteenth century. BHS is another large shop, part of which retains the facades of 1883 (by John Baird and John Mercer). The shop was erected in 1984 to plans of Ian Burke & Partners. Behind BHS, overlooking the river, are flats built in a modern baronial style.

The west side of High Street, from the Fish Cross to the Kirk Port, is occupied by a group of shops forming what is known locally as the Isle. Behind the centre block of buildings is a lane, known fancifully as Hope Street, but better known locally as the Back o' the Isle. The buildings on the Isle are all quite distinctive. Those facing the Fish Cross are traditional shops. On the High Street side is the former Cross Keys Inn, the crossed keys still evident on the carved stonework above, but now occupied by a shop. Next door is the former banking premises with its pillars. This building dates from 1937 and was designed by Eric A. Sutherland. Next again is a rather fine baronial building, the ground floor of which has been modernised to create a shop. The upper floors retain their traditional style, with corbels and turrets. The building was erected in 1886 to plans of Allan Stevenson. On the south wall of this building is a niche containing a small statue of Sir William Wallace, the work of William Reid in 1810. This was located in an earlier building on the same site. The great patriot was captured by English soldiers and held in a prison that formerly stood here; this was the original Laigh Tolbooth of the burgh. Wallace was found in his cell one morning apparently dead, and his 'corpse' was thrown out into the midden. However, his former nursemaid found it and managed to revive him.

The Clydesdale Bank building is a fine Georgian structure, dating from 1844. It is known as Winton Buildings and was built on the site of the old Meal Market. At its south end, where Hope Street rejoins the High Street, is a modern sculpture depicting two headless bodies, one holding an open book, the other a large sphere depicting the world. This was the work of Doug Cocker and is entitled 'The Poet and the World'. It was erected in 1996. The shops in Hope Street are all quite traditional and, while some modern replacements have been built, they retain the scale and appearance of older buildings.

On the east side of the High Street there is a narrow lane known as the Kirk Port. This roadway leads to the old Church of St John the Baptist, or Ayr parish church. At the top of the lane is the lych gate, a vaulted structure that was erected in 1656. Within the gateway hang some old iron mort-safes, used in the early nineteenth century when body snatching was rife. Here also is a guide to where a number of acquaintances of Robert Burns are buried. The old graveyard is a most interesting place to visit; there are hundreds of old stones, and the memorials reflect the long history of the town. Here can be seen stones commemorating those who worked in various trades, sometimes the symbolism indicating this. There are a good number of local and Ayrshire-wide landowners buried here, and in some cases the memorials bear their arms. A stone nearer the river commemorates seven martyrs for the Covenant, who were taken at the Battle of Rullion Green and sentenced in Edinburgh to be executed in Ayr. The tale of the hangman disappearing and the deed having to be carried out by one of their number is recounted in the chapter on Irvine. They were hanged on 27 December 1666. The Burns connections in the graveyard are numerous. Here are buried Robert Aiken, first patron of Robert Burns, Provost William Fergusson, his father's employer for a time, Dr George Charles, a childhood playmate, Revd Dr William MacGill, mentioned in the 'Kirk's Alarm' and author of *Practical Essay on the Death of Christ*, which resulted in him being charged with heresy, Revd Dr William Dalrymple, who baptised the poet and others. Other notable folk interred here include Charles Abercrombie (d. 1817), a civil engineer and James Smith (1759-1848) the 'father of Scottish botany'. There is also the grave of Brigadier-General James George Smith Neill (1810–47), a war hero at the relief of Lucknow; a statue in Ayr's Wellington Square also commemorates him.

The Auld Kirk is a magnificent building. Cruciform in plan, it was erected in 1654 at the time of the Commonwealth, when Cromwell's soldiers had taken over the original old church of St John – in Ayr's Fort area – and used it for their own purposes. A 'donation' of £600 was obtained, which helped to pay for the erection of a new church. The building has a number of interesting memorials on the external walls, including one commemorating William Adair (d. 1684), the first minister in the new church. Inside the church is a fine treasure house of antiquity, including a rare 'Obit' board on which money donated to the poor was recorded. There are three lofts supported on Corinthian columns. The church was restored in 1836 under the watchful guidance of David Bryce (1803–76), a prominent Scottish architect.

High Street continues south from the Kirk Port, gradually narrowing. The Carrick Arcade occupies the line of another narrow lane that left the street on the west side. Nile Court is on the east side again, reached through an arched pend. The lane has a few older buildings within it, though the tall flats at the bottom are modern, erected in 2000–1 in a traditional style.

Carrick Street is the next street to leave High Street, this time to the west. The start of the street is narrow, where it had to make its way between two burgage plots, but it widens once it leaves the site of the old backriggs behind. Most of this street has been redeveloped over the years. On the corner of Carrick Street and Boswell Park is the Gaiety Theatre, which was built in 1902 to plans by J. MacHardy Young, replacing an older timber building that stood here. The Popplewell family operated the theatre for most of its life, but South Ayrshire Council has owned and operated it since 1973. The new extension on the west side of the original building was added in 1996. The Gaiety has since its inception been one of Scotland's premier variety theatres and many stars have trod its boards including George Formby, Will Fyffe, Andy Stewart and Harry Lauder. The Gaiety Whirl, a revue that started in 1930, has become one of its most popular and enduring institutions.

The Wallace Tower stands to the side of High Street at the top of Mill Street and occupies the site of an ancient tower that was originally known as the Auld Tour. Latterly, for some unknown reason, the tower became associated with Sir William Wallace, and when the replacement tower was erected a wooden statue of the patriot was included. The present tower dates from 1834 and was the work of Thomas Hamilton. It rises 115 feet above the level of the street and is one of the most prominent landmarks in the town. On a niche overlooking the street is a statue of Wallace in stone, sculpted by James Thom. Originally the ground floor of the tower was closed in, but when it was threatened by a street-widening scheme, this was opened up and became part of the pavement, preventing the need to remove the tower.

Mill Street headed for the Nether Mill, though anything of any historical significance has gone. Only Christina's Bar is of any age, the rest of the street and most of Mill Street hereabouts having been redeveloped in the 1960s and 1970s. The wall of Boots the chemist has various carvings on it, representing artefacts associated with the Black Friars who had a friary on this site. The church hall for the Auld Kirk is located off Mill Street, and a public pathway can be followed through the modern houses built on the site of Turner's Brewery to Turner's Bridge. This was erected in 1900 by A. M. Turner to allow his workers a quicker route to work from the houses on the north side of the river. He owned the Ayr and Newton Breweries located at the southern side of the bridge.

Shortly after the junction with Mill Street can be found the Tam o' Shanter Inn. Despite its name, the inn has no connection with the hero of Burns's epic poem. In all probability it acquired its title in the early nineteenth century when an enterprising landlord decided to cash in on the tale. Nevertheless, the reputed connection has resulted in its preservation. The building was probably erected in the early eighteenth century as a domestic dwelling. The roof is thatched, one of the few buildings in Ayrshire that still uses this material. The inn was closed in 1957 and for a number of years the building served as the Tam o' Shanter Museum but this proved to be financially impractical and, in 1993, it was converted back into a public house.

High Street ends shortly after this, at the junction with Alloway and Kyle streets. Kyle Street was the original main road east from the town, but when the railway station was opened a more direct route was formed by way of Alloway Street to Burns Statue Square. Kyle Street has a number of older buildings within it, mainly of the nineteenth century, though there are some modern developments on its southern side.

Alloway Street is a continuation of the shopping centre of the High Street. On its west side is Hourstons, a large department store, erected in 1896 to plans by Allan Stevenson. David Hourston founded the store, but it was later sold and went through a variety of owners – including House of Fraser – before it was decided to revert to its older name, by which many locals still knew it. On the east side is the modern façade of the Clydesdale Bank, the sandstone frontage broken by a glass section. This was designed by Cowie, Torry & Partners and erected in 1987.

Alloway Street ends at Burns Statue Square, known locally as the 'top of the town'. The Square was never really square in the true sense and, for many years, the south side was rather open, before being occupied by a large garage. This space is now filled by the Odeon Cinema (erected in 1937 to plans by Andrew Mather), and the tall Burns House, a hideous multi-storey office block used by South Ayrshire Council. The eponymous statue was unveiled on 8 July 1891 and was the work of George A. Lawson; the pedestal was designed by James A. Morris. On the four sides of its Aberdeen-granite base are plaques depicting scenes from the life and works of Burns. The other memorial in the Square commemorates soldiers from the Royal Scots Fusiliers who were killed in action, mainly during the Boer and other African wars. The memorial comprises a statue by Thomas Brock on a pedestal, erected in 1902.

On the east side of Burns Statue Square is the railway station, though the Station Hotel dominates the scene. This was Ayr's 'new' passenger station, completed in 1886 and replacing two older ones: one was located on the north side of the harbour and the second station was in Kyle Street. The hotel also opened in 1886 to plans of Andrew Galloway, who was the chief engineer for the Glasgow & South Western railway company. The railway passes to the east side of the hotel, the line south heading ultimately for Stranraer. The line north from Ayr is now electrified, and is a very busy commuter line into Glasgow.

*

The Sandgate passes through Ayr town centre on a north-south axis. Although the street technically does not start at the New Bridge, our trip up the Sandgate will begin there. The New Bridge is the second bridge to occupy this site. The first New Bridge was erected in 1786–8 to plans of Robert Adam, with Alexander Stevens as engineer. Adam's drawings show a bridge similar to that erected, but there are some differences, indicating that perhaps Stevens redesigned the bridge. In any case it proved to be insufficiently strong and in a storm in 1877 it was washed away; the prediction by Burns that it would become a 'shapeless cairn' had come true. The present New Bridge was erected in 1877–9 to plans of Blyth & Cunningham. It is a much flatter structure, built with durability in mind, and has survived the growing traffic and all the storms that have been thrown at it since.

This part of the main road is officially New Bridge Street; it runs from the bridge to the front of the Town Hall, or where the High Tolbooth stood. On the east side of the street, overlooking the bridge, is a fine bow-fronted building that was erected in 1787 by Stevens for himself, and also to form something of an ornament to those approaching the town from the north. The west side of the street has some older buildings along it also, but none so old. Most date from the nineteenth century.

The Boat Vennel today is a narrow roadway but it was originally the main route from the town centre to the harbour. On the south side of the vennel is Loudoun Hall, a town house dating from around 1513 and Ayr's oldest building. Built by James Tait it was later acquired by the Campbells of Loudoun as their town house (the Campbells held the Hereditary Sheriffdom of Ayrshire), since when the building became known as Loudoun Hall. Ownership passed through various hands and eventually the building fell into the slum category. The Marquis of Bute, however, recog-

Ayr: the New Bridge,
New Bridge Street and spire of
the town hall

nised its architectural merit and was instrumental in saving it from demolition. A restoration plan was drawn up and the building was returned to a sound condition once more. Loudoun Hall is open to the public on occasion, but is mainly used by various local groups for holding meetings. Some of the ground floor is vaulted, and on the first floor is the main hall, in the interior wall of which is a carved stone aumbry.

The town hall stands at the corner of New Bridge Street with High Street. The building was erected in 1827–32 to plans of Thomas Hamilton. A large neo-classical building, the hall is adorned by a tall spire that is visible for miles around, although modern building has tended to obscure some of the more distant views. The extension along High Street was added in 1878–81 to plans of Campbell Douglas & Sellars. The interior of the building was the work of J. K. Hunter in 1901, following a destructive fire. On the opposite side of the street from the town hall is a fine classical building, erected around 1830 to plans of Thomas Hamilton for the Ayrshire Bank. This banking company was founded in 1830 by Quintin Kennedy and was taken over in 1845 by the Western Bank.

Academy Street strikes west from the Sandgate, leading of course to Ayr Academy. The street is narrow, the buildings alongside it being quite old and traditional. Here can be found the business of Corney & Barrow, which took over from an older company, Whighams of Ayr.

Whighams were importers of wine, and the ground floor of their build-ing has some old vaulted cellars. It has been discovered that the firm was involved in the free trade or smuggling business in its infant years. Cathcart Street is the next street to strike west from the Sandgate. At the east end of the street is an old building known as Lady Cathcart's House. This probably dates from the early seventeenth century and was the town house of the McAdams of Waterhead. The house was under threat of demolition, but it was acquired by the Scottish Historic Buildings Trust and restored from 1991 to plans of Simpson & Brown – the date and initials are on the new window heads. Next door to Lady Cathcart's House is the Bank of Scotland building, dating from 1877 and designed by Alexander Petrie. The Royal Bank building is of 1973, by Gratton MacLean & Partners.

The pioneer road-maker, John Loudon McAdam (1756–1836) was born in Lady Cathcart's House, his parents' main home of Lagwyne Castle at Carsphairn having been destroyed by fire at that time. The young McAdam trained with his uncle in New York, where he made a fortune as a merchant, but returned to Scotland in 1783 and settled at Sauchrie House, in Maybole parish. He opened a tar works at Muirkirk, held a number of local offices and carried out many experiments to find a more suitable surface for Ayrshire's roads. In 1798, in order to meet business debts he was forced to sell his estate at Sauchrie, and moved to England where he became General Surveyor to many turnpike trusts. He continued his experiments and, in 1818, published his influential tome *A Practical Essay in the Scientific Repair and Preservation of Roads*. As a result of his advice the main streets of London, Dublin, Edinburgh and other centres were 'macadamised'. McAdam was awarded a govern-ment pension and grants for his work in road improvement. He turned down a knighthood in 1834 due to his age, having it conferred instead on his second son. McAdam died in 1836 and was buried at Moffat. 'Macadamised' road surfaces were adopted throughout Europe and the USA and proved highly effective in the new industrial age.

Newmarket Street leaves the Sandgate on the east side, taking a dog-leg route back to High Street at the Isle. The street is pedestrianised now, making it a very pleasant shopping area. Most of the buildings are quite traditional in style, and one is adorned with heads representing John Knox, Robert the Bruce and William Wallace. This building housed the Ayr Public Library when it was built in 1870. At the corner of Newmarket Street and the Sandgate is the quaint old corner known as Queen's Court. This was an old part of the town where there were some back lanes linking old stables and courtyards. These were saved from demolition and converted into a small shopping area, with little craft and gift shops, restaurants and cobbled seating areas.

St John Street strikes west from the Sandgate. Half way along this road was the Kirk Port, the gate that allowed access to the old church of St John. On the east side of the Sandgate is the former post office building, a sandstone baronial structure erected in 1893 to plans of W. W. Robertson. The present post office is a distinctly unattractive structure, having been erected in 1968 at the corner of the Sandgate with Boswell Park. The former Liberal Club, at 67–71 Sandgate, was erected in 1911 to plans of J. R. Johnstone.

Boswell Park, which runs east from the Sandgate, takes its name from the Boswell of Auchinleck family who used to own Sandgate House, which stood where the present post office building is now. The street runs through what was once open ground to link the Sandgate with Carrick Street. Here can be found the Mecca bingo hall, formerly Green's Playhouse cinema, constructed in 1931.

The Westkirk pub in the Sandgate occupies the former Ayr Free Church, which was erected in 1845 to plans of William Gale and is Norman in style. A plaque on the wall of the shop on the north side of the former church marks the site of John Murdoch's school, which Robert Burns attended for three weeks in 1773 'to revise his English grammar'. The school was demolished in 1894 when the present building was erected to plans by H. V. Eaglesham.

Sandgate continues to the south, ending at the mini roundabout at the junction of four main roads: Fullarton Street, Wellington Square, Fort Street and the Sandgate itself. Fullarton Street runs parallel with Boswell Park, and also links the Sandgate with Carrick Street. Here is Ayr bus station, as well as the rather fine Holy Trinity Episcopal Church. This building was erected in 1898 to plans of John L. Pearson, and it is regarded as his finest work in Scotland. The tower, which is quite a landmark locally, was not added until 1964, by which time it was decided to construct it from concrete. The church contains some fine stained glass by Clayton & Bell, a pulpit of Caen stone and some balusters from the original Auld Brig of Ayr.

Fort Street heads north from the mini roundabout to the top end of Ayr harbour. The Baptist Church was originally erected in 1815 as the Theatre Royal, and was converted into a church in 1887. The rear of the Westkirk inn can be seen on the east side of the street. This part of the former church was erected in 1878. Further north is the former New Church, a fine classical building dating from 1807–10 and designed by David Hamilton. The church was renamed the Cathcart Church when it amalgamated with the Cathcart Street Church in 1951 but was itself closed in 1981 and is now used as a dance studio. The memorial gateway still survives. Next door is Ayr Academy, the oldest surviving part of which dates from 1880, although there has been an educational establishment with this name in Ayr since the late eighteenth century. The school was designed by Clarke & Bell in a Grecian style and contains carved representations of Burns, Watt and Wilkie. The school has been extended a number of times since, including 1907 by James Morris, and although there have been proposals to close the building and move the pupils to more modern schools in the town, nothing has yet come of it.

At the junction of Fort and Cathcart streets is the former Cathcart Street Relief Church, which has now been converted into flats. The building was erected in 1816, but it later became the church hall for Cathcart Church. It closed as a hall in 1981 and was a warehouse before being converted into its present use. Further north is the former Custom House, dating from around 1810. The flats on the corner are modern, though were built with a traditional appearance. At the foot of Fort Street, by the harbour side, is the Boathouse restaurant. This occupies the old lifeboat station that opened in 1803 but was closed in 1932.

Some older buildings occupy South Harbour Street to begin with, including some traditional inns with names like Ye Olde Forte Bar and the Steamboat Tavern. Soon a tall wall, marking the northern limits of the old Cromwellian fort, replaces the street side. A gap site follows, formerly occupied by large stores, before the sloping walls of the fort are reached. This corner of the fort is occupied by a little turret that was added sometime in the second half of the nineteenth century by an eccentric local businessman, 'Baron' John Miller (1820–1910). It is known locally as Miller's Folly. The sloping walls below, which extend westward alongside South Beach Road and beyond, were part of Cromwell's fort, of which more later.

The Citadel Leisure Centre is located by the side of South Beach Road. This building incorporates the Ayr Baths building of 1972, designed by Cowie, Torry & Partners. The baths were extended with the addition of games halls and other facilities in 1997. The south harbour is today no longer used by ships or fishing boats. The wharves are now home to a variety of modern flats, including Mariners' Pointe and Citadel Quay. The style of these buildings is quite unique. Around the former slipway of Ayr dockyard can be seen a number of sculptures indicative of a maritime past, as well as a real fishing boat, *Watchful*, taken from the Maidens, and perched on two stands.

The story of Ayr harbour is long and interesting. No doubt fishermen have used the mouth of the river for many centuries. The building of boats naturally co-existed with this, but large-scale shipbuilding did not come until later. There were a number of yards alongside the harbour, but the largest was created in 1881 on the south side, the slip dock of which survives. Many vessels were launched from here, including the *Drake*, which was the largest at 1,597 tons. The yard was closed after the Second World War. Port business is now undertaken from the north harbour side, where the large Newton dock can be found. This was excavated in 1878. Nearby can be seen Ayr lighthouse, a cylindrical tower erected in 1841 to plans of Robert Paton, with lighthouse keeper's cottage adjoining. Off the north breakwater, about two hundred yards from the harbour mouth, the cargo vessel *Kaffir* ran aground on 23 September 1974 after having been taken illegally from Ayr harbour by the engineer. The vessel, which is not large, can still be seen at times from the shore.

Ayr Fort was constructed between 1652–3 by soldiers in Cromwell's army. Five citadels were established across Scotland, of which Ayr was one. A high revetted wall was constructed around the site, which included the parish church of St John. This was requisitioned for use as a store, the tower being useful as a lookout. Various barracks were erected within the walls, as well as a brewery, kitchens, parade ground, bakery and the other facilities required by a group of soldiers. Of the fort, the only surviving remains are the walls that can be seen along South Beach Road, and behind Arran Terrace and Ailsa Place. The eastern walls have been removed, although in Academy Lane there survives the former arched gateway into the fort, now much lower in height due to the ground level having risen over the years.

The fort was abandoned by 1660 and was subsequently granted to the Earl of Eglinton as compensation for his losses during the Commonwealth. A Burgh of Barony named Montgomeriestoun was established, with the intention of rivalling Ayr, but little came of this plan. Eventually, in 1852 the barony was acquired by John Miller who converted what remained of St John's Tower into a mock Gothic castle, named Fort Castle. This survived until 1924 when the Marquis of Bute was instrumental in restoring the tower to its original style. St John's Tower is open to the public on occasion. Within can be found some old sarcophagi, discovered during excavations here. There are a couple of gravestones in the old churchyard that surrounded the tower, and tradition has it that Maggie Osborne, the legendary Ayr witch, was interred here.

The streets within the Fort area have names associated with the history of the town. Montgomerie and Eglinton recall the owner of the barony, whereas Arran and Ailsa are named after the views of the two islands. Bruce Crescent was named from Robert the Bruce, who held a meeting of the Scottish parliament here in 1314, the first after his victory at Bannockburn, at which the succession was settled.

*

The area south of the Fort was developed in a grid fashion in the early nineteenth century. Charlotte Street, for example, was named in honour of Princess Charlotte, daughter of the future King George IV, in 1813. Here can be found the former Charlotte Street School, or Lady Jane Hamilton's School, which dates from 1843, and the old police station, erected in 1858.

Wellington Square lies further south, and is one of Ayr's finest Georgian streetscapes. The square was laid out in 1806 and named for the victor of Waterloo, Arthur Wellesley, Duke of Wellington. The north side of the square has some fine Georgian townhouses, most of which are now occupied by offices. The south side is similar in appearance and here, at number 25, can be found the oldest building in the square, Wellington House of 1806. In the centre of the square can be found Ayr's cenotaph, a foursquare memorial designed by James Kennedy Hunter and erected in 1924. Here also are various statues depicting a number of eminent figures from the nobility and various heroes of the British Empire. They include the 13th Earl of Eglinton (1812–61), the 'Tournament Earl' (sculpted by Matthew Noble, 1865), Brigadier-General James Neill of Swindridgemuir (1810–1857), who fell at the Relief of Lucknow (sculpted by Matthew Noble, 1859) and Sir James Fergusson of Kilkerran (1832–1907), governor of South Australia, New Zealand and Bombay at different times and postmaster general (sculpted by Sir Goscombe John, 1910). Lesser memorials commemorate John Loudon McAdam (unveiled 1936 by the Institution of Municipal and County Engineers) and Primrose William Kennedy of Drumellan (1799–1863), provost of Ayr 1855–61, unveiled at the junction of Sandgate and Fort Street in 1868.

The County Buildings and Sheriff Court dominate the seaward side of the square. The courthouse is the older of the two, and it faces the square. Designed in 1818–22 by Robert Wallace, it is a fine classical building with a dome. The County Buildings behind, which have their own façade facing the Low Green area, were erected in 1931–5 to plans by Alex Mair. The Duke of York, later King George VI, on 10 July 1931, as noted by a plaque on the south side, laid the foundation stone. The County Buildings occupy the site of Ayr's gaol, which had been erected in 1822. On the west side of the County Buildings is a garden area, with a fine cast-iron fountain gifted to the burgh by James Steven of Skeldon House. Here also is a war memorial commemorating the soldiers of the Royal Scots Fusiliers who served in various wars. The memorial comprises of a statue by Pilkington Jackson on top of a plinth with inscribed wall behind. The memorial was erected in 1960, the regiment having been amalgamated with the Highland Light Infantry in 1959 to form the Royal Highland Fusiliers.

On the south side of Pavilion Road stands the Pavilion, a magnificent if eclectic building dominated by four square-towers at the corner. This building was erected as a theatre and dance hall in 1910–11 to plans of James Kennedy Hunter, but is now used a children's entertainment centre. Also by the roadside is a memorial celebrating the gift of the Low Green – an impressive sward of grass adjacent to Ayr beach – to the inhabitants of Ayr by William the Lion in the fourteenth century.

Barns Street strikes east from Wellington Square and continues into the dogleg of Dalblair Road towards Burns Statue Square. Barns Street is lined with fine terraced houses, though the multi-storeyed Ramada Jarvis Caledonian Hotel dominates the aspect down the street. This was erected in 1971. Dalblair Road has been redeveloped over much of its length. The Dalblair Arcade shopping centre (now renamed the Arran Mall) was completed in 1967. Dalblair House stood where Hourston's department store now stands. Barns Street was named after Barns House, still extant at the end of Barns Park and Barns Crescent. This elegant house is one of the oldest of its type in Ayr, dating from around 1800 and still in private ownership. Barns Terrace dates from 1845–60 and overlooks Alloway Place, the continuation south of Sandgate and the main route towards Doonfoot.

The area south of Barns Street and Wellington Square, stretching to Belleisle Park, is one dominated by large houses and salubrious hotels. The Fairfield House Hotel is located in Fairfield Road, built for a Glasgow merchant. The Gartferry Hotel, in Racecourse Road, dates from 1867 and was designed by Andrew MacLachlan as a house for Robert Paton. Built into the stone wall surrounding the hotel grounds are stones originally used to affix the gibbet to the Over Tolbooth. In the street known as Savoy Park can be found Wellsbourne, designed by the Ayr architect James Morris, whose own house, Savoy Croft, is located nearby. Savoy Park was a large house for Charles Orr Ewing MP, also by James Morris and erected in 1884–6. It has some fine panelling within, and the dining room has some painted armorial panels; this house is also now a hotel.

Gargowan House, also in Racecourse Road, is now part of the

Ayrshire Hospice. The house was erected in 1823, but in 1995 was purchased by the trust and extended to form the present hospice. The Ayrshire Hospice trust had been founded in November 1983 and, after buying the house, put up a fifteen-bed residential unit to the rear. Over the years further fundraising allowed more bedrooms to be added, and in 1998 the adjoining property was added. The hospice exists to care for those suffering from cancer or the later stages of motor neurone disease.

Down Blackburn Road are a few large buildings of note. In Craigweil Road are three houses, Carlton Turrets, Craigweil and Westfield, the first two of which are mirror images of each other. They were designed by John Murdoch and erected in 1879. Craigweil was the home of John Sword, founder of the Western SMT Bus Company. Craigweil was for many years Ayr's youth hostel, but, in 2001, it was closed and the building was acquired by Wellington School, which already owned the two other buildings, as well as Hartfield and Hartree houses. Wellington School is a private establishment that was founded in 1839 as a girls' school by Mrs Gross, the name coming from Wellington Square, where the first school was located. It has a number of famous former pupils including the two Kirstys: television presenter Kirsty Wark and supermodel Kirsty Hume. The school became co-educational in 1994.

Miller Road links Alloway Place and Racecourse Road with Burns Statue Square. The road was laid out in 1852 by Mrs Nicholson of Barns House and was built up with large terraced or detached buildings. Some of these are now hotels or commercial premises. South of here is the Park Circus and Bellevue Crescent area, again occupied by desirable properties. These were erected from 1860 onward. In Park Circus is St Andrew's Church, a massive Perpendicular Gothic building with a tall spire, dating from 1893. The architect was John B. Wilson, and the church contains stained glass by John Blyth.

Midton Road makes its way through the centre of this affluent area. The road starts at the junction with Carrick Road, in the gusset of which stands Ayr Grammar School. This was erected in 1868. Further along the road St Columba's Church occupies another gusset. This church was erected in 1902 as the Trinity Church to plans of John B. Wilson and again is dominated by a spire in which is a carillon of bells. The organ is of 1904 by J. J. Binns. Stained glass includes work by C. C. Baillie, Susan Bradbury and Sidney Holmes. Carrick Road continues south to a gusset of its own, where St Leonard's Road and Monument Road separate, and a church with a spire also occupies this spot. This is St Leonard's Church, erected in 1886 to plans by John Murdoch. The chancel was added in 1911. The organ is by Harrison & Harrison.

The St Leonard's area is mainly residential, with some large houses located here and there. Nothing of Corsehill House (which was located off Monument Road) survives, but the gardens are used by the council as a nursery. These are open to the public. At the junction of Monument Road and Chapelpark Road can be seen a stone representation of Ayr's coat of arms. This was taken from the original New Bridge of 1785. St Leonard's Road continues into Maybole Road, one of the main routes south from the town centre. Most of this area is residential, beyond Ewenfield Road being relatively modern. The Laigh Glengall estate was erected from 1959 onward.

Doonfoot Road is the continuation of Racecourse Road south of Racecourse View. Seafield Hospital was here, but closed in 1991. The hospital was centred on Seafield House, erected in 1860 to plans of Clarke & Bell for Sir William Arrol (1831–1913), famous as the engineer who built the Forth Bridge. The hospital opened in 1921. On the other side of the road is the Viewhouse, originally erected as a pavilion and viewing platform for the racecourse that existed here. The racing of horses has long been popular in Ayr, and in 1770 it was decided to formally lay out a racetrack here. The course was closed in 1904 when the present racecourse on the north side of the river was opened.

Belleisle Estate occupies the east of Doonfoot Road. This is now a fine public-park with two golf courses. Belleisle House was erected in 1787 for Hugh Hamilton of Pinmore but, in 1829, it was rebuilt for Colonel Alexander West Hamilton to plans of William Burn. The local council purchased the grounds in 1926. The house is now Belleisle House Hotel, and within can be seen a rather fine fireplace in the panelled hall. The grounds are mainly occupied by the two golf courses, known as Belleisle and Seafield. The former is one of the finest inland courses in Scotland and has hosted many prestigious tournaments; it is an 18-hole course, 6,431 yards in length, par 71. The latter is 5,246 yards, with a par of 68. Belleisle also has some highly attractive gardens, and its conservatory is home to a fine selection of plants and a statue by W. Pfohl. Within the gardens can be seen an obelisk inscribed with prayers. Here also is an aviary and pet corner, where birds and small animals can be seen in cages. A deer park occupies the slopes down to Doonfoot Road.

Two main roads pass through that part of Ayr east of the railway line – Castlehill Road and Holmston Road. Castlehill Road, or the A713, heads for Dalmellington, and begins at the roundabouts adjacent to Ayr station. Here can be seen a traditional pub, the Market Inn, which was saved from demolition when the Safeway supermarket was being constructed in the 1990s. The inn dates from 1910. In Mossgiel

Road is the Church of Jesus Christ of Latter Day Saints, erected in 1962. Castlehill Church itself is located further south, erected in 1958. Castlehill House is now gone, having been erected in 1804 for Patrick Ballantine, but demolished in the 1960s. The earlier house was home to John Ballantine, lawyer in Ayr, who was an associate of Burns, and to whom he inscribed 'The Brigs of Ayr'.

Belmont Road leads back to Ewenfield Road, making its way over the railway by a level crossing. Off Belmont Road is Belmont Academy, dating from 1960. In Peggieshill Road is St Paul's RC Church, erected in 1966–7. The altar, lectern and ambo are constructed of Creetown granite. Queen Margaret Academy is located at the end of Dalmellington Road, just short of the bypass. The school was opened in January 1976 to serve the Roman Catholic secondary children in the town. On the other side of the road from here is the Kincaidston housing estate, erected in 1973. Kincaidston Primary School is located at the foot of Cranesbill Court within the estate, and was opened in 1975.

Holmston Road (A70) leaves the railway-station roundabouts and heads eastward for Cumnock and ultimately Edinburgh. Near the start can be seen Holmston House, built in 1857–60 to plans of William Lambie Moffat as the Kyle Combination Poorhouse; it is now used as offices by the Social Work department. The former Ayr County Hospital of 1880 (by John Murdoch) has been demolished and replaced by modern flats in 1999–2000. On the opposite side of the road is Holmston Primary School, erected in 1884. Holmston cemetery is the largest burial ground in Ayr, established in 1860 and still used. The gates at the entrance contain the Ayr arms, and were designed by John Murdoch in 1862. The cemetery contains a number of memorials of interest, but its sheer size means that it is sometimes difficult to track down a particular grave. Assistance can sometimes be had from the office. Here is buried George Douglas Brown (1869–1902), author of *The House with the Green Shutters*, James MacNaughton of Smithfield, who built the railway from Dundee to Newtyle in 1826–32, victims of the Ayr Carpet Works fire of 1876, the dead from two world wars and many locals, known and unknown.

The other side of Holmston Road is lined with trees, with the river Ayr walk passing alongside. This provides an attractive stroll alongside the river, and the route can be followed as far as Auchincruive estate. By the side of the pathway, behind the houses of Holmston Crescent, can be found Wallace's Heel, a spring by the riverside where the patriot reputedly escaped from English soldiers, leaving the imprint of his heel on the rock. Nearby is an old limekiln.

Kyle Academy stands to the north of Holmston Road. It was opened in August 1979. South of Holmston Road are the suburbs of Masonhill and Forehill. Forehill Primary School is located in Caledonia Road, opened in 1968.

# 16

# Ayr: Newton, Alloway and beyond

THAT PART OF AYR which lies on the north side of the river Ayr was originally totally independent of the larger burgh to the south. The river formed the parish boundary between Ayr and Prestwick, though in 1779 the southern part of Prestwick was separated from it and a new parish, named Newton upon Ayr, was created. In 1873 the boundary of the burgh of Ayr was extended to include Newton and other places on the north side of the river. In 1895 Newton parish, St Quivox parish and the parish of Ayr were joined together to create the present Ayr parish.

Newton upon Ayr is the part of the town that extends along Main Street and Prestwick Road towards Prestwick Toll. The old part of the village was located on Main Street, which originally had an open burn or drain running down its centre. Main Street is still a busy route today, but is no longer the major shopping street it once was. The street starts at the north end of the New Bridge. In a small garden area is the old Newton market cross, dating from 1675 and rebuilt in 1775, according to the eroded inscription.

On the left, at the junction with North Harbour Street, is the former Darlington Place Church, now used by Borderline Theatre Company as their practice area and theatre. The church was erected in 1860 to plans of Clarke & Bell and converted in 1986 by J. Wetton Brown. Next door to the former church are a few traditional nineteenth century buildings before the modern brick-built MFI furniture shop is found. Further along the street is Babylon nightclub, originally the Orient cinema of 1932 by Albert V. Gardner.

On the opposite side of the street are a few traditional premises followed by the sandstone Carnegie Library, which is the main library in the area and is operated by South Ayrshire Council. Andrew Carnegie gifted £10,000 towards the construction of this building in 1893. Campbell Douglas & Morrison designed a renaissance structure that is adorned with arched windows on the first floor and inscribed panels. Inside, on the staircase, can be seen a window by Stephen Adam & Co on which the figure of Knowledge has six toes on her foot!

Now located on a traffic island in Main Street is the Newton Steeple, dated 1795. This was originally part of the burgh tolbooth and council rooms, the arched entranceway giving access to Newton Parish Church and kirkyard. When the new road was being created here in

1963, it was agreed after a long campaign to retain the structure, which is a simple foursquare tower adorned with a steeple and clock. The building of the road also meant the demolition of the former Newton Church of 1777 and its parish kirkyard, the graves of which were relocated. The present Newton Parish Church (built as Newton Free Church) is located to the north, erected in 1862 to plans of William Clarke. The large halls adjoining were erected in 1971.

A variety of commercial premises line Main Street north of here to its end at Damside and New Road junction. At the foot of Damside is the former Unionist Club, built in 1891 by James A. Morris. The former Salvation Army citadel is nearby, constructed in 1905 by Arthur Hamilton in a style reminiscent of Glasgow architects of the period.

The area west of Main Street, as far as the harbour, was feued out in the early nineteenth century in a grid pattern. Green Street was named after the Newton Green, which was located here. Most of these streets and associated lanes are filled by commercial and industrial premises, but here and there are some buildings of interest. The former Newton Academy, used as a school until 1970 and now council offices, was erected in Green Street to plans of William Cowie in 1911. Off Weir Road is the later Newton Green burial ground.

Behind the older buildings on the east side of Newton's Main Street the town has been virtually redeveloped since the Second World War. This is Wallacetown, a separate community of sorts established by the Wallaces of Craigie, who had their seat at Newton Castle. This old tower house no longer exists – it stood where Asda car park is now – but Garden Street recalls the former garden. Most of the community was demolished in the 1960s and replaced by an unattractive grid of modern flats, only little bits of the old place surviving. River Street, by the side of the Ayr, is one of these. This links the New Bridge with the Auld Brig. Among old traditional inns can be found the former River Street Mission Hall, erected in 1878. The Black Bull Inn has associations with Burns, to whom it was known as Simpson's Inn. Here his father interviewed John Murdoch as a possible teacher for Alloway, and Burns himself later wrote some letters here. Asda is located next door, a 1987 brick-built structure by Cowie, Torry & Partners, with a glass frontage to Gordon Place. This little street is now only open to pedestrians, the Ayr Martyrs Free Church of 1832 being located at the side of the main road. By the side of the Auld Brig is Ramsay Garden, named in honour of John Ramsay, a local illusionist of note. Cowie, Torry and Partners erected Riverside House, another undistinguished modern structure used by South Ayrshire Council, in 1975. The riverside walk can be followed further east.

John Street is now a busy dual carriageway, forming part of the town centre ring-road. It starts at the King Street roundabout and heads south east to the Victoria Bridge. Here can be found St Margaret's RC Church, erected in 1826 to plans of James Dempster. It has a modern church-hall adjoining, though this one seems to fit in nicely. Behind it, though access is difficult, is a little burial ground. Wallacetown Parish Church is located further along the street, erected in 1834 to plans of John Kay. On the opposite side of the street is the Riverside Evangelical Church, a simple Gothic building of 1860, originally Wallacetown Free Church. The tall towers of Riverside Place were erected in 1969–70 to plans of Cowie, Torry and Partners, but in 1992 they were refaced and topped with mock pediments. At the end of the street is the fire station, standing on the site of Content House. J. & J. A. Carrick designed this in 1963. Content House was the home of the MacIlwraith family. The former Robertson Memorial Church of 1901, designed by Allan Stevenson, was in 1950–4 converted into the present Civic Theatre. On the east side of the roundabout is the older block of Ayr College, a utilitarian building of 1966 by Charles Toner, with a more recent building of 1999–2000 by Boswell, Mitchell & Johnson across the road.

Within the older part of Wallacetown, at George Street and Limond's Wynd, can be found the former Morrison Congregational Church of 1779, restyled in 1901 by J. K. Hunter. Beyond, the redevelopment has created a grid pattern, with blocks of flats and sheltered housing, interspersed with Wallacetown School (1875), Church of God and the traditional Horseshoe Inn.

The north side of King Street has also been redeveloped, this time a bit later, in 1973. Russell Street School dates from 1890. Here also is the woollen mill of Begg of Ayr, noted for the manufacture of woollens since 1900. Allison Street has the modern police station at its southern end, erected in 1975. At the east end of King Street, at what was originally the busy junction with Russell, George and Queen streets, can be found two small cemeteries: the Seceders' Graveyard and Wallacetown cemetery. The former is located in the angle formed by King and Russell streets and is the older of the two. Wallacetown cemetery is located on the opposite side of what was Russell Street from the old graveyard, next to the railway line. This cemetery was established when the old kirkyard around the parish church became full. Within the cemetery can be seen a statue commemorating John Taylor (1805–1842), a notable Chartist who was imprisoned for his radical beliefs. He was arrested in 1839 for inciting a riot in Birmingham, serving a few weeks. The statue was erected in 1850.

North of Tam's Brig, as the railway crossing in Prestwick Road is known, is a continuation of Newton that was developed in the nineteenth century. Here are the more pleasant suburbs of Woodfield, Heathfield and Falkland, linking Ayr with Prestwick. Near Tam's Brig is St James' Church, its tower a distinctive landmark. This was erected in 1883–5 to plans of John Murdoch in the Early English style. The hall was added in 1933 to plans of Alex Mair. In McCall's Avenue was Gray's Carpet works, a major employer in the town from 1876 until 1974. Newton on Ayr station was opened in 1839 and still serves commuters on the Ayr to Glasgow line. Newton Park is a welcome open area in what is quite a dense area of busy streets. The park is home to tennis courts, bowling greens and a boating pond.

Within this northern Newton area can be found three smaller churches, the Ayr United Free Church, located in Kirkholm Avenue. This church was erected in 1930 following the Union of the United Free Church with the Church of Scotland when a number refused to join, and formed the UF Church (Continuing). The Assembly of God Church is found in Prestwick Road, next to Woodfield Crescent. New Prestwick Baptist Church is found further along Prestwick Road, erected in 1900. There are a few places of interest in this area, including the Territorial Army centre in Seaforth Road, the ambulance depot in Maryfield Road, and Heathfield Primary School of 1931. Heathfield Road is a busy artery, linking Prestwick Toll with the bypass and routes east. The former Heathfield Hospital was provided in 1905 to treat infectious diseases. The hospital was closed in 1991 and most services transferred to the new Ayr Hospital. Heathfield Clinic survives.

There is a number of industrial and retail premises built in the eastern Heathfield area. Part of this was, at one time, an aerodrome, created in 1941. There was a serious crash here on 14 August 1941, in which twenty-two were killed, including Arthur Purvis, who was regarded as one of the most influential figures in persuading the Americans to support Britain in the early days of the Second World War. The graves of the victims can be seen in the Holmston cemetery in Ayr. The present Heathfield retail park is located in what is known as Liberator Drive, commemorating the air crash, and at the entrance is a propeller from an aeroplane. An earlier representation of a complete aeroplane suffered in strong winds.

East of Wallacetown, Whitletts Road is an important route in and out of the northern half of Ayr. On crossing the railway line at the end of King Street, the areas of Hawkhill and Lochside are reached. Somerset Park is home to Ayr United Football Club, which has played here since 1910, when the club was formed by the merger of Ayr

Parkhouse and Ayr Football Club (whose home ground it had been since 1888). The record crowd at the stadium is 25,225 for a league game against Rangers in 1969, which Ayr won by two goals to one. Under Ally MacLeod, an inspirational manager, the club's most consistent period came in the 1960s and 1970s when Ayr were formidable opponents for any team, particularly at Somerset. The present stadium is not up to modern standards and, although there have been recent proposals to move to a new ground at Heathfield, these have been hampered by the highly restrictive planning policies of the Scottish Executive in Edinburgh. While Ayr United has never won a major trophy the team came close in the spring of 2002 when, in the same week, it contested the League Cup final against Rangers and a Scottish Cup semi final against Celtic. Inevitably however both games were lost to clubs with resources far in excess of those available to a provincial side.

Next to Somerset Park is the yard of W. G. Walker & Co., which was established by William Walker in 1878. His son, John Walker, is credited with inventing the method of laying tarred roads, having experimented with this in 1894. Miller Road in Ayr was the first local road to be treated in this way. On the other side of the street is James Dickie's stamping works, known locally as the 'Wee' Stampworks. This foundry was established in 1913. The former Hawkhill Post Office at the corner of Somerset Road with Back Hawkhill Avenue dates from 1857, and is now a newsagents and store. Hawkhill Avenue and the first developments on Whitletts Road date from the mid-to-late nineteenth century. Lochside Road strikes in a north-easterly direction from here, this scheme of houses being developed from 1932 onward. Here is found the Lochside Church of 1940 and Braehead Primary School of 1951.

On the south side of Whitletts Road is Ayr Racecourse, one of only five major horseracing venues in Scotland, and the only one with Group One status. The course dates from 1907, replacing the more cramped course at Belleisle. The Ayr Gold Cup, which was instituted in 1804, is held here every September and is Scotland's most important flat race. The Scottish Grand National, which moved here from Irvine in 1966, is run in the spring. The course has a number of pavilions overlooking it, including the Eglinton stand of 1967 designed by J & J. A. Carrick, and the Princess Royal stand of 1995–6, designed by Carrick Cowie Torry. At the west end of the course is the Western House, a fine building of 1919 designed by Harold O. Tarbolton to be the clubhouse of the Western Meeting Club. Today the house is used as a venue for weddings, corporate entertainment and other events. Within the course is a statue of Red Rum, the famous racehorse which won both the Grand National

Ayr Racecourse: the Eglinton stand

at Aintree and the Scottish version at Ayr. It was sculpted by Annette Yarrow and was unveiled in 1975.

Whitletts is today a suburb of Ayr, but it began its life as a separate village almost two miles from the town centre. Originally it was a small rural community with a public house and smithy, but with the development of coal mining in the area the community grew with the erection of a number of miners' houses. The present Whitletts has lost much of its heart, the original Main Road being redeveloped, leaving few older buildings. Whitletts Primary School was designed by A. C. Thomson and erected in 1910. The Thistle Inn was built in 1937 to plans of J. R. Johnstone. At the junction of Low and High roads can be found the village war memorial, a simple granite cross. Dalmilling Parish Church is located in Dalmilling Road. This church was erected in 1953 and designed by Cowie & Torry. Further along Dalmilling Road is the Roman Catholic Cathedral of the Good Shepherd, erected in 1955 to plans of Fred Torry. Since 1961 this has been the seat of the Bishop of Galloway. In 1985 the inside was refurbished, using many items rescued from St Robert Bellarmine church in Glasgow, and stained glass from Our Lady & St Margaret in Kinning Park. In common with many other churches it has suffered from falling congregations over the years and, in 2002, there were even proposals that it should be demolished.

Mainholm Academy was erected in 1965, and is one of the largest secondary schools in Ayr. In Harthall is Dalmilling Primary School, opened in 1959, and in Westwood Avenue is Westwood Nursery School, opened in 1977. Next to this is Dalmilling golf course, an 18-hole, 5,457 yards, par 68, municipal course, created in 1960. Thornyflat Maternity Hospital was located at the foot of Thornyflat Avenue. This was opened in 1944, but was demolished in the late 1980s and the site used for housing.

Mainholm Road can be followed past the academy and round the east end of the racecourse into the suburb of Craigie. The housing estate was developed from 1947 onward, occupying the lands associated with Craigie House. This mansion still survives, perched on a prominent site overlooking the river Ayr and is at the heart of a very pleasant complex of gardens and woods. The first house was built around 1730 by the Wallace family but, in the 1780s, a fine Palladian mansion was erected for Sir William Campbell, who had bought the estate in 1783. A massive Doric porch was added around 1837, W. H. Playfair being claimed as the architect. The house was latterly used as a hotel, then to provide additional rooms for Craigie College and, since 1998, has been used as the Ayrshire Business Centre.

Craigie College was established in 1964 as a teacher-training establishment. The buildings were new, erected on the lands of Craigie to plans of A. Buchanan Campbell. The halls of residence were added in 1967, designed by Boswell, Mitchell & Johnson. The college invariably seemed to be under the threat of closure but, in 1993, was taken over by Paisley University, and now forms the Ayr campus of that centre of education. The Craigie Horticultural centre is located in the lower grounds of the estate. Here is a garden visitor centre, with glasshouses containing plants from different climates. The centre has a sales area and tearoom. Nearby is the Ayrshire Archives centre, where many important documents and objects from Ayrshire's past are preserved and available for inspection. A caravan site occupies one of the fields behind Ayr College.

*

East of Ayr bypass is the rural countryside of St Quivox and Auchincruive. The tiny village of St Quivox lies around its old churchyard and parish church. Worship has taken place here since at least the thirteenth century. The present church dates from 1596 and was extended in 1767 for the Oswalds of Auchincruive. It is a simple, single-storey building, with a small belfry at one end. The churchyard contains a number of old stones of interest, including that in memory of Richard Oswald (of whom more shortly), as well as the mausoleum of the Campbells of Craigie, designed by W. H. Playfair in 1822. The old manse building nearby dates from 1823.

The Hannah Research Institute lies south west of St Quivox. This was established in 1928 as a dairy research institute, the funds for which were gifted by John Hannah of Girvanmains. The institute was designed by A. G. Ingham and has been extended over the years. Here also is the Kevoca business centre, the named Kevoca being a derivative of Quivox, rather than a Scandinavian name! Within the grounds can be seen a small bronze sculpture entitled 'The Milkmaid', the work of Denys Mitchell.

On the south side of the B743, the main Ayr to Mauchline road, is Auchincruive estate, location of part of the Scottish Agricultural College. Auchincruive was anciently a seat of the Wallaces, and Sir William Wallace is reckoned to have hidden in the woods hereabouts on a number of occasions. The Murrays of Broughton latterly owned Auchincruive, but in 1764 Richard Oswald purchased the estate. The Oswalds of Auchincruive were a prominent family locally, and some of them found fame internationally. Richard Oswald (1705–84) was celebrated for his part in helping negotiate the American Declaration of Independence, but was held in less regard for his part in the African slave trade. Richard Oswald erected the present mansion house in 1767, using plans supplied by Robert Adam. The house was extended later, but has been restored internally and renamed Oswald Hall. The estate extends to 665 acres and contains a number of college buildings. Among these is the original stable block of the estate, the tower of which contains a doocot. This block was probably erected in the eighteenth century. The college buildings date from 1927 onward, and include the fine Wilson Hall, designed by D. S. MacPhail in 1956 in a semi-baronial style.

North of Auchincruive are the Brickrow smallholdings, and at Kirklandholm Farm is the landscaped site of the Auchencruive Nos. 1, 2 and 3 coal mine, which operated until 1960. Fulshawwood Farm was the site of a Second World War camp. A track from Auchincruive passes through the Newbarns Wood and links onto the Mainholm Road, where there are a number of smallholdings. This minor road is unusual in that it has a couple of milestones along it, one of them at Newbarns, at this point no longer a public highway.

The A70 road leaves Ayr at the Holmston roundabout and heads for Coylton. The Old Toll area is soon reached, where can be found a number of cottages, toll site and disused quarry. The Belston Quarry is also long-since disused, and is now a pleasant loch that attracts wildlife. At

Whitefordhill is Ayr cattle market, established here in 1993. This replaced the old market in Ayr, which is now occupied by the Safeway supermarket in Castlehill Road. The firm of James Craig has operated the market since 1889.

MacNairston Road strikes south from the Old Toll and passes Sandyhill Terrace before turning sharply south-east. On the right is Ayr crematorium, erected in 1966 to plans of Douglas Hay. The surrounding grounds are laid out with pleasant lawns and bushes, with memorial gardens. The Crofthead caravan park occupies the site of the former Crofthead Hospital, built in 1903 as a joint smallpox hospital, but never used as such. It was to serve as a children's hospital for a time. Mac-Nairston Road continues past Friarland and Abbothill farms to the south, names that recall the fact that there was at one time a friary nearby at Loch Fergus. A cottage known as Wee MacNairston has a small private observatory. Loch Fergus itself is a small kettle-hole lochan located on the boundary of Ayr parish. The loch has an islet within it which was the site of a monastery of which very little is known. No sign of this can be found there today. The name Fergus is thought to derive from one of the Scottish kings who defeated King Cole.

The Dalmellington Road (A713) climbs from the Kincaidston round-about. It soon reaches some houses and the Ailsa Hospital, which was built in 1866–9 as the Glengall Asylum. The architect was Charles Edward, who won a competition to design it. The hospital is still functioning. Due south of the Ailsa Hospital is Ayr Hospital, a large brick built modern hospital of 1991, designed by Keppie Henderson architects. Originally having 301 beds, the hospital cost £31 million to erect. This replaced the former Ayr County Hospital, Heathfield Hospital and Seafield Children's Hospital, all of which were located in the town. The hospital has been extended a couple of times since, including a chapel that includes stained glass taken from the Biggart Hospital. Further on the Dalmellington Road is the Carrick Glen private hospital, erected in 1991–2 to plans of the Elliott Manning Partnership. The Independent British Hospital Association operates this hospital, which has twenty-two beds and offers a range of surgical and outpatient facilities.

The A713 continues to climb and arrives on the summit of the Cock Hill. Here is the large Mosshill Industrial Estate, established in 1973 in an attempt to improve the economy of the Doon valley, but which attracted more employees from Ayr. The main factory here was the Digital Equipment computer factory, established in 1976, later taken over by Compaq and closed in 2002.

A minor road strikes west from Mosshill passing the Ayrshire

Equitation Centre. Further on is Mount Fergusson farm, named after William Fergusson of Doonholm, twice provost of Ayr from 1759–61 and 1763–5. A minor road strikes south from the Corton Road and heads for the former Dalrymple Station. It passes Mount Oliphant Farm, home from 1766–77 to Robert Burns. He was only seven years of age when he moved here, and eighteen when he moved on to Lochlea.

Dalrymple railway station was located one mile from the village itself, in Ayr parish. The station opened in 1856 and was closed to passengers in 1954. Carcluie Farm is located at what was a crossroads, the roadway north over Barrhill no longer being open to vehicles. It passes the little Carcluie Loch, a small pool in the hollow. To the west of Carcluie are the two large reservoirs created from 1855 onward as part of the Ayr waterworks. Blackhill Farm, which sits by the side of the busy A77 next to Monkwood Bridge, is now better known by its new name and use as the Riverside Inn.

*

The A77 heads north back towards Ayr, but a road strikes west into Alloway. This passes Doonholm Farm and gatehouse, the lands of Doonholm being gradually built on by an ever-expanding town. Doonholm House is located in a bend of the river Doon. It is a fine Georgian house dating from around 1760 and built for William Fergusson. Extensions were added in 1819 for John Hunter and in the 1850s, but in the early 1980s these were removed and the house restored to something like its original state. The stable block is dated 1881, and was erected for J. Kennedy, whose coat of arms appears over the archway. At the West Lodge can be seen the Alloway Mote Hill, a relic of a Norman place of defence.

The village of Alloway was at one time the centre of its own parish, but in January 1691 this was absorbed into that of Ayr. The village did not grow for centuries, and it is only in recent years, when Ayr has expanded considerably, that it became a highly desirable suburb. As a result there are now many housing estates around it, though these tend to be of larger bungalows and villas.

Doonholm Road crosses the disused Maidens and Dunure branch railway and soon passes the library and primary school, the latter erected in 1896, the former in 1974. At the foot of the road is the old village proper, where the most interesting buildings can be found, including Burns Cottage, without doubt the most famous building in Ayrshire and one of the most popular tourist-attractions in Scotland. A single-storey thatched cottage, it survives on the west side of the street. The cottage

Alloway: Burns Cottage

was as an inn for a time, before being purchased in 1881 and returned to its original condition. In the garden area surrounding it is the cottage museum, erected in 1900, which contains many artefacts and early manuscripts of Burns.

Robert Burns was born on 25 January 1759, one of seven children. His parents were William Burnes, a struggling tenant-farmer, and Agnes Broun. Some historians have argued that he may not have been born in the cottage that bears his name but in another dwelling behind, and that the extant cottage was erected soon after his birth when a stormy 'Januar' win" blew down the older one. The storm in question is mentioned in the poem 'There was a Lad', and it is said that his father built the present cottage shortly after. After a short education at Kirkoswald and Ayr, Burns was required to work on the farms that his father leased, firstly at Mount Oliphant, east of Alloway, then at Lochlea and Mossgiel, the latter two near Mauchline. Burns wrote poetry from an early age, but it was not until 1786 when the first collection of his work, *Poems Chiefly in the Scottish Dialect*, was published in Kilmarnock that he achieved any success. He became celebrated across the country as the 'ploughman poet' and was invited to Edinburgh, where a second edition of his works increased his fame. With the money he earned he toured the Borders and, on more than one occasion, the Highlands, which became a source of inspiration for his later work.

Abandoning plans to emigrate at this time, Burns remained in Scotland, writing more poems and songs. He also collected old tunes and songs on behalf of James Johnson, in many cases reworking these into a higher standard. Although he had found success, he failed to make his fortune, and remained a poor farmer. He subsequently moved to Dumfries, settling in a house in the town, from where he worked as an excise officer for a time, before his untimely death in 1796 of endocarditis.

Burns's greatest works are his poems, such as 'Tam o' Shanter', 'To a Mouse', 'The Cottar's Saturday Night' and 'Holy Willie's Prayer'. His best work was written in the Scottish vernacular and used the language and rhythms of everyday speech. His songs are not far behind in terms of quality. They include 'Auld Lang Syne', 'My Love is like a red, red rose' and 'Ae Fond Kiss'. He has been translated into many languages, and is popular in Russia and Japan, as well as throughout the English-speaking world. The cult of Burns has grown enormously over the years and his birthday is celebrated across the world on Burns Night, 25 January, invariably at a traditional Burns Supper.

Robert Burns (1759–1796)

Emphasising his status as a friend of the common man, he is frequently referred to as Rabbie Burns. Many of the places associated with him across the county have been mentioned in the relevant chapter.

On the other side of the street from Burns Cottage is Alloway village hall, a fine little building of 1849, when it was used as a school. This was restored in 1929–30 to plans of Sir Robert Lorimer. Within can be seen a fine mural depicting scenes from Burns poems, as well as a bust of the poet. The wall facing the street contains Alloway's war memorial, designed in 1920 by James A. Morris.

North of here the village is soon left behind, and the estate grounds of Rozelle and Belleisle give some separation from Ayr. The Ivy House, adjacent to Belleisle Golf Course, is now a fine hotel, originally known as North Parks, and dating from 1754 but extended into a sizeable house in 1900. Rozelle House is now a gallery of artefacts and paintings belonging to the people of Ayr. The house probably dates from 1770 and was erected by Robert Hamilton of Bourtreehill. It was extended to plans by David Bryce around 1835. In 1968 John Hamilton gifted it to the Burgh of Ayr for use as a gallery, its grounds to be a public park. The Alexander Goudie paintings depicting the pursuit of Tam o' Shanter by the witches were purchased in 1999 by a consortium of three benefactors and are on view in the gallery. The grounds contain some fine woods, walks and two large ponds. There are some items of sculpture on display in the grounds, including works by Ronald Rae. Adjoining Rozelle House is the MacLaurin Art Gallery, established in 1976 following a bequest from Mary Ellen MacLaurin, where an ever-changing exhibition takes place. Perhaps the best known in recent years was the display of paintings in 2002 by local artist Peter Howson, which included a number of pop star Madonna. Howson's exhibition attracted more than 12,000 visitors.

The Alloway church is located to the south of the old village centre. The old kirk in its graveyard is located on the west side of the road, the present parish church to the east. The old kirk probably dates from the sixteenth century in its present form, and was used until the mid-eighteenth century. It then became a school of sorts, but by the time of Burns was a ruin. The kirkyard contains a number of old stones of interest, including a headstone commemorating Burns's father, William Burnes (1721–1784). A large sarcophagus commemorates David Cathcart, Lord Alloway (1764–1829), and other local gentry buried here include Crawford of Doonside and Hughes of Mount Charles. An old iron mort-safe can be seen, dating from the time of the body snatchers.

The present Alloway parish church was erected in 1858 to plans of Campbell Douglas, and extended in 1877 and again in 1890. It has some rather fine stained glass, the work of Stephen Adam, Susan Bradbury, Clayton & Bell, W. & J. J. Keir and Gordon Webster. A booklet, *Through a Glass Brightly* (1999) by Revd J. Walter MacGinty, gives details. One of the windows is by Douglas MacLundie and commemorates D. F. McIntyre, the pilot who made the first flight over Everest in 1933. The present church has a small burial ground behind it where the grave of its benefactor, James Baird of Cambusdoon and Auchmedden (1802–1876), can be seen. It was he who accumulated such a fortune from the iron and steel industry that he was able to form the Baird Trust, which still makes grants to Christian organisations. He lived at Cambusdoon House, which no longer survives, but which he erected in 1853, probably to plans of David Bryce. It was latterly used as a boys' school, but was destroyed by fire in 1970. Only a fragment of an archway survives; it can be found in an open area down Shanter Way. An ancient early Christian cross, dating from some time between the eighth and twelfth centuries, was found in the grounds. It is now protected by South Ayrshire Council's museums' service.

Alloway railway station was in operation from May 1906 until 19

December 1930. Its site is now a pleasant open area leading to the Tam o' Shanter Experience, a visitor centre dedicated to the life and works of Robert Burns. The centre was opened in 1975 and extended in 1995. Here is an attractive café, gift shop and gardens.

The Brig o' Doon Hotel was rebuilt in the late 1990s, but incorporates part of the old Burns Monument Hotel, itself a rebuilding of the Burns Arms Inn, which was built in 1829 to cater for tourists visiting places associated with the bard. The Burns Monument itself is located in an attractive garden area, which is open to the public. Sir Alexander Boswell of Auchinleck (1775–1822) was responsible for instigating this memorial, which took three years to build. He laid the foundation stone on 25 January 1820. An elegant Greek structure, designed by Thomas Hamilton, it rises over three levels. The triangular base represents Carrick, Kyle and Cunninghame, the nine Corinthian columns representing the muses. Within can be seen a number of artefacts associated with the poet, including Highland Mary's Bible and Jean Armour's wedding ring.

The Old Bridge of Doon is, according to a poem written by Burns, where Tam o' Shanter finally managed to lose the witches who were pursuing him, although one of the harridans managed to pull the tale from his grey mare. The bridge is a high single-arch crossing of the Doon, dating from the fifteenth century. The New Bridge of Doon was erected in 1813. Ayr Rugby Club has its ground upstream of the Old Bridge. The club was founded in 1899 and has played at Alloway since 1962.

Greenfield Avenue strikes west from Alloway towards Doonfoot. The father of Robert Burns constructed this roadway in 1755–6. Among the houses to the south can be found a simple cairn, marking a Bronze Age cairn that is referred to in *Tam o' Shanter*. The cairn was rebuilt in 1965, when the surrounding houses were erected. Within Mountcharles Crescent can be seen Mount Charles House itself, dating from 1754–7. This was erected for Charles Dalrymple of Orangefield. The house was extended in 1829, creating the present classical front. A lodge of the latter date survives at Greenfield Avenue. Mount Charles and its stables have been divided into lesser houses. Alloway Mill lies by the side of the Doon. This dates from a rebuild in 1903. The Dutch, or Doonside, Mill was located further upstream and here William Burnes lodged for a time prior to building Burns Cottage.

Doonfoot consists of a group of housing estates located, as its name states, at the mouth of the river Doon. Most of the houses are modern, but here and there are properties that have a degree of antiquity. A small restaurant, the Secret Garden, is located in an older cottage. Next to the restaurant is Doonfoot Bridge, originally erected in 1772 by James

Armour and Adam Smith, according to an old stone inscription that was located on it. Armour is thought to have been the future father-in-law of Burns. The bridge was rebuilt in 1881. The Balgarth Hotel was erected as a private house in 1892, and extended in 1898, the architect being James Morris on both occasions. At the foot of Stonefield Park can be seen an ancient standing stone. Doonfoot Primary School is located off Abbots Way. The school was erected in 1974 to serve a growing population.

There are parking areas on the front at Doonfoot, from where a pleasant walk can be made to the interesting ruins of Greenan Castle, perched precariously on its cliff to the west. The castle is a simple tower-house erected by John Kennedy of Baltersan, probably in 1603. The tower formerly had courtyard buildings attached. The castle occupies a very ancient site, and is surrounded by extensive earthworks. Indeed it is often claimed that it was one of the early locations of Camelot. Greenan House was a fine Georgian building dating from the 1740s. There were plans to turn this into a clubhouse for a proposed golf course, but the mansion was gutted by fire in 1990 and had to be demolished. High Greenan dates from 1910, the work of James Hunter in an Arts & Crafts style.

The Craig Tara Holiday Park, which is located just south of Greenan, was originally founded as an army camp, HMS *Scotia*, in 1942. This base was used for the training of navy personnel in signals, communications and other skills. After the war was over it was acquired by Billy Butlin who converted it into one of his famous holiday camps. The old barrack blocks were rebuilt as holiday chalets, and various places of entertainment were created to keep the holidaymakers happy. Among these were swimming pool, amusements, theatre, church, railways and a ski lift, linking the upper car park with the camp itself. Butlins ran the camp until 1998, by which time it had become known as Wonderwest World, but it was sold to Haven Holidays who have demolished most of the chalets and replaced them with static caravans.

# 17

# Dalrymple, Patna and Dalmellington

THE RIVER DOON RISES in the Galloway Highlands and flows north-west to the sea at Doonfoot, south of Ayr. This chapter will deal with that part of the river's valley from Dalrymple upstream.

Dalrymple parish extends to 7,960 acres, occupying land on the north side of the river Doon from its major bend at Cassillis in the west, to the high moors of Kilmein Hill to the east. Dalrymple itself is a vil-lage built on the banks of the river, where a number of roads merge in order to cross the Dalrymple Bridge. The church lies to the west of the bridge, a rather simple structure of 1849, designed by David Cousin of Edinburgh. The surrounding graveyard has few stones of any real antiq-uity. A second church in the village, the former Free Church, existed from 1863 until 1936. The building was later adapted and converted into the present White Horse Inn.

Main Street extends northward from the Dalrymple Bridge to the junction in front of the Kirkton Inn and is lined with attractive eighteenth-century housing. The village hall, adorned by its clock, was erected around 1870, having been the gift of James Stephen to the village. Near to it is the Kirkton Inn, an old coaching establishment that was rebuilt in the nineteenth century.

Opposite the Kirkton Inn is the junction with Garden Street, which leads past the former Dalrymple station and makes for Ayr. This street is also lined with traditional cottages, most of which were originally thatched and date from 1799 onwards. Beyond the village boundary the road climbs Knockjarder Hill steadily to its summit, where the Knockjarder water filters are located. These were created in 1886 as part of the new water supply for Ayr. A farm track strikes south by the side of the filters, towards Woodland and Dalrymple Wood, part of the Cassillis House policies. At Woodland the remains of an ancient fort can still be made out immediately north of the house.

East of the Garden and Main streets junction is a curved road leading to the other main junction in the village. Along this road are the former smithy, dated 1868, and the post office. In the open area where the roads meet is Dalrymple war memorial, an octagonal cross bearing the names of thirty men killed in the First World War, and five from the Second World War. It was designed by James Miller and created by William Vickers. Dalrymple School is located behind the main road. It dates from 1962, replacing an older school of 1875 in Barbieston Road. There is quite a bit of new building going on around Dalrymple, with housing estates being erected in various spaces. Barbieston Road is where the community centre of 1964 is located, the 1875 date stone on the cairn in front of it having been rescued from the old school.

Off Barbieston Terrace is Barbieston Courtyard, now converted into housing. This is supposed to occupy the site of Barbieston Castle, which may date from the fourteenth century. The castle was a seat of the Dalrymples and Kennedys but was demolished around 1845.

Skeldon estate lies to the east of Dalrymple. Skeldon House is a fine mansion of around 1780, built for Major General John Fullarton (d. 1804), who was reputed to have named Patna on the Doon after Patna in India. The house rises over three storeys, with pediments to front and rear. The house was altered in 1908 to plans of James Miller, the ornate pillared and domed porch dating from this time. Within the policies around it are the remains of Skeldon Castle, now forming part of Castle Cottage. This castle was a seat of the Craufurds of Kerse.

The B7034 heads east from Dalrymple towards the village of Holly-bush. It passes Balgreen Farm, now part of Skeldon estate. The farm has a courtyard steading, which was improved in the late nineteenth-century, and is distinguished by its tower. Robert Ingram designed this in 1882. On the opposite side of the road is Skeldon Mills, at one time famous for making the renowned Ayrshire Blanket. The works were extended in 1842 and ownership passed through a variety of hands until they closed in the 1950s. The mills are now converted for other purposes. Auchendoon House was built for the mill manager.

Hollybush village is a small community that today comprises a number of modern villas and bungalows. There was a railway station here from 1856–1964, which led to a small community growing up around it. A school for pupils in the eastern part of Dalrymple parish operated here from 1875 until 1962, the building surviving and now converted for another use.

Hollybush House has served as the Queen Mother Home for Disabled Ex-Servicemen since 1985. Previously it was a hotel, but the house was originally erected in 1853 for Henry Leck. The architect was Robert Paton who used an Elizabethan style. Leck's daughter, Jane Leck (d. 1913), was a noted author and poet in her day. An older building occupied the site of Hollybush, and it was originally known as Over Skeldon, a Campbell property.

North of Hollybush the A713 takes one back towards Ayr, crossing a rather hillocky stretch of countryside. The Hollybush Inn is a simple stone cottage that has been extended and converted into a public house and restaurant for passing traffic. Nearby is the Benston Smithy. On the lands of Farden is the Mote Knowe, perhaps an ancient Norman defence.

Although fragmentary, there is more to be seen of Martnaham Castle, which occupies a promontory in Loch Martnaham. The castle perhaps dates from the fourteenth century, but has been in ruins for many years. The structure appears to have been 100 feet by 30 feet in size, and it is claimed that it was the original seat of Old King Cole. Loch Martnaham is a natural loch, the largest in the area. It measures approximately one-and-a-quarter miles by a quarter mile, and is twenty-six feet at its deepest point, which is located due south of Martnaham Lodge. The Snipe Loch lies to the west of Loch Martnaham, and is a smaller kettle-hole lochan now used for fishing.

A minor road links the A713 with the B742, passing Purclewan Mill. Nellie Kilpatrick lived here, the earliest love of Robert Burns. His first attempt at a poem, 'Handsome Nell', was written in her honour in 1773. Purclewan Smiddy was run by James MacCandlish, whom Burns described as 'one of the worthiest fellows that ever any man called by the name of friend.'

Heading back into Dalrymple on the B742 one passes the small Lindston Loch. On the hill above it is Lindston Farm, the summit of the hill formerly occupied by a circular earthwork, perhaps some form of hill fort. The B742 passes below the Burnton Viaduct, which carries the Doon valley line over the Purclewan Burn. This viaduct is a notable feature hereabouts, having sixteen arches. More earthworks were located on the hill above Old Knockjarder Farm.

From Hollybush the A713 enters the upper valley of the river Doon, where the valley floor is narrower and the surrounding countryside is wilder. The first community reached is Polnessan, just a single row of houses by the side of the road. These were erected for the local mineworkers, replacing older miners' rows that were located all around this area. The tips and bings that litter the moor around here testify that this was a major mining area. On the B730, just north of Polnessan, was the mining community known as Kerse Square, which at one time had twenty-two houses and a small co-operative store. Another mining community was located near Knockshinnoch Farm. This was known as Cairntable, and at one time there was even a railway station here. The Coylton Coal Company erected the houses in 1911. Broom Hill to the west was the site of a late minor coal mine, but in recent years has been subject to opencast working.

At the foot of Broom Hill, between it and the greater height of the

Craigs of Kyle, is the Kerse Loch, another of the kettle-hollow lochans hereabouts. At one time there was a Kerse Castle in the vicinity, a seat of the Craufurd family, but of this no remnants survive, the family moving to Skeldon. The earliest reference to the castle is dated 1281, and the Craufurds were active in local and national affairs. Fergus Craufurd was taken prisoner at the Battle of Dunbar in 1346. The 'Flitting of the Sow' is an old tale of a feud between the Craufurds and their neighbours, the Kennedys. It is said the last fragment of Kerse Castle blew down in 1797.

There is a prehistoric burial cairn on the low hill known as the Carline Knowe, immediately south of where Cairntable was. The moors to the south are now afforested, but previously they were a hive of activity, with mineral lines criss-crossing them, linking coal mines. Below the Bow Hill, within Dalrymple parish, were the Bowhill mines, as well as the Houldsworth Pit. When this opened in 1899 it was the deepest mine in the county, with a shaft 206 fathoms below ground. Dalrymple parish rises to the east of here, reaching its highest point at Kilmein Hill, 1,408 feet above sea level.

*

Shortly after Polnessan the village of Patna is reached, a fairly large village consisting mainly of council housing from the 1950s and 1960s. These were provided to rehouse miners from the old rows that existed on the hillside to the east of the village. The old part of Patna is located along Main Street, the road that links Patna with Kirkmichael. Here can be found the parish church, a building of 1839. A second church existed in Patna, the United Free Church, erected in 1901–3 to the plans of John B. Wilson. It was partially destroyed by fire in 1999 and has remained closed.

There are few old buildings surviving in the village, only the River Doon Hotel and a few other houses. At the top end of the street is a simple granite pillar, or cross. A second memorial is a granite structure, located in front of the village's band hall. A. Barclay Walker gifted this in 1872 as a fountain.

Patna cemetery lies on the minor road that heads towards Shankston and Carnochan farms. There are no particularly old graves here, but there are some commemorating men killed in the mines. On the side of the afforested Patna Hill is the war memorial. Shankston Loch is another of the local kettle-drum lochans. Kirkmichael Road climbs over the pass below Patna Hill before dropping into the valley of the Dyrock Burn. At Dalvennan is a country sports centre, with fishing and clay pigeon shooting.

The houses of Patna extend to the south of Main Street, occupying the low-lying ground of Carskeoch Farm. The primary school was opened in 1959, again replacing an older school. There is a caravan and camping site at Carskeoch. On the hillside above, now hidden in the trees, can be found remain of old quarries where limestone was dug. Also in the woods here are Chapel Hill and Chapel Well, recalling the fact that a place of worship existed here at one time or other.

The river Doon separates Patna into two distinct halves. The eastern half is the more linear, following the A713. Here are some modern bung-alows among the council housing, as well as a large factory and two nursing homes, one of which was added onto Doonbank House. The Doon Valley Golf Club occupies the ground east of the railway line. The nine-hole course is 5,856 yards in length, par 70. The site of Patna rail-way station is nearby, which was opened in 1856 but closed in 1964.

A minor road climbs from near Downieston Farm up onto the moors to the east of Patna. This was where most of the original residents came from, before being rehoused in the valley. Miners' rows were built next to their place of work, hence Burnfoothill and Lethanhill villages were over 800 feet above sea level. Little remains to mark their site, though the old schoolhouse of Lethanhill is still occupied. The war memorial at Lethanhill remains, the site of the main rows now planted in trees. Again many small railway lines, linking the various coal mines, crossed this high stretch of ground.

After Patna, the next village one reaches on heading up the Doon valley, is Waterside, also known as Dunaskin. This community grew up round the Dalmellington Ironworks, which were established here in 1847 by Henry Houldsworth. The arrival of the ironworks led to the development of the rural glen, previous to which was just a quiet upland valley with little population. At its peak, more than two thousand men were employed here. There were eight furnaces, providing employment both directly and indirectly for 1,400 people. The furnaces were closed down in 1921, after which the site was developed as a brickworks. The last brick was made here in 1976.

Today the site of the ironworks has been developed as the Dunaskin heritage centre, and here over half of the 110 acres have been scheduled as a Ancient Monument, being one of the finest remaining examples of a Victorian ironworks. The museum is open regularly, and here the visitor will see the recreated manager's office, old engineers' workshops, the Craigton Mine experience, blowing engine house and the quiet Dunaskin Glen. Some of the older buildings are of interest, including the engine house of 1847, which was extended in 1865, and Ardoon House, erected around 1860 as the general manager's home. There is a tearoom, gift shop, and children's play area, and on certain Sundays steam trains operate between here and Minnivey.

The Waterside Church, which was opened on 3 February 1895 to accommodate 360 worshippers, still exists. The architect was James B. Wilson. A former public school, now St Xavier's RC Primary School lies east of the railway. The Catholic church of St Francis Xavier is the building furthest to the east in the village. This brick-built structure was opened on 14 September 1895 at a cost of £25,000. Catholics from Patna and Dalmellington now use the church. A school formerly adjoined the chapel, and to its south stood a convent, demolished in November 1994. In the row of houses alongside are two cottages preserved as they were in 1915, when ironworkers occupied them. There are box beds, front room, scullery and various household goods from the period. The cottages are often open to the public.

The hillside to the east of Waterside has a few places worth exploring. An ancient tumulus of unknown vintage crowns the summit of Green Hill. In Dunaskin Glen, on a high promontory, are the ruins of Laight Castle, which measured fifty feet by thirty-five feet. The Craufurds probably erected this some time in the fourteenth century. The walls are supposed to have been demolished in 1770 for the purpose of building dykes. Tradition claims that the ancient King Alpin was slain in battle here in AD 843, hence the name 'Laight-Alpin'.

The west side of the Doon valley from Waterside is occupied by Keirs Farm. Here the fragments of Keirs Castle are built into the present farmhouse, although the mound on which the tower stood is still visible. Keirs was a Shaw seat, the last block of masonry being removed in the 1950s. Keirs Hill is afforested, but there are some interesting place names around it, hinting at a troublesome past, such as Spy Knowe and Horseman's Knowe. Wallace Moor may have some connection with the great patriot.

At Waterside are two rough roadside stones on which the words 'In memory of the Unemployed 1921, 22, 23' are painted. These recall the hard times in the valley when the ironworkers were laid off and the works closed. Coupled with the General Strike of 1926, it was a disastrous time in the Doon valley.

*

The main road into Dalmellington from Waterside crosses the Sillyhole Moss, part of which is now protected as a nature reserve. Dalmellington is an old community, one that existed long before the arrival of the ironworks, but for centuries was only a minor village in an upland countryside. There is still an ancient motte hill in the town, a sizeable mound rising above the Muck Water. A second mound is known as Dame Helen's Castle, located further up the same valley, its provenance unknown, although there are some who argue that the name Dalmellington comes from 'Dame Helen's Town'.

The old part of the town is located at the foot of the motte hill, next to a bridge across the Muck Water. Behind the houses, next to the modern library building of 1982 (designed by Roy Maitland), can be found the old kirkyard, site of the village's early church. The only building within it today is the MacAdam of Craigengillan mausoleum. Here also is a simple granite memorial commemorating all the local Covenanters, although it does not name any. Dalmellington has many associations with the time of the Covenant and, being upland and wild, many Covenanters hid in this area. The kirkyard contains a number of interesting old stones.

Three streets radiate from the town centre. The Low Main Street heads for Ayr Road. Here is the former Lamloch Church, erected in 1851 to plans by David Millar, but closed in 1974. The Royal Bank building is by Peddie & Kinnear. On the Ayr Road itself are a number of houses, as well as an access road leading to Dalmellington's schools. These include Doon Academy, a secondary school opened in 1976. The school has a small swimming pool that is open to the public. Further along the road are a running track and other sports facilities.

At the former Dame Helen's Nursery School is the base for Dalmellington Book Town. Dalmellington entered for, but lost, the competition to be designated Scotland's official Book Town, but Richard Booth, founder of the original Book Town of Hay on Wye, decided that Dalmellington should have won. He opened a shop in the village and soon was joined by a few others, creating a second Book Town, which specialises in the sale of second hand and antiquarian books.

High Street makes its way past some of the older buildings in Dalmellington, before heading up Glen Muck. Here can be found Ye Old Castle House, formerly an inn, which probably dates from the eighteenth century. The Dalmellington Inn dated from the seventeenth century but was rebuilt in the nineteenth. Townhead climbs to the south, at one time the main road into the village. By the side of this road, next to the motte, was the Roman Catholic Church of Our Lady and St Barbara. Barbara is the patron saint of miners. The church was erected in 1959–61, its modern style rather unusual, but the dwindling congregation meant that it became too expensive to keep, and it was closed in the 1990s and demolished in 2003.

High Street reaches Bellsbank Road, which skirts around Dalmellington to the south. A number of twentieth century properties are located here, as well as the village war memorial, perched on a low hill next to Bellsbank House. A memorial to the mineworkers of the Doon valley was unveiled next to the war memorial on 31 March 1996. The stone has the inscription: ' "It well recalls the triumphs past" Dedicated To The Mineworkers Of The Doon Valley', below a carving indicating a miners' lamp. Sculptor Kevin Roberts carved the memorial.

A narrow lane runs along the south side of the Muck Water from the Square, heading to the King George V Park. On the left hand side are some low single-storey cottages, one of which is Cathcartston, an old weaver's cottage of 1744. This is now converted to a visitor centre, where displays on weaving, mining and other aspects of local history can be seen.

Bellsbank is a modern housing estate erected from 1948 onward to re-house miners who lived in the rows on the high moorland round about. The community is separated from Dalmellington proper by about half a mile of open countryside, which was the Town's Common, giving it a rather independent air. Here can be found Bellsbank Primary School, Bellsbank Lamloch Church, built in 1956 and dedicated in 1958, a post office and some shops.

High Main Street leaves Dalmellington Square and climbs up to the Gillies' Knowe. There are some older properties at the foot of this street,

most of which have been restored. A plaque on the wall of one building marks the birthplace of Robert Hettrick (1769–1849), known as the 'Blacksmith poet'. He wrote a number of verses, some of which were collected into a book published in 1826.

The street climbs to the parish church, known also as the Kirk of the Covenant. This was erected in 1846 to plans of Patrick Wilson. A neo-Norman building, it has a tall tower, which with the addition of its elevated location, makes it a prominent local landmark. Heading south along the street known as Knowehead from the parish church, one reaches the present church-hall. This was in fact the former

Dalmellington: the parish church

church of 1766, built by James Armour, the father-in-law of Robert Burns. Churchhill climbs to the east, some of the buildings within it being quite old, in particular one with corbie-stepped gables.

Either this road, or a lane to the north of the parish church, can be followed to the present cemetery. Here can be found a number of graves to mining victims. On the moor beyond is an old man-made earthwork known as Pickan's Dyke. When this was made is unknown: some claim it was erected by the Picts and was part of the Deil's Dyke that borders Galloway, whereas others think it may have been some form of boundary wall protecting a deer park surrounding the old motte hill.

The Gillies' Knowe is now a small industrial estate. To the west are the miners' rows of Broomknowe, these ones being later houses of 1910–12 and classed as 'model' houses when built, even although they still had an outside toilet. At the west end of the rows is the Sillyhole Bridge, where a minor road strikes across country to Burnton, another former mining community. The houses here were designed to replace older rows at Craigmark, which lay slightly further north. Nothing of these survives, other than the former co-operative store, which is now a public house. At Craigmark is the Scottish Industrial Railway Museum, located at the former Craigmark mine. The pit operated from 1866 until 1927. The museum is home to a number of steam and diesel locomotives, and most summer weekends there are a couple in steam, giving rides along a length of track.

Beyond Craigmark a minor road climbs steadily up the hillside, leading to the former mining villages of Benquhat and Corbie Craigs. Corbie Craigs was the lower of the two villages, a row of houses at the head of the Dunaskin Glen. At one time there were fifty people living in ten houses here. In the 1940s the miners were rehoused in Dalmellington and Bellsbank. Benquhat, or Benwhat, lay even higher up, on the lower slopes of Benquhat Hill itself, which rises to 1,427 feet above sea level. Benquhat had a co-op store, post office, miners' institute and mission hall. In 1881 the population was 772. Again the 131 houses have been demolished and opencast working has removed the site of some. However, the war memorial still stands proudly, high on the slopes of Benquhat Hill. The hillside here is littered with old pit-bings and the remains of collieries. These were the Corbie Craigs pits, which operated from 1850 until 1919. The Chalmerston opencast coal site covers hundreds of acres of hillside, the workings removing any remains that existed there.

The B741 leaves Dalmellington in a northerly direction, passing the Gillies' Knowe before dropping once more to the site of the former manse and some new housing where a caravan site once existed. From the Gillies' Knowe a former estate drive heads east, along the south side of the Cummock Burn. Along the way can be found the Spider's Web, a large stone that has a natural pattern on it, reminiscent of a web. Camlarg House no longer exists, having been demolished in the early 1950s due to mining subsidence. The house was on an ancient site, for here the Craufurds lived for centuries. In later years the estate was owned by the Logans, and was latterly acquired by the coal companies.

North of Camlarg is a large coal-bing, known for years as the Burning Bing due to the fact that there were burning coals within it. Snow would rarely lie on the surface, and during heavy rain it could be seen steaming. The bing was associated with Pennyvenie Nos. 2 and 3 Colliery, which lay at its eastern end, operating from 1881 until around 1978. A few miners' rows still exist at Pennyvenie, including Sighthill. Near Glenview, on the opposite side of the Cummock Burn, is a chalybeate spring. The miners' rows of High Pennyvenie were located further up the glen, but the rows there have long gone. A school existed at the foot of the Pennyvenie Glen. A number of old mines were located north of Pennyvenie, including Beoch No. 4, which operated from 1936 until the 1960s. This was one of the highest pits in the area, the surface buildings being 1,100 feet above sea level, and linked to High Pennyvenie by a tramway. At Benbain cottage was an old rifle range.

Benbeoch, or *Beinn a' Bheathaich* in Gaelic, means mountain of the birch trees. This hill rises to 1,522 feet above sea level, its south-eastern slope being distinguished by its massive rock face. This comprises basaltic columns, making it similar to Arthur's Seat in Edinburgh. Below Benbeoch Craig, as it is known, is the Fox Yird, an ancient stonewalled enclosure that was created to prevent foxes from mauling sheep. A spring of fine water flows from its lowest end. North of Benbeoch is the Headmark Moss, location of an air crash when a Hawker Hurricane landed and sank into the moss.

The B741 heads west from Dalmellington to Straiton. On leaving the village it has to cross the boggy ground alongside the Doon, before it climbs up towards Auchenroy Farm. Auchenroy Hill, which is over 1,200 feet above sea level, has a Bronze Age burial cairn on its southern summit. Grimmet Farm lies off the road to the north. In Grimmet Glen beyond the house can be found a number of waterfalls, including the Grimmet Linns.

At the west end of the Doon Bridge a minor road strikes south, heading for Dalcairnie Farm. It passes the west side of the Bogton Loch, a shallow loch surrounded by wet and marshy ground. Beyond Dalcairnie Farm a track can be followed to Dalcairnie Bridge, below which is the Dalcairnie Linn, at one time a popular waterfall for tourists to visit. The fall is forty feet in height, with a sheer drop of twenty, tumbling down through a dark and narrow gully. On the Wee Cairn Hill above can be found the Dalcairnie Cairn, another Bronze Age burial site.

The A713 strikes south from Dalmellington up the side of the Muck Water, heading over the hill into Galloway. At Mossdale Farm the Mossdale Burn was dammed in 1886 to catch water for Dalmellington. In the late 1920s a larger dam was constructed, to form the Corbie Craig Reservoir. The hills here get rougher and higher as the road heads further south, and Glen Muck becomes a narrow gorge. Most of the hills around here have been afforested. Half way up the glen is a natural spring that was often used in the days when horses were the only means of transport and they were glad of a drink at the Carrier's Well. The glen opens out again further south, near to Glenmuck Farm.

Loch Muck is a moorland stretch of water, the surface level of which is about 950 feet above sea level. The loch does not drain into the Muck Water, as one would expect, instead the Muck Burn flows from the south into Loch Doon. Ayrshire is left behind at Eriff, the road heading south through the parish of Carsphairn and the Stewartry of Kirkcudbright. On Little Eriff Hill, which lies on the west side of Loch Muck, but which is little more than a high point on the moor, is the Cairnennock Bronze Age cairn.

Back at Mossdale a minor road strikes west, climbing through the Bellsbank Plantation and heading for Loch Doon. More ancient burial cairns can be discovered on Pennyarthur Rigg and to the east side of the road, where the Bubbly Cairn is lost in the trees. On leaving the forest the traveller is given a fine view down Strath Doon towards the Bogton Loch, and across the river towards Craigengillan House, perched on the hillside opposite.

Craigengillan incorporates an old tower house known as Berbeth, but when the MacAdam family acquired the estate they named it after their former estate in Carsphairn parish. The older part of the house can be seen to the rear, dating from around 1780, where a thin spiral stair with a turret overlooks the garden. The house was extended around 1820, when the new crow-stepped and glazed entrance front was added, as well as the tall square tower. The Georgian stable block is a rather fine courtyard building, complete with domed clock tower. Robert Burns was friendly with John MacAdam and wrote an epistle to him.

The immediate surroundings of Craigengillan are finely wooded, and the Glessel Burn has an attractive waterfall in the glen. The moor above has a couple of small lochans on it, including Wee Berbeth Loch, which has an old boathouse. Further out onto the moor can be found more lochans, the Widow's, Little and Black Loch, although these drain into the Water of Girvan. The first two are tiny pools of water, the Black Loch large enough to have had a boathouse. Another, unnamed, lochan lies west of the hill known as Carwaur.

The river Doon issues from the dam that raised the water level of Loch Doon, and flows down through Glen Ness, or Ness Glen as it is more often known. Glen Ness means 'glen of the waterfall', and the Pike Fall is one of the main falls in what is a turbulent stretch of water. A footpath down through the glen, below the Craigs of Ness, was at one time regarded as one of the finest country walks in the district, but the pathway is no longer there, and the glen is wild and overgrown.

The minor road from Mossdale crosses the dam at the foot of Loch Doon and ends up on its western shores. Here can be found a small parking area, toilets and some local information. Loch Doon is Ayrshire's largest loch, but its surface area was increased considerably when the dam was built as part of the Galloway hydroelectric scheme. The dam was erected in 1935, and a second dam was required at the foot of the Muck Burn, to prevent the waters from escaping into the Carsphairn Lane. The resultant reservoir raised the water level by twenty-seven feet. As part of the hydro scheme, a tunnel was cut beneath Cullendoch Hill, allowing water to flow from the loch out into the Carsphairn Lane, and thus pass down through the hydroelectric power stations at Kendoon, Carsfad, Earlstoun and Tongland. A tunnel also exists to allow water to be captured from the Bow Burn and Water of Deugh and fed into the loch. All this is outwith Ayrshire, however.

The minor road along the west side of Loch Doon passes Beoch and Lamdoughty farms on its way to the head of the loch. Near to the dam is an area of ground known as Macnabstone. This is said to commemorate a heroic Scot who managed to burst the dam the English soldiers had built in an attempt to capture Loch Doon Castle. Connected with this story is the piece of land on the east side of the loch, below Muckle Eriff Hill, which is known as the Englishman's Stair. West of Macnabstone is a Bronze Age cairn known as the White Laise.

At Macnabstone one can see a number of derelict concrete structures by the side of Loch Doon. These are all that remain of one of the most profligate uses of money that has ever taken place in Ayrshire. During the First World War it was decided to create a school of aerial gunnery at Turnberry aerodrome, and an outpost for target practice was created here. On the opposite side of the loch large blocks of concrete mark the line of a little railway that had carriages running along it, complete with moving targets. Aeroplanes were expected to fly towards these targets and fire at them, but it was soon discovered that the targets moved too slowly to be an effective representation of enemy aircraft.

To the north of Beoch Farm a whole community connected with the gunnery school was built, complete with prisoner-of-war camp, huts, wharf, stables and even a cinema. A light railway was built through the grounds of Craigengillan to take building materials to the site.

The Loch Doon road continues south, crossing the Garpel Burn by a long causeway and bridge. The Garpel rises in Loch Finlas, another natural loch that has been dammed. The dam was constructed in 1887 to hold water for Ayr and its height raised in 1916. At its western end the little Derclach Loch is linked to Loch Finlas by a short watercourse. To the south of Lamdoughty Farm, by the side of the loch, is an islet known as Donald's Isle. When the level of the loch is high this is totally covered, but when the level drops the island become accessible. On the islet stone foundations can be discerned, said to belong to an ancient hall house or some other building. The roadway passes below the Wee Hill of Craigmulloch (1,382 feet) a lesser height of Craiglee, which at 1,715 feet is one of the highest hills hereabouts. Most of the lower ground around Craiglee is afforested.

Loch Doon Castle

Loch Doon Castle soon comes into view. This is one of the oldest and finest castles in the county. The building consists of eleven uneven sides, with a pointed arched gateway on the north face. Within the courtyard can be seen the remains of a spiral staircase and a chimney at what would have been first floor level. On the east side, overlooking the loch, is a narrow lancet window. Loch Doon Castle, or Balloch Castle as it was known at times in the past, is thought to date from the thirteenth century. It was here Sir Christopher Seton, a follower of the Bruce, retired for safety after the Battle of Methven in 1306. The castle was attacked by the English and Seton taken prisoner, to be hanged in Dumfries as a traitor. In 1510 William Craufurd of Lochnoreis attacked the Kennedy stronghold.

The castle we see today is not located on its true location, for it used to sit on an island within the loch. When the hydroelectric scheme was being created, it was realised that much of the building would be submerged and so it was decided to move the castle stone by stone to the west bank. The castle was built with the same alignment, hence the present entrance facing away from the road. The cost of moving the castle was £4,000. When the level of the water is low, the original castle island can be seen out in the loch. There is still quite a bit of masonry left there, for only the dressed stones of the walls were moved. Some later stonework that was not thought worthy of moving also remains on the islet. At low water there are other islands in the loch. These include Pickmaw Island, one of the largest, as well as another that was reputedly used as a prison by the keepers of the castle.

Craigmalloch cottage, which is just to the south of Loch Doon Castle, is now an outdoor centre, much used by youth and fishing groups. At Craigmalloch Farm is the Byre, a small café and craft shop. The public road stops just beyond here, but it is possible to keep driving as far as Lochhead, although the track is rough. The way passes Starr cottage, another outdoor centre, but which was at one time famous for its mutton. It was claimed that the shepherd at Starr had 7,777 acres to cover. Lochhead is technically on the Kirkcudbright side of the loch, but in 1993 the boundary was redrawn to include it and some ground in Ayrshire. At one time a borstal institution used the cottage, but it is now back in private hands.

A forest drive can be taken from Craigmalloch westwards through the Carrick Forest to Ballochbeatties and the public road once more. A toll is payable to use this road, but it allows the visitor to experience some of the wildest countryside in the area. Most of the ground is afforested, but there are odd views of the little Loch Gower, little more than a widening of the Whitespout Lane, and the larger Loch Riecawr. This loch was a natural loch, sometimes known as Loch Recar, but it was dammed in 1953 and used to supply Ayr with fresh water. An islet within the loch is known as Peden's Isle, a hiding place for the famous Covenanter.

There is a massive stretch of untamed countryside extending south of here, accessible only to the keen hill walker. Here is the wild Loch Macaterick, a loch with a very unusual shape. The rivers hereabouts, as in much of the Galloway Highlands, are known as 'lanes', including the major Eglin and Gala lanes. Tunskeen is a hill walker's bothy, located in the wild granite cauldron known as the Dungeon of Buchan. The Eglin Lane rises in Loch Enoch, the waters of which are in Kirkcudbright, but the northern shores and outflow is in Ayrshire. This loch is 1,617 feet above sea level. North of this loch is Mullwharchar, a granite peak 2,270 feet in height. During the 1970s this hill was considered as a dump for nuclear waste, as the granite was thought suitable for storage purposes. At a later date the hill came under threat again as the possible site of a large ground-aerial. Fortunately neither of these schemes came to anything, and the hill survives as wild and remote as ever.

# 18

# Maybole and Kirkoswald

MAYBOLE IS AN OLD TOWN, one that claims to be the 'Capital of Carrick'. A Burgh of Barony since 1516, the town lies inland, where a variety of roads meet, but there was a community here long before recognised roads were formed. The present community still exudes an air of antiquity, and some of the buildings within the town are of a considerable age. The village is also the centre of a large parish, one that extends north as far as Alloway, and which takes in the coast at Dunure, in all around 22,647 acres.

Maybole was anciently a weaving village, but by 1850 this trade had collapsed. The manufacture of boots and shoes then took over, and by 1890 there were no fewer than ten factories producing footwear. At that time 1,500 workers were employed in the trade, and the annual output was valued at £250,000. The trade has diminished considerably, the last large factory closing in 1962.

The town of Maybole is today blighted by the incessant traffic trying to make its way along the narrow main street (which is effectively part of the busy trunk road, the A77). This street – which has four names along its length – is probably the town's finest, and here most of the old buildings can be found. Starting at the north-east end, the one that is entered from Ayr, we pass Lyonston Farm on the south, just before entering the town at Cassillis Road. An ancient standing stone can be seen here, in a field south of the road. The town begins with some modern housing on the right, and some older terraced buildings on the left. On the right the former Jack agricultural-implement factory is soon reached, now used by a packaging firm. Alexander Jack erected the factory in 1852 to his own plans. Next to this is the parish church, a rather unusual building with a small steeple. The church was erected in 1808 to plans of Robert MacLachlan.

Cassillis Road narrows now, the buildings standing on the pavement, and the density increasing. Just beyond the crossroads can be seen Maybole Castle, surrounded to one side by a stretch of walled garden. The castle is the finest building in the town, dating from around 1620, although some say that it existed from before 1545. It is a tall L-plan tower house of four floors, the lower floors rather plain, but the upper floors have a number of decorative features on the exterior walls. Here are some fine turrets and oriel windows, one of them being famous as the location from where the Countess of Cassillis eloped with Sir John

Maybole Castle

Faa, one of the so-called 'raggle taggle gypsies' according to the old ballad. To one side of the tower is a later wing, but it is built in a similar style, and again is adorned with an oriel window. Maybole Castle was probably built as the town house of John Kennedy, 6th Earl of Cassillis, and it is still the property of the Kennedy family, now represented by the Marquis of Ailsa. The castle operates as the estate offices, but the upper floors are tenanted as a home. At one time it was much larger, extending over the ground occupied by the post office and old library, but in 1812 this was cleared away to allow the main road to pass through.

On the opposite side of the street from the castle is the former Carnegie public library. This dates from 1905–6 and the great philanthropist donated £2,500 towards the cost. Recreation rooms were also added at this time, the cost defrayed by Robert MacQuater. The architect was J. K. Hunter who used a Scots renaissance style. The health centre is a modern building of 1990 although, being built in a traditional manner, it fits in well with the streetscape. The post office was erected in 1912, the use of corbie stepped gables and pedimented dormer windows making it an attractive Renaissance building.

The town hall was erected in 1887 to plans of Robert Ingram. The baronial style building is still used for various meetings. The corner turret is rather unusual, with its large windows and corbelled detail. On the south-west side of the building, and joined to it, is an older tower-house of the seventeenth century that was originally the town house of the Kennedys of Blairquhan. This has a door at ground-floor level that was obviously created from an ancient double-arched window. The upper floors are corbelled out, the whole topped by a more modern parapet and steeple with clock. The castle was latterly used as a court and tolbooth.

Whitehall is the continuation of High Street beyond John Knox Street, said to be named from the White, or Carmelite, Friars who had a preaching station here. In this street can be found some attractive buildings from the nineteenth century. Among these is the Royal Bank building of 1857, designed by Peddie & Kinnear. Near to it is the dis-used police station, the work of John Murdoch in 1868.

Kirkland Street leaves Cassillis Road at a sharp angle, dropping down to the lower end of the town. Here can be found St Cuthbert's RC Primary and Cairn Primary, located just off it in Cairnfield Avenue. The latter was erected in 1898 to plans of J. K. Hunter in style reminiscent of the Cotswolds. Beyond the junction with Crosshill Road is the grave-yard associated with the ancient collegiate church, the ruins of which still exist. The church was founded in 1193 by Duncan MacDowall, Lord of Carrick, and dedicated to St Cuthbert. The present ruins date from 1371, having been built by Sir John Kennedy of Dunure, and are now protected as an ancient monument by Historic Scotland. The church comprises of ruined walls with a fine Norman doorway. Over this is a worn block containing the Kennedy crest. The last interment in the graveyard took place in 1914. On 12 September 1993 an ecumenical service was held to commemorate eight centuries of Christian worship in Maybole. The old church is the burial place of the Earls of Cassillis. In the kirkyard can be seen the grave of John MacLymont, a Covenanter, as well as the grave of William Niven, a childhood friends of Burns.

A number of narrow lanes, such as Kirkwynd and John Knox Street, lead back up to the High Street from here. On a wall in John Knox Street a plaque marks the spot where Knox and the Abbot of Crossraguel debated for three days in 1562 on the relevant merits of Roman Catholicism and Protestantism. The debate was inconclusive, but the subject of transubstan-tiation seems to have been one of the sticking points.

Ladywell Road continues westward, the houses here more modern. It is joined on the right by Welltrees Street, dropping down from Whitehall. At Allan's Hill is Our Lady and St Cuthbert's RC Church, erected between 1876-9. This is a Gothic-style building, distinguished by its tall tower and spire. Adjoining the church is the former school and manse, the use of trefoil-shaped window heads being rather distinctive.

Miller Terrace and Coral Glen lead back up to the west end of

Whitehall. In Coral Glen is the West Parish Church, a simple T-plan block, designed by George Meikle Kemp (the architect of the Scott Monument in Edinburgh) and erected between 1836–40, the cost met in the main by Sir Charles Fergusson of Kilkerran. The bellcote on its corbelled course is one of the building's main features. The manse may also have been the work of Kemp. A path from Coral Glen leads up to the summit of the low hill, whereon stands Maybole's war memorial. The surroundings form part of the War Memorial Park, much of which is occupied by the 9-hole golf course. This 5,304 yard, par 66, course was opened on 17 May 1924, the clubhouse located adjacent to the bowling green. An earlier golf course existed at Kilhenzie, established in 1905. Carrick Street is a short road linking Whitehall with Culzean Road. Here can be found the small but quaint Baptist Church, erected in 1914 at a cost of £1,720. The brick-built church has a sandstone façade.

The Greenside is a pleasant corner of the town, originally known as the Ballgreen. Here the sports of archery and bowls were played, and a fair held. In 1892 the green was fenced in to become a small park, and a fountain was erected in 1881 to commemorate Thomas Dykes, factor to the Marquis of Ailsa and the first senior magistrate in Maybole. Overlooking the green is the Greenside Inn, dating from around 1900, an 'improved' public house. Here also is the former poorhouse, a simple block of 1863 designed by John Bowman.

Culzean Road heads back towards Maybole Castle. At one time there was a church at the east end, known as the Cargill Free Church, erected in 1843 and named after Donald Cargill, a noted Covenanter. Within the wall was part of a boulder at which Cargill had preached. This formerly stood at Cargilston Farm, also named after Cargill, and the site is now marked by an obelisk. The Cargill Church has been demolished and the site is now occupied by housing.

The railway arrived in Maybole in 1859, but the present station buildings date from 1880. East of the town the railway passes a spot known as Maybole Junction, but there is no junction, this never being built. The town has spread north of the railway, new housing and other developments being built on what was Kincraig Farm. One of the earliest buildings to jump the railway was St Oswald's Church, erected in 1883. This is a very small Gothic building, used by the Episcopal Church.

\*

Maybole is the main town in an extensive rural hinterland. There are many roads radiating from the town, and the following paragraphs will

follow these in turn, starting with the main Ayr road, the A77. Beyond
Lyonston Farm is Drumellan House, an old Georgian house of the late
eighteenth century, which was extended in the 1920s by Mr Craufurd,
a shoe manufacturer. This was the home of Primrose William Kennedy,
provost of Ayr, who is commemorated by a fountain in the county town.
The road meanders between a few low hills to the north of here, and
shortly after passing Hogg's Corner arrives at the small village of
Minishant. Some of the older road signs in the county spell this
Minnyshant. The village is little more than a line of houses along the
west side of the road, but it is an interesting place all the same. At the
north end of the village is the former Coats Memorial Church, now sec-
ularised and converted into a private house. The church was erected in
1877–8 to the plans of Thomson & Turnbull for Sir Peter Coats of
Auchendrane in memory of his wife, Lady Gloriana. The church closed
in the mid-1980s. The village to the south of here comprises a few older
buildings, including the little Minishant Inn. More modern housing lies
further south, set back from the road. Here is a fine terrace of wooden
cottages, the primary school and some modern housing dating from
1999 onward. Minishant was originally known as Culroy, a name now
transferred to a hamlet further up the Culroy, or Polnatibber, Burn.

Monkwood House lies to the east of Minishant, by the banks of the
river Doon. The house is a simple Georgian building of around 1720.
The house became the home of James Paterson (1805–1876), author of
the important *History of the County of Ayr*. In this book he recounts
the history of Ayrshire's parishes, and provides genealogical accounts of
the main landed families. For a time the house was known as Paterson
House, but has now reverted to its original name. In the grounds are a
large fishing-pond and the usual walled gardens associated with country
houses. Monkwood Grove cottage was at one time the home of James
Smith (1759–1848), who is regarded as 'the father of Scottish botany',
according to his gravestone in Ayr's old kirkyard. Another writer, Hugh
Douglas (1928–2003) was born at Monkwood Mains Farm. He was the
author of a number of Scottish books, in particular accounts of Bonnie
Prince Charlie, Robert Burns and Flora MacDonald.

South of Monkwood House, by the side of the river Doon, is an
ancient dun, perched high above the river on Stewart's Craig. This for-
talice (small fort) is shown on some maps as a motte hill and is known
locally as the Mote Knowe. The central enclosure is about fifty feet in
diameter, surrounded by a rampart around fifteen-feet thick. The
entrance may have been on the south east, but this is uncertain.

Auchendrane House lies next along the A77, between Monkwood

and the Monkwood Bridge over the river. Auchendrane is one of the best-known estate names in Ayrshire, due to its long and bloody history. The 'Auchendrane Tragedy' was the result of a feud between the Kennedys and Mures of Auchendrane in the sixteenth century. Sir Walter Scott in one of his long poems, 'Auchendrane or the Ayrshire Tragedy', recorded the entire affair. The castle was later acquired by the Fergusson family, and in 1868 was sold to Sir Peter Coats, of Paisley thread-making fame. In 1905 Sir James Coats was created a Baronet of Auchendrane. He was a director of J. & P. Coats Ltd, sewing-cotton manufacturers. The present building is an amalgam of many periods and alterations, but is essentially a baronial building. The old Monkwood Bridge dates from 1798, erected by John and James Rutherford. Spanning the Doon, it leads back into Ayr parish.

An alternative route from Maybole to Ayr is the B7024, known locally as the 'high road', which leaves Maybole from a more elevated position and crosses the lower slopes of the Carrick Hills before dropping down to Alloway. On the outskirts of Maybole a former school is passed, attractively located within its wooded grounds. Behind the school the Lover's Lane footpath drops back down to Lyonston. The road passes the Grange area of the parish. Holmes House is a modern building erected on a low area of ground, the pond a man-made feature. At Low Milton Farm is the ancient St Helen's Well, long since covered over. Grange House is an attractive Georgian house, dating from the late eighteenth century. A minor road can be followed over the low hill back into Minishant.

After Grange the little village of Culroy is reached, little more than a few houses at the Culroy Bridge. At one time there was a smithy here (the village was often known as Culroy Smithy or Culroy Bridge before Minishant became accepted as the name for Culroy) and a popular inn. A minor road through the trees leads up to Burnhouse and on to Otterden House. This house was erected in the simple Scots Georgian style around 1780.

At Blairston Mains can be found an ancient boulder known as Wallace's Stone. This marks the spot where Sir William Wallace is said regularly to have halted before entering Ayr. On the boulder is a carved representation of his sword, but this is more likely to be an early Christian cross, and the boulder would have been a wayside cross marking a pilgrimage route.

Beyond Blairston Mains is the Nether Auchendrane estate. Here is the old Nether Auchendrane House, originally known as Blairston. The present building incorporates an ancient tower house, but most of the surviving work was added in the second half of the nineteenth century by a variety of architects. The house was latterly a nursing home. Within the grounds are some modern private houses, as well as an activity centre owned by the Guide Association. By the side of the river Doon, in a similar location to that at Monkwood, is another ancient dun. This one is known as Craigmuir Mote.

On the opposite side of the B7024 from Nether Auchendrane is the Newark estate. A gatehouse protects the drive leading up to the rather grand baronial castle, still in private hands. The Kennedys of Bargany built Newark Castle in the sixteenth century, when it was known as the New Wark of Bargany. The castle was built on a high rock, overlooking the low ground occupied by Ayr and Alloway. The Craufurds of Camlarg acquired the castle in 1601 and made extensions to the old tower around 1687. The castle was sold to the Earl of Cassillis in 1763. The tower was extended again in 1848–9 to plans by David Cousin. A further extension was made in 1907–8 to plans of James Miller. Today the Walker family owns the castle.

The B7024 drops down to the Bridge of Doon and enters Alloway. On the right, before it crosses the bridge and leaves Maybole parish, is a gateway and drive leading into what was Doonside House. This was erected in 1884–9 to plans of J. MacVicar Anderson and demolished in 1961. It replaced an earlier Classical mansion of the eighteenth century that was destroyed by fire around 1880. Some of the second Doonside House's sculpted pieces and panelling are incorporated in the present house, created from the former Home Farm in 1961–2 by James A. Carrick for the Dunlops. Still to be found, however, are the fragmentary remains of Brigend Castle, perched on a rock above the river Doon. This was a sixteenth century building owned by the Montgomeries. The old doocot is also a survivor.

From Culroy a minor road climbs past Bryden's Cottage and Knockdon (at one time an estate in its own right) to another minor road that leaves the Maybole–Alloway road near to High Grange. This road leads to the Carrick Hills, and it reaches the height of 685 feet above sea level before dropping quickly to the Heads of Ayr. At Breek is a drive leading into Sauchrie House, which stands on a low eminence above the glen of the Sauchrie Burn. Sauchrie House dates from around 1775, being a rather undistinguished Georgian building. Sauchrie became the home of John Loudon McAdam between 1783 and 1787, and it is claimed that the first roads constructed to his specification were within the estate grounds. The countryside around Sauchrie is well wooded, the little burns passing through attractively wooded gorges. In the glen above the house is a sizeable waterfall. Another can be found at High Pinmore Farm, in the Pinmore Glen. West of Craigskean Farm is the Bride's Well, a natural spring at the foot of a rock face.

The road through the Carrick Hills climbs into open moorland beyond Sauchrie, reaching a viewpoint at the highest point on the road. From here a magnificent view is obtained over the town of Ayr, Ayr Bay as far as Troon and Irvine, and over the Firth of Clyde to Arran and the mountains of Argyll. A track leads up the slopes of the Brown Carrick Hill as far as the police wireless-masts, from which the actual summit (at 940 feet) is a further half-mile to the west. Some of the ground to the west has been covered in forestry plantations.

The road drops down from the peak of the Carrick Hills past Carwinshoch to Genoch Farm, where it joins the A719, the coast road from Ayr to Turnberry. Carwinshoch House, located by the side of the minor road that crosses Brown Carrick Hill south-east of Genoch Farm, dates from 1981–4. It is a much-enlarged cottage originally occupied by the gamekeeper of the Sauchrie estate. The architect was Ian MacGill of Cowie Torry & Partners. On the opposite side of the road are the Heads of Ayr, a hill of 258 feet that drops suddenly in tall cliffs to the sea. On the southern slopes of Bower Hill (which is what the Heads hill is called) is the site of an ancient chapel, of which nothing remains. Laigh Kyleston Farm is now the Heads of Ayr Farm Park, where visitors are welcome to look at the animals. Perryston House, located at Perryston Farm off the A719, is a rather grand modern building of 1939, designed by Ninian Johnston and built for Archibald Newall. At Low Glenayes is the Bracken Bay holiday park, one of a number of caravan sites along this popular coast. The track past the site can be taken down to Bracken Bay, an attractive shingle beach to the west of the Heads.

The A719 makes its way westward, climbing up to Lagg Farm. Just beyond here is the small Fisherton Church, erected in 1838 as a chapel of ease for the residents of Dunure and district. In 1912 the church was rebuilt and extended, the architects being J. & H. V. Eaglesham. The manse was located further west, at Fisherton Farm. Fisherton is a name that is sometimes used with Dunure to describe this area. The upper part of Dunure village is properly described as Fisherton, but the name Dunure is today becoming more popular. Fisherton School serves the local children of primary age.

On the hill above Fisherton can be seen the tall tower of Dunduff Castle. This tower stands on a low knoll and construction is said to have started in the fifteenth century. Tradition claims that work on the castle was stopped in 1696, and that it stood little more than one storey high for centuries thereafter. However, in the late 1980s the upper floors were added in a traditional style to create the present attractive building. The architect who produced the design for the restoration was Ian Begg. West of the castle, in the field above the post office radio station, are the remains of a prehistoric earthwork.

Just west of Dunduff Farm are the scanty ruins of Kirkbride, an ancient church that is still surrounded by its old kirkyard. The church dates from pre-Reformation times but was abandoned when its parish was united with that of Maybole. The gravestones that surround the church are few in number, a more modern cemetery for Dunure area being established by the side of the A719. Dunduff farmhouse is a large late eighteenth century building, distinguished by its projecting bow front.

From Fisherton a minor road drops down to the charming village of Dunure. The roadside is lined with a number of attractive cottages, including one with a rather distinctive series of bows, perhaps inspired by nautical themes. The old part of the village is built around the little harbour, little more than a square basin protected from the sea by a short breakwater. Even the 'lighthouse' at the pier end is little more than a cylindrical tower topped by a guiding light. The Earl of Cassillis rebuilt Dunure harbour in 1811 at a cost of £50,000 as a stimulus to trade. The village developed slowly, but thereafter grew rapidly and, at one time, was the busiest fishing-centre on the west coast of Scotland. Today, however, the harbour is home only to a few pleasure craft and lobster fishermen.

The Anchorage Inn overlooks the harbour. This row of buildings is the older part of Dunure which, with the row of cottages known as Sea View, forms the original village. The Kennedy Hall is dated 1881 and is hidden among the old cottages. Dunure House is a fine building of around 1800, its large bow front being a distinctive feature. The smelting of limestone was at one time carried on in the village. The remains of the limekilns can be seen next to a path linking the old village with the castle. This path also passes the ancient doocot, a beehive-style building that was used to keep pigeons for eating. This one is thought to date from the early seventeenth century.

Dunure Castle is a spectacular ruin, perched high on a cliff. The oldest part, which takes an irregular plan, is thought to be as old as the fourteenth century, but the southern wing was added in the fifteenth and sixteenth centuries. The castle seems to have been occupied in 1610, but by 1696 it was described as ruinous. During the 1990s the castle was partially excavated, and the ruins made stable to allow access to the public. Iron stairs and walkways were created, giving access to what was for many years

Dunure Castle

one of the best known, but most inaccessible, castles in Ayrshire. Dunure was always a Kennedy seat, and was occupied until the mid-seventeenth century. There is a well-known story that Gilbert Kennedy, 4th Earl of Cassillis, captured Allan Stewart, the Commendator of Crossraguel Abbey and took him back to the castle. There he was held prisoner, and perhaps even roasted in the Black Vault, in order to force him to hand over the rich abbey lands. Whether or not the last part is true, history certainly records the passing of lands from Allan Stewart to the 4th Earl in the 1570s. The Kennedy Park surrounds the castle, forming an attractive area for summer visitors. Here can be found toilets, parking areas, swings and tennis courts. On the hillside above the old village, south of the road, are some post-war council houses, built in levels up the hillside.

North of Dunure harbour the *Iron Duke* ran aground after her engine failed in a storm in December 1883. The crew managed to swim ashore, but Captain MacBride was drowned and his body found on the shore the following day. On the same night the wooden barque, *Valkyrien*, was forced onto the shore, just to the north of the *Iron Duke*. Again, only one member of the ship's crew was drowned.

The road through Dunure village heads south and swings round to return to the A719 at Dunure Mains. The old Dunure Mill is a rather fine building, distinguished by its bipartite windows and crosses on the apex of the corbie-stepped gables. The building may date from the late eighteenth century. Dunure Mains is a typical modern farm, but is revered in history as the final home of the 'Baron of Buchlyvie'. This was a Clydesdale horse that was owned jointly by James Kilpatrick and William Dunlop of Dunure Mains. However, Kilpatrick agreed to sell his half share to Dunlop, but the price caused trouble between them and the case was eventually taken to the House of Lords. As a compromise the horse was put up for sale in 1911, and was bought by an anonymous bidder on behalf of Dunlop for £9,500. Unfortunately, the horse later suffered injury from a kick and had to be put down in June 1914. Originally buried here, the bones were later dug up and displayed in Glasgow's Kelvingrove Museum.

The A719 heads south along the hillside, high above the cliff-lined shore, before heading inland. On its way it traverses the Croy Brae, otherwise known as the 'Electric' Brae. This slight gradient on the road is famous for its optical illusion, which makes travellers think that they are going downhill when in fact they are going up. The mind tends to think that when travelling from west to east on the brae that the road should naturally drop to the bridge at the Craigencroy Burn. However, the road actually ascends to the bridge. Should a car be stopped on the brae and the handbrake released, passengers are amazed to discover that the vehicle begins to roll uphill! An inscribed boulder by the side of the road gives details of the phenomenon.

From Knoweside Farm a minor road drops down to Croy Shore. It passes a caravan site formed on the old railway line, and reaches the shore at another caravan site at Croyburnfoot. North of this site is an old spring known as the Fairy's Well. Croy House is a smallish mansion that served as a hotel at one time. South of it is a parking area, popular with picnickers who come to enjoy the magnificent sandy beach.

The A719 makes its way back inland, past the Castlehill Wood and Humeston Farm to the junction at Pennyglen. From here the B7023 is followed back into Maybole, passing through the woods of Enoch. Enoch Lodge is a fine cottage, the style being inspired by Adam's work at Culzean. Before dropping down into Maybole again, the B7023 crosses the Gallow Hill, site of a number of hangings in the early history of the parish.

From Enoch Lodge the Ladycross road can be used to bypass Maybole and return to the B7024, Alloway Road, at Cassillis View. The first crossroads reached is known as the Ladycross, for it is said that a wayside cross dedicated to the Virgin Mary stood here. It was here that a skirmish between the 5th Earl of Cassillis and Gilbert Kennedy of Bargany took place in 1601, at which a number of their followers were killed. Bargany died of his wounds a few hours later.

East of Ladycross is a roadside memorial marking the site of the

Cargill Stone, at which the Revd Donald Cargill preached an important Conventicle in May 1681. This was attended by hundreds of people from the surrounding county and, in the nineteenth century, an obelisk was erected to commemorate this event. To the north east of the memorial are Mid and East Brockloch farms. Between the two, in the wood surrounding the Brockloch Burn, can be found the scanty remains of Brockloch Castle.

A minor road strikes north from Ladycross, passing Steylea cottage and climbing the Preaching Brae. To the west, near the disused Howmoor whinstone quarry, can be found the remains of another dun, occupying an elevated position on the hillside. North of here, by the side of the hill, is the disused Howmoor rifle range. Parts of the targets and associated buildings can still be found on the ground. The minor road takes a sharp right turn and drops past Glenalmond and Garryhorn farms towards Culroy.

Following the A77 westwards out of Maybole, the parish is left behind just half a mile beyond the Academy. Beyond the Parish March Bridge, and its modern successor, one enters Kirkoswald parish, which will be dealt with later in this chapter. A minor road strikes south from Maybole, heading for the Girvan valley. An older road took a slightly higher route to the west of the present road, but this has been abandoned over much of its length.

Kilhenzie Castle is the first main place of interest reached after the outskirts of Maybole are left behind. This is a small, but interesting old building, originally erected as a fortified house in the late sixteenth century but extended in the seventeenth. Built for the Baird family, it was later acquired by the Kennedys and then the Fergussons. The house was extended again and restored around 1850–5 for a tenant on the Kilkerran estate, of which it was part.

Half a mile to the south of Kilhenzie Castle lodge house, just beyond Capenoch Bridge, a minor road can be followed in a southwesterly direction to Spring Garden Farm. This passes along the south side of Kildoon Hill, a prominent little basalt summit that reaches 590 feet above sea level. A tall obelisk commemorating Sir Charles Fergusson of Kilkerran (1800–49), erected in 1853, marks the east end of the summit. Fergusson, a local philanthropist, was responsible for a number of churches and schools. An ancient hill fort, known as Kildoon, crowns the summit of Kildoon Hill. This has been a vitrified structure, the ramparts protecting an area of around 150 feet by 100 feet. The west side of the fort, where the ridge joins other hills, had the additional protection of two ramparts, which included a ditch cut into the solid rock.

The rolling countryside on either side of Kildoon Hill is occupied by a number of farms and some old quarries. At Glenside is a disused reservoir, created in the nineteenth century to supply Maybole with water, and at Lochspouts is another reservoir, considerably larger and used until the 1940s. It is on the boundary between the parishes of Maybole and Kirkoswald. In Lochspouts was found a crannog, which was excavated at one time when the reservoir was drained. Within it was found an oak platform.

Below Lochspouts is the Ghaist Glen, a narrow glen associated with ancient tales of bogles. The minor road past the Capenoch Bridge meanders among woodland, passing through the Carsloe Wood before leaving the parish behind at Little Craigfin. Craigfin Hill is a low eminence 745 feet in height.

In the holm of the Water of Girvan, by the side of the Barlewan Burn, is Dalduff Farm. Here can be found fragmentary remains of Dalduff Castle, an ancient fortress of the sixteenth century.

There are two other roads striking out of Maybole in a south-easterly direction. Crosshill Road is the B7023, and shortly after leaving Maybole behind it passes the present cemetery. Kirkmichael Road passes the early nineteenth century St John's Cottage and crosses country to Kirkmichael village. Between these two roads are some small lochans, two of which are named the Heart Loch and Chapelton Loch. The third does not appear to have a name, even although it is the largest.

*

Kirkoswald parish is a rural part of the county, extending to 15,444 acres. There are three small villages within it, Kirkoswald itself, originally known as Kirkoswald of Turnberry, the Maidens and Turnberry. Kirkoswald is an old community lying by the side of the main A77. The old ruins of Kirk Oswald itself can be found in the old kirkyard at the west end of the village. The church is said to date from 1244, the monks of Crossraguel building a chapel on a site where St Oswald is thought to have fought a battle in 634 AD.

In the kirkyard are many old and interesting gravestones. Here can be found the graves of Douglas Graham, John Davidson, 'Kirkton' Jean Kennedy, (the originals from *Tam o' Shanter*), Hugh Rodger, schoolmaster in the village, and the maternal grandparents of Robert Burns, Gilbert Broun and Agnes Rennie. There can also be found the gravestone of Scipio, an African servant or slave who was employed by the Kennedys at Culzean Castle. An ancient font in the church is said to have been used to baptise Robert the Bruce. Here also is the parish war memorial.

The present parish church lies south of the village, on a farm road leading to Corrieston. The church was built in 1777, and it is claimed that Robert Adam was in the area at the time it was being built and advised the masons on how to improve its appearance. As a result, quoins, urns, pediments and round windows were added and the whole church achieved a more luxurious Georgian appearance. The church bell dates from 1677. Among the well-known visitors to the church are Robert Burns and President Eisenhower. The church was restored in 1997 following a fire. On the opposite side of the Kirkbrae is Glebe House, the former manse, erected in 1771.

A few old cottages line the roadside at Kirkoswald, including Kirkton Jean's Inn of 1792. This was originally Kirkton Jean's house, for the original Kirkton Jean's Inn has been demolished. The former Free Church, or John Knox Church, opened in 1851, is located on Kirkland Hill. It closed in 1931, after the union of the Church of Scotland and the Free Church in 1929, becoming a hall thereafter, and is now a private house. Souter Johnnie's Cottage, erected in 1786, survives. This was the home of John Davidson (1728–1806), who worked as a souter, or shoe-maker, in the village. He is mentioned in Burns's epic poem, *Tam o' Shanter*, and as a result his cottage was deemed worthy of saving. The cottage was restored by a local group in 1920 but, in 1932, was gifted to the National Trust for Scotland, who have maintained it ever since. It is a single storey building, the roof covered with thatch. Within can be seen some late eighteenth-century furniture, a few Burns relics and a souter's workshop. In the restored alehouse to the rear are statues of Tam, Johnnie, the innkeeper and his wife. James Thom, the Ayrshire sculptor, carved these.

Burns spent the summer of 1775 at Kirkoswald, learning mathe-matics from Hugh Rodger. He lodged with his uncle, Samuel Brown, at Ballochniel Farm, which lies a mile to the south west of the village. Burns's mother, Agnes Broun, was born at Craigenton Farm in 1732, which lies about a mile and a half east of Turnberry.

The primary school at Kirkoswald is now disused. It was completed in 1874 and built on the site of an earlier structure. East of the school is a more modern group of cottages, work on which started in the 1920s. At the junction with Balvaird Road is the Richmond Hall, a fine building in an eclectic style, designed by James Miller. Erected in 1925, it was the gift of Sir John R. Richmond of Blanefield to the village.

Blanefield House stands in its wooded policies to the east of Kirkoswald. The present house was erected in 1913 for J. R. Richmond, also to the plans of Miller, who created a fine English manorial building. At one time the estate was the property of the Blane family, who in 1812 were created Baronets of Blanefield. The first baronet was Physician-in-Ordinary to kings George III, George IV and William IV. In more recent years the Earl of Cassillis occupied the house, but it has been sold. Part of the estate extends to the south-east, as far as Craigdow Loch and the modern forestry plantations. Craigdow Loch is a natural circular loch. Craigdow Hill was the location of a massive conventicle, held in August 1678, and attended by seven thousand Covenanters.

Either the road past Auchenblane, or the busy A77, can be followed eastward towards Crossraguel Abbey, one of the most important historical

Crossraguel Abbey: the gatehouse and doocot

sites in Ayrshire. The abbey was founded in 1240 by Duncan, 1st Earl of Carrick, but has been extended and rebuilt over the years. It was eventually abandoned in the sixteenth century, and the ruins were further reduced by people stealing the stone. However, the remains were eventually protected and have been in the care of Historic Scotland and its predecessors for many years. Visitors to the abbey can wander among the well-kept grounds, admiring the quality of the work. In the sacristy can be found some ancient gravestones, including one commemorating Egidia Blair, Lady Row, of the early sixteenth century. The chapter house of the abbey still retains its vaulted room, and within these are preserved some ancient stones. One of the best-preserved parts of the abbey is the gatehouse building, which is quite like a small fortified-tower. A spiral stair can be climbed up through three storeys, the roof having been restored to its former glory.

The old tower at the south-east corner of the abbey precincts was in fact a proper fortified dwelling of around 1530. Unfortunately one side and the ground floor vaulting have collapsed. Still to be found within the ruins are the stream passing below the building, allowing the latrines to be flushed, and an old doocot, perhaps dating from the sixteenth century. Within the large complex can be seen the remains of a bakehouse, Abbot's House, kitchens, common hall, treasury and other buildings. Crossraguel Abbey was a Cluniac establishment, a daughter house to Paisley Abbey. In 1404 it was granted a Charter of Regality, meaning that the abbots had the right of jurisdiction over their lands. The last Abbot of Crossraguel, Quintin Kennedy, took part in a three day long debate with John Knox over the Doctrine of the Mass, on 28–30 November 1562. Each man had forty supporters, who were to supply quotations from books and to record the proceedings. The debate ended with neither side winning, but the people of Maybole later burned all Kennedy's books on the village green.

The ruins of Baltersan Castle can be seen further east, standing in the middle of a field to the south of the A77. This L-plan tower was built around 1584 by David Kennedy of Pennyglen. The tower is quite complete, rising to the chimney heads at one point, and here and there the corbels for a turret and cap house survive. The Great Hall measures thirty-six feet by nineteen feet and incorporates a spy-hole from the stairway. James Brown commenced restoration work in the 1990s.

To the north of Crossraguel is the Mochrum area. Mochrum Loch is an elliptical stretch of water, lying in a low stretch of ground. Beyond it is Mochrum Farm and rising behind is the prominent Mochrum Hill. This rises steeply from the surrounding countryside but flattens off at the top, creating a table effect. The hill is 886 feet in height, which is quite high so near the sea. Although the hill is prominent and an ideal viewpoint, there appears to be no signs of it having been fortified in pre-historic times.

West of Mochrum Hill is the magnificent Culzean estate, one of the most popular historical attractions in Scotland. Most of this, or at least 563 acres, is now protected by the National Trust for Scotland, which was gifted the property in 1945 by the 5th Marquis of Ailsa. Culzean had always been a Kennedy seat, although not always the main one. Early maps place Coif, or Cove Castle here, and the name Culzean may have been transferred to this place in the seventeenth century. The old tower house of Culzean probably dated from the fifteenth century, but in 1776 the 10th Earl of Cassillis commissioned Robert Adam to rebuild it and create a new country seat for himself. Adam came up with what is perhaps his masterpiece, encasing the old tower in a new Gothic castle. A courtyard building was designed, with a fine circular tower built high on the cliff top. Because of the caves beneath the castle, Adam had to build pillars and other supports in order to carry the weight of the new building. As time went on it was realised that the small courtyard would be of little use, and would be little more than a dank space, and it was at this point that Adam came up with his pièce de résistance: the oval staircase. The castle was extended in 1875–8, when Wardrop & Reid were commissioned to build the west wing. They copied Adam's style, but made it slightly more baronial in appearance.

Culzean Castle

Visitors to the castle begin their tour at the entrance hall of 1879, which leads into the armoury. Here can be seen a vast collection of swords and rifles, originally belonging to the West Lowland Fencible Regiment, raised by the 12th Earl of Cassillis when there was a threat of invasion from France. The old eating-room follows, occupying the ground floor of the original tower. This room has been used variously as a dining room, library and is now furnished as a sitting room. The dining room lies beyond, a fine Adam-style apartment. The oval staircase is one of Culzean's gems. Here a stair makes its way up through the centre of the building, the upper floors supported by Corinthian columns. Beyond the vestibule is the circular saloon, perched on the cliff top. A few smaller rooms follow before the green, or first drawing room is reached. The long drawing room, or picture room, occupies the great hall of the original castle. The tour continues through some bedrooms before reaching the Eisenhower presentation. General Dwight Eisenhower was gifted the guest flat at Culzean in 1945 by the Trust as a thank you for his part in the Second World War. Here the story of the D-Day landings is recounted.

The grounds around Culzean now form a country park. There are numerous fine walks through the woods, and down to the shore. Culzean Harbour is a quiet spot below the castle where there survives a wooden boathouse and small wharf. Here the 3rd Marquis built some boats before the business took off and he moved the works to the Maidens. Immediately west of here is the Dolphin House, a former laundry that has recently been restored and extended to form a bunkhouse and outdoor centre. On the cliff above is a small powder-house, dating from 1812 when Napoleon was thought to be considering invading Britain.

Paths meander through the woods westward to the Swan Pond, a large man-made lochan. On its southern shores can be found a small visitor centre with aviary, toilets, kiosk, play area and other facilities. This building was erected around 1820 to the plans of Robert Lugar. On the lower slopes of Barwhin Hill can be seen the pagoda, a rather unusual Gothic block used for kennels, dating from the 1820s. Barwhin Hill is said to derive its name from the fact that it was here the servant of Robert the Bruce was supposed to have landed from Arran and sent the signal back whether it was worth him coming over or not. Unfortunately someone was burning whin bushes at the time and when the Bruce saw the fire and mistook it as a signal that the folk of the district were ready to rally to his support, he arrived on the Ayrshire coast to find it overrun with English soldiers. He managed to escape to the Galloway hills where he commenced his guerrilla campaign, winning battles at Glentrool and Clatteringshaws, which ultimately led to his victory at Bannockburn in 1314.

From the Swan Pond a drive through the woods leads back to the large walled-gardens, part of which is now used for plant sales. The gardens are attractive and are home to a variety of crops. Near the main car park is the Camellia House, a magnificent glass-fronted building originally used for growing camellias and other delicate plants. It was erected in 1818 to plans of James Donaldson. This building was the subject of a recent restoration project. South of the car park is the deer park, an extensive field where a herd of deer can be seen.

In front of the castle itself is the Fountain Park, a rather grand garden built on terraces below the castle. In the centre of the lawn is a large fountain, and at the west end is the orangery of 1792. A path leads from here round to the west lawn, which has a few cannon pointing seaward. At the east end of the Fountain Park is the viaduct, one of Adam's finest creations. Access to the castle would have been difficult for carriages due to the low-lying ground between what was obviously a defensive site and the rest of the countryside. Adam designed a series of bridges and a causeway to link the two levels of ground, finishing it off to look like a ruined part of the castle. From the entrance arch, which has a circular tower on one side and a square tower at the other, the viaduct leads past what looks like old dungeons and an ice house to a large arched-gateway, the latter surmounted by the Kennedy crest of a dolphin. To the right is a courtyard block, formerly the stables, but now a shop and restaurant, as well as further estate offices. Its clock-bearing tower distinguishes it.

The former Home Farm was another Adam creation of 1777. Four T-shaped blocks were built around an open courtyard, each one linked by an arched gateway. This was restored in 1973 to plans of Boys Jarvis Partnership to create another restaurant, visitor centre and shop. The stone barn is used for smaller exhibitions. There are a number of other interesting buildings on the estate, including the old gasworks, which have been restored as a memorial to William Murdoch, born at Bello Mill in this county, the Cat Gates of 1802 (topped with Coade stone leopards) and Hoolity Ha' of around 1800.

On the A719 east of Culzean a minor road leaves the road at Balchriston Lodge and meanders down to the beach, at what is known locally as Maybole Shore. The road crosses the old railway, the Rancleugh Viaduct of which has been demolished. Down by the shore is Goatsgreen, an old cottage of around 1875 that was restored and extended by Duncan MacFarlane in 1963 for his own use.

Thomaston Castle stands in ruins next to Culzean Kennels, outwith the National Trust property. The castle dates from the early sixteenth century and was built for the Corrys of Kelwood, who obtained the lands in 1507. Tradition claims, however, that the original castle, or a predecessor, was built by Thomas Bruce (hence its name), nephew of King Robert I. An L-plan building, the walls are complete to the corbelled wallheads. By 1632 the castle was owned by the MacIlvaines of Grimmet, who had married the Corry heiress. The Kennels House is a fine Gothic building of around 1820. Beyond the woods, in a field below Thomaston Farm, is the Lady Well.

*

The A719 heads past Thomaston Castle and drops slowly towards the Maidens. Fine farms and various plantations occupy much of the countryside around here. In the Knockaniddling Wood is an old curling pond. As the Maidens is neared a number of caravan sites make an appearance, this being a popular spot for holidaymakers.

The Maidens of Turnberry, to give the place its full name, is a small, mainly modern, community established along the shore of Maidenhead Bay. There is a little harbour at the west end of the village, dating from the eighteenth century, created by building a long pier and breakwater out towards the Maidenhead Rocks, or the Maidens after which the village received its name. Fishing is no longer an important source of employment, and the harbour tends even to be empty even of pleasure craft. There can be found a few relics of the days of fishing at the harbour headland however, including old cast-iron basins in which nets were boiled.

Of the older buildings in Maidens, one of the few is the small church, a simple building originally used in the summer months as the holidaymakers' church. Ardlochan Road makes its way along the side of the beach, heading for Ardlochan House (now an inn) and more caravan sites. The old school in Turnberry Road has been replaced by a modern building in Shanter Road, opened in 1975. The old school was converted into a community centre.

A short track winds its way from near the toilets at Harbour Road towards Port Murray, a 'modern' house of 1960–3, designed by Peter Womersley. This is a flat-roofed building with glazed and cedar walls, perched on a stone basement beneath the cliffs. At Port Murray can be seen an old slipway, used at one time when boat building took place at the Maidens. This yard belonged to the firm of Alexander MacCredie, established in 1883 to build steamers. On the slopes of Bain's Hill to the south can be found an ancient standing-stone.

Shanter Road leads to Shanter Farm, at one time the home of Douglas Graham (1738–1811), who Burns named Tam o' Shanter in his famous poem with that title. Tradition claims that Graham had a boat at the Maidens, the *Tam o' Shanter*, which he used to run illicit goods ashore. Today the farm is home to a horse-riding centre. On the slopes of the hill to the east is the Shanter Knowe, a circular mound that was constructed as a motte hill sometime in the Norman period.

The road south from the Maidens passes the modern hotel and nursing home complex of Malin Court. Soon the remains of Turnberry Airfield are apparent, the large runways still surviving between the whin bushes. The airfield at Turnberry was established in 1917 as a School of Aerial Gunnery, used in connection with Loch Doon. Three main runways were created, of 2,010 yards, 1,400 yards and 1,250 yards, forming a triangle. On the Lands of Turnberry hard-standing areas were created where aircraft could be parked. In Tauchet Wood, south of Little Turnberry, the former bomb stores can still be found.

The Royal Flying Corps, Royal Air Force, Australian and United States air forces used Turnberry airfield. A war memorial in the form of a granite cross with a carved sword can be found on a low knoll near to the lighthouse. The memorial lists thirty-nine names and was erected to the plans of Colonel Hugh R. Wallace of Cloncaird and Busby. The memorial was unveiled in May 1923. During the Second World War the Coastal Command used Turnberry as a training unit, but the airfield was closed at the cessation of hostilities in 1945 and the five hangars and other buildings were demolished.

Turnberry lighthouse, looking to the island of Arran

Turnberry Lighthouse dates from 1873. It was built of brick to the plans of Thomas Stevenson, father of Robert Louis Stevenson. The adjoining lighthouse-keepers' cottages are no longer occupied, as the whole set up is now automated. The lighthouse occupies the site of part of Turnberry Castle. Only fragmentary remains of the castle can be made out, the stonework having been battered for years by the waves. The ruins are perched precariously on the cliff tops, and access to them is difficult. The castle is one of the oldest in the area, and was probably abandoned sometime in the fourteenth century. There is a legend that Robert the Bruce was born here in 1274, his mother, the Dowager Countess of Carrick, having kidnapped his father from near Lochmaben Castle. He eventually succumbed to her charms and they were married in 1271.

Turnberry today is celebrated for its hotel and golf courses. The Glasgow & South Western Railway Company established these in 1904 and the hotel was quick to gain its reputation. The hotel building was designed by James Miller, and originally the trains that brought the holidaymakers to the hotel alighted at a station in front of the hotel. The railway line was closed in 1942. The hotel was owned by the railway company and its successors until 1983. It is now owned by the Westin group and has been extended considerably over the years. Today the hotel boasts 132 rooms, four bars, three restaurants and a health spa.

The lands to the west of the hotel, as far as the lighthouse, form the Turnberry golf courses. There are two of these – the Ailsa and the Kintyre – both of eighteen holes. The Ailsa course was designed by Mackenzie Ross in the 1950s. The ninth hole, known as Bruce's Castle, has one of the most spectacular tees in the world, being perched on a rock. The course extends to 6,440 yards and is a par 69. The Kintyre course was created in the 1990s, being designed by Donald Steel. It replaced the former Arran course. This course is 6,638 yards in length, par 74. The first Open Championship to be held at Turnberry took place in 1977, when Tom Watson beat Jack Nicklaus by one stroke in one of the most exciting tournaments in history. Known to golfing aficionados as the 'Duel in the Sun', Nicklaus and Watson matched each other shot for shot almost from start to finish. Indeed the outcome was still in doubt right up to the eighteenth hole on the final day. Opens have also been staged there in 1986, when Greg Norman won, and in 1994, the winner being Nick Price. The Duke of York opened the new clubhouse in 1993.

The village of Turnberry, or Milton of Turnberry as it was at one time known, comprises of a number of large bungalows and houses at the junction of the A719 with the A77. More bungalows are located up Drumdow Road, which lies south of the Milton Burn. The village has a small post office with store. Turnberry Lodge is a Gothic building of around 1840.

The A77 heads south from Turnberry, making its way along the raised beach towards Girvan. This area is famed for its early Ayrshire potatoes, and at certain times of the year large sheets of polythene can be seen covering acres of ground, helping to bring the potatoes on.

On the low hills above the road can be found a few interesting ancient earthworks, including the Fairy Knowe on the southern slopes of Balkenna Hill, and the Dowhill Mount, a Norman motte. This has a series of defensive ditches on the landward side. On the highest point of the motte can be seen a circular ring of stones, which may have been the masonry base to a wooden tower (a most unusual feature if this is the case) or else the remains of a stone-built dun.

At the foot of the Drumbain Burn is the large alginate factory, established in 1934. Kelp and other brown seaweed is brought here from all over Scotland and processed into alginates. This is in demand by the food, drinks, paper and pharmaceutical industries. Alginate Industries Limited originally opened the factory, but in 1979 this company merged with Kelco International of California.

Kirkoswald parish is left behind just beyond Dunnymuck Farm. However, there is a large area of farmland inland from the Balkenna shore that forms part of the parish. Most of this is rolling countryside, occupied by numerous farms and small woodlands. Here and there can be found items of interest, including Ladybank House. The Lady Burn has as one of its sources the Lady Well, a natural spring. Another stream, the Chapelton Burn, passes through a deep gorge known as the Balsarrock Glen, where a notable waterfall can be seen. The chapel referred to by Chapelton no longer exists, but it was probably located on the lands of Chapelton Farm. There also can be found the large boulder known as the Sturdy Stone. At Townhead is the former Townhead School, erected in 1875 but closed in 1958.

An old road can be followed beyond East Threave Farm, to the pass below Craigens Hill, where there is a Bronze Age burial cairn. Another is located near to Craigdow Farm, though access to there is usually made from the Maybole side, passing the Ghaist Glen. More antiquities can be seen on the Prop Hill, which is crowned with a mast. The Hollowshean camp is a large prehistoric fort covering a few acres. The fort is 240 feet long by 150 feet and may originally have been protected by ramparts shored up by stone; however most of this has been stolen. Protecting the fort on the western side, where the ridge is joined to the surrounding land, are three ramparts, perhaps originally laced with timber.

There is a strange stretch of Kirkoswald parish dropping down into the Girvan valley, but it will be dealt with in Chapter 20, as it falls more naturally into the area covered by that chapter.

# 19

# Kirkmichael, Crosshill and Straiton

KIRKMICHAEL AND STRAITON ARE two inland parishes, both of which are rural in nature and which extend over many acres of upland. Kirkmichael is the smaller, being 16,114 acres in extent, located in the valley of the Water of Girvan. Straiton is much larger, comprising 52,249 acres, mainly of moorlands and forestry plantations. A considerable amount of Straiton parish is located in the Doon valley, for Patna, Keirs, Loch Doon and much of the uplands as far as Mullwharchar, mentioned in Chapter 17, fall within this parish.

Kirkmichael parish has two villages within it, Kirkmichael itself and Crosshill. Kirkmichael stands by the side of the Dyrock Burn, the older part of the village lying on the north bank. The village became a popular location for weavers to set up in business, and many of the old weavers' homes can still be seen.

Kirkmichael Church

At the east end of the village is the parish church, a building of 1787 erected by Hugh Cairncross, situated in its kirkyard. The belfry was rebuilt in 1887. This is reached through the rare, for Ayrshire and

Scotland, lichgate, which probably dates from around 1700. Within it is an old bell of 1702. The T-plan church is still in use, and boasts three lofts for the local lairds. James A. Morris and Hugh Wallace designed the pulpit, which is a stone structure depicting Saints Andrew, George, Michael and Patrick. This was erected in 1919 as a war memorial. Stained glass includes work by Christopher Whitworth Whall. The church occupies an ancient site, dedicated to St Michael, one that has been used for worship since the thirteenth century. The graveyard around the church is one of the most interesting old burial grounds in Ayrshire. Here can be seen a number of eighteenth-century stones with various trade and mortality symbols. The present village cemetery is located at Hillhead, half a mile west of the village.

Patna Road extends west from the church to the foot of the village joining the B7045, which links Maybole and Straiton. Along this road are some old cottages, and single-storey buildings like Jock's Restaurant. Here also is the MacCosh Hall, erected in 1898 to plans by John Baxter. This has a distinctive clock tower and was the gift of Dr David MacCosh. A drive leads up to the manse, a fine Tudoresque house erected in 1838 at a cost of £968. Straiton Road contains another group of old buildings. Most of the newer houses are located in Bolestyle Road, which links Patna and Straiton roads, forming a triangle. At the south end of the village is the school. Straiton Road was formed as a sort of bypass to Kirkmichael, crossing Dyrock Burn by the New Bridge. The Portcheck Bridge over the Dyrock Burn, at the top end of Bolestyle Road, is a narrow and hump-backed construction, erected in 1775.

West of Kirkmichael, located within wooded policies, is Kirkmichael House. This incorporates an old tower house of the seventeenth century, but the building seen today is in essence a Jacobean building of 1830. To this was added a mock tower house in 1861. Kirkmichael was originally a Kennedy seat, remaining in their hands for at least five centuries until 1920. In recent years the house was converted into a residential school, but this has closed. In the grounds are a sizeable pond and old walled garden. Just south of Kirkmichael village is Aitkenhead, a group of buildings by the banks of the Girvan. There was at one time a mill here, but in recent years a warehouse has been built on the site.

East and north of Kirkmichael the parish climbs up to Guiltree Hill, an eminence 635 feet in height. The Dalrymple Road climbs over this hill, a wonderful upland route that affords fine views in all directions. On the western slopes of Guiltree Hill is a circular earthwork of unknown vintage. A second one on Guiltreehill Farm has been lost, as has another at Cassington. On the Downan's Hill above Dunree Farm can be seen another earthwork, in this case a circular dun. The surrounding wall is around six feet in height, in places up to twenty feet thick, but averaging around ten feet. This protects a central area measuring around 120 feet by 100 feet. Access to this was made through an entrance on the south-west side. This little hill is known as Cassillis Downans in the work of Burns, where he reckons fairies are wont to gather. The name Dunree, however, is from the Gaelic meaning 'king's fort'. In the valley below, near Lindsayston Farm, the Chapel Knowe recalls the fact that a pre-Reformation chapel stood here.

Cassillis House, or castle, lies below Downan's Hill, by the side of the river Doon. Cassillis is pronounced 'cassels', although there are many who mispronounce the name with three syllables. Cassillis is in fact one of the finest castles in the county, a great tower house of the fourteenth century, to which various additions have been made. The oldest part of the castle is the tall tower, which has walls sixteen feet thick in places. Additions were made to this in the seventeenth century and again in 1830 when Thomas Brown was employed to extend the house. The main turnpike stair in the old tower has a hollow central column in which it was possible to climb to freedom, should the castle be forced. Cassillis is the seat of the Marquis of Ailsa, his son and heir taking the title Earl of Cassillis. The Kennedy family has owned this estate since 1373 when Sir John Kennedy married the heiress, Marjory de Montgomerie. Sir Gilbert Kennedy was created Lord Kennedy in 1452 and his grandson, David, 3rd Lord Kennedy, was created Earl of Cassillis in 1509. He was to suffer at Flodden. In 1831 Archibald, 12th Earl, was created Marquis of Ailsa.

Along Patna Road, near Dyrockbank, a track climbs up past Glenside Farm towards the Loch Spallander waterworks and dam. Loch Spallander was a natural loch that was dammed in 1970 to create a sizeable reservoir, serving Maybole, Girvan and most of the intervening villages. Near the Barracks Bridge two old limekilns can be seen.

Crosshill village lies to the south west of Kirkmichael, located in a hollow formed by low hills, south of the Water of Girvan. The village was established around 1808 by the owner of Dalhowan estate, and became a noted weaving community. The handloom weavers built many of the old roadside cottages that survive. Most of the incoming weavers were Irish, 800 of the 1,000 inhabitants in 1838 being from that country.

The parish church is located up Milton Street. This building dates from 1838 and was established as a chapel-of-ease for the Crosshill parishioners. A T-shaped building, it has a small belfry on top of the west gable. In 1853 it became a *quoad sacra* parish of its own. Off Milton Street is a recreation ground. The war memorial is a foursquare pillar, the column covered in names of those who fell, the upper part carved with a sword and Celtic-style ornament. Colonel Hugh R. Wallace of Cloncaird and Busby designed this. Crosshill Primary School is a modern building of 1968, designed by Robert B. Rankin & Associates. This replaced the old school, which itself replaced an old building established by the laird at the time the village was laid out. The village hall dates from 1892 and the church hall is of 1847, owing its origins to being a Free Church.

Dalhowan Street, with its fine row of weavers' cottages, leads south, past the new cemetery, to the crossroads at Cloyntie. Beyond this is the Kirkbride estate, the house built high on a hilltop. This was erected in 1861 in a manorial style. The house was extended in 1924 but some of this was later removed in the late 1970s. William Houldsworth, of the iron and coal family, owned the house at one time. At Balgreggan Farm are former limestone quarries, and the remains of kilns can be found. Longhill farmhouse to the north of here has now been extended considerably to form a small country house.

From Kirkbride a minor hill road climbs uphill steadily, attaining a height of 1,040 feet before dropping down to the valley of the river Stinchar. Shortly after Kirkbride gates it passes the former Auchalton Toll cottage, but no fee now requires to be paid. Higher still is the wildlife reserve known as Auchalton Meadow.

The road climbs steadily, entering the large forestry plantations of the Carrick Forest. A long projection of land belonging to Kirkmichael strikes south here, taking in Clauchrie Hill and the Back Fell of Glenalla. At the 'Ayr 16' milestone the road takes a sharp turning and crosses a small bridge. This spot is known as the De'il's Elbow. The Fore Fell of Glenalla is actually the highest of the three fells here, reaching 1,404 feet above sea level.

The road from Kirkmichael to Straiton is the B7045. After Aitkenhead it begins to meander considerably among the small hillocks, woods and plantations, making its way up the Girvan valley. Just beyond Aitkenhead is a bridge across the Girvan, leading to the long drive making its way to Blairquhan Castle. This is the route tourists follow when visiting the house. The drive follows the Water of Girvan, but the woods and plantations mean that the river is only glimpsed here and there. There are some smaller falls in the river, the lower of which is known as the Tranew Linn. The upper falls don't seem to have an official name. Blairquhan actually lies much nearer Straiton, and will be mentioned shortly.

The public road to Straiton passes by Cloncaird Castle, which can be seen standing by the side of the Water of Girvan, on a small promontory of land formed between the Girvan and the Kelse Burn. From the public road the castle looks like a nineteenth-century Gothic building, which in fact it is, being designed by Robert Wallace and erected in 1814 for Henry Ritchie, but the older tower of the sixteenth century Cloncaird Castle survives within. The main entrance is located in an unusual cylindrical tower positioned at one corner, giving the castle a rather unique appearance. The Ritchies owned Cloncaird until 1843 when his nephew, William Wallace, succeeded. In 1947 the castle became a convalescent home. The castle was later returned to private ownership, and is once more a fine country house. At Drumfad, high above the castle, are the remains of a doocot dating from the eighteenth century.

\*

The road into Straiton meanders among plantations and low hills before dropping down to the large floodplain on which the village stands. Straiton is a charming village, situated on the edge of the better quality land, and serves as a gateway to the Galloway Highlands, which seem to rise up beyond it. The hills in the immediate locality are not particularly high, but they rise steeply, giving an indication that this is the start of a major group of hills.

The village itself is small, little more than a single street of cottages, although there are one or two more houses around it. Thomas, Earl of Cassillis, established the village in the mid-eighteenth century. Main Street runs from the church at the west end to the war memorial at the east end. The church and its churchyard are both interesting. The present church dates from 1758, a fairly simple building, incorporating a foursquare tower, added at the time of the restoration in 1901. The restoration work was carried out by John Kinross, the tower designed by Ayr architect John Murdoch. To the rear of the church is a much older wing, which incorporates the Kennedy of Blairquhan tomb. This dates from around 1510. The piscina

Straiton

of the predecessor is visible on the east wall. A slab indicates that this was the burial place of the Keirs family, from 1712 until 1796. Within can be seen a stained glass window by Sadie MacLellan of 1977.

The kirkyard has a number of interesting old stones. Here can be found two headstones marking the grave of the Covenanting martyr, Thomas MacHaffie. Near to them is a stone depicting a family of nine children, all of whom must have died around the same time. There can also be found a fine selection of eighteenth-century stones bearing symbolism, including an Adam and Eve stone. Next to the church is the village hall, known as the MacCandlish Hall. This was erected in 1912 to the plans of Thomas Jack in the American colonial-style, with its timbered loggia. Further along the street is the old Black Bull Inn, on which can be seen a 1766 date stone. This inn featured in a television advert in the 1970s.

At the east end of the village street is the war memorial. The 'main' road makes a sharp right turn here, starting out on the hill road to Newton Stewart. Behind the memorial are the gates leading into Traboyack House, an attractive small mansion of 1792. This is in fact the former manse for the parish.

There are a few other houses on the Dalmellington road, as well as back towards Kirkmichael. The long row of houses running alongside the Lambdoughty Burn is known as Fowler's Croft. This is a modern development of 1984, designed by Robert Allan & Partners, successfully extending the village in a sympathetic way.

The Blairquhan estate surrounds Straiton to some extent. The castle and its policies lie to the west of the village, perched on a bluff over looking the Water of Girvan. Blairquhan Castle was a MacWhirter then Kennedy seat, and for centuries an ancient tower house in the Scots style stood here, not unlike Fyvie Castle in appearance. Nineteenth-century taste, however, decided that this should be replaced with a more 'up to date' Gothic fantasy. William Burn, the noted Edinburgh architect of the period, designed the present castle, a Tudor Gothic structure, noted for its lantern tower, and it was erected between 1820 and 1824. A few carved stones from the old tower were incorporated in the kitchen courtyard walls. The castle is open to the public during the summer months, and here one can see a fine array of rooms.

Entry is made through the grand porte-cochère, leading to the entrance hall. Beyond this is the central saloon, which rises to the top of the lantern tower, sixty feet above. From here a series of rooms are viewed, including the small drawing room, drawing room and the main stairs. Upstairs are some bedroom suites, and the tour returns to the ground floor where the sumptuous dining room is visited. The rooms below stairs are then viewed, and here is a modern collection of work by Scottish Colourists, including Fergusson, Peploe, Cadell and Hunter. The billiard room is now a museum of oddities from the history of the estate, including various plans, old games, and letters. The grounds of Blairquhan are extensive. The walled garden is well maintained, and was formed in the 1820s by John Tweedie (1775–1862), who worked at Castlehill in Ayr and later at Eglinton Castle. The gardens include a glasshouse, and north of it is the pinetum of 1860, surrounding the peaceful garden pond. North of this again is the restored icehouse. Between the kitchen courtyard and the stable block is the old Dool Tree.

The Whitefoord family acquired Blairquhan in the early seventeenth century but they lost a lot of money in the Ayr Bank crash of 1772 and the estate had to be sold in 1798. Sir Adam Whitefoord was created Baronet of Blairquhan around 1742, but the title became extinct. Sir David Hunter bought the estate, and the family (now Hunter Blair) have remained here ever since. They hold a baronetcy (of Dunskey Castle in Wigtownshire) created in 1786, but the present laird is a younger brother.

The road east from Straiton, heading to Dalmellington, is the B741. On leaving Straiton it climbs steadily, passing by the side of the Lambdoughty Glen. This is afforested, but there is an attractive woodland walk through the glen, named Lady Hunter Blair's Walk. This passes by the side of a series of waterfalls, one of which is known as the Black, or Rossetti, Linn for it is said that Dante Gabriel Rossetti (1828–82), a leading Pre-Raphaelite painter and poet, once contemplated suicide here. East of here the open moorland is crossed, much of which is afforested now, before dropping back down to Dalmellington and the Doon valley.

Situated south of Straiton is the primary school, and further on is the present cemetery. Between the two a track begins to climb up into the Barbellie Wood, from where a footpath climbs steeply to the summit of Craigengower. This is surmounted by a fifty-five-feet-tall obelisk in memory of Colonel James Hunter Blair MP (1817–54), erected in 1856 to plans of William Burn. James Hunter Blair was killed at Inkerman, in the Crimea.

The valley of the Girvan takes the form of a real glen here, having a wide and level bottom, the sides of which rise up steeply to the surrounding hills. Many of the faces are steep and rocky, including the notable Craigencallie, or the rock of the old woman. On the Doonans Hill are two summits, known as The Doonans, which derive from the Gaelic *dunan*. These were two ancient hill forts that, being 971 feet above sea level, would have been ideal in times of attack, but unsuitable for everyday living. In the valley below are the remains of ancient burial cairns, one of which is located on the better ground at Dalmorton Farm. On the west side of the valley is Balbeg House, built in the nineteenth century as a simple farmhouse, but extended in 1908 and 1923 to form a shooting lodge. The first extensions were for Sir Charles Fergusson of Kilkerran, the second for Sir Gerald Healey.

The hill road to Newton Stewart keeps following the Girvan as far as the Tairlaw Bridge, where it strikes south, and begins its ascent over the hills. Just north of the bridge is Baing Farm, which sits by the side of the Baing Burn. This stream has a number of waterfalls on its lower stretches, as well as one larger fall, the Drummore Linn. A tributary of this stream is known as the Chapel Burn, but whether there was ever a place of worship here is unknown. More definite is the remnant of a burial cairn, which is located next to a sheepfank near to the Baing Loch.

A minor road leaves the Newton Stewart hill road at the Tairlaw Bridge and keeps true to the Girvan valley. The Girvan, at this point, passes through the Tairlaw Glen, at the head of which is the Tairlaw Linn, a series of falls. More antiquities can be searched out on the ground around Knockdon Farm, for due west of the farm, next to a track leading into the forest, is a burial cairn. Another cairn can be found east of the farm, on a low knoll of the Knockdon Craig, and north of here is a prehistoric enclosure.

The minor road can be followed further up the Girvan valley, past the Bradan waterworks, to the dam that creates Loch Bradan reservoir. Loch Bradan was a natural loch, but it was dammed in 1909–13 to hold water for the burgh of Troon. In 1972 a second, longer and higher dam was built, creating a much larger loch. Before the first dam was built, Loch Bradan had an island in the centre of it on which was an ancient building, deemed to be a castle. This was not as important as the castle in Loch Doon, so unfortunately Lochbradan Castle has been lost, drowned in the waters. Loch Bradan had a sister loch to the west, now incorporated within the larger reservoir. The sister loch was known as Loch Lure.

Back at the Tairlaw Bridge, the hill road can be followed past the forestry workers cottages at Tairlaw and past Tairlaw Toll. The forest proper is entered here, for the plantations continue south for some miles. Just beyond Tallaminnock a track can be followed eastward to the second dam on Loch Bradan, built to prevent the waters overflowing westward into the Stinchar basin.

In the Balloch Plantation of the Carrick Forest is a sizeable loch, known as the Linfern Loch. This lies 980 feet above sea level and is used for fishing. The Linfern Loch drains out into the Stinchar, the Linfern Loch Burn passing close to the ancient burial cairn known as Cairnannock.

The Barr to Loch Doon cycle route passes through the forest, following forest roads. At the Stinchar Bridge, on the hill road once more, is a popular picnic site. Here a number of forest walks can be made, of various lengths. One of these leads to the site of Craiglure Lodge, used when this was free of forests and was a gentleman's stalking and shooting estate. From Stinchar Bridge a minor road heads east through the forest, crosses the infant Girvan and ends at a picnic spot on the southern side of Loch Bradan. The Girvan passes through little Loch Skelloch, which is a popular fishing venue. An old track continues northward to the shores of the loch. It formerly ended at Lochlure Lodge, a fishing lodge, which has long gone, the remains submerged below the waters.

Ballochbeatties Farm lies at the southern tip of Loch Bradan, and beyond it, hidden in the trees, is Balloch Lodge, used by the Balloch Fishing Club. Three early members of the club, Claud Hamilton, John Lockhart and Charles Inglis, are commemorated on a cairn that can be found in the forest above the forest drive back to Loch Doon. This road leads towards Loch Riecawr, mentioned in Chapter 17. A branch can be followed on foot through the trees southward towards a Rocking Stone, hidden in the trees and difficult to find. The Loch Slochy that appears on the maps is little more than a boggy reed-bed in the middle of the forest.

The hills here are wild and open, rising to the highest point at Shalloch on Minnoch. This summit is 2,543 feet above sea level, the east face of which drops steeply down into the centre of wild Grey Galloway. On its northern slopes are the headwaters of two major Ayrshire rivers, the Girvan and Stinchar. These have their source on the slopes of Caerloch Dhu, a northern summit of the hill, and are only three-quarters of a mile apart. The Girvan drops to the east, soon entering the little Loch Girvan Eye, which lies in a hollow of the hills. The stream then flows down to the Cornish Loch, an objective of one of the footpaths from Stinchar Bridge. The Girvan leaves this loch, which is only seven feet deep at the most, tumbling over a few falls before heading north towards lochs Skelloch and Bradan.

At Stinchar Bridge, Straiton parish is left behind, but it is probably best to deal with this part of the county at this point. From the bridge the hill road continues south, heading for the Minnoch valley. This stream actually drains into the Cree and thence into the Solway Firth, making it a rather cheeky addition to Ayrshire. The hill road leaves the forest behind, for it has climbed as high as 1,421 feet above sea level. Just after it leaves the forest, to the right, can be found a small memorial commemorating Agnes Hannah, a nurse who died here in a blizzard.

The Minnoch valley is mainly covered by trees, this being part of the large Glentrool Forest. Here and there in the forest are some open areas, where little cottages or farms still exist. The first of these is Waterhead on Minnoch, which at one time sold teas and home baking to passing travellers. Beyond Waterhead the infant Water of Minnoch is crossed by Maggie Osborne's Bridge, named after the infamous Ayr witch, who it is said performed her black arts hereabouts.

The hill road is joined by the Nick of the Balloch road at the Rowantree Burn and near here was the Rowantree Toll, another tollhouse. Between the High and Laigh Rowantree Bridges is a foursquare cairn on the top of which is a bas-relief in bronze of the Galloway hills. This was erected to commemorate David E. T. Bell (1907–65), who was a keen cyclist and explorer of these hills. He regularly contributed a column on his exploits to the *Ayrshire Post* over thirty years, using the pen-name, 'The Highwayman', of which two volumes have been published.

South of Rowantree Toll, of which only a few stones forming a wall can be seen, is Craigenrae. There used to be a school here, long since closed. Here can be found an outdoor centre operated by the council and the Duke of Edinburgh's Award Scheme, located in a shepherd's cottage. In the forest to the east of the outdoor centre is the Murder Hole, a marshy depression that is said to be the original Murder Hole used in the novel *The Grey Man* by S. R. Crockett. To suit his needs, he transposed this to the wilder countryside at Loch Neldricken.

There is not much of the Ayrshire countryside to be found south of here, before the county is left behind and the Stewartry of Kirkcudbright is entered. This takes place at a little bridge over a small burn that drains down from Loch Moan. Loch Moan, although it is on the boundary between the two counties, is officially in Kirkcudbright, the county boundary being drawn along the northern shores. This spot is known as Suie Toll but, like Rowantree Toll, only a few roadside boulders remain to mark the site of the tollhouse. Of the Rowantree Inn nothing can be found. This was at one time a traveller's rest, and must have been located somewhere between Suie and Rowantree tolls.

In the woods can be found a couple of ancient burial cairns. Cairnfore is located west of the hill road, and the remains of another lies north of Tarfessock Farm. Tarfessock is named after another of the mountains in the so-called Awful Hand range, of which Shalloch on Minnoch is the most northerly. Tarfessock rises to 2,287 feet above sea level. The next mountain to the south of here is Kirriereoch Hill, which is located on the county boundary. This summit is 2,579 feet in height, the highest point of the county.

# 20

# Girvan and Dailly

THE TOWN OF GIRVAN is a popular seaside resort, though it doesn't attract the long-term holidaymaker like it once did, for it is now too easy to fly abroad for the sun. The town remains a popular destination for day-trippers and weekend breaks, however, and in the summer months the shore and main street are busy with incomers. It is the centre of a parish of 14,954 acres.

Although Girvan was an ancient town, created a Burgh of Barony for Boyd of Penkill in 1668, it was actually rebuilt in the eighteenth century, when the planned part of the town was established, with Dalrymple and Henrietta streets forming the main north–south axes, and Ailsa and Hamilton streets running east–west. The oldest part of the town was located around the parish church, which stood where the old kirkyard survives. The church was abandoned in 1780. The triumphal arch and gateway was erected in 1908 to plans by James A. Morris to commemorate William Johnstone. In the graveyard are a few stones of interest, including that to Alexander Ross, special constable, of whom more later. Behind the churchyard is the former manse, now known as Strathavon, and dating from 1818. Here also is a caravan site.

The car park opposite the kirkyard is an ideal spot to begin an exploration of the town. This used to be occupied by small lanes and tightly packed buildings, but all of this has now gone, leaving Girvan's High Street as little more than a short pedestrian footpath. A tourist information centre is located here.

Bridge Street leads to the crossroads, a busy junction with traffic lights. Here can be seen the tower of Old Stumpy, the former tolbooth of the burgh. This building dates from the eighteenth century and was originally surrounded by the burgh's buildings. The tower rises foursquare to a corbelled parapet, above which is a carved pediment with clock, surmounted by an octagonal bell tower with spire. In 1909 the town buildings were removed and the MacMaster Hall was built, a fine classical building donated to the town by John MacMaster, banker in Canterbury but a native of Kirkoswald. Its architect was W. J. Jennings of Canterbury. Opened in August 1911, the hall was gutted by fire in 1939 and demolished in 1956, leaving Old Stumpy to stand alone.

Heading east, or inland from here, is Hamilton Street, which leads to Church Square. Along this street are a few banks, but no buildings of any real distinction. The banking premises include the Halifax, erected around 1870 in a French Renaissance style. Peddie & Kinnear designed the former Britannia branch in 1856, and the Woolwich dates from around 1860. Off the square in Montgomerie Street is the prominent North Parish Church, distinguished by its 150-feet-tall spire, the highest in the county. This was erected in 1883–4 to plans of William G. Rowan at a cost of £4,000. It is a fine Gothic building in red sandstone. On the south side of the square is St Andrew's Church, erected in 1870 to plans by Clarke & Bell. This church is adorned with pinnacles and a spire. In the Square is the Hugh MacCubbin fountain, presented in 1911.

The Avenue starts with the police station, erected in 1923 to plans of A. C. Thomson. The Avenue was created around 1820 to be the residence of the better-off residents of the town. There are some fine Georgian and Victorian houses here, in a mix of styles. The Avenue continues in a south-easterly direction, passing the Davidson Cottage Hospital. This was gifted to the burgh in 1921 by the Davidson family in memory of their parents. The building is an attractive grey-stone structure, designed by Watson, Salmond & Gray. Further along this road is Girvan Academy, a substantial building.

Knockcushan Street heads west from the crossroads, making its way towards the harbour. The street gets its name from a low hill, formerly the hill of justice from 1186 until 1639, which is now occupied by a public garden and aviary. Here is a small memorial recollecting the fact that Robert the Bruce is said to have held court here in 1328. The council offices were built in the nineteenth century in an Italian style.

Girvan harbour is located in a widening of the mouth of the Water of Girvan. Apart from the wharves, there is little more than a timber jetty and the pier, heading out to the lighthouse. The harbour was rebuilt in 1869–70 and extended in 1881–3 at a cost of £80,000. Girvan is still a popular port for landing fish, and pleasure craft make it their base. A lifeboat station is situated on the slopes of the harbour side.

The strange building on the side of the harbour is a sewage pumping station, erected in 1991. It is adorned with carvings of maritime objects. The leisure pool is located in a modern, but unattractive block on the harbour side. This was erected in 1972 to plans of Cowie Torry & Partners. Here also are a few shops. The boating pond lies to the south of here, and there are swings and chutes to entertain young children.

Girvan's main street is known as Dalrymple Street. It strikes south from the major crossroads and here can be found the main shops and services of a rural town. The King's Arms Hotel is a former coaching establishment. The Chalmers Arcade stands on the site of the former Chalmers Free Church.

Girvan: the harbour

The MacKechnie Institute is located on the corner of Dalrymple Street and Ailsa Street West. It was designed by James MacKissack and erected in 1887–8. The building is a mix of styles, including baronial, Renaissance and Jacobean. Robert and Thomas MacKechnie donated around £6,500 to the burgh, £3,000 of which was used to build the institute. Here can be found a small museum, dedicated to the Girvan and south Carrick areas. On display are various natural history items, including birds and rocks, and there is room for a changing exhibition. The bank premises include the Royal Bank, erected in 1863 to plans of David MacGibbon, the noted architectural historian; the Bank of Scotland dates from 1879, and the Clydesdale Bank is of 1910.

In Ailsa Street East is the Baptist Church, erected in 1960 to replace an earlier building destroyed by fire. This street becomes North Park Avenue, the houses overlooking the Victory Park. This was gifted to the burgh in 1920 by the Dalrymple-Hamiltons to commemorate the victory in the Great War.

At the junction of Dalrymple Street with Wesley Road the Methodist Church can be found. This was constructed in 1902 to plans by Watson & Salmond, a fine building, seemingly all roof, built in the Arts & Crafts style. Between Wesley and Wreck roads, behind the shops of Dalrymple Street, is the former Girvan Academy building. This was a fine example of 1930s styling, complete with drum towers, long glazed panels and a flat roof, designed by William Cowie & Torry. The design began in 1938 but work was halted by the outbreak of war and it was not executed until 1948–55.

After the Duff Street/Wreck Road crossroads, Dalrymple Street changes its name to Glendoune Street. Here the street is lined with smaller cottages, many of which were built by the weavers who made Girvan their home. The street continues south to the roundabout on the southern edge of town, where the A714 and A77 meet. In Piedmont Street, off Glendoune Street, is St John's Episcopal Church, erected in 1859 to plans of Alexander G. Thomson. Partially erected might be more accurate, for the church has never been completed. The nave was put up in 1857–9, but the proposed transepts were not built, the adjoining arches filled with concrete. The tower was added in 1911 to plans of James Chalmers, but again this terminates abruptly. Inside can be seen a sixteenth century chancel screen, originally incorporated in an Italian church.

Kirkpatrick and Henrietta streets, one the continuation of the other, form another main route through the town. This route passes the Doune cemetery, opened in 1861. Interred here is William Jackson, composer of 'The Bonnie Lass o' Ballochmyle' and 'The Dear Little Shamrock'. At one point the street has an open area of grassland to the west, or shore, side, which is Stair Park. In the centre is the burgh war memorial, a large obelisk designed by James A. Morris in 1922.

At the corner of Henrietta and Duncan streets is the South Parish Church, a plain building of 1842, erected as a chapel of ease. In 1875 it was raised to quoad sacra status. Further north along the street is the Roman Catholic Church of the Sacred Hearts of Jesus and Mary, with St Joseph's Convent alongside. The Gothic-style church was erected in 1860–5. Stevenson & Ferguson added the modern entrance porch in 1959. The stained glass is contemporaneous with the original building. The convent dates from 1890 and was extended in 1908. The Roman Catholic school, Sacred Heart Primary, is located in the former Doune Public School of 1874, erected to plans of John Murdoch. Girvan Primary was opened in 1912 as the town's High School, William Cowie being the architect. The building is a Renaissance structure in red sandstone.

Girvan promenade heads south from the harbour to the south end of the town, where there is a stretch of grassland known as Ainslie Park between the houses and the sea.

The area south of Victory Park, bounded by Coalpots Road – which forms an eastern bypass of sorts around Girvan – is occupied by an extensive housing estate. Yet here among the modern houses can be found places of interest, for Mote Hill Road commemorates the motte hill that still exists here. The road has to take a wide arc around the hill, which rises above the surrounding land. On Doune Knoll, which rises between Piedmont Road and Glendoune Street, there was a further earthwork. It has been said that you can hardly dig your garden in the Girvan area without disturbing some form of archaeological site. When the houses at Todd Street were being built in April 1961 a Bronze Age burial site was discovered. This was excavated and various burial pits containing urns were found. Numerous other sites have been discovered in later construction work throughout the district.

The present Girvan Academy occupies the site of the ancient Ballochtoul Castle, which was the home of the Boyds, owners of the barony. The castle was five storeys in height, but there was no inter-connecting stair. On the opposite side of the railway from the Academy was the Carrick District and Girvan Burgh Combination Hospital, which was used for infectious diseases. This has been demolished.

Glendoune House is located in the woods at the south-east side of Girvan, at the foot of the Doune Burn's glen. The house was erected around 1800 for Spencer Boyd of Penkill, supposedly on the site of a monastic settlement. Ownership passed to George Kirkpatrick Young around 1846 and he added the three storey Italianate tower to one side of the old block. A second tower for the other side was planned, but never built. The walled garden survives, as does a Victorian stable block. In the grounds is an ancient tree, supposedly planted by Mary Queen of Scots. At Low Troweir to the north of Glendoune is a large mound known as Troweir Mote, perhaps some form of hill fort.

From the old kirkyard at Old Street, Vicarton Street strikes east, lined with attractive cottages dating from around 1840. At the east end of the street is Girvan railway station, opened in 1877 and still functioning. The buildings were rebuilt after 1946. Before the present station was opened, there was an earlier station behind the graveyard, for the Stranraer line was not opened until 1877, but the line into Girvan harbour was opened in 1860. This was later converted to a goods station but has been closed for many years. On the other side of the railway is Hamilton Park, home of Girvan Amateur Football Club.

Almost at the large roundabout at the junction of the A77 with the B734 is a roadside memorial commemorating Alexander Ross, a special constable who was shot and killed in a riot between Catholics and Orangemen that took place on 12 July 1831. He was later buried in the old churchyard. His killer, Samuel Waugh, was captured at Suie Toll and later hanged in Ayr on 19 January 1832.

On the north side of the Water of Girvan from Girvan itself is a small community that has the name Newton Kennedy. This was estab-lished by the Kennedys of Dunure as a possible rival to the larger town on the south side of the river, but it was never as successful. Today the community has little more than a few older rows of cottages, and the Victorian terrace of Golf Course Road, built at the time when Girvan was noted as a holiday resort, as opposed to a major port. The golf course extends north from here, the 18-hole course being 5,064 yards in length, par 64. The boat-building yard of Alexander Noble & Sons lies on the north side of the harbour. Fishing boats and other craft have been built here since 1946, when the yard was established.

The countryside north of Girvan is home to many other antiquities, some of which are buried below the present soil levels. Beyond the site of the Bridge Mill is Girvan Mains Farm, a name that is important in the early history of Carrick. The Kennedys of Girvan Mains were involved in many of the clan feuds that existed. They were granted a baronetcy in 1672 but it became extinct shortly after. The name Girvan Mains would indicate to some extent that there was a Girvan Castle at one time. On the lands of Girvan Mains is the site of a Roman Camp, the evidence for which is usually only seen by aerial photography. North of the farm itself is the Gallow Hill, the place where the Kennedy's dispensed their justice. The A77 road heads north from Girvan Mains, keeping to the landward side of the raised beach. After Girvan Mains the first farm passed is Chapeldonan. This is named after the ancient chapel of St Donan, the fragmentary remains of which can be found in the field north of the farm. It had a font at the door and a sacristy behind.

East of Chapeldonan in the Ladywell valley are nine large bonded warehouses, used by the Grant's whisky company. The distillery is located south of the warehouses, on the B741, Maybole road. This was initially erected in 1963–73 to plans prepared by Cowan & Linn. The distillery produces grain spirit, which is mixed with malts brought from highland distilleries and blended to form a variety of whiskies, most notably Grant's Standfast. A number of other spirits are produced at this plant, including vodka. There are some other industries in the Grangestone Industrial Estate, where the whisky distillery is located.

East of Grangestone is the Trochrague estate, anciently a Boyd seat. The present mansion is a Gothic castle, part of which dates from 1803, but which was extended later. The original Georgian block was added to in 1883 in the baronial style, and again in 1910–23 when a mock tower house was added to plans by J. J. Burnet. He was also responsible for the porte cochère. The walled garden is located east of the house, at Nether Trochrague.

The next estate east of Trochrague is Killochan, where the castle is another of Ayrshire's hidden gems. According to an inscription over the original entrance door, 'This work was begun the 1 of Merche 1586 be

Ihone Cathcart of Carltovn and Helene Wallace his spouse. The name of the Lord is ane strang tovr and the rytheovs in thair trovblis rinnis into it and findith refuge.' The tower is L-shaped in plan, with a large circular tower on the outward angle, and a square stair-tower (with entrance) on the inner. Turrets adorn the external corners. Lower extensions to the castle were made in the eighteenth century. The lands of Killochan were granted to the Cathcarts in the fourteenth century, King Robert I granted a charter of confirmation in 1324. The Cathcarts were granted a baronetcy (styled of Carleton, their ancestral tower) in 1703, and the family held Killochan until 1954. To the west of Killochan Castle is the Baron's Stone of Killochan, a massive boulder that is thought to weigh thirty-seven tons. Composed of granite, it was dumped here by a glacier flowing from above Loch Doon. It later formed the justice hill of the Barons of Killochan.

Craighead Hill lies north of Killochan. The hill is not particularly high, being only 551 feet above sea level, but it rises steadily above Girvan vale. On its eastern slopes are a number of old quarries, originally used to obtain limestone for the adjacent lime works. These have long-since closed, but the quarries are popular with geologists, for they contain many interesting features, including fossils.

There was at one time an important coal-mining industry in the immediate area, a remote outlier of the Ayrshire coalfield. Old bings associated with the Killochan Pit are located in the northern woods of Bargany estate, next to the railway line, from where a branch led into the pithead buildings. At one time there were 160 miners employed here, but the pit closed in 1967. A number of old shafts can be found in the Kilgrammie Plantation, which lies north of the B741 and railway. Kilgrammie is a small clachan of cottages located on the north side of the plantation, built along a low ridge. At the foot of the brae, where the road passes beneath the railway, was Dailly station, which opened in 1869.

*

The B741 strikes south and makes its way to Dailly, located on the opposite side of the Girvan. En route it passes the remains of an old coal mine. The Dailly Bridge is dated 1873. Dailly is a former mining village, enlarged and rebuilt after 1825. The parish of Dailly, or Dalmaolkeran as it was once known, extends to 18,078 acres. At one time the parish of Barr was part of it, but this was removed in 1653.

Just short of the Dailly Bridge is a road heading into the Brunston Castle Golf Club. This is a modern course, designed by Donald Steel, and built on lands that were part of the Bargany estate. The 18-hole course is 6,662 yards in length, par 72, and a modern clubhouse overlooks the course. Here also are a number of houses, built as part of the development scheme.

Brunston Castle itself is an old ruin that stands on a knoll by the side of the Water of Girvan. The castle was erected in the seventeenth century by the Kennedy family, but was abandoned sometime in the eighteenth century. The castle was T-plan in style, with a stair tower centrally placed. Additions were made to the castle at a later date, but today the ruin is scanty and overgrown.

The village of Dailly was established in the 1760s as New Dailly, for there is a clachan known as Old Dailly further west. A planned village, the proposed grid was slow to fill up. Main Street is located parallel to the river, linking Dailly Bridge with Roan Bridge to the east. The street comprises of a number of old cottages, many of which date from the eighteenth century. Here also is the primary school. The war memorial is located in a small square next to the church, the fine obelisk on a stepped base being the work of James A. Morris in 1922.

The parish church is a T-plan building erected in Main Street in 1776. It is Georgian in style and has a rather distinctive tower. The manse is located off Linfern Road. The Revd John Thomson (d. 1799) had two sons born here, Thomas (1768–1852), a noted lawyer and antiquarian, and Revd John Thomson, better known as 'Thomson of Duddingston' (1778–1840). The latter succeeded his father as minister in 1800, but studied art under Alexander Nasmyth and became a successful painter in his own right. The kirkyard has a number of interesting old stones. Here lies John Brown, who was trapped for twenty-three days in Kilgrammie Pit when a rock fall blocked his exit. A rescue party managed to get him out, but he died after three days on 3 November 1835, aged 66. The modern cemetery is located up The Loaning, next to Upper Roan Bridge. At one time there was also a Free Church in Dailly. Back Street runs parallel with Main Street, part of the original feu scheme. The rest of the village comprises modern council houses in Hadyard Terrace and elsewhere.

On the north side of the Girvan from Dailly is Dalquharran Castle. There are in fact two castles, for standing on a knoll by a bend of the river is the old castle, which dates from the fifteenth century, and further up the hill is the eighteenth-century castle, sadly now also in ruins. The Kennedy family built the old castle, which has a vaulted ground floor. The tower is the oldest part, the long wing and round tower added around 1679.

New Dalquharran Castle was built in 1785 to plans provided by

Robert Adam. The client was Thomas Kennedy of Dunure, who had married Adam's niece. It has been claimed that this grand country seat was every bit as magnificent as Culzean, and that the interior furnishings were even more sumptuous. There was even a circular drawing room and library included within the large central bastion tower, which is similar to that at Culzean. The castle was extended in 1881 to plans of Wardrop & Reid for F. T. R. Kennedy. Unfortunately, the castle was too big for the family and in 1936 it was converted into a youth hostel. The hostel was later closed and in 1970 the roof of the mansion was removed, leaving it to succumb to the elements. Nevertheless, the massive structure is still an impressive sight in Girvan dale. The new castle stands on the slopes of the little knoll known as Cairn Hill. This gets its name from the prehistoric cairn that can be seen on its summit. Fragmentary remains of a third castle can be found in the immediate vicinity. Lochmodie Castle stood by the side of the Quarrelhill Burn, the little that can be seen of it now being lost in the lower part of Mossgennoch Wood. Today, there is a row of cottages by the roadside.

At Dalquharran Mains was another coal mine in the Dailly coalfield. This was Maxwell Pit, owned by South Ayrshire Collieries Ltd, which operated until 1973. On the opposite side of the railway from the old pit is Wallacetown, a little clachan of houses by the roadside. At one time there was a tile works here, located by the side of the Burninghill Wood. This wood got its name from an incident in December 1849 when a pit here collapsed, and the coal dust caught fire. The heat began to burn the surrounding coal, and the fire continued to rage underground for fifty years. On the surface the steam and smoke from the fire was often seen percolating through the rocks and soil.

At Wallacetown a minor road leaves the valley bottom and climbs up the hillside, passing through the Kilcase Wood before emerging again on the high moors of central Carrick. The road can actually be followed over the hill to Kirkoswald. Above the road, on the Kirk Hill, is an old earthwork known as the Plantation Bank. This is a circular structure that may have been some form of hill fort.

Beyond High Newlands, standing next to an old road that linked Maybole with the Girvan valley, is the Drummochreen Cairn. Drummochreen Farm lies lower down the valley, but an even older building lies next to the Water of Girvan. This was a sixteenth-century castle, owned by the MacAlexanders. Half-a-mile upstream are the ruins of Drummochreen Mill.

At the Captain's Bridge, below Drummochreen Farm, is an ancient earthwork that is thought to be a dun. Drumburle House dates from around 1770 and is a fine small mansion that incorporates a large arched-window. At one time the Hunter Blairs owned the estate. In the grounds is a small doocot. East of Baldrennan Burn one finds oneself in a distant part of Kirkoswald parish. Here is the little clachan known as the Roan of Craigoch. At one time there was a station here, known as Kilkerran. The station opened in 1869. There is also a mill here. In the Glenshalloch Wood, which clothes the hillside to the north, can be found remains of old coal workings. By the side of the road, just short of the parish boundary, was an acid works.

The clachan of Ruglen lies on the south side of the railway, off a connecting route that links the north Girvan vale road with the southern. The Drumgirnan Bridge over the Girvan dates from 1799 and can be crossed, bringing one to the Kilkerran estate, a gatehouse to which lies on the south side of the bridge. In the low-lying fields by the side of the river is a private airstrip. The B741 crosses the Water of Girvan by two other bridges, the Hamilton Bridge of 1825 and the Aird Bridge of 1817. Before these last two bridges were erected the public road went through the centre of the Kilkerran estate, and much closer to the house.

Kilkerran is a large estate, long owned by the Fergusson family, who were created Baronets of Kilkerran in 1703. The 1st baronet was an eminent advocate; his successor was a Lord of Session, taking his title Kilkerran. The present mansion dates from around 1730, having been erected by Sir James Fergusson, 2nd Baronet, Lord Kilkerran. His eighth son, George, was created Lord Hermand. The architect may have been James Smith. The house has been extended a number of times, including in 1818 when James Gillespie Graham added the bowed wings, and in 1854 when David Bryce added the billiard room. It was recently restored following a serious fire in April 1994. This is not the real Kilkerran, for the old castle of that name lies further south, hidden up the Lindsayston glen. The present Kilkerran incorporates the old tower house of Barclanachan, where the countryside was more pleasant and fertile than the steep gullies of the old Kilkerran, resulting in the family deciding to move their seat here.

The policies of the estate are extensive, and are finely wooded. At the east end is the house of Ladyburn, at one time the dower house but now a private hotel. The Lady Burn flows down through the beautiful Lady Glen, through which a number of woodland walks can be made. The name comes from the old Lady Chapel, the ruins of which are perched on the south side of the glen. This chapel dates from pre-Reformation times. The walled garden at Kilkerran is now a caravan and camping site. Brown & Wardrop erected the stable block in 1875 to their plans. Some of the lodges were the work of Gillespie Graham, the landscape garden being designed by John Hay of Edinburgh in 1814.

On the moor south of Kilkerran are some old quarries, used for extracting limestone from the northern slopes of the Barony Hill. The private drive through Kilkerran's policies returns to the B741 at the Woodend Bridge. Just beyond this a minor road strikes south, ultimately reaching Barr and the Stinchar valley. The first farm on the left is Whitehill, where, in a field south-east of the farmhouse is an ancient burial ground known as Machar-a-kill. This has connections with St Macarius, and within the walled enclosure can be found some ancient carved stones, including a baptismal font.

Just short of the Lindsayston Burn is a farm road, striking uphill past Drumwhirn. This leads towards the ancient Kilkerran Castle, little more than a gable of masonry perched high above the Lindsayston Burn. However, it is possible to note that the ground floor was vaulted and that there were three floors above it. The Fergussons erected this old tower around 1500. In the glen below the castle are some impressive waterfalls. Further up the stream is an ancient earthwork known as the Mote Knowe. This may have been the site of an even earlier stronghold of the Fergusson clan. By the side of the B741, near Moorston, is a little roadside memorial recording that 'John Aitken died here, 2d Jany. 1861'. He lived at Midton nearby and was employed to maintain the local roads. It is thought that he died at this spot of a heart attack at the age of 70.

The road returns into Dailly. If the southern road in the valley is followed, it soon enters the Bargany estate woodlands at Maxwellston Farm. North of the road at Maxwellston, on part of Brunston Castle golf course, is an ancient mound mostly covered in trees. What this was is not exactly known. Maxwellston Hill lies on the southern side of the road, climbing steeply to 1,030 feet above sea level. This height so near the coast was an ideal place to defend, and consequently the remains of a hill fort crown the summit. This measures around 275 feet by 230 feet. Two ramparts surround the central enclosure, rising to a height of around four feet. They may never have been much higher, for it has been speculated that this fort was unfinished. On the north-west side of the fort the ramparts are missing, again hinting that the fort was abandoned before it was complete. East of Maxwellston Hill is the greater height of Hadyard Hill, the highest point of which is known as Pheelie and which is 1,069 feet above sea level.

The Bargany policies are extensive, and the gardens are attractive. These are open to the public throughout the summer months, and here the visitor can delight in the display of azaleas and rhododendrons in season. The little lochan can be walked round, a peaceful spot in which to contemplate. The Weaver's Glen has a path through it built as a job creation scheme for unemployed weavers. Crossing the Girvan below the house is the Duke's Bridge, a balustraded structure of 1756, later named in honour of the Duke de Coigny who married Henrietta Dalrymple-Hamilton. The estate was later owned by the Earl of Stair, but passed to his second son, and remains in Dalrymple-Hamilton ownership.

Bargany House is an old building, originally erected in 1681 but incorporating decorative masonry from its sixteenth-century predecessor. The house was remodelled in 1747, the entrance being moved to the north-east, but it was returned to the courtyard on the south-east when the mansion was extended in 1845–6 by William Burn. The house was eventually abandoned somewhat in the 1970s. It was acquired by a private trust and was restored to plans by Patrick Lorimer in 1988–91, now forming a rather grand country-house. Bargany was anciently a Kennedy seat, and the Kennedys of Bargany appear prominently throughout Carrick history. The estate was later acquired by the Dalrymple-Hamilton family, who still own it, the mansion and a few acres around it having been sold to save it from demolition.

A cottage on the estate was the birthplace in the eighteenth century of two poets of local renown. The cottage, which stood at the top of the Butler's Brae on the north side of the Girvan, no longer exists. Hew Ainslie (1792–1878) emigrated to the United States where he became a builder of breweries. His most acclaimed piece of work was 'The Rover of Loch Ryan', which was regarded as the best Scottish sea-song. Hamilton Paul (1773–1854) became an assistant editor of the *Ayr Advertiser* then a minister, though his verses are regarded as rather poor. He is buried at Broughton churchyard in Peeblesshire, where he ministered.

The village of Old Dailly lies by the side of the Penwhapple Burn. The ancient ruined church can still be seen in its graveyard, surrounded by many old stones. The church probably dates from the seventeenth century, but this occupies an even older site. It was abandoned in 1766 when the church was moved to New Dailly. Within the kirk can be seen the Lifting Stanes, two ancient boulders weighing around 300 pounds each that were used as a test of strength by the local lads. Also known as the Charter or Blue Stones, in recent years they have been anchored down to prevent them from being stolen.

The kirkyard has many old stones of interest. Adjoining the kirk are the mausoleums and burial grounds of the Boyds, Cathcarts and Kennedys. On the wall of the Kennedy mausoleum but in the Boyd plot is a memorial to William Bell Scott (1811–90), a respected artist. Scott was born in Edinburgh and trained as an engraver. He had an interest in writing poetry, his first volume being published in 1838. He became known for his murals, the work at Wallington Hall in Northumbria being his most notable. In 1859 he met Alice Boyd of Penkill, who became his lifelong companion. He painted the murals at Penkill between 1865–8. He died at Penkill on 22 November 1890. There is also a number of Covenanters buried at Old Dailly. In the Mote Wood, west of Old Dailly, is a prehistoric mound, the origin of which is obscure. Some maps simply note it as a mound, others claim it to be a burial cairn, and yet the name of the wood would lead us to think it was a motte hill. West of here is Camregan Farm. In the little Camregan Glen are the remains of Camregan Castle, little more than a mound and some boulders. Within a mile or so we return back to Girvan.

The B734 climbs south from Old Dailly, following the glen of the Penwhapple Burn. Just over half a mile from the village is a small gate-house forming the entry into Penkill Castle. This is one of Ayrshire's finest little castles, perched high above the gullies formed by two minor streams. The castle, which has a square shape, was built in the sixteenth century and extended to the east in 1628. By the nineteenth century the tower had fallen into ruins, but in 1857 the building was inherited by Spencer Boyd and the work of restoration begun. It was at this time that the rather fanciful drum-tower was added, to plans by Alexander George Thomson, its parapet rather too large to look original, but at least the building was saved. The castle became the haunt of the pre-Raphaelite art set, which loved to come here and live in relative solitude. Indeed, so quiet did the owner wish this place to be that it was said that he insisted that it was not named on Ordnance Survey maps. Spencer and Alice Boyd, his sister, were friends of William Bell Scott, and through him invited many of the pre-Raphaelite artists to Penkill. Among these were Dante Gabriel Rossetti, William Morris and Christina Rossetti.

Inside the castle are a number of fine murals, painted by William Bell Scott, including the 'King's Quair' on the spiral stair. The outside of the building, facing the courtyard is the more decorative of the fronts, adorned by the tower, the chapel building and a large carved owl. The sides facing the gorge are simple and plain, little more than high walls of masonry. The gardens are sometimes open to the public. In the deep glen below the castle is a Covenanter's Cave, latterly used by the artists and poets associated with Penkill, notably Dante Gabriel Rossetti, who wrote some sonnets within it.

The Penwhapple Burn rises in the Penwhapple Reservoir, used to store water for Girvan and the surrounding area. A short dam erected in 1935 creates a largish loch. Above Penwhapple dam is the Green Hill, on which is a lower knoll known as the Spy Knowe. On the summit of the latter is a Bronze Age burial cairn. Another can be found on the low summit north of Balcletchie Farm, on the south side of Penwhapple Glen.

*

From near Penkill a minor road passes down through Penwhapple Glen to the Penwhapple Bridge, before climbing up on the south side of the valley. This road leads through the vale of Assel to Pinmore and the Stinchar dale. In the valley is the large whinstone Tormitchell Quarry.

Between here and Girvan is a range of hills which, though they are of no great height, seem to be larger than they are due to their proximity to the sea. The highest summit is Troweir Hill, at 971 feet, but Saugh Hill is virtually as tall. There are two prehistoric remains to be found on Saugh Hill, which is the nearest of the two summits to Girvan. One of these is a burial cairn, found on a western projection. The other is a tumulus, located on the summit. An ancient cairn also crowns Troweir Hill, but this has been altered so much over the years by visitors to the summit that little of the Bronze Age survives. To the south of Troweir Hill is a high pass, through which an ancient hill path makes its way. This passes by the tiny Laggan Loch, little more than a large pool of water.

The path from Glendoune up to the Laggan Loch passes below the Dow Hill, a low knoll on the side of Laggan Hill. This summit is crowned by an ancient fort and dun, the summit of the hill being steep and rocky on a few sides, adding to its defensive properties. This hilltop is 522 feet above sea level, but most of the ramparts have been robbed or flattened. The central area may have been around fifty feet in diameter, indicative of a dun. The external fort measured around 130 feet by 50 feet, the east neck of land having further ramparts.

The A714 leaves the southern end of Girvan and winds uphill to cross over to the Stinchar valley. Behind the low Shalloch Hill is a cemetery. The road passes by the Glendrissaig Reservoir, created to store water for Girvan. A second reservoir is located further south, at Pinmacher. The road crosses the railway at the head of the glen, but here the railway takes a route below the hill, passing through a tunnel 500 yards long. This was excavated in 1876. To the south of Pinmore is the Kinclaer Viaduct, where the railway crosses a small valley by means of eleven arches. The main road has to follow the contours of the ground, and in consequence passes through the viaduct in two directions. On the north side of the tunnel is the large Dinvin motte. This is perhaps better described as a large hill fort, around which are a number of concentric ditches.

The road and railway descends to Pinmore, a tiny clachan formed where there was at one time a railway station. The station opened in 1876 to serve a dispersed community, but was closed in the sixties. Similarly, Assel Primary School no longer functions. The road from Penkill past Tormitchell meets the A714 here. Beyond Pinmore one enters the Stinchar valley, which will be covered in the following chapter.

From Pinmore a minor road crosses the remote country around Knocklaugh before dropping down through the valley of the Lendal to the sea. Near High Letterpin is a large prehistoric settlement, the remains of which can be made out on the ground. The Water of Lendal is not a particularly large stream. It rises near to Loch Lochton and flows steadily down through the shallow valley to Lendalfoot. On the way it passes Lendal Lodge. Knockdaw Farm lies south of the water, and here are the fragmentary remains of Knockdaw Castle.

Beyond the Cundry Mill Bridge is a small caravan site, reminding us that we are back at the coast, and in an area much frequented by day-trippers and holidaymakers. Lendalfoot is a small village comprising a few cottages at the foot of the Water of Lendal. At one time there was a school here, but this is now used as an outdoor centre. South of the original village are rows of holiday homes, known as Carleton Terrace. Many of these were originally wooden buildings, but over the years most have been rebuilt or built around to form more permanent buildings. The first houses date from 1933 when the Hamilton estates offered feus on which to build holiday homes. Carleton Fishery lies just to the south west of the terrace. The fishery was built in 1832 according to a date stone built into the wall. More holiday huts and buildings can be found further along the coast at The Whilk.

The name Carleton comes from Carleton Castle, the ruins of which can be seen on the hillside south of Lendalfoot. This tower was a Cathcart seat, and it was erected in the fifteenth century. The tower is now in ruins, one corner of the building collapsing. At one time a walled enclosure with smaller towers enclosed the promontory between the streams. There is a baronetcy in the name Cathcart of Carleton, but by the time this was granted the family were resident in Killochan Castle.

On the opposite side of the road from Little Carleton Farm can be seen a motte hill, probably the predecessor of settlement in this area.

Below Carleton is a memorial standing on a low knoll next to the Lendal. This commemorates Charles Berry (1872–1909), who lived nearby. He was a noted naturalist in the area, and was a keen ornithologist. He was often the first to record the arrival of the wheatear to Scotland each summer, and could predict within a few days when it was due. Berry was buried in the churchyard at Colmonell, where his gravestone is adorned with a carved bird in a nest and a plant climbing over a rough-hewn rock to represent geology.

Carleton and Balsalloch hills rise steeply to the south of Lendalfoot, attaining a height of 613 feet at the latter, although they are really the same hill. On Carleton Hill are some ancient earthworks, which were perhaps some form of fort.

The road back to Girvan from Lendalfoot has to make its way between the hills and the sea. Just north of Lendalfoot is a roadside memorial commemorating Archibald Hamilton and his crew, who came from Kings Cross on Arran. Their ship was wrecked on 11 September 1711 and their lives lost. The bodies were washed up on the shore here. Little else is known about them.

For a mile to the north of Lendalfoot the road crosses a raised beach, the stumps of former sea stacks abandoned in fields of grass. Near the Pinbain Bridge the old road began to climb the hillside, leaving the coast behind. This route crossed the slopes of Pinbain Hill before dropping past Kilranny to rejoin the present route near Ardwell. By the roadside is the Kittyfrist Well, a natural spring used by travellers to slake their thirst. In 1831 T. F. Kennedy of Dalquharran decided to create a new route, lower down the hillside. This had to make its way through a narrow gap in the cliffs, and from the builder of the road this was named Kennedy's Pass. This road has been widened by blasting many times over the years, so that now Kennedy's Pass is little more than a name by the roadside.

To the north of Ardwell is Ardmillan, where an old castle stood, built by the Kennedy family in the sixteenth century. The castle was a tower of three storeys with unusual circular towers to one side. In the eighteenth century the castle was extended to create a Georgian mansion, but from 1910 its fortunes began to wane when the castle suffered a fire. The Georgian wing was rebuilt in a baronial guise for the owner, Peter MacCallum Lang. A second major fire occurred in 1972, killing the lady owner. The remains were eventually demolished in 1991. Today a caravan site occupies the grounds. The only indication that there was at one time a castle and estate here is the former gatehouse, a neo-baronial building erected in 1908.

The Kennedys owned Ardmillan until 1658 when an heiress married James Craufurd of Baidland. A later James Craufurd (1805–76) was created Lord Ardmillan in 1855. A path behind the site of the castle climbs through the woods and up to Main Hill. Here can be found the remains of a memorial commemorating Archibald Craufurd (d. 1878).

He was an active soldier, serving in India and taking part in the capture of the Cape of Good Hope in 1795. His wife made many benefactions in the Girvan area.

The Byne Hill lies north of the memorial. This is Girvan's peak, and dominates views of the south end of the town. The summit is 702 feet above the sea, and is crowned by a viewpoint pillar. The Byne Hill is composed of gabbro, an igneous rock that is magnetic.

The Ailsa Craig lies off the shores of Ayrshire, ten miles out from Girvan. The island is part of Dailly parish, which is an unusual situation, considering that Dailly has no shoreline of its own. According to local legend, the Devil lifted a massive scoop of rock out of Dailly parish and hurled it into the firth, creating the island, thus explaining the situation. The island measures approximately one mile in diameter, and rises steeply to 1,110 feet in height. Most of the island is surrounded by cliffs, the Barestack being 625 feet tall, making it one of Britain's highest and most spectacular. Many of the cliffs are columnar. Given its impressive physical characteristics, it is hardly surprising that Ailsa Craig is one of Ayrshire's most recognisable places.

On the east hillside of Ailsa Craig is Ailsa Castle, a small tower-house that probably dates from 1597 when Thomas Hamilton was appointed keeper of the island. The ground floor is vaulted, and a stair in the east end of the castle rises up to the first floor. This is also vaulted and comprises two chambers. A spiral stair climbs higher to the second floor, the roof of which has long gone. A trap door at the foot of the main stair gives the only means of access to the vaulted basement. There is a tiny enclosure on the north side of the castle. The castle is thought to have been erected as a preventative measure against pirates. The Castle Well is located on the hillside above the castle.

Ailsa Craig has always been something of a problem for ships, often appearing suddenly out of the mist. On the eastern shore, where the only stretch of level ground can be found, is the lighthouse, erected in 1883–6 by D. & T. Stevenson. This is thirty-five feet in height and has been automated since 1990. Here also are the former lighthouse keepers' cottages and a gasworks. The latter was used to drive the two foghorns that existed at the north and south end of the island. There have been many shipwrecks around the island. These include the *Duke of Edinburgh* (1870), *Dreamland* (1878), *Nith* (1879), *Clan Campbell* (1881), *Austria* (1884), *Lincoln* (1888), *Pennon* (1889), *Eliza* (1892), *Frederick Cornelis* (1901), *Earl Mulgrave* (1903), *Beta* (1910), *Walrus* (1910), *Stars* (1912) and *Margareta* (1952). This last vessel was subsequently salvaged and repaired.

The Ailsa Craig has been used for quarrying granite for many years. The stone is finer than most granites and was in great demand for the manufacture of curling stones. Quarrying has mainly taken place at the north end of the island, to where a small railway line ran from near the lighthouse. Although quarrying has long-since ceased, pieces of granite are still taken from the island to make the bases for curling stones at Mauchline (*see* Chapter 9).

# 21

# Barr, Colmonell and Ballantrae

THE RIVER STINCHAR DRAINS a considerable area of Carrick. The source of the river can be found on the slopes of Caerloch Dhu of Shalloch on Minnoch (mentioned in Chapter 19) and the area around the headwaters have been described there. Our tour of the Stinchar basin will commence at Balloch, where the Stinchar emerges from the Carrick Forest and begins its more open course, passing through attractive dales where farms occupy the valley floor, sheep graze on the surrounding hillsides and the high moors are generally afforested.

The Stinchar Falls are located within the forest, and form an attractive destination for a few forest walks. The falls are located just below where the Linfern Loch Burn meets the Stinchar. Soon the river leaves the forest behind and enters the flatter ground at Aldinna. The hillsides to either side are afforested, and the little streams that drop down into the river have a number of smaller waterfalls on them. One of these streams, the Loch Burn, drains the Aldinna Loch, which lies on the open moors north of Rowantree Toll.

Above the White Row is the Whiterow Scaurs, a rocky outcrop on the slopes of the Craig of Dalwine, a prominent hill hereabouts. The highest point the public can drive to in the valley is to the North Balloch Bridge, where North and South Balloch farms lie on opposite sides of the river. The name Balloch derives from the Gaelic, *bealach*, meaning 'pass', and there are two main hill crossings here. To the south the public road climbs steadily through the Nick of the Balloch, reaching a high point of 1,276 feet. The route begins by passing Pinvalley Farm, in a field of which is an ancient homestead. On entering the forest the road passes by a chambered cairn. Another burial cairn can be seen on the summit of Pinbreck Hill, which rises to 1,637 feet on the east side of the road. The public road crosses the Witch's Bridge, said to have connections with Ayr's Maggie Osborne, and enters the Nick of the Balloch proper. Just beyond the top of the pass is the natural spring known as the Brandy Well. On the west side of the pass is Rowantree Hill and Craigenreoch, the latter 1,854 feet in height. The northern slopes of these hills are drained by the Balloch Burn, which tumbles over the Linn of the Darkness waterfall at one point. The Haggis Hill dominates the west side of its glen.

From North Balloch a minor road heads over the De'il's Elbow road to Crosshill. At Dalquhairn Farm a Bronze Age cairn can be seen in the field south of the farm. The road crosses the Dalquhairn Burn at Sally Pollock's Bridge from where it climbs steadily to the summit at 1,106 feet. From South Balloch the minor road down Stinchar vale meanders along the valley bottom, passing little cottages and the odd farm, before reaching the village of Barr. At Knockeen Farm, behind a small fir wood, is a Bronze Age cairn. A farm road strikes north from near Knockeen and crosses the Stinchar by a bridge before reaching Daljedburgh Farm, where there is a memorial commemorating a farmer's wife who was buried here. Daljedburgh Hill rises steeply behind, attaining a height of 1,227 feet. Rock outcrops break through its southern slopes.

Beyond Pynannot Farm a minor road joins the Barr Road across the Milton Bridge. This road climbs steeply over the hill to Delamford Farm, above Dailly. Glengennet farmhouse is a considerable building, dating from the early nineteenth-century. The road climbs steeply up the ridge of Milton Hill, and at the head of the Milton Burn gorge passes over a cattle grid and enters Delamford ground. In the forest plantation to the west of the road is a burial cairn.

From the Milton Bridge it is a short journey of one mile, passing Upper and Nether Barr farms, before the village of Barr is reached. Locally this is known as 'The Barr'. Barr is the centre of an upland parish of 55,190 acres. The village is tiny, however, and has never really grown to any extent. The parish church is located at the north side of the bridge over the Water of Gregg. Built in 1878 in the Early Gothic style to plans of Allan Stevenson, it replaced the old church that stood in the kirkyard that still exists in the centre of the village. The older church dated from 1652. The former Angus Memorial Free Church dates from 1891–2; it was designed by Alexander Petrie and is adorned by a tower. This building is now a private house. Barr's old kirkyard is reached through the Dods memorial gateway and it has a number of interesting old stones including the graves of a few Covenanters. Outside the kirkyard is a memorial fountain to John MacTaggart who was killed at Bloemfontein in the Boer War in 1901.

Barr's centre is located at the junction of Stinchar, Changue and Glengennet roads. Here can be found an attractive row of traditional cottages. The post office is located in Glengennet Road, and the village primary school in Changue Road. The King's Arms Hotel dates from the early 1800s. John Arthur, using a style that looks slightly out of place, designed the Institute in 1913.

Changue Road is a dead end, heading up the Water of Gregg valley. Off it lies Dinmurchie Farm, birthplace of James Dalrymple (1619–95), created Viscount Stair in 1690. It was he who compiled *Institutions of*

Barr

*the Law of Scotland* in 1681, one of the most important books on Scots law ever written. A parking and picnic area is located at the edge of the Changue Plantation of the Carrick Forest, where a number of forest walks start. Here also is the beginning of the Barr to Loch Doon cycle route, which makes its way through the forests. A forest road can be followed up through the Gregg valley and into the Howe of Laggan, where two memorials can be seen. These commemorate two shepherds who were overcome by blizzards and perished on the hill. The first of these is found near to an old set of buchts (sheep pens) at the foot of the Mid Hill Burn. It commemorates Christopher MacTaggart (1893–1913). The second memorial is in the form of a cairn, and is located in a clearing of the forest near to the Lead Mine Burn. This one commemorates James MacTaggart (1888–1943). The brothers are both buried in Barr churchyard.

The Lead Mine Burn recalls the fact that lead was once worked here, but to no great extent. The burn forms the eastern side of an old hill road that once made its way across the hills here. Between Cairn and Pinbreck hills the pass is known as the Nick of Darley, and it is amazing to think that this was at one time one of the main routes from Ayrshire into Galloway. It was always a difficult route to follow, as an early map points out: 'At the Nick of Darlae & half a Mile West the Road leads on the Side of a very steep Hill, its not above two feet broad, and if you stumble you must fall almost Perpendicular six or seven Hundred Feet.' Cairn Hill is 1,578 feet in height and gets its name from the Bronze Age cairn on its summit.

The Stinchar at Barr is quite a substantial watercourse, crossed by the Stinchar Bridge at the bottom end of the village. This is a rusticated structure of 1787. On the other side is Alton Albany House, a country house located by the side of the river and surrounded to the rear by woodland. The house was erected in the 1830s but extended in 1861 to plans by John Murdoch for Henry Hughes-Onslow. The Tudoresque lodge dates from around 1860. From the Stinchar Bridge the B734 winds up the side of Auchensoul Hill, taking a route known with some justification as 'The Screws'. The B734 heads down Stinchar vale in the opposite direction from the Screws road. There are a number of sizeable farmsteads here, each with an area of good ground by the side of the river, and a high stretch of land suitable for grazing sheep. In many cases this upper ground has been partially afforested.

A minor road leads across the Stinchar to Kirkland Farm. This gets its name from the fact that the remains of Kirkdominae are located here, between Kirkland and Auchensoul. Kirkdominae was a pre-Reformation chapel that was dedicated to the Holy Trinity. The remains are fragmentary, but the site is ancient, and well renowned in local lore, for here the legendary Kirkdominae, or Kirkdamdy, Fair was held on the last Saturday of May. This no doubt started as a celebratory fair held on a saint's day, but in later years it degenerated into little more than a drunken brawl, as many fairs did. On the hillside above the ruins of the chapel is the Struil Well, an ancient water source associated with the chapel.

There are a couple of interesting objects at Balligmorrie Farm. On the low knoll that lies to the north of the steading, on the opposite side of the road, is a Bronze Age burial cairn, known as the Cairn o' Cairnwhin. South-east of the farm, on the summit of Balligmorrie Hill is a small cairn bearing the date 1960, erected by the Sloan brothers using stone taken from a bridge over the Stinchar that collapsed.

Downstream from Balligmorrie is Pinmore, where the Water of Assel joins the Stinchar. Here stood Pinmore Castle, a tower house of the sixteenth century. Pinmore was erected by the Hamilton family. The castle was gutted by fire in 1876 after which it was rebuilt and extended to plans by Allan Stevenson, but was eventually demolished in 1982. A new house occupies the site.

The B734 crosses the Stinchar by means of Pinmore Bridge, which dates from 1802 and was erected by Hugh Hamilton of Pinmore. The builders were Gilbert MacLymont, Robert Carswell and Alex Jordan. On the other side of the river the A714 is joined, making its way south from Girvan. At Holmhead is a small church by the side of the road. This is an interdenominational chapel, erected in 1878 by Hugh

Hamilton of Pinmore, using Allan Stevenson as architect, and is now owned by the Coltman Family Trust. In the kirkyard is a memorial to Captain Hugh Hamilton. From Holmhead a winding track makes its way up through the Oak Wood to High Aldons, where the remains of old quarry-workings are found.

The A714 road passes beneath the railway and arrives at Daljarrock Hotel. This building is quite old, dating from around 1750, but perhaps with an older core. Reginald Fairlie designed alterations in 1928. At one time there was even a post office here, serving the rural community. The house was struck by fire in 1986 after which many of the later additions were removed. The main road crosses the Stinchar for the first time at Daljarrock Bridge, and re-crosses the railway once more.

The railway crosses the Daljarrock Viaduct, which was erected in 1876–7. This was the second attempt at bridging the valley, for whilst the structure was being erected in 1875 a great flood washed it away. Pinwherry Station was opened at this time, but as with all the small halts on this line, it was closed in the middle of the 1960s.

The road soon reaches the junction with the B734 at Hallowchapel, where a few houses and cottages exist. A few hundred yards further on one reaches Pinwherry village, which lies on both sides of the Duisk River, near its confluence with the Stinchar. The Duisk is the main tributary of the Stinchar, and drains a wild moorland basin. Pinwherry has the ruins of an old castle. This dates from around 1596, and was built by the Kennedy family. It passed through various Kennedy hands until it came into the ownership of the chief, Earl of Carrick. The tower is L-shaped in plan, but most of the walls are today obscured by thick ivy. Nevertheless, it still rises four storeys in height and has a number of turrets and spiral staircases. The castle had been abandoned by 1800 and replaced by the nearby Pinwherry House.

At Pinwherry School a minor road gives access to the Muck Water valley. This is a little known glen, and yet has a number of sizeable farms within it. The Muck Bridge, from where a farm track leads to Glenduisk Farm, crosses the Muck. Here can be found the remains of a burial cairn occupying the summit of a low knoll in the fields. The minor road meanders up the Muck valley, surfaced almost as far as Mark Farm. From Docherneil Farm a track climbs up to Glake Cottage, perched high on the moors. On the low summit to the west of the cottage is a prehistoric standing stone, known as the Glake, or Gleik, Stone, on which are ancient cup depressions. There are few other antiquities in this glen, but beyond Mark a forest road can be taken into the Galloway forest where a burial cairn can be found next to a pit below the Pindonnan Craigs.

The A714 makes its way up Glen Duisk towards the village of Barrhill. At Alticane Farm the Alticane Glen is wooded and contains a couple of attractive waterfalls. At Sixpence a minor road crosses the hill by way of Ballaird and Craigbrae into the valley formed by the Burn of Lig. Loch Lig is an egg-shaped loch in the valley bottom. South of here, on Farden Farm, are the Black Loch and the little Kirkie Loch.

Ballochmorrie lies further up the glen. This was at one time the home of W. McAdam, grandson of John Loudon McAdam of roadmaking fame. Ballochmorrie House was built in 1833, with an older block to the rear. The lodge house is dated 1909. The next small country house along the road is Glentachur, formerly Madajosa, which is now a country house hotel with caravan site.

The former estate of Kildonan occupies the north side of the Duisk River. The country house was erected in 1914–23, one of the last great houses of its type to be built. It was built for Euan Wallace MP, who inherited the estate and was compelled by the will to make it his home. The architect chosen was James Miller, who created a massive English Manorial building, its tall grouped chimneys being a distinctive feature. The Wallaces did not occupy the house for long, and in 1941 it was converted into a convent for the Sisters of St Joseph of Cluny. This was closed in 1976 and it has passed through various hands since then. The stable block, with its clock tower, was also the work of Miller.

On the hillside above Kildonan are a couple of farms and various woodland plantations. By the side of the Knockmalloch Wood is an ancient homestead. The Mill Burn was dammed to create the Mill Loch, storing water in order to turn the millwheel. There are a few natural lochans in the forest beyond, including the Near Eyes Stanks and Loch Farroch, which is the largest. The Duisk Lodge is located in woods on the south side of the Duisk. In the holm below the lodge is a Bronze Age cairn. A second cairn is located on the moors south west of the lodge, beyond White Cairn Farm.

*

The first indication of the village of Barrhill is the church, known as Arnsheen Church, standing on a low knoll above the Stinchar. The church was erected in 1887 as a chapel-of-ease for the large Colmonell parish. A baronial-style building, its tower rises fifty-five feet above ground level. The architect was Robert Ingram. A Free Church formerly existed nearby, but was later converted into a store.

Soon the village is entered, passing the primary school on the right.

Barrhill is little more than one long street, built to either side of the Cross Water, which passes beneath Main Street by a bridge of 1811. The buildings generally date from the nineteenth century, and are traditional in style. Only at the southern end, at Wallace Terrace, are there groups of more modern houses. The Memorial Hall was erected in 1924 to plans by James Miller. A path from Barrhill leads up the side of the Cross Water to a Covenanters' tomb, located in the wood. On the north side of the Duisk from Barrhill is Balluskie Farm, reached by a minor road that crosses the Wauk Mill Bridge. The Wauk, or Walk, Mill was used for dressing flax.

Gowlands Terrace is followed south from Barrhill up past the auction market and a new cemetery to Barrhill station, which is on the Ayr to Stranraer railway line. This station is one of few that has survived, being opened in 1877. North of the station is a pool in the wood known as the Curling Pond, where the roaring game was played with gusto. Here also is the eminence of Barr Hill, after which the village was named.

The Cross Water runs down to the village from this area, dropping over the Linn Dhu falls at the head of an attractive wooded glen. The minor road continues over the moors and through the forests to Glenluce in Wigtownshire, but Ayrshire is left behind beyond Chirmorie Farm. The Chirmorie Loch is an elliptical stretch of water lying to the east of the farm. A track through the forest leads to Dochroyle and Laggish, between which is the White Cairn, a prehistoric burial mound. East of Dochroyle, on the north side of the Pollgowan Burn, can be found remains of a hut circle and associated field system.

The Arecleoch Forest lies on the high moors to the south west of Barrhill. This is a major stretch of sitka-spruce plantations, most of which is owned by the Forestry Commission. Within the forest are a few items of interest, but these are difficult to find. The Water of Tig has its source in the woods, on the northern slopes of Strawarren Fell. Downstream from there is a spot where a number of old shielings can be found, left in a clearing of the forest. North of the shielings, in the Glenour part of the forest, can be found a prehistoric standing-stone. Other antiquities include a burial cairn on the summit of the Cairn Hill of the Moil, and a chambered cairn at the Wee Fell.

At the east end of Barrhill village the road splits, the A714 taking the northern side of the Duisk, the B7027 the southern. Both routes actually rejoin at Challoch near to Newton Stewart. The B7027 passes the Altercannoch farms, winding its way up the valley. The Waulkmill is an old mill building of the early nineteenth century, still with its tall chimney.

The road continues past Lochton Mill to Knockycoid Farm.

Between the two is Loch Duisk, a tiny widening of the river and surrounding marshland. This is really the start of the Duisk, for above here
the headwaters are known as the Pollgowan and Lavery burns. Most of
the Pollgowan and Pullower burns' drainage basin is afforested, but
within it can be found five small lochs. These are the Cow Loch, Long
Loch, Black Loch, Craigie Loch and Loch Martle, the latter having an
old boathouse. South-east of Loch Martle is a Bronze Age burial cairn,
and a second can be found in the woods at Craigance.

South of Knockycoid the lands of Drumlamford are reached. This
estate occupies the moors surrounding the numerous lochs that occupy
the hollows between the howes. These lochs are quite sizeable, the two
largest being on the boundary between Ayrshire and Wigtownshire. Of
these two, Loch Maberry lies further west, and only about one quarter
of it lies within Ayrshire. The larger part of the loch lies in the county
to the south, and this includes the ruins of Lochmaberry Castle, which can
be found on an islet within the loch. This was a very ancient structure, the
walls six feet thick and rising just as high.

Loch Dornal lies east of the B7027, a many-winged loch. Where
Loch Maberry drains into the river Bladnoch, the waters of Loch Dornal
run into the Carrick Burn and thence into the river Cree. The Carrick
Burn is so called because it forms the boundary between Galloway and
Carrick. The stream runs into the Cree at a spot known as Carrick
Burnfoot, downstream from the ruinous Carrick Mill. The other lochs
in the Drumlamford estate are Loch Gower, Loch Nahinie,
Drumlamford Loch and Loch Mabrennie. Only Drumlamford Loch is
of any great size.

Drumlamford House is a massive Italianate building constructed of
large blocks of Galloway granite. The house was erected in 1830–41 to
plans by W. Frazer for Rigby Wason. Sir William Beale MP, who was created a Baronet of Whitehall Court in Westminster and of Drumlamford in
1912, later owned the estate.

A minor road from the B7027 at Marberry Cottage heads east, passing
through the plantations and fields of Dornal towards Barwinnock,
Barjarg and Dalnaw farms. Barwinnock Farm has a herb garden that is
open to the public. Here a variety of Scots and exotic herbs and other
plants are grown and offered for sale. There is also an exhibition on
rural life and the use of medicinal plants. Barjarg Farm lies by the side
of the Cree, on the Ayrshire side, whereas Dalnaw is reached by crossing
a bridge, the farm being located in Kirkcudbrightshire. The three counties (Ayr, Wigtown and Kirkcudbright) meet at Carrick Burnfoot, just
south of here.

The A714 from Barrhill makes its way past Blair, Artnoch and Killantringan farms before reaching Corwar estate. The name Killantringan derives from the 'church of St Ninian', indicating that hereabouts was an ancient religious site. A lodge at the end of the drive marks the way into Corwar House, which stands in the midst of a wood. The house was originally built of Creetown granite in 1838 for Rigby Wason, who had already built Drumlamford House nearby. The architect was W. Frazer. In 1892 the house was extended for Hugh Elliot to plans of Richard Park. In 1974 the original house was demolished, leaving only the Victorian wing.

The A714 passes Eldrick and Creeside farms before crossing the River Cree at the Wheeb Bridge. This marks the boundary of the county. The Cree is still a sizeable watercourse this far from the sea, and it makes a tumble over the Moor Linn near here. In the woods south of Arnimean is a Bronze Age cairn. In the forest north of Creeside is Loch Goosey, a fair sized loch.

From near Blair Farm a minor road climbs up the side of the Feoch Burn and crosses the heavily afforested moors. It terminates at Black Clauchrie, a large shooting lodge far out on the moors, though much of the surrounding land is now afforested. At Laggan can be seen some waterfalls on the Feoch Burn. On the higher ground behind the house is Laggan Loch, a little pool in the woods, and the Laggan cairn, an ancient burial mound. Darnaconnar Farm is still operational, virtually surrounded by forests.

To the north of Darnaconnar is Balmalloch, beyond which is a megalithic chambered-cairn. Here two cists can be seen radiating from the centre of a robbed cairn. The cists are well preserved, the larger having large slabs and dry stone masonry forming the walls, and a large slab over the top. The other cist is not so fine, but is covered by a slab six feet in length. Another Bronze Age cairn is located on the moor north of Darnaconnar.

The minor road continues past little Loch Nevan and crosses the Clauchrie Burn to arrive at Black Clauchrie. This house was erected in 1898–1901 as a shooting lodge for the Austen family to plans of James K. Hunter in a mix of Scots baronial and English styles. A South House is a few hundred yards south of the main house. A track continues over the moors to the east of Black Clauchrie, passing the former farms of Clachrierob and Clauchrieskaig. Near the latter is a round pool known as Skaig Loch. The moors around here are all afforested now, but within them can be found a few ancient cairns. One of these lies on the low hill known as the Standard, another is in the forest west of White Clauchrie.

The Stinchar valley from Pinwherry down to Ballantrae is a rich stretch of countryside, with fine estates and rich farmland by the riverside. The B734 makes its way along the north side of the river, linking Pinwherry with the attractive village of Colmonell. Just west of the bridge across the Stinchar is the farm of Almont, the name probably deriving from 'Auld mount', being descriptive of the motte hill that lies immediately to the north east of the farm. On this motte can be seen a memorial commemorating John Snell (1629–79). This was erected in 1875 to plans by Hugh MacCall. Snell was born here, the son of the local smith, and trained as a lawyer. 'By diligence and prudence' he rose to high office, becoming Seal Bearer to King Charles II. At his death he left a considerable amount of money to found the Snell Exhibition Bursary, by which the leading student at Glasgow University has the opportunity of attending Balliol College, Oxford. This is still awarded annually. Among those who have won the award over the years are Adam Smith, George Douglas Brown, Professor John Wilson and John Gibson Lockhart.

Glessal Hill and Breaker Hill lie to the north of Almont and are afforested. Bargain Hill is still open, its summit marked by the remains of a prehistoric hill-fort. On the southern slopes an old quarry can be seen breaking its way into the hillside, and in the glen to the west is a small waterfall at the head of an attractive wooded glen.

The little clachan of Poundland lies at the foot of the Poundland Burn, overlooked by Poundland House. On the south side of the river from here is Dangart House, also known in the past as Lugarvale Lodge. Another large house lies off the B734: Craig House. This is a two-and-a-half storey laird's house of the late eighteenth century, built for the Kennedys of Craig. An adjoining cottage may be the old sixteenth century predecessor built by David Graham.

Near Garnaburn Farm a minor road strikes north, climbing up the valley of the Garna Burn and crossing the hill before dropping past Carleton Castle and arriving at Lendalfoot. In the Garna glen a man-made lochan has been created, forming the Pinbraid Fishery

The village of Colmonell comes into sight, the first indications of a village being the isolated cemetery. Behind this, on a scar above the Stinchar, are the remains of a prehistoric mound, known as the Tongue Cairn. Colmonell consists of little more than a single street, though at the west end it takes a sharp dog-leg. Only the cul-de-sac of Craigneil Road lies beyond. At the east end is the village school and the former Free Church, its tower a local landmark. Unfortunately the rest of the building has been rebuilt as a garage. This church was erected in 1898 to plans by Alexander Petrie. The older houses in Colmonell occupy the northern side of the road, the south being built up later, when Hyslop Crescent was built. Next to the kirkyard is a house known as The Yett, erected in 1905 but incorporating older work of 1596 and 1795.

At the west end of the village, where Main Street bends into Rowantree Street, the little Manse Road can be followed to the parish church. Tradition has it that St Colman of Ella established his cell here around AD 600. The present building is an interesting structure, quite simple in style, with a small open belfry at its eastern end. The church dates from 1772, replacing an older building. It was rebuilt in 1849 and again in 1899, the latter time by Sir Robert Lorimer. The oak pulpit, organ screen and chancel are Lorimer's designs. Inside can be seen stained glass by Louis Davis and Douglas Strachan, and a mural memorial to John Snell.

The churchyard has a number of old stones of interest, including the martyr's grave commemorating the Covenanter, Matthew MacIlwraith. It is thought that MacIlwraith may have suggested the name 'Mucklewrath' to Sir Walter Scott in his Covenanting novel, *Old Mortality*. Here also is the grave of Charles Berry (1872–1909) a local naturalist, and the burial place of the MacCubbins and MacConnels of Knockdolian. This old enclosure has the MacCubbin arms on it, with the date 1663. In the south-east corner is a flat stone marking the grave of Andro Snell, father of John Snell, which the scholar erected in 1664. Another memorial commemorates members of John Loudon McAdam's family.

Within the angle of the dogleg is Kirkhill House, a fine Elizabethan building of 1843–5, perhaps designed by David Rhind at the same time as he was working at Knockdolian Castle. It was built by Lieutenant-Colonel Barton of Ballaird. Next to it, and separated from it by only a few yards, is Kirkhill Castle, an L-plan tower house erected in 1589 for Thomas Kennedy and his wife Janet, according to a date stone. The tower has a rare scale-and-platt stairway, and bartizans at the corners. Sir Thomas Kennedy of Kirkhill was Lord Provost of Edinburgh in 1680, but was renowned for making his fortune in supplying arms in the Covenanting period. Later owners were the Bartons of Ballaird. The castle was abandoned when the new house was erected. Next to the woods to the north of Kirkhill is the large boulder known as the Deaf Stone. Another named boulder is the Cloven Rock, which lies near to the summit of Pyet Craig.

A minor road strikes south from Colmonell's Main Street, passes the park and the village war memorial (designed by Robert Lorimer in 1922), and crosses the Stinchar by a bridge, erected in 1867 to designs by Hugh MacCall. A minor road on the south side of the river can be followed, meandering through the countryside, westward towards Ballantrae. A few small roads head back upstream from the bridge, one of these passing Dalreoch House and making its way towards Dangart House. Dalreoch House is a fine late Victorian building. The Dalreoch Burn makes a steep gully to the west of Dalreoch Hill, a lowish summit of 594 feet. A second minor road climbs uphill past Bardrochat House to the open moors south of Dalreoch Hill, giving access to a number of remote farms. Bardrochat House is a fine mansion of 1893, designed by George M. Watson and extended in 1906–8 to plans by Sir Robert Lorimer. The house was long owned by the MacEwen family. Sir John MacEwen was a notable politician, serving as MP for Berwick and Haddington from 1931–45. He was created a Baronet of Marchmont (his other seat in the Borders) and of Bardrochat in 1953.

The land south of Dalreoch has been farmed fairly intensely, but there are now many abandoned steadings on the moors. South of Wheeb Farm the track drops to cross the Water of Tig, a Stinchar tributary, and back up to Glenour. By the side of the water is Peden's Mount, one of the locations where the leading Covenanter, Alexander Peden, is known to have hidden. In the river below here is a fair sized waterfall.

West of Bardrochat are the lands of Craigneil, the remains of Craigneil Castle standing high above a disused quarry. Although the castle was in ruins by the time the quarry was established, workings below the tower resulted in part of it collapsing in 1886. Craigneil was a Kennedy seat, erected sometime in the fourteenth century. On the floodplain of the Stinchar to the north of the castle is an ancient burial cairn, and by the side of the road west of the farm is the former Craigneil Toll.

Knockdolian Castle stands by the side of the Stinchar, a mile and a half to the west of Colmonell. There are two buildings of this name, the old tower house of around 1650, still virtually entire, and the present country-seat, erected in 1842 by Alexander MacCubbin Cathcart to plans by David Rhind. Knockdolian was anciently a seat of the Graham family, and part of the earlier castle may be incorporated in the present old tower. The new castle is a fine Tudoresque mansion, the entrance doorway adorned by the MacCubbin and Cathcart arms. In the river is a large boulder known as the Mermaid's Stone, reputedly the spot where a mermaid sat and sang all night. The lady of the castle had the stone destroyed, after which the mermaid only returned once, to sing a swan-song, in which she cursed the family, resulting in the young heir being killed and the family becoming extinct.

Knockdolian gets its name from the prominent hill of that name, which rises steeply above the Stinchar to the south west of the castle.

The name is thought to mean the 'false craig', from it looking not unlike the Ailsa Craig from the sea, and thus causing many ships to become disorientated and run ashore on the rocks near Ballantrae. The hill is steep, and rugged, and reaches a height of 869 feet above sea level. On the summit is a Bronze Age cairn. On the northern slopes of Knockdolian is a rocky hillock known as Duniewick. This is in fact an ancient dun, measuring approximately 100 feet by 85 feet, the stones of which have fallen considerably. The original entrance to the dun appears to have been on the south-west side of the fortress.

On the south side of Knockdolian Hill are Macherquhat and Balnowlart farms, at the latter being the ruins of a fairly modern house, built in the traditional Scots style. Balnowlart House was erected in 1905, the architects being J. Jerdan & Son. At first glance the house looks as though it was an ancient Scots tower house, which was exactly the image that its owner wished to present. Sadly, it has been abandoned and now lies in a sorry state within its wood. On the low summit of Balnowlart Hill are the remains of a Bronze Age cairn.

The south side of the Stinchar hereabouts is a most interesting stretch of countryside, but one that needs to be reached from either Colmonell in the east or Ballantrae to the west. The only means of crossing the Stinchar between the two, other than by wading, is by the private footbridge at Knockdolian Castle. This area is known as Innertig, and it was here that the original village centre for what is now the parish of Ballantrae was located. The old churchyard and ruins of St Cuthbert's Church of this clachan can be found at Kirkholm Farm, near to the confluence of the Tig and Stinchar. This place was known as Kirkcudbright Innertig, as opposed to the better-known Kirkcudbright. The old church dates from pre-Reformation times but was abandoned when a new church for the parish was erected at Ballantrae in 1604. The kirkyard still has some old stones around it.

A number of prehistoric cairns can be found around here. Two of these lie fairly close to the minor road, the Polcardoch Cairn, which has been partially removed, and the Sallochan Cairn, which lies further north. A third cairn is located on the summit of Cairn Hill to the east. North of Cairn Hill is the ruin of Knockdhu Cottage, known in Covenanting annals as the place where Alexander Peden was captured.

The minor road on the south side of Stinchar crosses the Water of Tig at a spot known as Heronsford, where a tiny estate village is located. The Tig is an elusive stream, one that is difficult to see by the casual wanderer. It meanders down through an attractive wooded valley known as Glen Tig, access to which is difficult other than on foot.

On the south side of Tig are a few large country houses. Laggan House stands near the foot of the water, but today has lost its importance and surrounding estate. This was originally owned by the Earl of Stair, but in 1845 was purchased by Charles MacGibbon, whose son was David MacGibbon (1831–1902), the noted architect and historian. Along with Thomas Ross they compiled the five-volume *Castellated and Domestic Architecture of Scotland,* and the three-volume *Ecclesiastical Architecture of Scotland.* The MacGibbons left Laggan in 1902. Much of the old house, which may have been designed by MacGibbon's father, has been demolished, leaving only the 1913 wing by James Miller standing, alongside the ruin of the billiard room. A caravan site now occupies the lands around the old house.

East of Laggan House is Auchenflower House, a fine building of around 1860 erected by James MacIlwraith. The architect is unknown. Around 1910 James Miller added Scots domestic extensions for Reginald Hughes-Onslow. Further east is Balkissock House, built in 1933–5 to plans by James Miller for Reginald Hughes-Onslow. A modern-style country house, Balkissock is distinguished by its white harl, tall chimneys and wide windows. The farmhouse nearby, which was built in 1820, was the predecessor as a shooting lodge.

From Auchenflower a minor road meanders across country before degenerating into a track at Crailoch. This was originally a main route south, the old route still walkable across country towards Glen App. Along the old route can be found some milestones, looking rather out of place on such a wild road.

The estate of Auchairne lies to the south of Laggan, this house erected around 1820 by extending a farmhouse. At that time the Donaldson family were the owners. The house was later owned by Sir Bernard Fergusson, Lord Ballantrae (1911–1980). The walled garden is located at the Lady Knowe. Near to Laggan dairy is a small hillock known as the Mote Knowe, perhaps indicative of the fact that a motte hill once existed here.

*

Both roads on either side of the Stinchar make their way downstream to the village of Ballantrae, created in 1617 when a petition was sent to the king asking for permission to move the church here from Kirkcudbright Innertig. The new site, which had been created a Burgh of Barony for the Kennedys of Bargany in 1541, was regarded as having greater potential, for here a harbour and associated industries could be created.

The village did not become anything more than that, and today remains a small community often passed through by travellers on the busy A77.

The A77 crosses the Stinchar at the new Ballantrae Bridge, of 1964, bypassing the twin-arched bridge of 1770, which has become dangerous. On the north side of the crossing stands the ruins of Ardstinchar Castle, now little more that a tall block of masonry perched precariously on a rock outcrop. The castle was built around 1450 by Hugh Kennedy of Bargany, who made his fortune by befriending Charles VII of France. Mary Queen of Scots spent the night of 8 August 1566 in the castle. At one time the castle comprised of a three-storey tower with a large wall surrounding a courtyard. It was abandoned in the seventeenth century and much of the stone was stolen to build the present village.

Like Colmonell, Ballantrae's main thoroughfare takes a right-angle turn, near to which stands the parish church. The present little Gothic building dates from 1819, the small, but decorative, tower with clock being added in 1891. Within are memorials to David MacGibbon and another to Lord Ballantrae. Revd Thomas Burns, nephew of the poet, was minister here from 1826–30. The parish church replaced the older building, the ruins of which can be seen in the kirkyard across the road. Adjoining the ruins is the Kennedy mausoleum of around 1601, which has an inscription commemorating Gilbert Kennedy 'slain in feudal conflict' at Maybole by the Earl of Cassillis in 1601. Also in the kirkyard are some interesting old stones with carved symbolism, and a number of memorials commemorating folk drowned at sea. Among these is a military grave that simply records 'An unknown seaman, known unto God.'

Main Street, Ballantrae, runs on a north-south axis, the older properties at the southern end. Here is the Kings Arms Hotel, erected in 1770 using stones from Ardstinchar Castle. The manse building dates from 1736 and the former schoolmaster's house was erected in 1750.

Shore Road passes by the police station and inshore rescue-boat station and arrives at Foreland, the name of the street fronting the shore. At the north end of this road is the small harbour, little more than a pier built out on the rocky headland that allows some protection behind it. The pier was erected in 1847 using Arran freestone and for a time paddle steamers made Ballantrae one of their ports of call during Clyde cruises. This trade has long gone, and the harbour today is little more than a sandy haven for small pleasure craft and the odd lobster boat. Some of the old fishermen's cottages of the early nineteenth century survive.

Foreland can be followed south and round back to the church, passing the primary school. The shore gets rockier the further south one walks, and eventually becomes a spit of shingle, behind which are various salt-water pools. The mouth of the Stinchar has always been changing, and even a look at maps made over the past century reveals an ever-changing shape. The mouth of the river was preserved as a nature reserve by the Scottish Wildlife Trust, but this agreement has been relinquished.

From little Church Street a track and path can be followed up Mains and Mill hills, on the latter of which stand the remains of an old windmill. This is thought to date from 1696. At the eastern end of Mains Hill was an old Bronze Age burial cairn, remnants of which may still be visible on the ground.

The A77 leads north from Ballantrae, heading towards Girvan. The first few miles it takes the low route over the ancient raised beach north of the village. At one time there was a golf course here. There are few buildings on this beach, and even although the ground is excellent, the farm steadings were erected up on the summit of the bank at Balig and Corseclays. Just north of Corseclays are the remains of an ancient hill fort, perched on the edge of the former cliff top.

The A77 then climbs high up over Bennane Hill, before dropping back down to the shore again at Carleton Fishery, south of Lendalfoot. The road did not always go this way, for it is only in recent years that the way past Meikle Bennane has been taken. Previously the road kept much closer to the sea, but so precipitous were the cliffs above and below it that it was often closed due to rock falls. The old route can still be followed on foot.

At the southern end of the old road is the Bennane Cave, its entrance partially protected by a stone-built wall. This cave has been occupied for many centuries, and a cairn nearby commemorates its last regular resident. This was Henry Ewing Torbit (1912–83), who was better known as Snib Scott, after an earlier hermit who used to live there. Torbit was born near Dundee and trained to be a bank manager, but decided to leave the modern world behind and became a man of the road. He eventually settled in this cave, and lived in the neighbourhood until his death.

There are several antiquities on and around Bennane Head. The summit of Bennane Hill itself is home to an ancient enclosure, a circular earthwork on the highest point of the hill. At Little Bennane Farm is another ancient mound, marked as a tumulus on the map.

North of Little Bennane is a small bay known as Balcreuchan Port. High cliffs surround this, and the bay is only accessible by taking a winding path down to the bottom. This bay has a cave at its northern end, celebrated in local lore as Sawney Bean's Cave. There is a well-known local legend that a cannibal of that name lived here, perhaps in the seventeenth century. He and his family would attack travellers on the road above and take them down to the cave where they would eat them. Eventually they were captured and taken to Edinburgh for execution. Unfortunately there is no evidence for any of this.

The main road south of Ballantrae begins climbing up the hillside and eventually passes over into Glen App. On the way the route passes the wooded policies of Glenapp Castle, a massive baronial structure erected in 1870 to plans of David Bryce. The builder was James Hunter, who had purchased the estate in 1864 from the Earl of Orkney. The estate was sold in 1894. In 1922–4 Lord Inchcape had the castle extended, the architect probably being James Miller. The castle has a massive six-storey tower, as well as various other turrets, battlements and corbie-stepped gables. The gardens are attractive and used to be regularly open to the public. In 1919 Lord Inchcape began the building of the cottages at Smyrton, a small estate village by the side of the A77.

There are a few minor roads leading into the rural countryside west of Glenapp Castle, and in fact one of these was an early route taken by travellers between Ballantrae and Stranraer. There is a small community at Garleffin, a number of cottages randomly placed on the map. Here was a large stone circle, originally comprising eight stones. It was calculated that the circle recorded a solar eclipse that took place at noon on 31 December 2709 BC. Unfortunately, modern agricultural practices have removed most of these stones, so that today there is only a solitary remnant, surviving because it was in a cottage garden. At Colling Bridge is the modern cemetery for Ballantrae.

The landscape south of Ballantrae is one that is wild and remote. Near Downanhill can be found the remains of an ancient homestead. The minor road rejoins the A77 south of Glenapp Castle, passing close to Kilantringan Loch. This has been dammed to enlarge it, but the original dam burst, causing damage to the Currarie Glen. There is another man-made lochan to the south-west, known as Blackwater Loch.

Glen App itself is a fairly straight valley, its sides steep and the bottom narrow. The glen's straightness is due to the fact that it was formed by a fault in the earth's crust, for this is part of the south-western end of the Southern Upland Boundary Fault. The Water of App rises on the moors north of Beneraird, the highest hill in the locality. This summit is 1,440 feet high, but was crossed by a public road near to its highest point. This is no longer open to traffic, and is generally only used by walkers. Smyrton Hill, Benawhirn and Auchencrosh Hill bound the north side of the infant App. To the south is Beneraird and Milljoan Hill. This part of the glen is wooded and unoccupied.

Carlock House is located in that part of the glen where the A77 arrives over the pass from the north. Carlock House is not a particularly large mansion, being little more than a largish double storey villa, erected in 1909. However, this is now the main seat of Glenapp Estate, Lord Inchcape having sold Glenapp Castle.

Where the main road crosses the moors north of Carlock is an area renowned for snowdrifts. A number of old snow fences survive to either side of the road, but today the moors have been planted in trees, reducing the chance of drifting. It was during a snowstorm on 28 December 1908 that Robert Cunningham was killed. He was the postman at Ballantrae and had managed to carry out his round in the terrible conditions. At Carlock House he was told to stay, but he insisted on trying to make his way back to Ballantrae. Unfortunately he died in the storm, and his body was not found for a number of days. A memorial cross erected by the Postmens' Federation marks where his body was found, visible from the main road.

Much of Carlock Hill is now afforested. The remains of an ancient burial mound known as the Carlock Cairn crown the summit of the 1,060 feet high hill. There are a few other antiquities to be found on this range of hills along the north side of the glen. The Drumduff Cairn stands on a low ridge off the Green Benan, and a burial cairn surmounts the summit of Penderry Hill, which rises to 1,014 feet. At Blarbuie, north of Finnarts Farm, two standing stones, an ancient earthwork or enclosure and a burial cairn can be found.

The road down Glen App drops from near Carlock House down

Ballantrae: the village viewed from Garleffin, with Ailsa Craig beyond

into the valley bottom. Above Dupin Farm, where the high moors are afforested, is a Bronze Age cairn located within an old sheepfold. At Mark can be found Glenapp Church, a little place of worship perched on a low hillock. This church was erected in 1850 and endowed under the will of Isabella Caddell (d. 1829), who left £4,500 and fifteen acres of land to establish a church and school. It was a chapel-of-ease for the large Ballantrae parish, becoming *quoad sacra* in 1874 and having its own minister until 1940. The church was restored in 1910 under the supervision of P. MacGregor Chalmers. It is also known as Butter's Church and was restored once more in 1930 by the Mackays in memory of Elsie

Glenapp Church

Mackay. In the small kirkyard around it are memorials commemorating the 1st Earl of Inchcape, James Lyle Mackay (1852–1932). This memorial is adorned with carved figures of a lion, tiger, owl and eagle. The 2nd and 3rd Earls are also interred here. A small memorial commemorates James Lyle Mackay, killed climbing locally in 1941 at the age of seventeen. The church itself is an attractive building, complete with stained glass windows by Douglas Strachan and Kelley & Co. One of these commemorates Elsie Mackay, daughter of the 3rd Earl, who was killed in an attempt at flying the Atlantic in 1928. Another, 'The Stilling of the Tempest', commemorates the 1st Earl.

The old road took to the north side of the App, crossing the Bridge of the Mark, but today the A77 keeps to the south. The old route passed Craiganlea and the old mansion of Finnarts, sadly demolished. Finnarts

Farm survives, and here can be found an old doocot that was contemporary with the house. At the foot of the glen this old road crossed the App by an attractive old humpbacked bridge. At Finnarts Bay is a fish processing plant and a fish farm.

The headlands of Garry Point and Port Sally have the remains of a Second World War gun emplacement on them. This was part of the Loch Ryan military port scheme for here, during the Second World War, the sheltered loch was used as a seaplane base and the Mulberry Harbours were built prior to use for landing on the continent.

The A77 swings round at the foot of Glen App and makes its way along the side of Loch Ryan. On the hillside above are the remains of an ancient cairn. Around a mile from Finnarts Bay the road crosses the Galloway Bridge, which itself crosses the little Galloway Burn. This marks the southern extremity of Ayrshire, where Wigtownshire takes over. The hillside above is known as the Old Park of the Gleick.

There remains one final part of Ayrshire to be described. This part has, in fact, in recent years been 'stolen' by Dumfries and Galloway, but historically belongs to Ayrshire. Lagafater estate lies south of Beneraird, on the old hill road that made its way south towards Glen Luce. The estate lies in the water basin of the Luce, and access to Lagafater Lodge is made by road across the Wigtownshire moors, and for this reason the southern county does have quite a strong claim to it. There are many old antiquities on the moors hereabouts, as well as the remains of some more recent works. Near Drumahallan is Mirren's Stone, a large boulder out on the moors. South-east of here are two Bronze Age cairns, and a third is found south of Drumanwherran. On the Pinwherran Burn was an old dam, creating a reservoir that was quite short lived. There were a number of others on the moors here, many of which have been dismantled.

More cairns can be found on the moors near Shennas Farm, one near the Main Water of Luce, and two close together in the improved grassland at Laganabeastie and a third on the moor at Drummanmoan. Near Drumley the base of various hut circles have been discovered. North of Barnvannoch are the remains of another, larger dam, which formed a fair-sized reservoir on the Main Water of Luce. North of here is Lagafater Lodge, a remote hunting-lodge. For a number of years Sir Adrian Boult, the noted conductor, owned this. From Lagafater the old coach road makes its way north towards Beneraird and back into 'real' Ayrshire. Near the top this road passes a little cairn that marks the spot where James Henry was overcome by a blizzard and died on 1 April 1891. A plaque within Ballantrae church also commemorates Henry, who was a gamekeeper on the Lagafater estate for W. R. Collraith.

# Bibliography

Adamson, Archibald R., *Rambles Round Kilmarnock*, Kilmarnock Standard, 1875.

Allan, Revd Arthur, *Fairlie: Past and Present*, J. & R. Simpson, 1914.

Andrew, Ken, *Ken Andrew's Ayrshire Guide – Kyle & Carrick District*, Alloway Publishing, 1981.

*Old Prestwick*, Stenlake Publishing, 2000.

Baird, J. G. A., *Muirkirk in Bygone Days*, W. Shaw Smith, 1910.

Barber, Derek, *Steps through Stair – a History of Stair and Trabboch*, Stair Parish Church, 2000.

Barclay, Alistair, *The Bonnet Toun*, Stewarton Bonnet Guild, 1989.

Barr, James, *The Scottish Covenanters*, John Smith, 1946.

Baxter, David D., *The Parish of Largs*, Largs & District Historical Society, 1992.

Bayne, John F., *Dunlop Parish, a History of Church, Parish and Nobility*, Edinburgh University Press, 1935.

Beattie, Frank, *Kilmarnock in Old Picture Postcards*, European Library, 1984.

*Greetings from Kilmarnock*, Stenlake Publishing, 1994.

*Streets and Neuks: Old Kilmarnock*, Kilmarnock Standard, 2000.

Beattie, Robert, *Kilmaurs Past and Present*, Kilmaurs Historical Society, 1993.

Begg, Dr James A., *A Hundred Years of Health in Ayrshire*, 1999.

Blyth, Molly, *Old West Kilbride*, Stenlake Publishing, 1997.

Boyd, J., *Guide to Wemyss Bay, Skelmorlie, Inverkip and Largs*, Alexander Gardner, 1879.

Boyle, Andrew M., *The Ayrshire Book of Burns-Lore*, Alloway Publishing, 1985.

*Ayrshire Heritage*, Alloway Publishing, 1990.

Campbell, J. R. D., *Largs Through the Centuries*, Largs & District Historical Society, 1995.

Castle, Jeanette, *Ayr Memories*, Kyle & Carrick District Council, 1994.

Clements, James, *Stevenston – the Kernel of Cunninghame*, Burgh of Stevenston, 1974.

Close, Rob, *Ayrshire & Arran: An Illustrated Architectural Guide*, RIAS, 1992.

Cochrane, Drew, *The Story of Ayrshire Junior Football*, Drew Cochrane, 1989.

Cotter, Douglas, & Stewart, Alan, *Purple & Gold: the Story of Marr College and the C. K. Marr Educational Trust*, C. K. Marr Educational Trust, 1996.

Czerkawska, Catherine Lucy, *Fisherfolk of Carrick*, Molendinar Press, 1975.

*Dalry Remembered*, Dalry Local History Group, 1985.

Dalziel, Robert, & Harrison, Terry (Editors), *200 Years of Catrine & Sorn Parish – a Cotton Tale*, Countryside Publications, 1987.

Davis, Michael, C., *The Castles and Mansions of Ayrshire*, privately published, 1991.

Deans, Brian T., *Green Cars to Hurlford*, Scottish Tramway Museum Society, 1986.

Donnachie, Frank, *Old Fairlie*, Stenlake Publishing, 1999.

Donnelly, Frank, *The History of Kilmarnock Academy*, Kilmarnock Academy, 1998.

Douglas, Henrietta, & Douglas, Hugh, *Minishant is a Bonnie Wee Place*, Strathprint, Peterborough, 1982.

Duerden, John W. N., & MacNeill, Donald, *Heathfield Hospital, Ayr*, Ayrshire & Arran Health Board, 1991.

Dunlop, Annie I., *The Royal Burgh of Ayr*, Oliver & Boyd, 1953.

Farrell, Robert, *Benwhat and Corbie Craigs*, Cumnock & Doon Valley District Council, 1983.

Findlay, Robert & Swan, T. Sorbie, *Largs – a Short History*, Robert Findlay, 1980.

Findlay, Thomas, *Garan 1631 to Muirkirk 1950*, privately published, 1980.

*A Muirkirk Miscellany*, privately published, 1986.

Gillespie, Revd James H., *Dundonald, the Parish and its Setting*, John Wyllie, 1939.

Gow, Bill, *The Swirl of the Pipes*, Strathclyde Regional Council, 1996.

Gray, James T., *Maybole: Carrick's Capital*, Dragon Books, 1972.

Gunn, J. Thomson, *The Spell and the Glory of Largs*, Mercury Press, n.d.

Gurton, Owen A., *Fairlie Village Walks*, Largs & District Historical Society, 1998.

Guthrie, James A., *A Corner of Carrick*, Alexander Gardner, 1979.

Hay, John, *Kilwinning Parish – A short history*. Kilwinning Abbey Church, 1967.

Hendrie, Revd George S., *The Parish of Dalmellington*, William Murdoch, 1902.

Hill, George, *Tunnel & Dam - The Story of the Galloway Hydros*, South of Scotland Electricity Board, 1984.

*Historical Aspects of Newmilns*, Newmilns & Greenholm Community Council, 1990.

Hood, John, *Old Mauchline and Tarbolton*, Stenlake Publishing, 2001.

Hutton, Guthrie, *Mining – Ayrshire's Lost Industry*, Stenlake Publishing, 1996.

*Irvine Valley Scenes – Across Three Centuries*, Rotary Club of Loudoun, 2000.

House, Jack, *Stewarton*, Stewarton Bonnet Guild, c.1970.

Kennedy, R. & J., *Old Ayr*, Stenlake Publishing, 1992.

Ker, Revd William Lee, *Kilwinning*, A. W. Cross, 1900.

Kerr, I. B., *In and Around Largs*, Largs & District Historical Society, n.d.

Kinniburgh, Moira & Burke, Fiona, *Kilbirnie & Glengarnock – Shared Memories*, Kilbirnie District Library, 1995.

Kirk, Robert, *Pictorial History of Dundonald*, Alloway Publishing, 1989.

Kirkwood, Revd J., *Troon and Dundonald*, Mackie & Drennan, 1876.

Knox, James E., *Maps of Kilmarnock*, Kilmarnock & District History Group, 1993.

Lamb, John, *Annals of an Ayrshire Parish – West Kilbride*, John J. Rae, 1896.

*West Kilbride and Neighbourhood*, Arthur Guthrie, 1899.

Lauchlan, Roy, *Old Kilwinning*, Stenlake Publishing, 1998.

Laurenson, John, *Cumnock and New Cumnock in Old Picture Postcards*, European Library, 1983.

Lawson, Revd Roderick, *Ailsa Craig*, J. & R. Parlane, 1888.

*Places of Interest about Girvan*, J. & R. Parlane, 1892.

*Fifty-four Views of Carrick with Description*, J. & R. Parlane, 1894.

*The Covenanters of Ayrshire*, J. & R. Parlane, 1904.

Lewis, R. B., *Seafield Children's Hospital, Ayr*, Ayrshire and Arran Health Board, 1991.

Lindsay, Maurice, *The Burns Encyclopedia*, Robert Hale, 1959.

Loudoun, Craufuird C., *A History of the House of Loudoun and Associated Families*, C. C. Loudoun, 1996.

Love, Dane, *Scottish Kirkyards*, Robert Hale, 1989.

*History of Auchinleck – Village & Parish*, Carn Publishing, 1991.

*Pictorial History of Cumnock*, Alloway Publishing, 1992.

*Pictorial History of Ayr*, Alloway Publishing, 1995.

*Ayr Stories*, Fort Publishing, 2000.

*Ayrshire Coast*, Fort Publishing, 2001.

Lyell, D. I. (Editor), *Mauchline in Times Past*, Countryside Publications, 1986.

MacArthur, Wilson, *The River Doon*, Cassell, 1952.

McCallum, May Fife, *Fast and Bonnie – A History of William Fife and Son, Yachtbuilders*, John Donald, 1998.

McChesney, John S, *The Story of Dalrymple*, Dalrymple Community Council, 1992.

McEwen, Mae, *Troon Memories*, South Ayrshire Council, 1996.

*Memories of Auld Irvine*, John Geddes, 1997.

*Millennium Memories: I belong tae Yrwyn*, Westward Media, 1999.

MacIlvean, John Gardiner, *The Birth of Football in the Burns Country*, privately published, 1982.

MacIntosh, John, *Ayrshire Nights' Entertainments*, John Menzies, 1894.

McIver, Donald, *Old New Cumnock,* Stenlake Publishing, 1997.

*A Stroll through the Historic Past of New Cumnock*, New Cumnock Environmental Regeneration Volunteers, 2000.

MacJannet, Arnold, *The Royal Burgh of Irvine*, Civic Press, 1938.

Mackay, Archibald, *The History of Kilmarnock*, Archibald Mackay, 1880.

Mackay, James A., *Kilmarnock*, Alloway Publishing, 1992.

Mackenna, James, *Round About Girvan*, Hugh Wallace, 1906.

Mackintosh, Ian M., *Old Troon & District*, George Outram, 1969.

*Memories of Old Troon*, I. M. Mackintosh, 1972.

MacLeod, Alex G., *The Book of Old Darvel*, Walker & Connell, n.d.

McMeikan, James, *Girvan Memories*, Kyle & Carrick District Council, 1993.

MacNaught, D., *Kilmaurs Parish and Burgh*, Alexander Gardner, 1912.

MacPherson, Ian, *Old Troon*, Stenlake Publishing, 2000.

McQuillan, T. Courtney, *The Hill – its People and its Pits*, Cumnock & Doon Valley District Council, 1988.

McSherry, R. & M., *Old Saltcoats*, Stenlake Publishing, 1995.

*Old Largs*, Stenlake Publishing, 1997.

*Old Stevenston*, Stenlake Publishing, 1998.

McTaggart, Hugh & Hamilton, Armour, *Old Dalry*, Stenlake Publishing, 1999.

Mair, James, *Pictorial History of Galston*, Alloway Publishing, 1988.

*Pictorial History of Newmilns*, Alloway Publishing, 1988.

*Pictorial History of Darvel*, Alloway Publishing, 1989.

Malkin, John, *Sir Alexander Fleming – Man of Penicillin*, Alloway Publishing, 1981.

*Pictorial History of Kilmarnock*, Alloway Publishing 1989.

Maxwell, Hugh, *Old Darvel*, Stenlake Publishing, 2001.

*Old Galston*, Stenlake Publishing, 2001.

*Old Newmilns*, Stenlake Publishing, 2001.

*Maybole Past & Present*, Maybole Community Council, 2000.

Millar, A. H., *Castles and Mansions of Ayrshire*, William Paterson, 1885.

Milligan, Susan, *Old Maybole and North Carrick*, Stenlake Publishing, 2000.

*Old Stewarton, Dunlop and Lugton*, Stenlake Publishing, 2001.

Moir, Peter, & Crawford, Ian, *Clyde Shipwrecks*, Moir Crawford, 1988.

Moore, James M., *Ayr County Hospital*, Ayrshire & Arran Health Board, 1991.

Moore, John, *Gently Flows the Doon*, Dalmellington District Council, 1972.

*Ayr Gaiety: The Theatre Made Famous by the Popplewells*, Albyn Press, 1976.

*Among thy Green Braes*, Cumnock & Doon Valley District Council, 1977.

*Doon Valley Diary*, John Moore, 1980.

Morris, James A., *The Brig of Ayr*, Stephen & Pollock, 1912.

*The Auld Toon o' Ayr*, Stephen & Pollock, 1928.

*A Romance of Industrial Engineering*, Glenfield & Kennedy, 1939.

Morton, Jocelyn, *Three Generations in a Family Textile Firm*, Routledge, 1971.

*[New] Statistical Account of Scotland*, William Blackwood, 1842.

*Ordnance Gazetteer of Scotland*, 6 vols. William MacKenzie, nd.

*Our Village – the Story of West Kilbride*, West Kilbride Amenity Society, 1990.

Paterson, James, *History of the Counties of Ayr and Wigton*, Dick, 1847–52.

Paterson, John, *Reminiscences of Dalmellington*, W. Pomphrey, 1902.

Pettigrew, David, *Old Muirkirk*, Stenlake Publishing, 1996.

*Old Irvine*, Stenlake Publishing, 1997.

Reid, Denholm, & Andrew, Ken, *Ayr Remembered*, Stenlake Publishing, 2001.

Reid, Donald L., *Beith Supplement and Advertiser- The Story of Beith's Newspaper*, Beith Open Award Group, 2000.

*Old Beith*, Stenlake Publishing, 2000.

*In the Valley of Garnock*, Beith Open Award Group, 2001.

*Old Dalmellington, Patna & Waterside*, Stenlake Publishing, 2001.

*Doon Valley Memories*, Dunaskin Veterans Group, 2002.

Retter, Janet, *Drongan – the Story of a Mining Village*, Cumnock & Doon Valley District Council, 1978.

Robertson, William, *Historic Ayrshire*, Thomson, 1891–4.

*Ayrshire: Its History and Historic Families*, Dunlop & Drennan, 1908.

Rollie, Chris J., *Robert Burns and New Cumnock*, 1996.

Rowallan, Lord, *Rowallan: the Autobiography of Lord Rowallan*, Paul Harris, 1976.

Rowan, David, *Memorials of Ochiltree and Neighbourhood*, Aird & Coghill, 1879.

Sanderson, George, *New Cumnock – Long Ago and Far Away*, 1989.

*New Cumnock – Far and Away*, 1992.

Sanderson, Margaret H. B., *Ayrshire and the Reformation*, Tuckwell Press, 1997.

Shaw, James Edward, *Ayrshire, 1745–1950*, Oliver & Boyd, 1953.

Smart, W., *Skelmorlie*, Skelmorlie & Wemyss Bay Community Centre. 1968.

Smellie, Thomas, *Sketches of Old Kilmarnock*, T. Smellie, 1898.

Smith, David L., *Tales of the Glasgow & South Western Railway*, Ian Allan, 1962.

*The Dalmellington Iron Company: Its Engines and Men*, David & Charles, 1967.

*Legends of the Glasgow & South Western Railway in LMS Days*, David & Charles, 1980.

Snoddy, T. G., *Round About Greenock*, Allen Lithographic Co., 1950.

*Some Notes on an Ayrshire Parish – Stevenston Past and Present*, Archibald Wallace, 1902.

Steele, Elizabeth J., *Old Kilbirnie & Glengarnock*, Stenlake Publishing, 2001.

Steele, John, & Steele, Noreen, *Whispers of Horse Island*, Argyll Publishing, 1999.

Steven, Helen J., *The Cumnocks: Old and New*, Dunlop & Drennan, 1899.

Strawhorn, John, *History of Old Cumnock*, Cumnock Town Council, 1966.

*Ayrshire – the Story of a County*, Ayrshire Archaeological and Natural History Society, 1975.

*History of Irvine*, John Donald, 1985.

*History of Ayr*, John Donald, 1989.

*History of Prestwick*, John Donald, 1994.

Strawhorn, John & Andrew, Ken, *Discovering Ayrshire*, John Donald, 1988.

Strawhorn, John, & Boyd, William, *Third Statistical Account of Scotland – Ayrshire*, Oliver & Boyd, 1951.

Thomas, John, *Regional History of the Railways of Great Britain: Scotland – Lowlands and the Borders,* David & Charles, 1971

Torrie, E. P. Dennison & Coleman, Russel, *Historic Cumnock*, Historic Scotland, 1995.

Turnbull, George, *A South Ayrshire Parish*, Stephen & Pollock, 1908.

Warrick, John, *History of Old Cumnock*, Alexander Gardner, 1899.

Webster, Nicola, *Irvine in Old Picture Postcards*, European Library, 1983.

Welsh, Iain, *Prestwick in the 40s*, Kyle & Carrick District Council, 1992.

West Kilbride Amenity Society, *Our Village*, West Kilbride Amenity Society, 1990.

Wham, Alasdair, *The Lost Railway Lines of Ayrshire*, G. C. Book Publishers, 1997.

Whatley, Christopher A., *John Galt 1779–1979*, Ramsay Head Press, 1979.

Wilson, Rhona, *Old Catrine & Sorn,* Stenlake Publishing, 1997.

Woodburn, John, *A History of Darvel*, Walker & Connell, 1967.

Wyllie, Stewart C., & Wilson, James, *Troon in Old Picture Postcards*, European Library, 1990.

Young, Alex F., *Old Kilmaurs & Fenwick*, Stenlake Publishing, 2001.

In addition, numerous local guidebooks or histories have been consulted, in particular:

*Ayrshire Collections*, Vols. 1–13, Ayrshire Archaeological & Natural History Society, 1947–83.

*Ayrshire Monographs*, Ayrshire Archaeological & Natural History Society, 1987 to present.

*Ayrshire Notes*, Ayrshire Archaeological and Natural History Society and Ayrshire Federation of Historical Societies, 1991 to present.

*Castles:*

*Culzean Castle*, National Trust for Scotland, 1978.

*Dean Castle*, Kilmarnock & Loudoun District Council, nd.

*Hunterston Castle*, Pilgrim Press, 1975.

*Loudoun Castle*, Loudoun Castle Park, 1995.

*Churches:*

Agnew, Revd Hugh M., *United Free Church West, Cumnock*, Cumnock Chronicle, 1923.

Borrowman, Revd Alexander S., & Richmond, Robert, *Glencairn Church of Scotland, Kilmaurs*, 1940.

Brown, J., *Mansefield Church of Scotland*, 1961.

Couper, Revd W. J., *Kilbirnie West United Free Church*, 1923.

*Darvel Central Church, 1888–1988*, Darvel Central Church Centenary Publication Committee, 1989.

*Dreghorn & Pearston Old Parish Church, Bi-Centenary*, 1986.

Fergusson, Sir James, *The Parish Church of Dailly*, 1966.

Gibson, Revd A. Cameron, *A Guide to the Parish and Kirk of Fenwick*, 1985.

Hopkins, Irene, *Galston Parish Church*, 2000.

Hunter, James, *History of the Old High Kirk* [Kilmarnock], n.d.

*Kirk o' the Covenant, Dalmellington, 1846–1946*, 1946.

MacKenzie, Archibald, *An Ancient Church: The Pre-Reformation Church of St John the Baptist, Ayr*, 1935.

Morrice, Revd C. S., *A Brief History of Mauchline Parish Church*.

Reid, Beatrice, *The High Kirk of Stevenston, 1833–1983*, 1983.

*Local Booklets:*

Berry, Peter, *Airfield Focus: Prestwick*, GMS Enterprises, 2000.

Brash, Ronald W., *The Tramways of Ayr*, N.B. Traction, 1983.

Brash, Ronald W., & Leach, Allan, *Round Old Ayr*, Ayrshire Archaeological and Natural History Society, 1972.

Bryce, David, *Our Blood is on Their Hands*, 2001.

*Burns House Museum Mauchline*, n.d.

Faulds, Revd M. H. & Tweedie, William, *The Cherrypickers*, Cumnock & Doon Valley District Council, 1981.

*Historic Alloway*, Ayrshire Archaeological and Natural History Society, 2000.

*Historic Ayr*, Ayrshire Archaeological and Natural History Society, 1998.

Hutchison, Jennifer, *History and the Economic Development of the Village of Dunlop,* 1972.

Radford, C. A. Ralegh, *Crossraguel Abbey*, Historic Scotland, 1988.

# Index